DIGITALLY ARCHIVING CULTURAL OBJECTS

DIGITALLY ARCHIVING CULTURAL OBJECTS

Katsushi Ikeuchi
The University of Tokyo

Daisuke Miyazaki
The University of Tokyo

Katsushi Ikeuchi
The University of Tokyo
Institute of Industrial Science
4-6-1 Komaba, Meguro-ku
Tokyo, Japan
ki@cvl.iis.u-tokyo.ac.jp

Daisuke Miyazaki
The University of Tokyo
Institute of Industrial Science
4-6-1 Komaba, Meguro-ku
Tokyo, Japan
miyazaki@cvl.iis.u-tokyo.ac.jp

Digitally Archiving Cultural Objects
by Katsushi Ikeuchi and Daisuke Miyazaki

ISBN-13: 978-1-4419-4543-3   e-ISBN-13: 978-0-387-75807-7

Printed on acid-free paper.

9 8 7 6 5 4 3 2 1

springer.com

Preface

In 1898, the English writer H.G. Wells introduced the idea of time travel in his novel, The Time Machine. Here at the Ikeuchi Laboratory, the University of Tokyo, we have assembled a group of world-class engineers whose work in computer vision lets us travel back in time to the 7th century to the roots of our Japanese culture and to preserve cultural objects through the magic of three-dimensional digital conversion. The Great Buddha of Nara was originally built in the seventh century by order of the emperor, but it was burned down twice during civil wars in Japan. The current Buddha was rebuilt in the sixteenth century. Using advanced computer vision, computer graphics techniques, and historic knowledge from documents preserved in the Todaiji temple, we have reconstructed the Buddha and Buddha palace.

Another example of digital restoration is the work we have done with the Bayon Temple in Angkor Thom, Cambodia. This temple, which unites the Buddhist outlook of ancient India with Khmer tradition, is one of the master-pieces of historic architecture. Unfortunately, the structure is worsening day by day, and there is a high possibility of its collapsing in the near future. By using newly developed sensors and software, we have digitized this huge temple and obtained 3D digital data for restoration purposes.

Why are these restoration projects necessary? Unfortunately, many valuable objects that form part of our cultural heritage have been decayed by weathering and natural disasters such as Indonesia's recent earthquake. Other objects have been destroyed through man-made disasters such as the Taliban's destruction of the great Barmian Buddha in Afghanistan. But we can preserve our irreplaceable cultural heritage in 3D digital form for future generations using today's IT technologies. Images derived from 3D digital technology deepen our understandings of our cultural heritage and increase the identity and dignity of each nation.

This book presents an overview of the results of research on information and communication technologies devoted to digital preservation. It summarizes recent research results accumulated since the publication of our previous book,

Modeling From Reality. Our new book consists of four parts. Part I introduces our cutting-edge range sensors for scanning cultural objects. Part II presents our software algorithm, which integrates a large amount of range data into a unified mesh model. Part III explains techniques to analyze the color of the surfaces of cultural objects for preserving their "true surface color." Part IV provides examples of how to utilize these digital data for the "time-machine." We hope our readers enjoy their journey to this restored world.

Research results presented in this book are supported by three major research projects. We are deeply indebted to three leading program managers of the projects: Professor Masao Sakauchi of National Institute of Informatics for the Sin Program, Professor Makoto Nagao of National Library of Japanese Diets for the CREST program, and Professor Hiroshi Harashima of the University of Tokyo for the LP program for their guidance, management as well as financial supports. We extend our sincere appreciation to Dr. Joan Knapp, who revised our text; we could not have produced this book without her devoted help. We also thank our secretaries, Ms. Keiko Motoki, Ms. Yoshiko Matsuura, and Ms. Kaoru Kikuchi for putting our material in order. The cover of this book was designed by Tetsuya Kakuta. This research was financially supported in part by the Ministry of Education, Culture, Sports, Science, and Technology of the Japanese government, and in part by the Japan Science and Technology Agency.

KATSUSHI IKEUCHI

DAISUKE MIYAZAKI

Contents

List of Figures

List of Tables

Chapter 1

INTRODUCTION

Katsushi Ikeuchi and Daisuke Miyazaki

Introduction

Currently, a large number of cultural heritage objects around the world are deteriorating or being destroyed because of natural disasters, such as earthquakes and floods, or man-made disasters, such as civil wars and vandalism. Efforts to physically preserve and maintain these objects are being conducted all over the world, and these efforts are important and, indeed, essential. On the other hand, such daily physical efforts cannot stop the sudden loss of priceless objects, as was the case when the Taliban destroyed the Bamiyan Great Buddha or when an earthquake struck the Bam ruin in Iran. Thus, we have to develop methods to record and preserve current states of these reminders of our culture.

One of the best ways to record and preserve such objects is to obtain digital 3D data of them. 2D pictures have been a common method to record current appearances of heritage objects. However, 2D pictures, though they are impressive and beautiful, only provide appearances, and do not provide detailed information. Recent advancements in computer vision techniques enable us to obtain 3D digital data of these objects. Once these 3D data have been acquired, they can record 3D shapes of objects permanently and then safely pass these down to future generations. In addition, such digital 3D data are suitable for many applications, including simulation and restoration. Multimedia contents of objects can also be obtained from 3D data, and such digital contents can be viewed through the Internet from anywhere in the world, without moving the objects or visiting the sites.

We have been working to develop such digital archival methods by using computer vision and computer graphics technologies. Similar projects include Stanford's Michelangelo Project[2], IBM's Pieta Project[3], and Columbia's project[4], to name a few. Our project has a number of unique features; among them is its aim to digitize relatively large objects existing in the outdoors, such as the Kamakura great Buddha, and Cambodia's Bayon Temple. The size of target objects presents several challenges in terms of sensors used for data acquisitions and software to process the large amount of data. Also, our project aims to develop methods to record photometric information of outdoor objects. Strong sunlight and other environmental illuminations provide a challenge in processing photometric information.

This book summarizes our research efforts toward our preservation goal. It consists of four parts. Part 1 describes various sensors designed to obtain data. Part 2 contains a collection of papers that describe the geometric pipeline, converting obtained data into a consistent geometric model, through determining relative relations among digital data and connecting those data into a uniform representation. Part 3 concerns photometric issues, including how to map color pictures on a geometric model and how to remove the effect of sunlight in the pictures obtained. Part 4 reports on the effort to establish a digital museum to restore and display the original appearance of heritage objects as well as conduct analyses of obtained data for heritage research.

1.   Range Sensor

Part 1 contains papers on range sensors, specially designed in our project for measuring 3D shapes of cultural heritage objects. The process of obtaining 3D shape information of objects begins with collecting range data of objects by using various image/range sensors. Several computer vision techniques, such as traditional shape-from-X and binocular stereo, provide clouds of points of range information. Wide varieties of laser range sensors are also commercially available. On applying these established techniques or devices to objects in our project, however, we encountered several difficulties and challenges due to the scale of objects, complex structures of objects, and/or direct sunlight. Thus, we had to design several new types of sensors for our project.

Banno and Ikeuchi, in Chapter 2, report a balloon sensor, a new type of moving range sensor that hangs under a balloon. Large-scale objects require unusual viewpoints, such as very high viewpoints. Traditional scaffold methods, building scaffolds around the structures and bringing sensors on top of the scaffolds, do not work well due to the danger in high positions, vibration of the scaffolds, and inefficiency in bringing the sensors up and down. The balloon sensor provides freedom to choose any view by simply maneuvering a balloon to a desired position. This balloon method, however, poses a new challenge: the sensor swings during the range acquisition, and thus the resulting range data is distorted. Banno and Ikeuchi proposed to rectify such distorted range data by combining motion estimation from an image sensor mounted on the range sensor so that sensor motion predicted from an image sensor is consistent with the distortion of the range data. They introduced three constraints:

range data, bundle, and smoothness constraints, and derived a minimization formula to determine the sensor motion and to rectify the range data.

A moving 1D range sensor, referred to as a climbing sensor, was designed for obtaining range data of narrow corridors and hidden pediments, and is described by Ono, Matsui, and Ikeuchi in Chapter 3. Cultural heritage objects such as the Bayon Temple often have complex structures, with many hidden narrow corridors, due to modification of the structure during its long history and for defense purposes against an enemy's attack. For example, the Bayon Temple has double corridors around the building, narrow passages connecting fifty towers, and high surrounding walls. A range sensor prefers orthogonal views on the target surface for accurate measurement. In narrow areas, one view only provides limited orthogonal areas due to the distance between the sensor and the wall; other areas are visible, but heavily inclined. Chapter 3 describes a moving 1D range sensor to obtain orthogonal data along a moving direction. This type of sensor requires calculating the speed of the sensor to rectify the sampling intervals between views. Ono et al. developed an algorithm to determine the speed of the sensor using another 1D range sensor mounted on the orthogonal direction to the first 1D range sensor. The range images obtained by this second sensor are referred to as epipolar range images, following from epipolar-image analysis proposed by Bolles in the late 1980s.

Chapter 4 describes a range sensor to measure the surface of transparent or translucent objects, designed by Miyazaki and Ikeuchi. Some cultural heritage objects, such as necklaces with gems and traditional tableware, have transparent or translucent surfaces. The usual types of range sensors cannot measure shapes of this kind of surface because emitted laser light penetrates the surfaces from orthogonal directions. Miyazaki and Ikeuchi utilize the reflection from slanting directions on transparent surfaces. In order to separate the reflection light from the direct light penetrating and coming through the surface, polarization differences in reflected and direct light are used. This chapter presents an iterative method to obtain the object shape from analysis of reflected light obtained from the polarization analysis.

2. Range Data Analysis

2.1 Alignment

Part 2 begins with describing alignment, one of the two major steps in range data analysis. Each set of range data is obtained from arbitrary sensor locations and directions. Obtained 3D data is represented with respect to a sensor coordinate system. Usually a set of range data that covers an entire object's surface consists of multiple data sets obtained with respect to these relative coordinate systems. It is necessary to determine relative relations among these sensor coordinate systems. Some hardware, such as GPS, is available to determine the sensor coordinate system, but such currently available hardware is not accurate enough. Alignment algorithms determine these relations by comparing data similarity among possible overlapping areas.

Several simultaneous alignment algorithms are presented in succeeding chapters. Algorithms developed by Nishino and Ikeuchi are presented in Chapter 5, by Oishi and Ikeuchi in Chapters 6 and 7, and by Masuda, Hirota, Nishino, and Ikeuchi in Chapter 8. Traditional alignment algorithms employ pair-wise alignment to determine the relative relation between two views, and iteratively continue this process along the chain of range data to complete the whole set of range data. When handling a large number of data sets, error gradually accumulates along the chain, and a large gap may exist locally in the final result. To avoid error accumulation in a certain local part, the algorithms described aim to simultaneously determine all alignment relations within a data set for even distribution of errors among all the relations.

Nishino and Ikeuchi in Chapter 5 propose a robust alignment algorithm. Traditional alignment algorithms were designed mainly for relatively clean range data, obtained from indoor objects under controlled environments. On the other hand, range data obtained from outdoor structures, under direct sunlight, often contain a relatively large amount of outliers, compared with data from small indoor objects. Traditional alignment algorithms break down on being applied to such outlier-contaminated data, because they often employ a minimization strategy based on the least squares formulation. Nishino and Ikeuchi in Chapter 5 present a minimization strategy efficient and robust against outliers by using a conjugate gradient search utilizing M-estimator. For robustness, they also avoid using secondary information, i.e., surface normal, in their error metric.

Oishi and Ikeuchi in Chapter 6 consider a rapid alignment algorithm for on-site alignment. The Nishino-Ikeuchi algorithm in Chapter 5 is robust, but the algorithm is relatively slow. When work is being done onsite, a rapid alignment algorithm is desirable for data debugging and sensor planning, although this involves the sacrifice of some robustness. The most time-consuming step in alignment is to find pairs of data points. Oishi and Ikeuchi utilize a graphics processing unit, commonly available on recent PCs, for establishing pairs of data points. As a result, they achieve ten times the rapidity of the previous Nishino and Ikeuchi algorithm.

Oishi in Chapter 7 also extends the algorithm into a parallel implementation so as to be able to align a very large data set. Another issue in handling a large object is the huge number of data sets. The simultaneous algorithm, as originally designed, requires all range images to be read into memory; even when the computation is distributed over a PC cluster, the amount of memory used on each PC is not reduced. For parallel implementation, both time and memory performance have to be considered.

Masuda, Hirota, Nishino, and Ikeuchi in Chapter 8 extend the alignment algorithm to handle data deformation. The previous alignment algorithms, described in Chapters 5, 6, and 7, are concerned with rigid-body transformation parameters: three translation and three rotation parameters. Masuda et al. extend the algorithm so that it determines not only such rigid transformation parameters but also various deformation parameters. They model the deformation process using a deformation function with a small number of parameters. The minimization process in alignment determines these deformation parameters as well as rigid-body transformation parameters. Application areas of this deformation-alignment algorithm include shape parameter determination of old clay mathematical models using range data, comparison among old Japanese mirrors, and alignment between ground-based and balloon-sensor range data.

2.2   Merging

The second half of part 2 describes the step referred to as merging. As mentioned earlier, each range data set covers only a part of a whole object's surface. The previous alignment process determines relative relations among those partial data sets. Usually, 3D range data are represented as a mesh structure, connecting 3D data points with arcs, and forming triangular patches. It is necessary to connect those partial mesh representations into a uniform representation of a whole object's surface. The procedure of interconnecting these mesh structures is referred to as merging.

Merging is considered as extracting one surface from multiple overlapped surfaces. In the merging procedure, it is important to make the integration framework robust against any noise that may be in the scanned range images and can also be inherited from the registration procedure. Sagawa and Ikeuchi, in Chapters 9 and 10, merge a set of range images into a volumetric implicit-surface representation, which is converted to a surface mesh by using a variant of the marching-cubes algorithm [14]. Unlike previous techniques based on implicit-surface representations, this method estimates the signed distance to the object surface by determining a consensus of locally coherent observations of the surface. Chapter 9 mainly discusses a method to increase computational and memory efficiency using parallel computing techniques, while Chapter 10 extends the method for considering not only range data but also color information.

Merging is also considered as a process to reduce noise for a smoother surface. Chapters 11 and 12 consider methods to generate a smooth surface by considering two issues: data error and data lacking. Previously described methods assume error distributions are evenly distributed in space. Some range sensors, such as Cyrax, have less accuracy in the depth dimension than in the spanning dimensions, because the depth measurement is obtained by a laser returning a signal while the spanning dimensions are measured with encoders for mirror motions. Sagawa et. al. in Chapter 11 propose a method to reduce noise in range data by considering this anisotropic error distribution. Another issue in data error is how to fill small holes due to small occlusions. We have to interpolate over such holes for water-tight surfaces. Chapter 12 describes the method to fill such data holes by considering nearby signed distance fields and flipping signs of signed distance fields under certain conditions.

3.   Photometric Modelling

Photometric modeling, described in Part 3, provides color information about geometric models. Geometric models generated through range data analysis in Part 2 provide shape information about the objects. This shape information is useful for analyzing structures of objects and classifying them, but it is not enough for displaying them as multi-media contents. Part 3 examines methods for texturing, mapping such photometric information on geometric models.

One issue in texturing is how to map color pictures on geometric models while maintaining geometric integrity among color images. Ohkubo and Ikeuchi in Chapter 13 examine a mapping method for a large-scale object. When short-distance range sensors can be used, the most promising method is to calibrate the geometrical relationship between the image sensor and the range sensor before scanning, using a calibration object. However, this calibration-based method is accurate only around the position occupied by the calibration fixture. When a target object is very large, this method becomes unreliable due to lens distortion. This chapter employs the reflectance image, provided from a laser range sensor as a side product, as a vehicle for the alignment of range images with color images. In addition to this alignment between reflectance and color images, this paper also considers the simultaneous constraints among color images for avoiding error accumulation.

When an object is located outdoors, the color picture taken contains both illumination color and object color. In particular, when the target object is large, obtaining images takes a long time, and during image-taking, illumination conditions change; thus, the resulting photometric appearances are different from one part to another part. Such an effect can be removed by taking two color pictures of the same region under different illumination conditions, comparing them, and removing illumination colors. Kawakami, Tan, and Ikeuchi, in Chapter 14, focus shadow and non-shadow sub-regions in a single image of a common color region. This is possible because a shadow region, illuminated by sky light, and a non-shadow region, illuminated by both sky light and sunlight, provide two appearances of the same body color region under two different illumination conditions. Further, for reliably estimating the true color, they included the analysis of noise, and as a result, they produced an effective and robust algorithm.

The previous method separates illumination and surface reflection using three channels, RGB color components, whereas incoming light has a continuous spectral power distribution. Ikari, Kawakami, Tan, and Ikeuchi, in Chapter 15, propose a separation method to use this continuous spectral power distribution. They express illumination power distribution as a linear combination of three known basis functions. They also express spectral power distribution of surface reflection as a linear combination of three known basis functions. The resulting observed spectral power distribution is a product of these two linear combinations of six known basis functions. The authors set up a minimization formula to determine six unknown coefficients to the basis functions. They solve this minimization under three different cases: distribution from two different surface reflections under the same illumination, the same surface under different illumination conditions, and a surface of dichromatic reflection.

Another important issue in photometric modeling is how to store photometric information in an effective manner. Appearances of heritage objects and particularly indoor objects such as gems and gold plates depend on viewing and light-source directions and light-source color, mainly because of highlights on the surface. Appearances of highlights are not intrinsic characteristics of heritage objects. It is desirable to remove such highlights before archiving heritage objects, and to separately store those two factors for effective storage. Tan and Ikeuchi in Chapter 16 define the inverse-intensity chromaticity space to describe a linear correlation between image and illumination chromaticity. They derive an algorithm, based on an iterative framework, to generate a highlight-free image from a single input image. Chapter 17 extends the method to handle a textured surface. Shibata, Takahashi, Miyazaki, and Ikeuchi push this frontier further in Chapter 18. First, highlights and body reflections are separated, in this case using the difference in polarization characteristics of the two reflection components. Next, these two reflection components are analyzed using Nayar-Ikeuchi-Kanade reflection models. Extracted information is stored as parameters of the reflection model.

4. Utilizing Digital Data for Archaeological Investigation

Part 4 presents application examples of obtained digital data. We can categorize these examples into three classes: (1) analysis, (2) user interface, and (3) multimedia display.

Chapters 19 and 20 describe uses of digital data for analysis. The Bayon Temple's 173 faces are, from the JSA research based on the judgment of artists, classified into three categories: Deva, Devata, and Asura. Kamakura, Oishi, and Ikeuchi verify this hypothesis using PCA analysis on their digital data in Chapter 19. They also report that there are similarity groups in proximity areas. They conclude that this may support a hypothesis that there were multiple worker teams and these worker teams carved those faces in a parallel manner. Another example of analysis is in the area of photometric analysis. Illumination simulations often provide powerful evidence for archaeological investigation. In the research of cultural heritage objects such as wall sculptures and paintings, archaeologist have paid attention mainly to the appearance of the painting at the time it was created, and have argued about illumination conditions by observing such heritage objects. Instead of simple observations, simulations often provide more powerful evidence about illumination conditions. In order to demonstrate the ability of 3D digital data to provide such information, Masuda, Yamada, Kuchitsu, and Ikeuchi digitized actual shapes of caves and textured color pictures on the surface of digital models. They then demonstrated illumination simulation for archaeological investigation using a 3D geometric model from digitization of real caves, as described in Chapter 20. From the simulation, they were able to assert the possibility that the ancient artists could work inside the cave in sunlight if they chose the optimum season and time for work, as opposed to previous assumptions that these artists must have used artificial light.

Chapter 21 demonstrates the second class of 3D data applications: using 3D data as the interface of a database system. Okamoto, Oishi, and Ikeuchi propose editing, retrieving, and displaying a system of archeological information on a large 3D geometric model. They provide computer graphics models with various types of archeological information on those models. In order to efficiently handle large-scale models, they designed a system with multi-resolution mesh models. Users can associate those mesh models with user-defined archeological information and access the stored data from the models with easy mouse actions. They verify the effectiveness of the system with user study experiments.

Chapter 22 demonstrates the third class of applications: using 3D data for graphics contents for multimedia display. 3D data can be used on a real-image background for a mixed reality display. For the seamless integration of virtual and real objects, it is important to achieve consistency of illumination. Kakuta, Oishi, and Ikeuchi describe a method to represent shading and shadowing of virtual objects appropriate for architecture models in outdoor scenes. They developed a method to create the shadows of the virtual objects in a fast and efficient manner using a set of pre-rendered basis images and shadowing planes. They demonstrate the system in Asuka, an ancient capital of Japan.

Another example of multimedia display is explained in Chapter 23. One of the advantages of obtaining digital data of cultural heritage objects is to modify those data and display the original appearance of the object. The Nara great Buddha is one of the most important heritage objects in Japan. Originally the

Buddha statue was constructed in the 8th century, but was melted down twice due to Japanese civil wars. Oishi and Ikeuchi demonstrate the creation of the original appearance of the Buddha and Buddha palace from digital data of the current Buddha and Buddha palace.

Acknowledgments

This research was financially supported in part by the Ministry of Education, Culture, Sports, Science, and Technology of the Japanese government, and in part by the Japan Science and Technology Agency.

References

[1] K. Ikeuchi and Y. Sato, *Modeling from Reality*, Kluwer Academic Press, 2001.

[2] M. Levoy et. al., "The digital Michelangelo project," *SIGGRAPH 2000*, New Orleans.

[3] J. Wasserman, *Michelangelo's Florence Pieta*, Princeton University Press, 2003.

[4] I. Stamos and P. Allen, "Automatic registration of 2-D with 3-D imagery in urban environments," *ICCV2001*, Vancouver.

[5] P.J. Besl and N.D. McKay, "A method for registration of 3-d shapes," *IEEE Trans. Patt. Anal. Machine Intell.*, **14**(2):239-256, 1992.

[6] R. Benjemaa and F. Schmitt, "Fast global registration of 3D sampled surfaces using a multiple-z-buffer technique," *Int. Conf on Recent Advances in 3-D Digital Imaging and Modeling*, pp. 113-120, May 1997.

[7] P. Neugebauer, "Geometrical cloning of 3D objects via simultaneous registration of multiple range images," *Int. Conf on Shape Modeling and Application*, pp.130-139, March 1997.

[8] Y. Chen and G. Medioni, "Object modeling by registeration of multiple range images," *Image and Vision Computing*, **10**(3):145-155, April 1992.

[9] S. Rusinkiewicz and M. Levoy, "Efficient variants of the IPC algorithm," *Int. Conf 3-D Digital Imaging and Modeling*, pp.145-152, May 2001.

[10] H. Gagnon, M. Soucy, R. Bergevin, and D. Laurendeau, "Registration of multiple range views for automatic 3-D model building," *CVPR94*, pp.581-586.

[11] K. Nishino and K. Ikeuchi, "Robust simultaneous registration of multiple range images," *Fifth Asian Conference on Computer Vision ACCV '02*, pp.454-461, 2002.

[12] T. Oishi, R. Sagawa, A. Nakazawa, R. Kurazume, and K. Ikeuchi, "Parallel alignment of a large number of range images on PC cluster," *Int. Conf 3-D Digital Imaging and Modeling*, Oct 2003.

[13] M. D. Wheeler and K. Ikeuchi, "Sensor modeling, probabilistic hypothesis generation, and robust localization for object recognition," *IEEE PAMI*, **17**(3): 252-265, 1995.

[14] B. Curless and M. Levoy, "A volumetric method for building complex models from range images," *SIGGRAPH 96*, New Orleans, LA.

[15] M. Wheeler, Y. Sato, and K. Ikeuchi, "Consensus surfaces for modeling 3D object from multiple range images," *ICCV98*.

[16] R. Sagawa, K. Nishino, M.D. Wheeler and K. Ikeuchi, "Parallel processing of range data merging," *IEEE/RSJ International Conference on Intelligent Robots and Systems*, Vol. 1, pp.577-583, 2001.

[17] R. Sagawa, T. Masuda, and K. Ikeuchi, "Effective nearest neighbor search for aligning and merging range images," *Int. Conf 3-D Digital Imaging and Modeling*, Oct 2003.

[18] R. Sagawa and K. Ikeuchi, "Taking consensus of signed distance field for complementing unobservable surface," *Int. Conf 3-D Digital Imaging and Modeling*, Oct 2003.

[19] R. Kurazume, M. D. Wheeler, and K. Ikeuchi, "Mapping textures on 3D geometric model using reflectance image," *Data Fusion Workshop in IEEE Int. Conf. on Robotics and Automation*, 2001.

[20] R. Kurazume, K. Nishino, Z. Zhang, and K. Ikeuchi, "Simultaneous 2D images and 3D geometric model registration for texture mapping utilizing reflectance attribute," *Fifth Asian Conference on Computer Vision*, 2002.

[21] http://www.cvl.iis.u-tokyo.ac.jp/gallery_e/.

I

RANGE SENSOR

Chapter 2

SHAPE RECTIFICATION OF 3D DATA OBTAINED BY A MOVING RANGE SENSOR BY USING IMAGE SEQUENCES

Atsuhiko Banno and Katsushi Ikeuchi

Abstract   For a large object, scanning from the air is one of the most efficient methods of obtaining 3D data. We have been developing a novel 3D measurement system, the Flying Laser Range Sensor (FLRS), in which a range sensor is suspended beneath a balloon. The obtained data, however, have some distortion due to movement during the scanning process. Then we propose a novel method to rectify the shape data obtained by a moving range sensor. The method rectifies them by using image sequences. We are conducting the Digital Bayon Project, in which our algorithm is actually applied for range data processing and the results show the effectiveness of our methods. Our proposed method is applicable not only to our FLRS, but also to a general moving range sensor.

1.   Introduction

We have been conducting some projects to model large scale cultural heritage objects such as great Buddhas, historical buildings and suburban landscapes [21, 16]. Basically, to scan these large objects, a laser range finder is usually used with a tripod positioned on stable locations. In the case of scanning a large scale object, however, it often occurs that some part of the object is not visible from the laser range finder on the ground. In spite of such a difficulty, we have scanned large objects from scaffolds temporally constructed nearby the object. However, this scaffold method requires costly, tedious construction time. In addition, it may be impossible to scan some parts of the object due to the limitation of available space for scaffold-building.

We are now conducting a project [15] to model the Bayon Temple [33] in Cambodia; the temple's size is about 150×150 square meters with over 40 meters in height. Scanning such a huge scale object from several scaffolds is unrealistic. To overcome this problem, several methods have been proposed.

For example, aerial 3D measurements can be obtained by using a laser range sensor installed on a helicopter platform[31]. High frequency vibration of the platform, however, should be considered to ensure that we obtain highly accurate results. To avoid irrevocable destruction, the use of heavy equipment such as a crane should be eschewed when scanning a cultural heritage object.

Figure 2.1. The FLRS and the Bayon Temple

Based upon the above considerations, we proposed a novel 3D measurement system, a Flying Laser Range Sensor (FLRS)[14]. This system digitizes large scale objects from the air while suspended from the underside of a balloon platform (Fig.2.1). Our balloon platform is certainly free from high frequency vibration such as that of a helicopter engine. The obtained range data are, however, distorted because the laser range sensor itself is moving during the scanning processes (Fig.2.2).

In this study, we propose a method to rectify 3D range data obtained by a moving laser range sensor. Not only can this method be used in the case of our FLRS, it is also applicable to a general moving range sensor.

In this method based on "Structure from Motion", we use distorted range data obtained by a moving range sensor and image sequences obtained by a video camera mounted on the FLRS. The motion of the FLRS is roughly estimated only by the obtained images. And then the more refined parameters are estimated based on an optimization imposing some constraints, which include information derived from the distorted range data itself. Finally, using the refined camera motion parameters, the distorted range data are rectified.

Figure 2.2. An sample snap shot and the distorted range data obtained by the FLRS.

This method is not limited to the case of our FLRS but also applicable to a general moving range sensor that has smooth motion. In this study, we do not utilize physical sensor such as gyros, INS and GPS for estimation of self position and pose.

2. Full Perspective Factorization

Estimations of the shape of an object or of camera motion by using images are called "Shape from Motion " or "Structure from Motion ", and are main research fields in computer vision.

The factorization method proposed in [32] is one of the most effective algorithms for simultaneously recovering the shape of an object and the motion of the camera from an image sequence. Then the factorization was extended to several perspective approximations and applications [8, 23, 7, 25, 12, 11].

[25] also presented perspective refinement by using the solution under the para-perspective factorization as the initial value. In [12] a factorization method with a perspective camera model was proposed. Using the weak-perspective projection model, they iteratively estimated the shape and the camera motion under the perspective model.

2.1 Weak-Perspective Factorization

Given a sequence of F images, in which we have tracked P interest points over all frames, each interest point p corresponds to a single point $\vec{S_p}$ on the object. In image coordinates, the trajectories of each interest point are denoted as $\{(u_{fp}, v_{fp})| f = 1, ..., F, p = 1, ..., P, \ 2F \geq P\}$.

Using the horizontal coordinates u_{fp}, we can define an $F \times P$ matrix U. Each column of the matrix contains the horizontal coordinates of a single point in the frame order, while each row contains the horizontal coordinates for a single frame. Similarly, we can define an $F \times P$ matrix V from the vertical coordinates v_{fp}.

The combined matrix of $2F \times P$ becomes the measurement matrix as follow.

$$W = \left(\frac{U}{V} \right) \qquad (2.1)$$

Each frame f is taken at camera position $\vec{T}_f$ in the world coordinates. The camera pose is described by the orthonormal unit vectors $\vec{i}_f$, $\vec{j}_f$ and $\vec{k}_f$. The vectors $\vec{i}_f$ and $\vec{j}_f$ correspond to the x and y axes of the camera coordinates, while the vector $\vec{k}_f$ corresponds to the z axis along the direction perpendicular to the image plane (Fig.2.3).

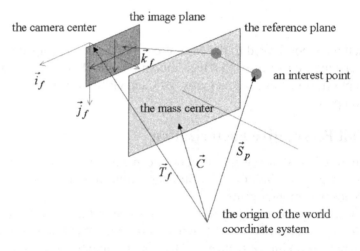

Figure 2.3. The Coordinate System: $\vec{T}_f$ denotes the position of the camera at time of frame f. The camera pose is determined by three unit basis vectors.

Under the weak-perspective camera model, a single point in the world coordinates $\vec{S}_p$ is projected onto the image plane f as (u_{fp}, v_{fp}).

$$u_{fp} = \frac{f}{z_f} \vec{i}_f^{\,t} \cdot (\vec{S}_p - \vec{T}_f) \qquad (2.2)$$

$$v_{fp} = \frac{f}{z_f} \vec{j}_f^{\,t} \cdot (\vec{S}_p - \vec{T}_f) \qquad (2.3)$$

$$where \quad z_f = \vec{k}_f^{\,t} \cdot (\vec{C} - \vec{T}_f) \qquad (2.4)$$

The vector $\vec{C}$ is the center of mass of all interesting points. Without loss of generality, the origin of the world coordinates can be placed at the centroid, that is $\vec{C} = 0$. Then this means that $z_f = -\vec{k}_f \cdot \vec{T}_f$ to simplify the expansion of the following formulation. To summarize,

$$\begin{cases} u_{fp} = \vec{m_f}^{\,t} \cdot \vec{S_p} + \mathbf{x_f} \\ v_{fp} = \vec{n_f}^{\,t} \cdot \vec{S_p} + \mathbf{y_f} \end{cases} \tag{2.5}$$

$$where \quad \vec{m_f} = \frac{f}{z_f}\vec{i_f}, \quad \mathbf{x_f} = -\frac{f}{z_f}\vec{i_f}^{\,t} \cdot \vec{t_f}$$

$$\vec{n_f} = \frac{f}{z_f}\vec{j_f}, \quad \mathbf{y_f} = -\frac{f}{z_f}\vec{j_f}^{\,t} \cdot \vec{t_f}$$

Using that the center of all interest points is the origin,

$$\sum_{p=1}^{P} u_{fp} = \sum_{p=1}^{P} \vec{m_f}^{\,t} \cdot \vec{s_p} + \sum_{p=1}^{P} \mathbf{x_f} = P\mathbf{x_f} \tag{2.6}$$

similarly,

$$\sum_{p=1}^{P} v_{fp} = P\mathbf{y_f} \tag{2.7}$$

We obtain the registered measurement matrix $\tilde{W}$, after translation $\tilde{W} = W - (\mathbf{x_1}\,\mathbf{x_2}\,\ldots\,\mathbf{x_F}\,\mathbf{y_1}\,\ldots\,\mathbf{y_F})^t$
$(1, \ldots 1)$ as a product of two matrices M and S.

$$\tilde{W} = M \cdot S \tag{2.8}$$

$$where \quad M : 2F \times 3 Matrix \quad S : 3 \times P Matrix$$

The rows of the matrix M represent the orientation of the camera coordinates axes throughout the sequence, while the columns of the matrix S represent the coordinates of the interest points in the world coordinates. Both matrices are at most rank 3. Therefore, by using the Singular Value Decomposition (SVD), we can find the best approximation to $\tilde{W}$.

2.2 Extension to Full-Perspective Factorization

The above formulation is under the weak perspective projection model, which is a linear approximation of the perspective model. Next, using an iterative framework, we obtain approximate solutions under the non-linear, full-perspective projection model.

Under the perspective projection model, the projective equations between the object point $\vec{S_p}$ in 3D world and the image coordinate (u_{fp}, v_{fp}) are written as

$$u_{fp} = f\frac{\vec{i_f}^{\,t} \cdot (\vec{S_p} - \vec{T_f})}{\vec{k_f}^{\,t} \cdot (\vec{S_p} - \vec{T_f})} \tag{2.9}$$

$$v_{fp} = f\frac{\vec{j_f}^{\,t} \cdot (\vec{S_p} - \vec{T_f})}{\vec{k_f}^{\,t} \cdot (\vec{S_p} - \vec{T_f})} \tag{2.10}$$

Replacing $z_f = -\vec{k_f}^t \cdot \vec{T_f}$, we obtain the following equations.

$$(\lambda_{fp} + 1)u_{fp} = \frac{f}{z_f}\vec{i_f}^t \cdot (\vec{S_p} - \vec{T_f}) \tag{2.11}$$

$$(\lambda_{fp} + 1)v_{fp} = \frac{f}{z_f}\vec{j_f}^t \cdot (\vec{S_p} - \vec{T_f}) \tag{2.12}$$

$$\lambda_{fp} = \frac{\vec{k_f}^t \cdot \vec{S_p}}{z_f} \tag{2.13}$$

Note that the right hand sides of Eq.2.11 and Eq.2.12 are the same form under the weak-perspective model (see Eq.2 and 3). This means, multiplying a image coordinate (u_{fp}, v_{fp}) by a real number λ_{fp} maps the coordinate in the full-perspective model space into the coordinate in the weak-perspective model space. Solving for the value of λ_{fp} iteratively, we can obtain motion parameters and coordinates of interest points under the full perspective projection model in the framework of weak-perspective factorization.

The entire algorithm of the perspective factorization is as follows:

Input: An image sequence of F frames tracking P interest points.

Output: The 3D positions of P interest points $\vec{S_p}$. The camera position $\vec{T_f}$ and poses $\vec{i_f}$, $\vec{j_f}$, $\vec{k_f}$ at each frame f.

1 Given $\lambda_{fp} = 0$

2 Supposing the Equations 2.11 and 2.12, solve for $\vec{S_p}, \vec{T_f}, \vec{i_f}, \vec{j_f}, \vec{k_f}$ and z_f through the weak-perspective factorization .

3 Calculate λ_{fp} by Equation 2.13.

4 Substitute λ_{fp} into step (2) and repeat the above procedure.

Until: λ_{fp}'s are close to ones at the previous iteration.

2.3   Tracking

As input, we need P interest points at each frame of a sequence, which are tracked identified points in the 3D world. There are several methods to derive interest points from images [22, 29]. Among them, we adopt *Harris operator* [13] and *SIFT key* [18] for derivation of interest points. SIFT key is robust against scale, rotation and affine transformation changes. The main reason why we adopt the method is its stability of points derivation and usefulness of the key, which has 128 dimensional elements and can be used for the identification for each point.

3.   Refinement

Without noise in the input, the factorization method leads to the excellent solution. As a result, the rectified 3D shape through the estimated camera parameters is valid. Real images, however, contain a bit of noise. Therefore, it is not sufficient to rectify range data obtained by the FLRS only through the factorization. For the sake of a more refined estimation of motion parameters, we impose three constraints: for tracking, movement, and range data. The refined camera motion can be found through the minimization of a global functional. To minimize the function, the solution by the full-perspective factorization is utilized as the initial value to avoid local minimums.

3.1   Tracking Constraint

As the most fundamental constraint, any interest point $\vec{S_p}$ must be projected at the coordinates (u_{fp}, v_{fp}) on each image plane. This constraint is well known as Bundle Adjustment [5]. When the structure, motion and shape have been roughly obtained, this technique is utilized to refine them through the image sequence. In our case, the constraint conducts the following function:

$$
F_A = \sum_{f=1}^{F} \sum_{p=1}^{P} \left(\left(u_{fp} - f \frac{\vec{i_f}^t \cdot (\vec{S_p} - \vec{T_f})}{\vec{k_f}^t \cdot (\vec{S_p} - \vec{T_f})} \right)^2 \right.
$$
$$
\left. + \left(v_{fp} - f \frac{\vec{j_f}^t \cdot (\vec{S_p} - \vec{T_f})}{\vec{k_f}^t \cdot (\vec{S_p} - \vec{T_f})} \right)^2 \right) \tag{2.14}
$$

The minimization of F_A leads to the correct tracking of fixed interest points by a moving camera. However, we can see that the presence of parameters we are trying to estimate in the denominator makes this equation a difficult one. We have to seek the optimal solution via some non-linear minimization techniques. Then, suppose that instead, we consider the following function:

$$
F_A' = \sum_{f=1}^{F} \sum_{p=1}^{P} \left(\left(\vec{k_f}^t \cdot (\vec{S_p} - \vec{T_f}) u_{fp} - f \cdot \vec{i_f}^t \cdot (\vec{S_p} - \vec{T_f}) \right)^2 \right.
$$
$$
\left. + \left(\vec{k_f}^t \cdot (\vec{S_p} - \vec{T_f}) v_{fp} - f \cdot \vec{j_f}^t \cdot (\vec{S_p} - \vec{T_f}) \right)^2 \right) \tag{2.15}
$$

The term $\vec{k_f}^t \cdot (\vec{S_p} - \vec{T_f})$ is the depth, the distance between the optical center of camera f and a plane, which is parallel to the image plane and include the point $\vec{S_p}$. The cost function F_A is the summation of squared distances on the image plane while the cost function F_A' is estimated on the plane of the point $\vec{S_p}$.

3.2   Smoothness Constraint

One of the most significant reasons for adopting a balloon platform is to be free from the high frequency that occurs with a helicopter platform [14]. A balloon platform is only under the influence of low frequency: the balloon of our FLRS is held with some wires swayed only by wind. This means that the movement of the balloon is expected to be smooth. Certainly, the movement of the balloon is free from rapid acceleration, rapid deceleration, or acute change in course. Taking this fact into account, we consider the following function:

$$F_B = \int \left(w_1 \left(\frac{\partial^2 \vec{T_f}}{\partial t^2} \right)^2 + w_2 \left(\frac{\partial^2 \mathbf{q}_f}{\partial t^2} \right)^2 \right) dt \qquad (2.16)$$

Here, $\vec{T_f}$ denotes the position of the camera, t is time, w_1, w_2 are weighted coefficients, and $\mathbf{q}_f$ is a unit quaternion that represents the camera pose. The first term of the above integrand represents smoothness with respect to the camera's translation while the second represents smoothness with respect to the camera's rotation. When the motion of the camera is smooth, the function F_B becomes a small value.

We implement in practice the following discrete form:

$$F'_B = \sum_{f=1}^{F} \left(w_1 \left(\frac{\partial^2 \vec{T_f}}{\partial t^2} \right)^2 + w_2 \left(\frac{\partial^2 \mathbf{q}_f}{\partial t^2} \right)^2 \right) \qquad (2.17)$$

3.3   Range Data Constraint

Taking a broad view of range data obtained by the FLRS, the data are distorted by the swing of the sensor. We can find, however, that these data contain instantaneous precise information locally; that information is utilized for refinement of the camera motion.

The FLRS re-radiates laser beams in raster scan order. This means that we can instantly obtain the time when each pixel in the range image is scanned because the camera and the range sensor are calibrated. If the video camera is synchronized with the range sensor, we can find the frame among the sequence when the pixel is scanned. With the video camera calibrated with the range sensor, we can also obtain the image coordinate of each interest point in the 3D world with respect to the instantaneous local coordinate.

Considering this constraint, we can compensate the camera motion.

When the range sensor scans interest point $\vec{S_p}$, we can conduct the third constraint to be minimized as follows:

$$F_C = \sum_{p=1}^{P} \left\| \mathbf{x}_{fp} - R^t (\vec{S_p} - \vec{T_{fp}}) \right\|^2 \qquad (2.18)$$

Here, the index fp denotes the frame number when the range sensor scans interest point $\vec{S_p}$. It is very significant to note that $\mathbf{x}_{fp}$ is the 3D coordinate values not described in the sensor-oriented coordinate system but in the camera-oriented one, which is rewritten based on the range data and camera-sensor calibration. In practice, we find sub-frame fp by using a linear interpolating technique for the motion of interest points between frames. The main purpose of the above constraint is to adjust the absolute scale.

As $\mathbf{x}_{fp} = (x_{fp}, y_{fp}, z_{fp})$, the above function can be rewritten as the stronger constraint:

$$
\begin{aligned}
F_C' &= \sum_{p=1}^{P} \left(\left(x_{fp} - \vec{i}_{fp}^{\;t} \cdot (\vec{S}_p - \vec{T}_{fp}) \right)^2 \right. \\
&\quad + \left(y_{fp} - \vec{j}_{fp}^{\;t} \cdot (\vec{S}_p - \vec{T}_{fp}) \right)^2 \\
&\quad \left. + \left(z_{fp} - \vec{k}_{fp}^{\;t} \cdot (\vec{S}_p - \vec{T}_{fp}) \right)^2 \right)
\end{aligned} \tag{2.19}
$$

3.4 The Global Cost Function

Based on the above considerations, we can understand that the next cost function should be minimized. Consequently, the weighted sum

$$
F = w_A F_A' + w_B F_B' + w_C F_C' \tag{2.20}
$$

leads to a global function. The coefficients w_A, w_B and w_C are determined experimentally, and we will discuss them later.

To minimize this function, we employ Fletcher-Reeves method or Polak-Ribiere method [26, 17, 30], which are types of the conjugate gradient method (in the next section, we explain the conjugate gradient method briefly). Then, we use the golden section search to determine the magnitude of gradient directions. For optimization, Levenberg-Marquardt method [19] is generally employed to minimize a functional value. Levenberg-Marquardt method is very effective in estimating function's parameters, especially in fitting a certain function. However in our function, minimizing the value of F_B' is not a parameter fitting problem. All we have to do is to simply decrease F_B'. Therefore we adopt the conjugate gradient method.

4. FLRS

FLRS(Flying Laser Range Sensor) has been developed to measure large objects from the air by using a balloon without constructing any scaffolds (Fig. 2.4).

We have two types of FLRSs. Each FLRS is composed of a scanner unit, a controller and a personal computer (PC). These three units are suspended beneath a balloon.

The scanner unit includes a laser range finder, especially designed to be suspended from a balloon. Figure 2.5 shows the interior of the scanner unit. It consists of a spot laser radar unit and two mirrors. We chose the LARA25200

Figure 2.4. The FLRS (25m sensor)

and LARA53500 supplied by Zoller+Fröhlich GmbH[2] as laser radar units because of their high sampling rate. Each laser radar unit is mounted on each FLRS scanner unit. Two systems equipped with Lara25200 and LARA53500 are respectively referred to as "25m sensor" and "50m sensor". The specifications of two units are shown in Table 2.1.

Table 2.1. The specifications of the 25m (LARA25200) and 50m (LARA53500) Sensors

	25m Sensor	50m Sensor
Ambiguity interval	25.2 m	53.5 m
Minimum range	1.0 m	1.0 m
Resolution	1.0 mm	1.0 mm
Sampling rate	$\leq$ 625,000 pix/s	$\leq$ 500,000 pix/s
Linearity error	$\leq$ 3 mm	$\leq$ 5mm
Range noise at 10m	$\geq$ 1.0 mm	$\geq$ 1.5mm
Range noise at 25m	$\geq$ 1.8 mm	$\geq$ 2.7mm
Laser output power	23 mW	32mW
Laser wavelength	780nm	780nm

Both sensors have the similar mirror configurations. There are two mirrors inside each unit to give a direction to the laser beam. One is a polygon mirror with 4 reflection surfaces, which determines the azimuth of the beam. In normal use, the polygon mirror, which rotates rapidly, controls the horizontal direction of the laser beam. Another is a plane mirror (swing mirror) which determines the elevation of the beam. The plane mirror swings slowly to controls the vertical direction of the laser beam.

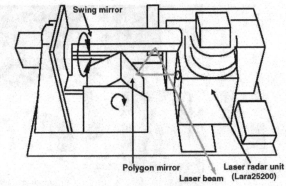

Figure 2.5. The interior of scanner unit (25m sensor)

The lase beam emitted from the LARA is hit on a surface of the polygon mirror at first. Then the polygon mirror reflects the laser beam onto the plane mirror. The plane mirror also reflects the beam outside the unit(lower of Fig.2.5).

The combination of two mirror demonstrate the specifications as in Table 2.

5. Experiments

We have been conducting the "Digital Bayon Project", in which the geometric and photometric information of the Bayon Temple is preserved in digital form. With respect to the acquisition of the geometric data, large parts of

Table 2.2.   The specifications of the 25m sensor and 50m sensor

	25m Sensor	50m Sensor
Angle Resolution		
Horizontal	0.05 deg	0.05 deg
Vertical	0.02 deg	0.02 deg
Horizontal field	$\leq$ 90 deg	$\leq$ 90 deg
Vertical field	$\leq$ 30 deg	$\leq$ 30 deg
Scanning period/image	$\leq$ 15 sec	$\leq$ 1 sec

the temple visible from the ground are scanned by range sensors placed on the ground. On the other hand, some parts invisible from the ground, for example, roofs and tops of towers, are scanned by our FLRS system.

The left side of Fig.2.6 shows a photo of the scanned area. On the right side of Fig.2.6, the dense fine model is the correct shape obtained by the Cyrax-2500 [1] fixed on the ground.

Figure 2.6.   A scene for this experiment. Left - a photo of an object; Right - 3D model obtained by the Cyrax-2500 fixed on the ground.

There are data missing in the model. To fill in the missing pieces of the model obtained by the sensor on the ground, we utilize our FLRS effectively. Figure 2.7 shows a sample image of the sequence obtained by the video camera. In this experimental data set, it takes one second for a range image: thirty pictures are saved in the meantime.

The result is shown in Fig.2.8. The upper shape in Fig.2.8 is the original one obtained from the FLRS. We can see that the shape is widely deformed. In the middle of Fig.2.8, the rectified shape by full-perspective factorization is shown. With respect to motion parameters, the ambiguity in scale is removed manually. At a glance, the factorization seems to rectify the shape properly. In

Figure 2.7. A sample shot of the image sequence

detail, however, the distortion in S shape is still left. Especially, the shape of the entrance is skewed. On the other hand, the lower shape is rectified correctly by our method. It is clear that the distortion in S shape is removed and the shape of the entrance is correctly recovered into a rectangle.

To evaluate the accuracy of our shape rectification algorithm, we compare the rectified shape with other data, which are obtained by a range finder, the Cyrax-2500, positioned on the ground. Aligning two data sets by using the conventional ICP algorithm [3] [6], we analyze the overlapping area.

Figure 2.9 indicates the point-to-point distances in the ICP algorithm. The region where the distances between them are less than 6.0 cm is colored light gray. The area where the distances are farther than 6.0 cm is displayed in dark gray. The upper figure shows the comparison between the correct shape and the original distorted one obtained by the FLRS. The middle one shows the rectified shape by the full-perspective factorization without ambiguity in scale. The lower shows the rectified shape by our method.

At a glance, the light gray region is clearly expanded by our rectification algorithm. Some parts of the rectified shape are colored dark gray because of the lack of corresponding points. Taking account of the fact that the correct shape of the parts invisible from the ground could not be measured, the proposed method could rectify the 3D shape correctly.

Table 2.3 shows a quantitative evaluation for our method. This table indicates the ratios of match region and the average distances between the Cyrax's model and the above three models. These numbers show that our method increases the match region and bring the distorted model by the FLRS to the correct one. We can see that our method was able to rectify the FLRS data properly.

Table 2.3. The evaluation of the rectified models. (a)The original distorted model. (b)The rectified model by the full-perspective factorization removing the scale ambiguity manually. (c)The rectified model by our method.

	(a)	(b)	(c)
match region (%)	37.2	49.8	62.7
error (average) [cm]	20.46	10.55	2.11

Figure 2.10 shows several samples of the method.

6.   Conclusions

In this chapter, we have described FLRS system and a proposed method to rectify 3D range data obtained by a moving laser range sensor.

We described how an outstanding measurement system FLRS was built to scan large objects from the air. This system allowed us to measure the large cultural heritage objects by using a balloon. To rectify the distorted shapes obtained from the FLRS, we proposed a rectification method based on the "Structure from Motion" techniques by using image sequences.

We utilized distorted range data obtained by a moving range sensor and image sequences obtained by a video camera mounted on the FLRS. First, the motion of the FLRS was estimated through full perspective factorization only by the obtained image sequences. Then the more refined parameters were estimated based on an optimization imposing three constraints: the tracking, smoothness and range data constraints. Finally, refined camera motion parameters rectified the distorted range data.

This method has shown proper performance and practical utilities.

Our method can be generally applied to a framework in which a range sensor moves during the scanning process, and is not limited to our FLRS because we impose only the smooth movement constraint.

Acknowledgments

This research was supported, in part, by Ministry of Education, Culture, Sports, Science and Technology under the Leading Project, "Development of High Fidelity Digitization Software for Large-Scale and Intangible Cultural Assets," and, in part, by Japan Science and Technology Agency, under the CREST program, "Automatic generation of virtual models of cultural heritage."

References

[1] www.leica-geosystems.com.

[2] www.zf-lase.com.

[3] P. J. Besl and N. D. McKay. A method for registration of 3-D shapes. *IEEE Trans. on PAMI*, 14:239–256, 1992.

[4] G. Blais and M. D. Levine. Registering multiview range data to crate 3D computer objects. *IEEE Trans. on PAMI*, 17(8):820–824, 1995.

[5] D. Brown. The bundle adjustment – progress and prospect. In *XIII Congress of the ISPRS*, Helsinki, 1976.

[6] Y. Chen and G. Medioni. Object modeling by registration of multiple range images. *Image and Vision Computing*, 10(3):145–155, 1992.

[7] S. Christy and R. Horaud. Euclidean shape and motion from multiple perspective views by affine iterations. *IEEE Trans. on PAMI*, 18(11):1098–1104, 1996.

[8] J. Costeira and T. Kanade. A multi-body factorization method for motion analysis. In *Proc. of ICCV1995*, pages 1071–1076, 1995.

[9] J. H. Friedman, J. L. Bentley, and R. A. Finkel. An algorithm for finding best-matches in logarithmic time. *ACM Trans. on Mathematical Software*, 3(3):209–226, 1977.

[10] P. Gill, W. Murray, and M. Wright. *Practical Optimization*. Academic Press, London, 1981.

[11] A. Gruber and Y. Weiss. Multibody factorization with uncertainty and missing data using the em algorithm. In *Proc. of CVPR2004*, volume 1, pages 707–714, 2004.

[12] M. Han and T. Kanade. Perspective factorization methods for euclidean reconstruction. Technical Report :CMU–RI–TR–99–22, Robotics Institute, Carnegie Mellon University, 1999.

[13] C. Harris and M. Stephens. A combined corner and edge detector. In *Proc. of Alvey Vision Conference*, pages 147–152, 1988.

[14] Y. Hirota, T. Masuda, R. Kurazume, K. Ogawara, K. Hasegawa, and K. Ikeuchi. Designing a laser range finder which is suspended beneath a balloon. In *Proc. of ACCV2004*, volume 2, pages 658–663, 2004.

[15] K. Ikeuchi, K. Hasegawa, A. Nakazawa, J. Takamatsu, T. Oishi, and T. Masuda. Bayon digital archival project. In *Proc. of VSMM2004*, pages 334–343, 2004.

[16] K. Ikeuchi, A. Nakazawa, K. Hasegawa, and T. Ohishi. The great buddha project: Modeling cultural heritage for VR systems through observation. In *Proc. of ISMAR2003*, 2003.

[17] D. A. Jacobs. *The State of the Art in Numerical Analysis*. Academic Press, London, 1977.

[18] D. G. Lowe. Distinctive image features from scale-invariant keypoints. *IJCV*, 60(2):91–110, 2004.

[19] D. W. Marquardt. An algorithm for least-squares estimation of nonlinear parameters. *Journal of the Society for Industrial and Applied Mathematics*, 11:431–441, 1963.

[20] T. Masuda, Y. Hirota, K. Nishino, and K. Ikeuchi. Simultaneous determination of registration and deformation parameters among 3D range images. In *Proc. of 3DIM2005*, pages 369–376, 2005.

[21] D. Miyazaki, T. Oishi, T. Nishikawa, R. Sagawa, K. Nishino, T. Tomomatsu, Y. Yakase, and K. Ikeuchi. The great buddha project: Modelling cultural heritage through observation. In *Proc. of VSMM2000*, pages 138–145, 2000.

[22] H. P. Moravec. Towards automatic visual obstacle avoidance. In *Proc. 5th International Joint Conference on Artificial Intelligence*, page 584, 1977.

[23] T. Morita and T. Kanade. A sequential factorization method for recovering shape and motion from image streams. *IEEE Trans. on PAMI*, 19(8):858–867, 1997.

[24] P. Neugebauer. Geometrical cloning of 3D objects via simultaneous registration of multiple range images. In *Proc. of the International Conference on Shape Modeling and Application*, pages 130–139, 1997.

[25] C. Poelmann and T. Kanade. A paraperspective factorization method for shape and motion recovery. *IEEE Trans. on PAMI*, 19(3):206–218, 1997.

[26] E. Polak. *Computational Methods in Optimization*. Academic Press, New York, 1971.

[27] W. H. Press, B. P. Flannery, S. A. Teukolsky, and W. T. Vetterling. *Numerical Recipes in C*. Cambridge University Press, 1988.

[28] S. Rusinkiewicz and M. Levoy. Efficient variant of the ICP algorithm. In *Proc. of 3DIM2001*, pages 145–152, 2001.

[29] S. M. Smith and M. Brady. SUSAN - a new approach to low level image processing. *IJCV*, 23(1):45–78, 1997.

[30] J. Stoer and R.Bulirsh. *Introduction to Numerical Analysis*. Springer-Verlag, New York, 1980.

[31] S. Thrun, M. Diel, and D. Haehnel. Scan alignment and 3-D surface modeling with a helicopter platform. In *Proc. of the 4th International Conference on Field and Service Robotics*, 2003.

[32] C. Tomasi and T. Kanade. Shape and motion from image streams under orthography: a factorization method. *IJCV*, 9(2):137–154, 1992.

[33] J. Visnovcova, L. Zhang, and A. Gruen. Generating a 3D model of a bayon tower using non-metric imagery. In *Proc. of the International Workshop Recreating the Past –Visualization and Animation of Cultural Heritage*, 2001.

[34] E. Walter and L. Prontazo. *Identification of Parametric Models from Experimental Data.* Springer, 1997.

[35] Z. Zhang. Iterative point matching for registration of free-form curves and surfaces. *IJCV*, 13:119–152, 1994.

Figure 2.8.   The upper figure shows the original distorted shape obtained by the FLRS. The middle one shows the rectified shape by the full-perspective factorization without ambiguity in scale. The lower shows the rectified shape by our method.

Figure 2.9. The upper figure shows the comparison between the correct shape and the original distorted one obtained by the FLRS. The light gray region indicates where the distance of two shapes is less than 6.0 cm. The middle one shows the rectified shape by the full-perspective factorization without ambiguity in scale. The lower shows the rectified shape by our method.

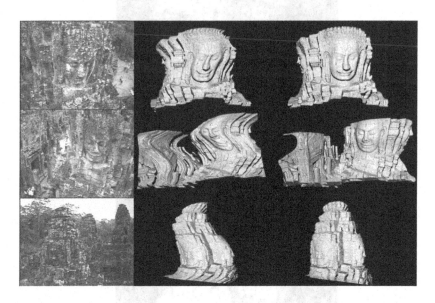

Figure 2.10. Some sample photos by FLRS (left), the original distorted data sets (center) and the rectified sets (right)

Chapter 3

THE CLIMBING SENSOR: 3D MODELING OF NARROW AREAS BY USING SPACE-TIME ANALYSIS

Shintaro Ono, Ken Matsui, and Katsushi Ikeuchi

Abstract In this chapter, we introduce a novel type of 3D scanning system, named 'Climbing Sensor'. This system has been designed especially for scanning narrow areas, which are hard or inconvenient to scan by a conventional, commercial scanning system due to its radial laser emission, dimension, and limitation of field angle in some cases.

Our system equips a moving platform with two 1D range sensors (main and sub units) on a ladder-style electromotive lift, and it scans the whole target while it moves downwards and upwards along the ladder. The main unit is used for scanning the target, which repeats scanning in a perpendicular direction to the moving direction of the platform. The sub unit is used for localizing the platform, and it repeats the scanning process in a parallel direction. By using the spatiotemporal range scans acquired from the sub unit, we can accurately estimate the motion of the moving platform, and a correct 3D model can be constructed from data scanned by the main unit.

We applied this system to the Bayon Temple in Angkor Thom, Cambodia. The scanning results proved that the system gives an accurate 3D model, and that the system and the speed of the estimating process are effective.

1.   Introduction

3D modeling of cultural heritage objects, especially large-scale and complex ones, involves various difficulties and challenges in observing the objects. Scanning elevated areas without occlusion is a typical example of these difficulties. An effective solution to this difficulty using a balloon has been proposed in the former chapter. Another issue is scanning narrow and tall or long areas. The goal of this chapter is to present the design of a novel range sensing system especially for such areas, to develop a localization algorithm required for realizing the system, and to apply the system to practical use for digital archiving of cultural heritage objects.

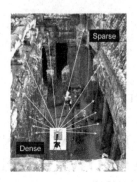

(a) Defects in the 3D model.   (b) Difference of point density.

Figure 3.1.   Narrow areas in the Bayon Temple.

In the case of scanning the Bayon Temple at Angkor Thom in the kingdom of Cambodia, a project in which we have been engaged for several years [1], the temple contains many narrow areas as passages and hidden pediments that were historically important for the defense of the temple. During our two scanning missions in 2003, most parts of the temple were successfully modeled by using several commercial sensors such as Cyrax 2500[14], Z+F IMAGER 5003[15], and our original sensing system, FLRS (Floating Laser Range Sensor)[2, 4, 5]. However, there still remained quite a few hole-like defects of range points in the 3D model as Fig. 3.1(a) shows, which are the areas that cannot reasonably be scanned by conventional systems. Since range sensors prefer orthogonal views on the target surface for accurate measurement, a sensor whose laser source is fixed when the scanning is going on cannot essentially solve the problem. In narrow areas, a view from a fixed point provides only limited orthogonal areas, and other areas are visible with heavy inclination — leading density and accuracy of range points are extremely deviated depending on the areas, as shown in Fig. 3.1(b)). These are not the only problems. Cyrax 2500 has a constraint in the width of its field angle, which causes considerable inefficiency in narrow areas. Although Z+F 5003 can scan the surroundings in a radial direction, a problem called distance ambiguity occurs. Also, the dimension of the device itself compared with the place to set it is a fairly difficult problem.

In order to model and scan such areas with uniform range point density and accuracy as far as possible, we developed a moving scanning system, 'Climbing Sensor,' a ladder-type laser scanning system. The system is equipped with a moving platform with a 1D range sensor (line-scanning unit) on a ladder-style electromotive lift, and it is able to scan the whole target while the platform moves upwards or downwards along the ladder.

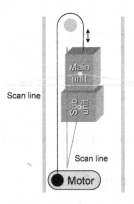

Figure 3.2. A basic illustration of the Climbing Sensor.

Although the motion of the platform can be regarded as uniform and straight during a single ascent and descent, our preliminary experiment proved that the speed value itself can vary among multiple ascents and descents, depending on how the ladder is set. There are various possible approaches for localizing the platform. In this instance, we developed an algorithm using another 1D range scanner mounted on the platform. The range images obtained by this scanner can be regarded as a kind of spatiotemporal range image, that we can analyze to determine the motion of the moving platform and create a 3D model with correct geometry. In the following, first we introduce a notion of the spatiotemporal range image, and describe the algorithm to localize the moving platform and obtain an accurate 3D model.

2. Spatiotemporal Range Image

2.1 Basic Design of the System

Since the Climbing Sensor developed in this chapter targets narrow and tall areas, we introduce a special moving platform with ladder-style guide rails and an electromotive lift, and put two 1D (line-scan) range sensors on the platform, a main and a sub unit.

The main unit is used purely for modeling targets. It is laid out on the platform so that its sweeping direction and moving direction become orthogonal. The sub unit is used for localizing the platform. It is laid out on the platform so that its sweeping direction and moving direction become parallel, and also the step bars of the ladder are observed. If the ladder is set vertically, the main unit repeats horizontal line scanning and the sub unit repeats vertical line scanning. Fig. 3.2 shows the basic illustration of the Climbing Sensor

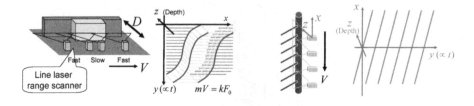

Figure 3.3. A basic idea of spatiotemporal range image.

2.2 Spatiotemporal Range Image

The simplest way to localize the platform is by matching the scanning results of the sub-scanning unit pairwise per each frame. However, such an approach cannot avoid accumulation of matching errors. Here, we propose a more simple, new, and original idea, a spatiotemporal range image[10]. By using this idea, the moving platform can be localized in a simple way with the error dispersed. We can avoid error accumulation throughout the whole process since this approach contains no matching process, and therefore a more accurate 3D model can be created.

The Spatiotemporal range image defined here is a kind of range image composed of a set of line-scanning range data. It can be assembled by placing the line range images next to each other per each frame with appropriate constant intervals, under the condition that the sweeping direction and moving direction of the scanning unit are parallel to each other. Fig. 3.3 illustrates the idea of spatiotemporal range image.

The spatiotemporal range image has some interesting features. It simultaneously represents the spatial characters of the targeted scene, which can be represented as x in Fig. 3.3, and the temporal continuity of the movement, which can be represented as y. In other words, by looking at the spatiotemporal range image along the y axis, one can determine how the sensor was moving in continuous time. Additionally, range points in the spatiotemporal range image cluster and compose some planes in most cases, due to the overlap of the scanning line and the difference in depth of the targeted scene from place to place.

The second feature described above implies that it is easy to extract edges from a spatiotemporal range image. The gradient of the edge m can be represented as a function of moving speed of the platform V by the following equation,

$$m = \frac{\Delta y}{\Delta x} = \frac{kF_0 \Delta t}{\Delta x} = \frac{kF_0}{V} \tag{3.1}$$

where the x-y-z coordinate is defined as in Fig. 3.3, i.e., x is a sweeping direction of scanning, y is a temporal axis, and z is a depth. F_0 is the scanning rate

Figure 3.4.   An example of spatiotemporal range image obtained from the Climbing Sensor.

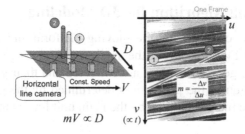

Figure 3.5.   Epipolar plane image (EPI).

of the sensor, and k is an interval between each scan in placing them next to each other along a temporal axis.

Fig. 3.4 is a real example of a spatiotemporal range image. Since the sub scanner can observe step bars of the ladder, edges can be seen clearly.

2.3   Contrast to EPI

It can be said that the spatiotemporal range image is a range-data version of the EPI (Epipolar Plane Image)[6, 7]. EPI is a color-data image that appears on a cutting face of a spatiotemporal volume composed of a sequence of color images captured by a moving camera, under the condition that the cutting plane is equal to an epipolar plane between each shot. In other words, it can be assembled by placing line color images next to each other per each frame, under the condition that image line and moving direction of the camera are parallel to each other (Fig. 3.5). EPI analysis is performed for estimating scene depth where the movement of the sensor is known. In contrast, spatiotemporal range image analysis is performed for estimating the movement where scene depth can be acquired by the scanning unit.

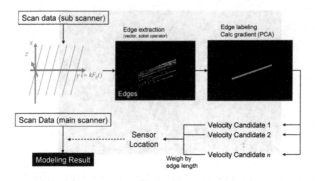

Figure 3.6.   Outline of the modeling process.

3.   Localizing Algorithm for 3D Modeling

The overall flow of localizing the moving platform and creating the 3D model is shown in Fig. 3.6. From the spatiotemporal range image prepared by the sub scanner, geometric edges are extracted and their gradients are calculated. The position of the platform is determined by the gradients, and is applied to the range image acquired by the main unit for 3D modeling.

3.1   Edge Extraction

We applied filtering by two constraints for extracting geometric edges from a spatiotemporal range image. One is based on spatial differential, and the other is based on angles between adjacent range points.

For spatial differential filtering, a simple Sobel filter is used. (Although such a filter is originally applied to color values in a 2D image, it is applied to depth values in a range image in this case. As the pixels in a 2D image are indexed as $I(u, v)$, the points in a spatiotemporal range image are indexed as $\vec{p}_{m,n}$, where m, n are an index number of the scan line and an index number of the range point in a specific line, respectively.) For angle-based filtering, whether the angle between $\vec{p}_{m-1,n} - \vec{p}_{m,n}$, $\vec{p}_{m+1,n} - \vec{p}_{m,n}$ and the angle between $\vec{p}_{m,n-1} - \vec{p}_{m,n}$, $\vec{p}_{m,n+1} - \vec{p}_{m,n}$ are within the thresholds is examined.

Points determined as edge points are labeled by clustering.

3.2   Calculating the Speed of the Moving Platform

The speed of the moving platform can be calculated from the gradient of the edges in the spatiotemporal range image. Considering the mechanism of the platform, the speed can be assumed as constant since it is moved in one way by an electromotive motor in the lift.

After labeling edge points, principal component analysis is applied to each edge. The gradient of the edge can be calculated from the direction of the

Figure 3.7. Overview of the Climbing Sensor.

primary component, and the moving speed is calculated back by Equation 3.1. The estimated value of the speed is calculated from every edge. In this system, in view of its mechanism, it can be considered that edges observed globally over a longer time period will have higher reliability in regard to the sensor movement, compared with edges observed locally over a shorter time period. Therefore, we took the weighted average of the estimated value by the length of each edge.

4. System Configuration

Fig. 3.7 shows the practical representation of the Climbing Sensor. This system is able to solve spatial limitations while keeping a sufficient width of field angle, and to regularize the density of range points to some extent.

4.1 Scanning Units

We chose SICK LMS200[17] for both main and sub scanning units. The specification is shown in Table 3.1. The reason that we used this is for its light weight, compactness, and wide scanning angle (FOV) with a sufficient scanning rate compared to the speed of movement of the platform. Especially, its dimension and weight belong to the smallest and lightest class among commercial laser range sensors, except for custom-designed products. This configuration solved the problem of the lack of space for scanning, since the small platform moves with a wide enough field angle and uniform point density.

4.2 Moving Mechanism

We chose Nobitec Lift NPL-4200[16] for the moving mechanism. The specification is shown in Table 3.2. This product is a telescopic ladder that can be expanded up to 3.2m. A power motor winch, which is installed at the foot of

Table 3.1. Specifications of the LMS200 Scanner.

Scanning principle	Time of flight, Line-scan
Range*	Max. 80m / 32m / 8m
Angular resolution*	0.25°/ 0.5°/ 1.0°
Field angle*	100°/ 180°
Response time*	53 / 26 / 13 ms
Measurement resolution	10 mm
System error	Typ. ±15mm (in mm-mode, range 1–8m)
	Typ. ±4cm (in cm-mode, range 1–20m)
Statistical error (1 sigma)	5 mm (at range ≤ 8m, reflectivity ≥ 10%, ≤ 5klux)
Data interface	RS-422/RS-232
Transfer rate	9.6 / 19.2 / 38.4 / 500 kBaud
Supply voltage	DC 24V ± 15 %
Power consumption	Approx. 20W (without output load)
Laser protection class	1 (eye-safe)
Operating ambient temp.	0 – 50°C
Weight	4.5 kg
Dimensions	L156 × W155 × H210 mm
Manufacturer	SICK AG, Germany

*Selectable by modes, but constraints exist in combinations.

Table 3.2. Specifications of the Nobitec Lift NPL-4200

Max. weight to ascent	100kgf
Max. height	3200mm
Supply voltage	AC100V 50/60Hz
Power consumption	870W
Speed of ascension	25m/min (0.417m/s)
Dimensions	H4380 × W1210 × D509mm
Manufacturer	KSS Corporation, Japan

the ladder, can roll up a wire. The moving platform with the sensing unit is connected to the wire and can slide along guides on a ladder.

This product is originally designed for lifting heavy loads to a higher place. It is possible to set the ladder nearly vertical while the platform moves upward and downward as originally used or to set it nearly horizontal while the platform moves forward and backward, depending on the condition of place and target for scanning.

Although the rolling speed of the winch is 25m/min according to the specification sheet, we did not use this value as a moving speed since it varies from case to case depending on conditions. Using the sub scanner, it is possible to obtain a more accurate speed of the sensor movement.

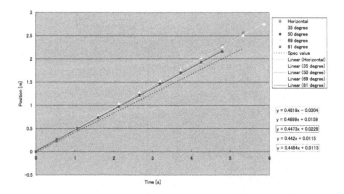

Figure 3.8. Verification of speed constancy of the moving platform.

4.3 Assumptions in Movement

We assume the following in regard to the movement of the platform in our system:

1 The platform moves in a straight direction.

2 The platform moves at a constant speed.

1. is based on the fact that the platform moves along the guides on the ladder. The gap between the guide and the platform is several millimeters at the maximum, which is more minute than the accuracy of the scanning unit. 2. is based on the fact that the movement of the system is driven by an electric motor, and that its load does not change during one scan since the setting condition of the ladder is constant.

To verify the second assumption, we recorded the movement of the platform by setting a video camera on the platform and capturing scale markings on a measuring tape attached along the ladder. The inclination angle of the ladder was changed in five levels, from horizontal to 81°. Fig. 3.8 is the result. Displacements in each scan were almost linear, and differences to the regression lines were less than 5mm. Meanwhile, the gradient of the regression line, i.e., an average movement speed, varied from case to case, and were different from the specified catalog value. These facts indicate that it is reasonable to adopt assumption 2, and to use this assumption to calculate the movement of the platform in each case of scanning.

5. Experiment and Modeling Results

The Climbing Sensor was put into practical use in modeling the Bayon Temple in Angkor Thom, Cambodia. The areas in which we used the Climbing Sensor in the temple are as follows.

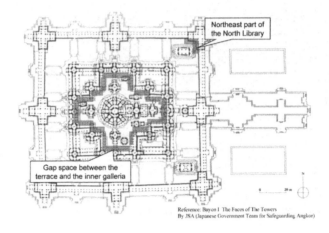

Figure 3.9. An example of area scanned by the Climbing Sensor.

  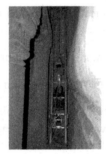 

(a) Gap space be-tween the terrace and the inner galle-ria.

(b) Northeast part of the North Library.

(c) Especially nar-row area.

(d) Nearly horizon-tal setting condi-tion.

Figure 3.10. Scanning situations in the Bayon Temple using the Climbing Sensor.

- Gap spaces between the terrace and the inner galleria: 173 scans.

- Northeast part of the North Library (a scripture house): 5 scans.

Fig. 3.9 shows the map of the scanned areas, and Fig. 3.10 shows our experi-mental scanning situation.

5.1   Modeling Result

Fig. 3.11 is an example of modeling result of the gap space between the terrace and inner galleria by the Climbing Sensor. Fig. 3.11(a) is a captured scene of the target by a camera. It can capture only a limited area of the scene because the space is so narrow that it is hard to keep enough distance to the tar-

  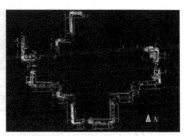

(a) Actual scene.   (b) Modeling result.   (c) Composite of all models in the gap areas.

Figure 3.11. Modeling result of the gap between the terrace and the inner galleria in the Bayon Temple.

(a) Before scanning by the Climbing Sensor.   (b) After scanning by the Climbing Sensor.

Figure 3.12. Modeling result of the northeast part of the North Library in the Bayon Temple.

get, and because the field angle of the camera is limited. Even in the case when using sensors such as Cyrax 2500, the area it can cover by scanning once is approximately the same level. Meanwhile, Fig. 3.11(b) is a 3D model acquired by scanning only once by using our system. Fig. 3.11(c) is the composite of all models scanned by the system in the gap areas between the terrace and the inner galleria. The reason why the northeast parts of the gap are lacking is because they include areas with a width less than 30cm, which is hard to set, even using our system.

Fig. 3.12 is an example of the modeling result of the northeast part of the North Library. The 3D model shown in Fig. 3.12(a) consists of the data scanned by Cyrax 2500. Though the circled part was hard to scan using Cyrax because of the spatial constraint of the setting, it was successfully filled by our system.

These results point out that the characteristics of the Climbing Sensor, its thin dimension and wide field angle, are effective.

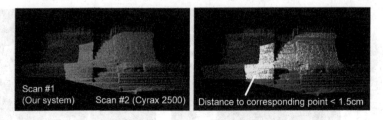

Figure 3.13.   Comparing 3D models obtained from the Climbing Sensor and Cyrax 2500.

5.2   Evaluation

In order to confirm the accuracy of the modeling result based on the estimated speed, we performed comparisons under two conditions.

First, we compared our modeling result with the basic standard model, using the Cyrax 2500 for the basic standard model. This model can be regarded as appropriate, since it is fixed on the ground and it assures the scanning error for the depth direction to be less than ± 6mm, which is accurate enough compared with that of LMS200. As a result of applying Oishi's fast alignment algorithm[8, 9] to the two models, the iterative calculation stably converged and they matched well. For most points in overlapping areas between the two models, the distance to the corresponding point (the nearest neighbor point in the counter model) became less than 1.5cm as shown in Fig. 3.13.

Second, we compared two modeling results both obtained by the Climbing Sensor. The histogram in Fig. 3.14 shows that the estimated speed varies from case to case. Comparing two models resulting from different values of estimated speeds is effective in proving the accuracy of each model. Fig. 3.15 shows the result of alignment. These are cases when the moving platform is assumed to move in (a) the specified speed, or (b) our estimated speed value. In (b), for most points in overlapping areas, the distance to the corresponding point became less than 2 cm. Although the speed differs considerably, two models based on different values of estimated speed were aligned well.

6.   Conclusion

In this chapter, we described the design of a new type of sensor named Climbing Sensor to model areas too narrow for ordinary commercial sensors. While the localization of the sensor in a specific time is one of the general problems in remote sensing, by using a scan parallel to the movement, we succeeded in obtaining accurate speeds of the moving sensors, avoiding error accumulation and dispersing them throughout the whole scan.

The results show that the 3D model was accurate enough, since aligning the model with a model acquired from a fixed sensor went well. Also, 3D

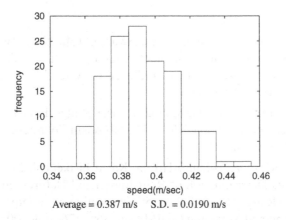

Average = 0.387 m/s   S.D. = 0.0190 m/s

Figure 3.14. The histogram of the estimated speed.

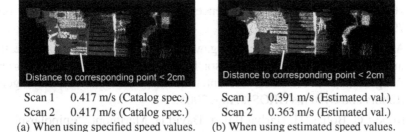

Scan 1 0.417 m/s (Catalog spec.)	Scan 1 0.391 m/s (Estimated val.)
Scan 2 0.417 m/s (Catalog spec.)	Scan 2 0.363 m/s (Estimated val.)
(a) When using specified speed values.	(b) When using estimated speed values.

Figure 3.15. Comparing 3D models both obtained from the Climbing Sensor, but with different values of estimated speed.

models obtained by the Climbing Sensor and rectified with different values of estimated speed matched well.

As a future project, we are planning to align the range images using deformable alignment[3]. By using this, the correct speed of the moving sensor could be analytically obtained under the condition that the range image has an overlap with another accurate range image. Also, it will be an interesting challenge to equip the moving platform with a camera and a light source, and create textured 3D models with true color.

Acknowledgments

This work was supported, in part, by Ministry of Education, Culture, Sports, Science and Technology, under the Leading Project "Development of High Fidelity Digitization Software for Large-Scale and Intangible Cultural Assets," and, in part, by Japan Science and Technology Agency, under the CREST program "Automatic generation of virtual models of cultural heritage."

References

[1] Katsushi Ikeuchi, Kazuhide Hasegawa, Atsushi Nakazawa, Jun Takamatsu, Takeshi Oishi, Tomohito Masuda, "Bayon digital archival project," Proc. International Conference on Virtual Systems and Multimedia (VSMM), Nov. 2004.

[2] Yuichiro Hirota et.al, "Designing a Laser Range Finder which is Suspended beneath a Balloon," Proc. The 6th Asian Conference on Computer Vision (ACCV), Jan. 2004.

[3] Tomohito Masuda, Yuichiro Hirota, Katsushi Ikeuchi, Ko Nishino, "Simultaneous Determination of Registration and Deformation Parameters among 3D Range Images," Proc. 5th International Conference on 3D Digital Imaging and Modeling (3DIM), pp. 369–376, Jun. 2005.

[4] Atsuhiko Banno, Katsushi Ikeuchi, "Shape Recovery of 3D Data Obtained from a Moving Range Sensor by Using Image Sequences," Proc. 10th IEEE International Conference on Computer Vision (ICCV), pp. 792–799, Oct. 2005.

[5] Atsuhiko Banno, Kazuhide Hasegawa, Katsushi Ikeuchi, "Motion Estimation of a Moving Range Sensor by Image Sequences and Distorted Range Data," Proc. IEEE/RSJ International Conference on Intelligent Robots and Systems (IROS), Aug. 2005.

[6] Robert C. Bolles, H. Harlyn Baker, David H. Marimont, "Epipolar-plane image analysis: an approach to determining structure from motion," International Journal on Computer Vision (IJCV), Vol. 1, No. 1, pp. 7–55, 1987.

[7] H. Harlyn Baker, Robert C. Bolles, "Generalizing epipolar plane image analysis on the spatio-temporal surface," International Journal on Computer Vision (IJCV), Vol. 3, No. 1, pp. 33–49, 1989.

[8] Takeshi Oishi, Katsushi Ikeuchi, Atsushi Nakazawa, Ryo Kurazume, "Fast Simultaneous Alignment of Multiple Range Images using Index Images," The 5th International Conference on 3D Digital Imaging and Modeling (3DIM), pp. 476–483, Jun. 2005.

[9] Takeshi Oishi, Ryusuke Sagawa, Atsushi Nakazawa, Ryo Kurazume, Katsushi Ikeuchi, "Parallel Simultaneous Alignment of a Large Number of Range Images on Distributed Memory System," IPSJ Transactions on Computer Vision and Image Media, Vol. 46, No. 9, pp. 2369–2378, Sep. 2005.

[10] Shintaro Ono, Katsushi Ikeuchi, "Self-Position Estimation for Virtual 3D City Model Construction with the Use of Horizontal Line Laser Scanning," International Journal of ITS Research (ITSJ), Vol. 2, No. 1, pp. 67–75, Oct. 2004.

[11] Christian Früh, and Avideh Zakhor, "3D Model Generation for Cities Using Aerial Photographs and Ground Level Laser Scans", Proc. IEEE Conference on Computer Vision and Pattern Recognition (CVPR), Vol. 2, pp. 31–38, Dec. 2001.

[12] Christian Früh and Avideh Zakhor. "Constructing 3D city models by merging ground-based and airborne views," Proc. IEEE Conference on Computer Vision and Pattern Recognition (CVPR), Vol. 2, pp. 562–569, Jun. 2003.

[13] Huijing Zhao and Ryosuke Shibaski, "Reconstructing Urban 3D Model using Vehicle-Borne Laser Range Scanners," Proc. International Conference on 3D Digital Imaging and Modeling (3DIM), pp. 349–356, May 2001.

[14] Cyrax 2500, Leica Geosystems, Switzerland. http://hds.leica-geosystems.com

[15] IMAGER 5003, Zoller+Fröhlich, Germany. http://www.zf-laser.com/e_bildgebende.html

[16] Nobitec Lift NP-4200, KSS Corporation, Japan. http://www.kss-co.jp/service/jisha/nobitec

[17] LMS200, SICK AG, Germany. http://www.sick.com

Chapter 4

INVERSE POLARIZATION RAYTRACING: ESTIMATING SURFACE SHAPES OF TRANSPARENT OBJECTS

Daisuke Miyazaki and Katsushi Ikeuchi

Abstract   We propose a novel method for estimating the surface shapes of transparent objects by analyzing the polarization state of the light. Existing methods do not fully consider the reflection, refraction, and transmission of the light occurring inside a transparent object. We employ a polarization raytracing method to compute both the path of the light and its polarization state. Our proposed iterative computation method estimates the surface shape of the transparent object by minimizing the difference between the polarization data rendered by the polarization raytracing method and the polarization data obtained from a real object.

1.   Introduction

There are many beautiful cultural assets made of glass, however, the risks that they will be damaged or lost are unavoidable. Especially, for art works made of glass, we cannot reconstruct its beauty if we once break it, because it is impossible to conceal all the cracks of the broken glass even if we try hard to attach its pieces together. Therefore, it is necessary to develop a technique to digitally preserve the 3D information of art works made of glass. However, in the field of computer vision, few methods have been proposed for estimating the shape of transparent objects, because of the difficulty of dealing with mutual reflection, which is the phenomenon that the light not only reflects at the surface of the transparent object but also transmits into the object and causes multiple reflections and transmissions inside it. In this chapter, we use the term "interreflection" for such internal reflection. Raytracer simulates the interreflection, and renders the 2D image from 3D shape:

$$\text{Image} = \text{Raytracer}(\text{Shape}) \quad . \tag{4.1}$$

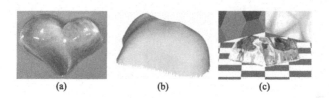

Figure 4.1.   Result for heart-shaped glass: (a) Target object, (b) result of proposed method, (c) raytracing image.

If an inverse function of raytracing were to exist, the 3D shape could be obtained straightforwardly from 2D data; however, there is no closed-form solution for the inverse problem of raytracing. This chapter presents a novel method for estimating the surface shape of transparent objects by numerically solving the inverse problem of raytracing and, at the same time, by analyzing the polarization of transparent objects.

An example for applying the proposed method is shown in Figure 4.1. Figure 4.1(a) is the target object, and Figure 4.1(b) is the result of proposed method. Figure 4.1(c) is a rendered example of the raytracing method by using the estimated shape.

Polarization is a phenomenon in which the light oscillates in one direction. Recently, research to estimate the shape of the object by using polarization has increased [1–5]. Saito et al. [6] and Miyazaki et al. [7, 8] estimated the surface shape of transparent objects by means of polarization analysis. Unfortunately, because these methods do not consider interreflection, they do not provide sufficient accuracy for estimating the shape of transparent objects. Other methods that estimate the 3D shape of transparent objects without using polarization have been proposed. Murase [9] estimated the shape of a water surface by analyzing the undulation of the water surface. Hata et al. [10] estimated the surface shape of transparent objects by analyzing the deformation of the light projected onto the transparent objects. Ohara et al. [11] estimated the depth of the edge of a transparent object by using shape-from-focus. Ben-Ezra and Nayar [12] estimated the parameterized surface shape of transparent objects by using structure-from-motion. Kutulakos [13] estimated both the depth and the surface normal of transparent objects by multiple viewpoints and multiple light sources. These methods, however, do not estimate arbitrary shapes of transparent objects.

There are other works that deal with transparent objects by using methods such as environment matting [14–19] and reflection separation [20–23]; however, they do not provide enough information about the shapes of the transparent objects.

We simulate the interreflection of transparent objects by using a method called polarization raytracing, and we use this method to estimate the surface shapes of transparent objects with arbitrary shapes. In this chapter, a forward-facing surface of the transparent object is called a front surface, and an object surface facing away from the camera is called a back surface. Our proposed method estimates the shape of the front surface by using polarization ray-tracing when the refractive index, the shape of the back surface, and the illumination distribution are given.

The rest of the chapter is organized as follows. In Section 2, we describe the theoretical background of the polarization raytracing method. In Section 3, we explain our estimation method, which solves the inverse problem of polarization raytracing method. Our measurement results are shown in Section 4, and our conclusions are presented in Section 5.

2. Polarization Raytracing

The theoretical details of the principle of polarization, which appears in this section, are presented in the literature [24, 25].

2.1 Conventional Raytracing

A conventional raytracing method renders a 2D image from 3D geometrical shape data of transparent objects or other kind of objects. The algorithm of the conventional raytracing method can be divided into two parts. The first part is the calculation of the propagation of the ray. The second part is the calculation of the intensity of the light.

Figure 4.2 describes the light reflected and transmitted between material 1 and material 2. Materials 1 and 2 may be, respectively, the air and the transparent object, and vice versa. Incidence angle, reflection angle, and transmission angle are defined in Figure 4.2. We assume that the surface of transparent objects is optically smooth; thus, the incidence angle is equal to the reflection angle. The transmission angle is related to the incidence angle as the following Snell's law:

$$\sin \theta = n \sin \theta' \quad , \tag{4.2}$$

where θ is the incidence angle, θ' is the transmission angle, and n is the ratio of the refractive index of material 2 to that of material 1. In this study, we assume that the refractive index of one object is a scalar value which is, at the same time, constant throughout any part of the object. The plane of incidence (POI) is a plane that includes the surface normal direction, the incident light direction, the reflected light direction, and the transmitted light direction.

The intensity ratio of reflected light to incident light is called intensity reflectivity R, and the intensity ratio of transmitted light to incident light is called intensity transmissivity T. Subscripts $\|$ and $\perp$ represent the components par-

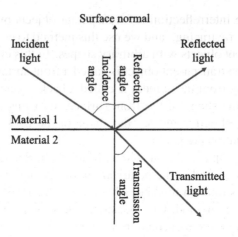

Figure 4.2. Reflection, refraction, and transmission.

allel and perpendicular to POI, respectively. Thus, parallel and perpendicular components of intensity reflectivity are represented as $R_\parallel$ and $R_\perp$, respectively, while those of intensity transmissivity are represented as $T_\parallel$ and $T_\perp$, respectively. These values are defined as follows:

$$R_\parallel = \frac{\tan^2(\theta - \theta')}{\tan^2(\theta + \theta')} \tag{4.3}$$

$$R_\perp = \frac{\sin^2(\theta - \theta')}{\sin^2(\theta + \theta')} \tag{4.4}$$

$$T_\parallel = \frac{\sin 2\theta \sin 2\theta'}{\sin^2(\theta + \theta') \cos^2(\theta - \theta')} \tag{4.5}$$

$$T_\perp = \frac{\sin 2\theta \sin 2\theta'}{\sin^2(\theta + \theta')} \tag{4.6}$$

If an incidence angle is larger than the critical angle, then the light does not transmit and totally reflects. This phenomenon is called total reflection and occurs when the incidence light is inside the object (namely, when material 1 is the object and material 2 is the air). Critical angle θ_C is defined as follows:

$$\sin \theta_c = n \tag{4.7}$$

For the total reflection, we must use $R_\parallel = R_\perp = 1$ and $T_\parallel = T_\perp = 0$.

The conventional raytracing method calculates the propagation of the ray by using the Snell's law (Equation (4.2)), and calculates the intensity of the light by using the total intensity reflectivity R and the total intensity transmissivity

T, which are defined as follows:

$$R = \frac{R_{\|} + R_{\perp}}{2}, \quad T = \frac{T_{\|} + T_{\perp}}{2}.$$ (4.8)

2.2   Mueller Calculus

In this chapter, we call the raytracing method that considers the polarization effect the polarization raytracing method. The algorithm of the polarization raytracing method can be divided into two parts. For the first part, the calculation of the propagation of the ray, we employ the same algorithm used in the conventional raytracing method. For the second part, the calculation of the polarization state of the light, there are three famous methods: Mueller calculus, Jones calculus, and the method that uses the coherence matrix. In this study, we employ Mueller calculus because of its simplicity of description, along with its ease of understanding and implementation. These three methods have almost identical functions; thus, all discussions presented in this chapter are also applicable to other calculi. Some researchers [26–28, 32, 31, 29, 30] also implemented and improved the polarization raytracing or improved these three methods, and also, there is some commercial software [33–35] that uses polarization raytracing.

In Mueller calculus, the polarization state of the light is represented as Stokes vector $\mathbf{s} = (s_0, s_1, s_2, s_3)^T$. The Stokes vector is a 4D vector. Its first component s_0 represents the intensity of the light; its second component s_1 represents the horizontal power of the linear polarization; its third component s_2 represents the +45°-oblique power of the linear polarization; and its fourth component s_3 represents the power of the right circular polarization. The Mueller matrix $\mathbf{M}$, which is a 4×4 matrix, represents how the object changes the polarization state of the light. The operation of Mueller calculus is a linear operation.

2.3   Mueller Matrices

In this section, we present an example of calculation using Mueller calculus.

Suppose the geometrical setup when the reflected and transmitted light is observed from the camera is as described in Figure 4.3. In this figure, there are two kinds of coordinates systems: $x'y'z'$ coordinates and xyz coordinates. Here, the z' axis and the z axis are the same. x' is included in the POI and is facing to the same side as the surface normal is facing. The angle between x' axis and x axis is called the POI angle ϕ in xyz coordinates.

In the case presented in Figure 4.3, observed light is a composition of reflected light and transmitted light. The Stokes vector $\mathbf{s}'$ of the observed light

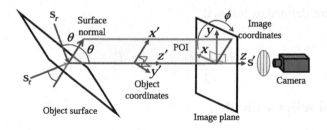

Figure 4.3. Reflected and transmitted light observed by the camera.

is calculated as follows:

$$\begin{aligned} \mathbf{s}' &= \mathbf{C}(\phi)\mathbf{D}(\delta;n)\mathbf{R}(\theta;n)\mathbf{C}(-\phi)\mathbf{s}_r \\ &+ \mathbf{C}(\phi)\mathbf{T}(\theta;n)\mathbf{C}(-\phi)\mathbf{s}_t \quad . \end{aligned} \tag{4.9}$$

Stokes vectors of the incident light are represented as $\mathbf{s}_r$ and $\mathbf{s}_t$, where $\mathbf{s}_r$ and $\mathbf{s}_t$ represent the lights that are set in the origin of the reflection and transmission, respectively. $\mathbf{C}$ is the rotation Mueller matrix and is given by:

$$\mathbf{C}(\phi) = \begin{pmatrix} 1 & 0 & 0 & 0 \\ 0 & \cos 2\phi & -\sin 2\phi & 0 \\ 0 & \sin 2\phi & \cos 2\phi & 0 \\ 0 & 0 & 0 & 1 \end{pmatrix} . \tag{4.10}$$

$\mathbf{R}$ and $\mathbf{T}$ are the reflection Mueller matrix and the transmission Mueller matrix, respectively, which are represented as follows:

$$\mathbf{R} = \begin{pmatrix} (R_{\|}+R_{\perp})/2 & (R_{\|}-R_{\perp})/2 & 0 & 0 \\ (R_{\|}-R_{\perp})/2 & (R_{\|}+R_{\perp})/2 & 0 & 0 \\ 0 & 0 & \sqrt{R_{\|}R_{\perp}} & 0 \\ 0 & 0 & 0 & \sqrt{R_{\|}R_{\perp}} \end{pmatrix} \tag{4.11}$$

$$\mathbf{T} = \begin{pmatrix} (T_{\|}+T_{\perp})/2 & (T_{\|}-T_{\perp})/2 & 0 & 0 \\ (T_{\|}-T_{\perp})/2 & (T_{\|}+T_{\perp})/2 & 0 & 0 \\ 0 & 0 & \sqrt{T_{\|}T_{\perp}} & 0 \\ 0 & 0 & 0 & \sqrt{T_{\|}T_{\perp}} \end{pmatrix} . \tag{4.12}$$

However, if the total reflection occurs, that is, if the incidence angle θ is larger than critical angle θ_C, then $\mathbf{R}$ and $\mathbf{T}$ are set to be identity matrix and zero matrix, respectively. **D** is the retardation Mueller matrix and is given as:

$$\mathbf{D}(\delta) = \begin{pmatrix} 1 & 0 & 0 & 0 \\ 0 & 1 & 0 & 0 \\ 0 & 0 & \cos\delta & \sin\delta \\ 0 & 0 & -\sin\delta & \cos\delta \end{pmatrix} , \tag{4.13}$$

where δ is the amount of the phase shift (*or* retardation). The phase of the reflected light shifts when the total reflection occurs. Thus, for the total reflection, δ in the following equation is used.

$$\tan\frac{\delta}{2} = \frac{\cos\theta\sqrt{\sin^2\theta - n^2}}{\sin^2\theta} . \tag{4.14}$$

The phase of the reflected light inverts when the incidence angle is smaller than the Brewster angle θ_B, which is defined as follows:

$$\tan\theta_B = n . \tag{4.15}$$

Thus, the value of δ is set as follows:

$$\delta = \begin{cases} \text{Eq.}(4.14) & \theta \geq \theta_C \\ 180° & \theta \leq \theta_B \\ 0° & \text{otherwise} \end{cases} . \tag{4.16}$$

2.4   Degree of Polarization

The polarization state of the light is calculated by observing the object with a monochrome camera, which has a linear polarizer in the front. For a certain pixel, we denote the maximum intensity observed by rotating the polarizer as $I_{\max}$ and the minimum as $I_{\min}$. The angle of the polarizer when the minimum intensity $I_{\min}$ is observed is called the phase angle ψ. This angle is defined as the angle from $+x$ axis to $+y$ axis in xyz coordinates (Figure 4.3).

Because the linear polarizer is used in this research, the fourth parameter s_3 of the Stokes vector cannot be determined. The relationship between the Stokes vector $(s_0, s_1, s_2)^T$ and $I_{\max}, I_{\min}, \psi$ is:

$$\begin{pmatrix} s_0 \\ s_1 \\ s_2 \end{pmatrix} = \begin{pmatrix} 1 & 0 & 0 \\ 0 & \cos 2\psi & -\sin 2\psi \\ 0 & \sin 2\psi & \cos 2\psi \end{pmatrix} \begin{pmatrix} I_{\max} + I_{\min} \\ I_{\max} - I_{\min} \\ 0 \end{pmatrix}. \tag{4.17}$$

The degree of polarization (DOP) represents how much the light is polarized and is defined as follows:

$$\hat{\rho} = \frac{\sqrt{s_1^2 + s_2^2 + s_3^2}}{s_0} . \tag{4.18}$$

However, linear polarizer can only calculate the following degenerated DOP:

$$\rho = \frac{I_{max} - I_{min}}{I_{max} + I_{min}} = \frac{\sqrt{s_1^2 + s_2^2}}{s_0} \quad . \tag{4.19}$$

For the remainder of this chapter, we refer to the ratio calculated by Equation (4.19) as DOP.

2.5   Illumination Distribution

In this study, we assume that all light sources are unpolarized. We also assume that the front surface of the object is uniformly illuminated with the same intensity in every direction, and that the back surface of the object is also uniformly illuminated with the same intensity in every direction but with a different intensity from the intensity that illuminates the front surface.

3.   Inverse Polarization Raytracing

In this section, we introduce our method for estimating the front surface shape of a transparent object using the DOP and the phase angle as inputs under the assumption that the refractive index, the shape of the back surface, and the illumination distribution are given. Details of numerical algorithms are shown in the literature [36].

We denote the input polarization data as I_E. Polarization data are represented as an image (2-dimensionally distributed data) where the DOP and phase angle are set for each pixel. The polarization raytracing explained in Section 2 can render the polarization data from the shape of the transparent object by tracing the light ray and by Mueller calculus. We denote this rendered polarization image as I_R. The shape of transparent objects is represented as the height H, set for each pixel. Heights partially differentiated by x and y are called gradients, and are represented as p and q, respectively:

$$p = H_x = \frac{\partial H}{\partial x}, \quad q = H_y = \frac{\partial H}{\partial y} \quad . \tag{4.20}$$

Surface normal $\mathbf{n} = (-p, -q, 1)^T$ is represented by these gradients.

The rendered polarization image I_R depends upon height and surface normal, so it can be represented as $I_R(H, p, q)$. Our problem is finding the best values to reconstruct a surface H that satisfies the following equation:

$$I_E = I_R(H, p, q) \quad . \tag{4.21}$$

We call this equation the "polarization raytracing equation" from the analogy of "image irradiance equation" used in the shape-from-shading problem.

A straightforward definition of the cost function, which we want to minimize, can be as follows:

$$\iint E_1(x, y)\,dx\,dy \quad , \tag{4.22}$$

where,

$$E_1 = (I_E - I_R(H, p, q))^2 \quad . \tag{4.23}$$

We will sometimes omit the variables (x, y) in the subsequent discussions for the simplicity of descriptions. I_R depends upon p, q, and H, while p, q, and H depend upon each other with Equation (4.20). Thus, the cost function must be modified as follows:

$$\iint (\lambda E_1 + E_2)\,dx\,dy \quad , \tag{4.24}$$

where,

$$E_2 = (H_x - p)^2 + (H_y - q)^2 \quad . \tag{4.25}$$

λ is a Lagrange undetermined multiplier.

Euler equations that minimize Equation (4.24) are derived as follows:

$$p = H_x - \frac{\lambda}{2}\frac{\partial E_1}{\partial p} \tag{4.26}$$

$$q = H_y - \frac{\lambda}{2}\frac{\partial E_1}{\partial q} \tag{4.27}$$

$$H = \bar{H} - \frac{1}{4}(p_x + q_y) - \frac{\lambda}{8}\frac{\partial E_1}{\partial H} \quad , \tag{4.28}$$

where $\bar{H}$ is a 4-neighbor average of H.

Each of the above equations can be decomposed into two steps:

$$p^{(k)} = H_x^{(k)} \tag{4.29}$$

$$p^{(k+1)} = p^{(k)} - \lambda_1^{(k+1)}\frac{\partial E_1^{(k)}}{\partial p} \tag{4.30}$$

$$q^{(k)} = H_y^{(k)} \tag{4.31}$$

$$q^{(k+1)} = q^{(k)} - \lambda_2^{(k+1)}\frac{\partial E_1^{(k)}}{\partial q} \tag{4.32}$$

$$H^{(k+1)} = \bar{H}^{(k)} - \frac{1}{4}\left(p_x^{(k+1)} + q_y^{(k+1)}\right) \tag{4.33}$$

$$H^{()} = H^{()} - \lambda_3^{()}\frac{\partial E_1^{()}}{\partial H} \quad . \tag{4.34}$$

Here, λ_1, λ_2, and λ_3 are scalar values that are determined for each pixel and for each iteration step. Superscript (k) represents the iteration number. We do not write down the iteration number for Equation (4.34) because we do not use this equation due to the following reasons. One reason is that the cost function E_1 depends upon the change of surface normal rather than on the change of height. Another reason is that the cost function E_1 smoothly changes when the surface normal changes, but it does not smoothly change when the height changes. This fact was empirically proved in the preliminary experiments.

The algorithm goes as follows. First, we set initial values of the shape H for each point of the front surface. Next, p and q are calculated by Equations (4.29)(4.31). Then, we solve Equations (4.30)(4.32). λ_1 and λ_2 should be optimal values; thus, we use Brent's method to determine λ_1 and λ_2, which minimizes the cost function E_1. After computing p and q at every pixel, we solve Equation (4.33) by the relaxation method [37, 38] to determine the height H. We use the alternating-direction implicit method to solve the relaxation problem.

To conclude, the front surface shape of the transparent object is estimated by an iterative computation, where each step of iteration solves Equations (4.29)–(4.33), and the iteration stops when Equation (4.22) is minimized. There are two reasons why we use Equations (4.29)–(4.33) instead of Equations (4.26)–(4.28): (1) If we solve Equations (4.26)–(4.28) simultaneously by setting an arbitrary value λ, a parameter tuning problem will occur where λ must be set to an optimal value in order to stably solve these equations; (2) We can apply adequate numerical algorithms for each of Equations (4.29)–(4.33).

4.   Measurement Result

4.1   Acquisition System

For obtaining polarization data, we developed an acquisition system, which we named "Cocoon" (Figure 4.4). The target object is set inside the center of the plastic sphere whose diameter is 35cm. This plastic sphere is illuminated by 36 incandescent lamps. These 36 light sources are almost uniformly distributed spatially around the plastic sphere. The plastic sphere diffuses the light that comes from the light sources, and it behaves as a spherical light source, which illuminates the target object from every direction. Note that the measurement is possible for arbitrary illumination conditions though the intensity and the polarization state of the illumination distribution must be known. The target object is observed by monochrome camera from the top of the plastic sphere, which has a hole on the top. Linear polarizer is set in front of the camera. We put the target object on the black pipe to make the incoming light from the back surface uniform and unpolarized. The camera, object, and light sources are fixed. From four images taken by rotating the polarizer at $0°$, $45°$, $90°$, and $135°$, we calculate I_{max}, I_{min}, and ψ (Section 2.4).

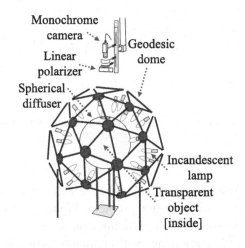

Figure 4.4. Acquisition System "Cocoon".

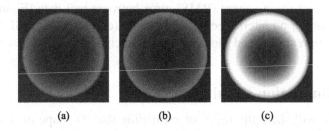

(a)   (b)   (c)

Figure 4.5. DOP image; (a) obtained from real object, (b) rendered by polarization raytracing, and (c) rendered by assuming that the internal interreflection does not occur.

4.2 Rendering Result

Before estimating the shape of the transparent object, we analyze the rendered image of forward polarization raytracing (Section 2). From the spherical part, we observe a transparent acrylic hemisphere, whose refractive index is 1.5 and diameter is 3cm. Obtained polarization image of the real object is shown in Figure 4.5(a). The figure represents the DOP, where DOP 0 and DOP 1 are represented as black and white, respectively.

The rendered polarization image of polarization raytracing is shown in Figure 4.5(b). The refractive index and the shape of the object are known. As for the illumination distribution, we have to obtain the ratio of the intensity of the light illuminating the front surface to that illuminating the back surface. Unfortunately, it is impossible to observe the light illuminating the back surface without moving the object out of the way. Therefore, we find the most appropriate value of the intensity of the back surface where the difference of

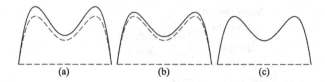

Figure 4.6. Simulation result of concave shape: (a) Initial state, (b)(c) result after 5, 20 loops, respectively.

the obtained DOP (Figure 4.5(a)) and the rendered DOP (Figure 4.5(b)) minimizes, by solving such minimization problem. Figure 4.5(b) is calculated by using the intensity obtained from such minimization.

For comparison, a rendered image with no interreflection is shown in Figure 4.5(c). This DOP image is rendered by assuming that the light reflected at the object's surface once is just observed and that the transmission does not occur. The root mean square (RMS) error between real data (Figure 4.5(a)) and DOP data of no interreflection (Figure 4.5(c)) was 0.48, while the RMS error between real data and polarization raytracing data (Figure 4.5(b)) was 0.055.

4.3 Simulation Result

Here, we will show the result of estimating the 2D shape of a simulated object for evaluating the robustness of our algorithm. This virtual transparent object is a concave shape whose refractive index is 1.5. The object is represented as a dotted line in Figure 4.6. We render the polarization data of the object observed from the upper position to the lower direction, and after that, we estimate the front surface shape of the concave object by using the rendered polarization data as input data. Illumination is distributed uniformly from every direction with the same intensity. The light is not illuminated at the bottom of the shape but is illuminated on the front surface. Illumination distribution, the back surface shape, and the refractive index are given.

The estimation result is illustrated in Figure 4.6. The dotted line is the true shape, and the solid line is the estimated shape. Figure 4.6(a) indicates the initial value, and Figure 4.6(b) and Figure 4.6(c) indicate the results after 5 and 20 loops of the proposed method. The shape, which is generated by scaling the true height by 1.2, is used as the initial state of the shape. The shape converged to the true shape at 20 loops. The average computation time was 14.8[sec] for 1 loop with 320 pixels by using Pentium4 3.4GHz. Here, the maximum number of tracings is 100 reflections or transmissions; however, if the energy of the light ray becomes less than a certain threshold, the tracing of the light ray is stopped.

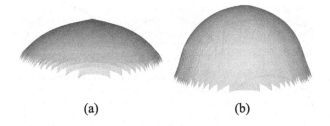

(a) (b)

Figure 4.7. Estimation result of hemisphere: (a) Initial state (result of previous method), (b) result after 10 loops.

4.4 Measurement Results of Real Object

4.4.1 Hemisphere

For the first measurement result, we observe an acrylic transparent hemisphere from the spherical part, which is also used in the rendering experiment (Section 4.2). We assume that the refractive index and the back surface shape are known. We use the same value for the intensity of the light source, which is obtained in Section 4.2. The value is obtained by observing the same object as Section 4.2, and we will provide a more objective result in the next section.

The estimation result is shown in Figure 4.7. Figure 4.7(a) represents the result of the previous method [6–8] and, at the same time, it represents the initial value. Figure 4.7(b) is the result after 10 loops of our method. The average computation time was 36[sec] for 1 loop with 7,854 pixels. Here, the maximum number of tracings is 10 reflections or transmissions.

More detailed evaluation is done in the 2D plane that is a cross section of the 3D object, which includes the center of the base circle and the line perpendicular to that circle. A light ray that is inside this plane does not go out, and a light ray that is outside this plane does not come in. The proposed algorithm estimates the front surface shape, a semicircle, by using the polarization data of the 2D plane as input data.

The result of applying the proposed method is given in Figure 4.8(1c) and Figure 4.8(2c). In Figure 4.8, the solid line represents the estimated shape, and the dotted line represents the true shape. For the estimated result shown in Figure 4.8(1c), the result of the previous method (Figure 4.8(1a)) is used for the initial state of the shape. For the estimated result shown in Figure 4.8(2c), the true shape, hemisphere (Figure 4.8(2a)), is used for the initial state of the shape. Figures 4.8(1b)(2b) and Figures 4.8(1c)(2c) are the result after 5 and 50 loops, respectively. The shapes converge to the same shape even if the initial shapes are different. The reason why there is a protruding noise at the top of the estimated shape might be the failure of considering the hole on top of the plastic sphere. Although we have assumed that the object is illuminated

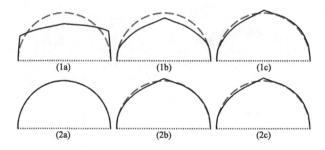

Figure 4.8. Estimation result: (1a) Initial state (result of previous method), (1b)(1c) results after 5 and 50 loops, (2a) initial state (true shape), (2b)(2c) results after 5 and 50 loops.

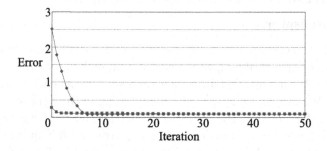

Figure 4.9. Error for each loop: (square) Result when true shape is initial value, (diamond) result when result of previous method is initial value.

uniformly with the same intensity from all directions, we now believe that this assumption might not strictly hold for this hole. Therefore, considering such illumination distribution will be our future work.

The value of the cost function (Equation (4.22)) per each iteration is plotted in Figure 4.9. The vertical axis in Figure 4.9 represents the value of Equation (4.22), while the horizontal axis represents the iteration number. A diamond mark is the value of the result whose initial state is the result of the previous method (Figures 4.8(1a)(1b)(1c)). A square mark is the value of the result whose initial state is the true shape (Figures 4.8(2a)(2b)(2c)). The leftmost value is the value of the cost function of the initial state. Both the value and the shape did not change after around 8 loops. The average computation time was 5.9[sec] for 1 loop with 320 pixels.

The RMS error between the estimated value and the true value is used to compare the accuracy between the proposed method and the previous method. The RMS error of the surface normal was 23.3° for previous method, 9.09° for our method when the initial state was the result of the previous method, and 8.86° for our method when the initial state was the true shape. The RMS error

Figure 4.10.   Bell-shaped transparent acrylic real object.

of the height was 2.70mm for the previous method, 0.672mm for our method when the initial state was the result of previous method, and 0.548mm for our method when the initial state was the true shape.

4.4.2   Bell-shaped Object

Finally, we observe the transparent object shown in Figure 4.10. This object is made of acrylic and is a body-of-revolution. Its refractive index is 1.5 and its diameter of the base is 24mm. The object is observed from the projected area of the object. The front surface is a curved surface and the back surface is a disk. The camera is set orthogonally to the disk. We assume that the refractive index and the back surface shape are known. We use the same value for the intensity of the light source that is obtained in Section 4.2. This chapter only concentrates on proposing a method to estimate the shapes of transparent objects, and obtaining the correct illumination distribution will be a future work.

We estimate the shape of a cross-section of the object to analyze the precision of the proposed method. The cross-section includes the center of the base circle and the line perpendicular to that circle. Figure 4.11(c) illustrates the estimated shape of the object. The solid curve represents the obtained front height, and the dotted line represents the given back height. The initial value is set to be a semicircle shown in Figure 4.11(a). The estimated shape after 5 and 20 loops is illustrated in Figure 4.11(b) and Figure 4.11(c), respectively. RMS of the height was 0.24mm, where the true shape was obtained from the silhouette extracted manually by a human operator from the photograph of the object taken from the side. The average computation time was 7.0[sec] for 1 loop with 320 pixels.

5.   Conclusion

In this chapter, we have proposed a novel method for estimating the surface shape of transparent objects by minimizing the difference between the input

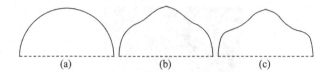

Figure 4.11.   Estimation result: (a) Initial value, (b)(c) result after 5, 20 loops.

polarization data taken by observing the transparent object and the computed polarization data rendered by the polarization raytracing method.

We estimated the shape of transparent objects by an iterative computation. We used a uniform illumination in this study; however, Hata et al. [10] estimated the shape of transparent objects by an iterative computation where the object was illuminated by structured light. Ben-Ezra and Nayar [12] estimated the shape of a transparent object observed from many viewpoints by an iterative computation. To improve the precision of measuring the surface shape of transparent objects, we should probably observe the target object from multiple viewpoints or under various types of illumination. In any case, the iterative computation is considered to be necessary. Our chapter provides the technique for measuring the surface shape of transparent objects using iterative computation, and this technique might be used as the basis for further developments.

Most of the artificial transparent objects have a planar base that enables them to stand by themselves. Also, the material (refractive index) of the artificial transparent objects is known in many cases. Thus, the assumption we adopted in this chapter, "back surface shape and refractive index are known," is effective in many cases. However, not all objects meet these conditions; thus, we intend to develop a method that can measure the back surface shape and refractive index at the same time as well as the front surface shape.

Acknowledgments

This research was supported, in part, by Ministry of Education, Culture, Sports, Science and Technology under the Leading Project, "Development of High Fidelity Digitization Software for Large-Scale and Intangible Cultural Assets," and, in part, by Japan Science and Technology Agency, under the CREST program, "Automatic generation of virtual models of cultural heritage." The authors thank Joan Knapp for proofreading and editing this chapter.

References

[1] K. Koshikawa and Y. Shirai, "A model-based recognition of glossy objects using their polarimetrical properties," *Advanced Robotics*, Vol. 2, No. 2, pp. 137-147, 1987.

[2] L. B. Wolff and T. E. Boult, "Constraining object features using a polarization reflectance model," *IEEE Trans. Patt. Anal. Mach. Intell.*, Vol. 13, No. 7, pp. 635-657, 1991.

[3] S. Rahmann and N. Canterakis, "Reconstruction of specular surfaces using polarization imaging," *Proc. IEEE Conf. Computer Vision and Pattern Recognition*, pp. 149-155, 2001.

[4] O. Drbohlav and R. Šára, "Unambiguous determination of shape from photometric stereo with unknown light sources," *Proc. IEEE Int'l Conf. Computer Vision*, pp. I:581-586, 2001.

[5] D. Miyazaki, R. T. Tan, K. Hara, and K. Ikeuchi, "Polarization-based inverse rendering from a single view," *Proc. IEEE Int'l Conf. Computer Vision*, pp. 982-987, 2003.

[6] M. Saito, Y. Sato, K. Ikeuchi, and H. Kashiwagi, "Measurement of surface orientations of transparent objects by use of polarization in highlight," *J. Opt. Soc. Am. A*, Vol. 16, No. 9, pp. 2286-2293, 1999.

[7] D. Miyazaki, M. Saito, Y. Sato, and K. Ikeuchi, "Determining surface orientations of transparent objects based on polarization degrees in visible and infrared wavelengths," *J. Opt. Soc. Am. A*, Vol. 19, No. 4, pp. 687-694, 2002.

[8] D. Miyazaki, M. Kagesawa, and K. Ikeuchi, "Transparent surface modeling from a pair of polarization images," *IEEE Trans. Patt. Anal. Mach. Intell.*, Vol. 26, No. 1, pp. 73-82, 2004.

[9] H. Murase, "Surface shape reconstruction of a nonrigid transparent object using refraction and motion," *IEEE Trans. Patt. Anal. Mach. Intell.*, Vol. 14, No. 10, pp. 1045-1052, 1992.

[10] S. Hata, Y. Saitoh, S. Kumamura, and K. Kaida, "Shape extraction of transparent object using genetic algorithm," *Proc. Int'l Conf. Pattern Recognition*, pp. 684-688, 1996.

[11] K. Ohara, M. Mizukawa, K. Ohba, and K. Taki, "3D modeling of micro transparent object with integrated vision," *Proc. IEEE Conf. Multisensor Fusion and Integration for Intelligent Systems*, pp. 107-112, 2003.

[12] M. Ben-Ezra and S. K. Nayar, "What does motion reveal about transparency?," *Proc. IEEE Int'l Conf. Computer Vision*, pp. 1025-1032, 2003.

[13] K. N. Kutulakos, "Refractive and specular 3D shape by light-path triangulation," *Proc. Int'l Symposium on the CREST Digital Archiving Project*, pp. 86-93, 2005.

[14] D. E. Zongker, D. M. Warner, B. Curless, and D. H. Salesin, "Environmental matting and compositing," *Proc. SIGGRAPH*, pp. 205-214, 1999.

[15] Y. Chuang, D. E. Zongker, J. Hindorff, B. Curless, D. H. Salesin, and R. Szeliski, "Environment matting extensions: towards higher accuracy and real-time capture," *Proc. SIGGRAPH*, pp. 121-130, 2000.

[16] Z. S. Hakura and J. M. Snyder, "Realistic reflections and refractions on graphics hardware with hybrid rendering and layered environment maps," *Proc. Eurographics Workshop on Rendering*, pp. 289-300, 2001.

[17] W. Matusik, H. Pfister, R. Ziegler, A. Ngan, and L. McMillan, "Acquisition and rendering of transparent and refractive objects," *Proc. Eurographics Workshop on Rendering*, pp. 267-278, 2002.

[18] Y. Wexler, A. W. Fitzgibbon, and A. Zisserman, "Image-based environment matting," *Proc. Eurographics Workshop on Rendering*, pp. 279-290, 2002.

[19] P. Peers and P. Dutré, "Wavelet environment matting," *Proc. Eurographics Workshop on Rendering*, pp. 157-166, 2003.

[20] Y. Y. Schechner, J. Shamir, and N. Kiryati, "Polarization and statistical analysis of scenes containing a semireflector," *J. Opt. Soc. Am. A*, Vol. 17, No. 2, pp. 276-284, 2000.

[21] Y. Y. Schechner, N. Kiryati, and R. Basri, "Separation of transparent layers using focus," *Int'l J. Computer Vision*, Vol. 39, No. 1, pp. 25-39, 2000.

[22] R. Szeliski, S. Avidan, and P. Anandan, "Layer extraction from multiple images containing reflections and transparency," *Proc. IEEE Conf. Computer Vision and Pattern Recognition*, pp. 246-253, 2000.

[23] H. Farid and E. H. Adelson, "Separating reflections from images by use of independent component analysis," *J. Opt. Soc. Am. A*, Vol. 16, No. 9, pp. 2136-2145, 1999.

[24] M. Born and E. Wolf, *Principles of optics*, Pergamon Press, 1959.

[25] W. A. Shurcliff, *Polarized light: production and use*, Harvard University Press, 1962.

[26] R. A. Chipman, "Mechanics of polarizaiton ray tracing," *Optical Engineering*, Vol. 34, No. 6, pp. 1636-1645, 1995.

[27] L. B. Wolff and D. J. Kurlander, "Ray tracing with polarization parameters," *IEEE Computer Graphics and Applications*, Vol. 10, No. 6, pp. 44-55, 1990.

[28] C. Gu and P. Yeh, "Extended Jones matrix method. II," *J. Opt. Soc. Am. A*, Vol. 10, No. 5, pp. 966-973, 1993.

[29] J. S. Gondek, G. W. Meyer, and J. G. Newman, "Wavelength dependent reflectance functions," *Proc. SIGGRAPH*, pp. 213-220, 1994.

[30] D. C. Tannenbaum, P. Tannenbaum, and M. J. Wozny, "Polarization and birefringency considerations in rendering," *Proc. SIGGRAPH*, pp. 221-222, 1994.

[31] A. Wilkie, R. F. Tobler, and W. Purgathofer, "Combined rendering of polarization and fluorescence effects," *Proc. Eurographics Workshop on Rendering*, pp. 197-204, 2001.

[32] S. Guy and C. Soler, "Graphics gems revisited: fast and physically-based rendering of gemstones," *Proc. SIGGRAPH*, pp. 231-238, 2004.

[33] LightTools, http://www.opticalres.com/.

[34] ZEMAX, http://www.zemax.com/.

[35] OptiCAD, http://www.opticad.com/.

[36] W. H. Press, S. A. Teukolsky, W. T. Vetterling, and B. P. Flannery, *Numerical recipes in C: the art of scientific computing*, Cambridge University Press, 1992.

[37] K. Ikeuchi, "Reconstructing a depth map from intensity maps," *Proc. Int'l Conf. Pattern Recognition*, pp. 736-738, 1984.

[38] B. K. P. Horn, "Height and Gradient from Shading," *Int'l J. Computer Vision*, Vol. 5, No. 1, pp. 37-75, 1990.

II

RANGE DATA ANALYSIS

Chapter 5

ROBUST SIMULTANEOUS REGISTRATION OF MULTIPLE RANGE IMAGES

Ko Nishino and Katsushi Ikeuchi

Abstract   The registration problem of multiple range images is fundamental for many applications that rely on precise geometric models. We propose a robust registration method that can align multiple range images comprised of a large number of data points. The proposed method minimizes an error function that is constructed to be global against all range images, providing the ability to diffusively distribute errors instead of accumulating them. The minimization strategy is designed to be efficient and robust against outliers by using conjugate gradient search utilizing M-estimator. Also, for "better" point correspondence search, the laser reflectance strength is used as an additional attribute of each 3D data point. For robustness against data noise, the framework is designed not to use secondary information, i.e. surface normals, in its error metric. We describe the details of the proposed method, and present experimental results applying the proposed method to real data.

1. Introduction

Registration of multiple point cloud range images is an important and fundamental research topic in both computer vision and computer graphics. Many applications and algorithms can be (are) developed on the assumption that accurate geometric models are obtained a priori, e.g., recognition, localization, tracking, appearance analysis, texture-mapping, metamorphism, and virtual/mixed reality systems in general, among others. Additionally, projects to construct precise geometric models based on observation of real world objects for the purpose of digital preservation of cultural heritage objects have drawn attention recently [3, 18, 21]. Because of their objective, these projects require very precise registration of multiple range images.

In this chapter, we propose a framework to register multiple range images robustly. Taking the point cloud images obtained through use of a range sensor, e.g., laser range scanner [8, 7, 20], light-stripe range finder [24], etc., as the input, we simultaneously register all range images to sit in one common coordinate system. We highly prioritize our efforts to make the resulting registered geometric model accurate compared with making the whole procedure computationally fast. For this reason, we design our registration procedure to be a simultaneous registration method based on an error metric computed from point-point distance, including additional attributes in its metric. Also, for robustness and efficiency, we adopt a conjugate gradient framework utilizing M-estimator to solve the least-square problem of minimizing the total errors through registration. Since we target large objects like the Great Buddha in Kamakura, the data size of each range image becomes huge. Thus, we employ k-d tree data structures for efficient point- point correspondence searches.

The remainder of this chapter is organized as follows. In section 2, we overview related work and present our framework. Section 3 describes how a point correspondence search will be accomplished efficiently; and we describe the details of how least- square minimization of the objective function, the core of our simultaneous registration framework, in section 4. We show results of applying our approach to real data in section 5, and section 6 concludes the chapter.

2.   Overview

2.1   Related Work

Past work on range image registration can be roughly classified with respect to the following three aspects.

Strategy: simultaneous[1] **or sequential** The basic strategy of registering multiple range images can be represented by two different approaches. The straightforward strategy is to focus on only two range images at a time, and register each range image to another [25]. After one range image pair is registered, a new pair including either range image in the former pair, positioned in the resulting coordinate, is registered. This is repeated till all range images are used. Since this sequential strategy requires only two range images for each registration stage, it can be implemented with less memory and the overall computational cost tends to be cheap. Also, the computational cost for each registration stage is not affected by the number of range images to be registered consequently.

However, this straightforward strategy is well known to be less accurate. In each range image pair registration stage, some error will be introduced due to data noise, etc. Since each range image will be fixed in the resulting position for each registration stage, this unavoidable error will be propagated to the latter registration stage and it will result in unaffordable error accumulated in the last range image position. Although the "gap" developed by this error accumulation can be small enough depending on the use of the resulting geometric model, it is much more preferable to avoid this theoretically, especially when the geometric model will be used as a basis of texture-mapping or appearance analysis, and so on.

Simultaneous registration solves this error accumulation problem by aligning all range images at once [1, 2, 5, 6, 10, 14, 19, 22, 23]. This can be accomplished by defining an error minimization problem by using an error metric common among all range images. This approach can diffusively distribute the registration error over all overlaps of each range image. The drawback is its large computational cost as opposed to that of sequential approaches.

Matching unit: features or points When registering range images, the problem is usually redesigned as an error (distance) minimization problem. The basis of the error to be measured can be features derived from the range images or points consisting of the range data. Feature-based methods extract some signatures around 3D points, invariant to Euclidean transformation, in each target range image and make correspondences among those features [6, 15, 16]. Based on the assumption that all correspondences are matched correctly, the transformation for registration can be computed in a closed form manner. On the other hand, if the signatures computed from the range images do not provide enough information and the matching of them cannot be done correctly, the registration stage can fail miserably. Point-based methods directly use the 3D points in an iterative manner. The point mates, the point correspondences to compute the error metric, are dynamically updated and several iterative steps are used to minimize the total error. One drawback of this point-based approach is that it requires an initial estimation of the rough transformation between the target range images, which is normally provided by human hand or interaction, while most feature-based approaches do not have this requirement.

Error metric: point-point distance or point-plane distance Originally, point-based approaches, such as the ICP algorithm [4, 28], set the error metric basis on the Euclidean distance between two points corresponding each other [11, 19]. However, since this error metric does not take the surface information into account, the point-based approaches based on point-point distance suffer from the inability to "slide" overlapping range images. An alternative to this distance metric is to use point-plane Euclidean distance, which can be computed by evaluating the distance between the point and its mate's tangent plane [6, 22]. By embedding the surface information into the error metric in this way, point-based approaches utilizing point-plane distance metric tend to be robust against local minima and converge quickly. However, computing the point-plane distance is computationally expensive compared with point-point distance computation; thus, methods using viewing direction to find the correspondence are also proposed for efficiency [1, 5, 22].

2.2   Our Approach

Taking into account the consideration described above, we have designed a registration algorithm which is i) based on the simultaneous strategy, ii) using points as matching units, iii) with the point-point distance metric. The framework is inspired by the work of Wheeler et al [26, 27], that applied similar techniques for object recognition and localization.

We want to construct the geometric model to be as accurate as possible. Also as future work, we would like to accomplish appearance analysis making considerable use of the geometry. For this reason, as a preliminary step, we attach more importance to robustness and accuracy than to computational expense in the registration method. This causes us to choose a simultaneous strategy, which is accurate in principle.

We employ points as matching units. Although the laser range scanner we use is quite accurate, the distance to the object is large and the measurement condition is poor in many cases. Because the scanned range images include noise, the information computed from them will be even more corrupted by the noise. Thus, we avoid using any secondary features derived from raw range data; instead, we directly use data points as matching units.

We use the point-point distance metric. Due to the noise problem, as mentioned above, we have to avoid obtaining secondary features, surface normals in this case, and thus, cannot use the point-plane metric that requires us to calculate surface normals. It is also true that point- point metric is less expensive in computational cost than the point- plane metric, and is preferable when the data set is very large.

The overall simultaneous registration framework can be described as an iteration of the following procedure until it converges.

Procedure OneStepOfSimultaneousRegistration
___

Array KDTrees, Scenes, PointMates, Transforms

foreach r in AllRangeImages
    KDTrees[r] = BuildKDTree(r)

foreach r in AllRangeImages

    foreach s in AllRangeImage-r
        Scenes[s] = s

    foreach i in Pointsof(r)
        foreach s in Scenes
            PointMates[i] += CorrespondenceSearch(i, KDTree[s])
    Transforms[r] = TransformationStep(PointMates)

TransformAll(AllRangeImages, Transforms)

We basically extend the framework of the pairwise ICP algorithm to handle multiple range images simultaneously. This is achieved by setting up an objective function to minimize globally, with respect to each of the range images. Defining *model* as the particular range image in interest and *scene* as one of the range images in the rest of range image set, in one simultaneous registration loop, each range image becomes a *model* once. Point mate search (search for nearest neighbor point) for each point in the *model* is done against all *scene* range images ($M-1$ if we have M range images), and they are stored in a global array. Rigid transformation for the current *model* is computed in a conjugate gradient search framework utilizing M-estimator, and is stored in a global array. After each range image has become a *model* once, all range images are transformed using the transformation stored in the global array. Note that each range image is not transformed immediately. Considering that each step transformation evaluated inside one simultaneous registration procedure will not be so large, this latency of transformation will not cause a problem. Furthermore, this timing of transformation saves us a large amount of computational time, since construction of k-d trees is required only once per range image in one simultaneous registration procedure. Details will be discussed in the following sections.

3.   Point Mate Search

3.1   K-D Tree

As we try to register range images that consist of a large amount of 3D points, finding correspondences for each point in each range image can easily dominate a critical portion of the overall computational time. To obtain point correspondences efficiently, we employ k-d tree structure to store the range images [12]. K-d tree's k-d abbreviates *k-dimensional* and it is a generalization of a binary-search tree for efficient search in high dimension space. The k-d tree is created by recursively splitting a data set down the middle of its dimension of greatest variance. The splitting continues until the leaf nodes contain a small enough number of data points.

The constructed k-d tree becomes a tree of depth $O(\log N)$ where N is the number of points stored. A nearest-neighbor search can be accomplished by following the appropriate branches of the tree until a leaf node is reached. A hyper-sphere centered at the key point with a radius of the distance to the current closest point can be used to determine which, if any, neighboring leaf nodes in the k-d tree must be checked for closer points. Once have we tested all the data in leaf nodes which could possibly be closer, we are guaranteed to have found the closest point in the tree. Though its worst case complexity is $O(N)$, the expected number of operations for the nearest-neighbor search is $O(\log N)$, which will be the case if the data is evenly distributed. For the cases of storing surfaces in 3D space in k-d trees, usually this even distribution assumption holds. The largest overhead involved in using k-d trees is that the k-d tree of range-image points must be built prior to the search. This operation costs $O(N \log N)$. To avoid making this computational expense critical, we update each range image position only once in one simultaneous registration procedure as listed in the pseudo code in section 2.2, requiring only M times of k-d tree rebuilds in one global iteration, where M is the number of range images.

3.2   Distance Metric

To utilize a nearest-neighbor search based on k-d tree structure, we need a measure of dissimilarity between a pair of points. The dissimilarity, Δ, between k-d points $\mathbf{x}$ and $\mathbf{y}$ must have the form

$$\Delta(\mathbf{x}, \mathbf{y}) = F(\sum_{i=1}^{k} f_i(\mathbf{x}_i, \mathbf{y}_i)) \tag{5.1}$$

where the functions f_i are symmetric functions over a single dimension and functions f_i and F are monotonic. All distances satisfy these conditions, including the Euclidean distance $\|\mathbf{x} - \mathbf{y}\|$. As mentioned in section 2.1, using point-plane distance as the error metric provides faster convergence . However, the point-plane distance, which can be computed by

$$\Delta(\mathbf{x}, \mathbf{y}) = (\mathbf{x} - \mathbf{y}) \cdot \mathbf{N_y} \tag{5.2}$$

does not satisfy the monotonic condition. To take advantage of the efficiency of the k-d tree structure, we use the point-point Euclidean distance as the dissimilarity measure. Also, we prefer point-point distance for the sake of robustness; avoiding the usage of secondary information derived from raw data, such as surface normals in point-plane, which can be sensitive to noise in the raw data points.

Figure 5.1 depicts an example of point correspondences in the case of using point-point distance metric and point-plane distance metric. While the point-point distance metric searches for the nearest neighboring point, meaning establishing a discrete mapping of one surface to another, the point-plane distance metric can be considered as a way to find the continuous mapping of one surface to another. In cases like Figure 5.1, where the *model* surface has to be "slid" to fit the *scene* surface, the point-plane approach succeeds in finding the correspondences that enable us to compute the rigid transformation close to the sliding direction, while the point-point approach tends to get stuck in a local minima because of the inability to find point mates in the sliding direction. This sliding ability of point-plane approaches provides faster convergence compared with using point-point distance metric.

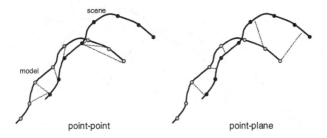

Figure 5.1. Point correspondences using point-point and point-plane distance metric.

Figure 5.2. Images using laser reflectance strength as pixel values.

To compensate for the inability of sliding in point-point based distance measurement, we need to attach, to the 3D points, some information that suggests better matches. For this purpose, we use the laser reflectance strength value (referred to as RSV for the rest of this chapter) as an attribute of each 3D point. Most laser range finders return the strength of the laser reflected at each surface point that it measured as an additional output value. Figure 5.2 shows two images with RSVs used as the pixel values. For better visualization, the images are histogram-equalized. As can be seen, the RSVs are mostly invariant against Euclidean transformation, since the dominant factor of the power of laser reflected at an object surface is its surface material. One common method to utilize two different sources of information in distance measurement, in this case the position distance and RSV distance, is to set up a combined metric, such as

$$\Delta(\mathbf{x}, \mathbf{y}) = [(x_{\mathbf{x}} - x_{\mathbf{y}})^2 + (y_{\mathbf{x}} - y_{\mathbf{y}})^2 + (z_{\mathbf{x}} - z_{\mathbf{y}})^2 + \lambda(r_{\mathbf{x}} - r_{\mathbf{y}})^2]^{\frac{1}{2}} \quad (5.3)$$

where r is RSV and λ is a constant scalar. However, this scalar introduces a tedious and ad hoc effort to determining the "best" λ. Instead, we use the reflectance to determine the best pair among candidates of closest points. Namely, we first search for multiple (m) closest points in the k-d tree, and

Figure 5.3. Point mates using point-point distance metric with reflectance strength values. Different shape marks indicate different reflectance strength values.

then evaluate the RSV distance for each of them to get the closest point with respect to laser reflectance strength value. We gradually reduce the number of the candidates m along the iteration so as to make it inversely proportional to the number of iterations. This utilization of the laser reflectance is similar to [17], which uses color attributes to narrow down the closest point candidates. Figure 5.3 depicts how the point-point distance metric utilizing RSV as additional attribute works in the example case depicted in Figure 5.1 ($m = 4$ in this example).

3.3   Speeding Up

Even though we employ k-d tree structure for efficient point correspondence search, when the number of points in the target range images is large, the computational cost becomes massive. In early stages of the simultaneous registration, when the range images are widely distributed, it is more important to get them close to each other than to accurately compute the rigid transformation for each registration step. To provide a way to speed up the registration, we subsample each range image to reduce the number of points used in the registration process. The points in each range image are given a sequential identification number $m = 0, .., M - 1$ and a uniformly distributed random number within the interval $[0, M - 1]$ is generated to pick up the points to be used. The seed number to generate the random numbers is common for all range images in one simultaneous registration procedure and updated once per one global registration step. In the current implementation, we allow the user to determine the percentile of points to be used in each range image interactively. In future implementation, this could be done automatically by first using small percentage and gradually increasing it to reach one hundred percent.

As the range images are set to be still in one iteration of simultaneous registration, it is very easy to make the whole framework run in a parallel manner. In our current implementation, constructing k-d trees and search point mates and computing transformation steps are done in threads, providing high scalability.

4. Least-square Minimization Strategy

4.1 Representing Transformation

Given a set of corresponding points $(\mathbf{x}_i, \mathbf{y}_i)$ where $i = 0, ..., N - 1$, the registration problem is to compute the rigid transformation which registers the *model* points $\mathbf{x}_i$ with their corresponding *scene* points $\mathbf{y}_i$. The rigid transformation can be specified by a pair of a 3×3 rotation matrix $\mathbf{R}$ and a 3D translation vector $\mathbf{t}$. When the corresponding points are aligned with each other, $\mathbf{y}_i$ can be written as

$$\mathbf{y}_i = \mathbf{R}\mathbf{x}_i + \mathbf{t} \qquad (5.4)$$

Since range data points will be contaminated by noise, the range image registration problem can be described as an error minimization problem with the error function as follows:

$$f(\mathbf{R}, \mathbf{t}) = \sum_i \|\mathbf{R}\mathbf{x}_i + \mathbf{t} - \mathbf{y}_i\|^2 \qquad (5.5)$$

to minimize with regard to $(\mathbf{R}\ \mathbf{t})$. As mentioned in section 2.2, i will stand for all point mates established from all pairs of range images (if there are M range images, i will include all point mates from $M \times (M - 1)$ range image pairs). Although it is convenient for vector computation to represent the rotation as a 3×3 matrix $\mathbf{R}$, $\mathbf{R}$ will be constrained in a non-linear way as follows (T stands for transpose):

$$\mathbf{R}\mathbf{R}^T = \mathbf{I}$$
$$|\mathbf{R}| = 1$$

It is difficult to take advantage of the linear matrix representation of rotation while satisfying these constraints. For this reason, we will use the quaternion representation for rotation, which is a well known solution to this rotation problem. (The benefits of using quaternion will be described later.) Thus, the position parameters of each range image and the rigid transformation to register all of them will be represented with seven element vectors as follows:

$$\mathbf{p} = [\mathbf{t}^T\ \mathbf{q}^T]^T \qquad (5.6)$$
$$where\ \mathbf{q} = [u\ v\ w\ s]^T$$

4.2 M-Estimator

As seen in section 4.1, the registration problem can be described as a least-square minimization problem with the objective function equation (5.5). Point correspondences are acquired using the techniques described in section 3. On solving this error minimization problem, we will have to deal with two problems,

Poor initial correspondences We must assume that the point correspondences established in the beginning will include a large number of mismatches.

Outliers Even when most of the point correspondences are correct, we still have to deal with outliers resulting from mismatches and noise-corrupted data points.

The underlying problem here is how to robustly reject outliers. The following three representative classes of solutions can be found in the field of robust statistics. The first class of solutions, outlier thresholding, is the simplest and most computationally cheap technique; thus it is the most common technique used in vision applications. The basic idea is to estimate the standard deviation σ of the errors in the data and to then eliminate data points which have errors larger than $|k\sigma|$ where k is typically greater than or equal to 3. The problem of outlier thresholding is that a hard threshold is determined to eliminate the outliers. This means that, regardless of where the threshold is chosen, some number of valid data points will be classified as outliers and some number of true outliers will be classified as valid. In this sense, it is unlikely that a perfect method for selecting the threshold exists unless the outliers are all known a priori.

The second class of robust estimators is the median/rank estimation method. The basic idea is to select the median or kth value (for some percentile k) with respect to the errors for each observation and to then use that value as our error estimate. The logic behind this is that the median is almost guaranteed not to be an outlier as long as half of the data is valid. An example of median estimators is the least-median-of-squares method (LMedS). LMedS computes the parameters of interest which minimize the median of the squared error computed from all data pairs using that parameter. Essentially, this requires an exhaustive search of possible values of the parameters by testing least-squares estimates using that parameter for all possible combinations of point correspondences. While these median-based techniques can be very robust, this exhaustive search remains a large drawback.

The third class of robust techniques is M-estimation; the technique we use. The general form of M-estimators allows us to define a probability distribution which can be maximized by minimizing a function of the form

$$E(z) = \sum_i \rho(z_i) \tag{5.7}$$

where $\rho(z)$ is an arbitrary function of the errors z_i in the data set. The M-estimate is the maximum-likelihood estimate of the probability distribution

P equivalent to $E(z)$. Least-squares estimation, such as minimizing (5.5), corresponds to M-estimation with $\rho(z) = z^2$.

$$P(z) = e^{-E(z)} = e^{-\sum_i z_i^2} \tag{5.8}$$

We can find the parameters $\mathbf{p}$ that minimize E by taking the derivative of E with respect to $\mathbf{p}$ and setting it to 0.

$$\frac{\partial E}{\partial \mathbf{p}} = \sum_i \frac{\partial \rho}{\partial z_i} \cdot \frac{\partial z_i}{\partial \mathbf{p}} = \sum_i w(z_i) z_i \frac{\partial z_i}{\partial \mathbf{p}} = 0 \tag{5.9}$$

where $w(z) = \frac{1}{z}\frac{\partial \rho}{\partial z}$

As can be seen in (5.9), M-estimation can be interpreted as weighted-least square minimization, with the weight function w being a function of data points z_i. In our current implementation, we use the Lorentz function as the M-estimator because we found it to work best with our range image data.

4.3 Putting It Together

Now, we can redefine our registration problem as follows: Given a set of corresponding points $(\mathbf{x}_i, \mathbf{y}_i)$ (i=0,...,N-1), we will minimize

$$E(\mathbf{p}) = \frac{1}{N}\sum_i^N \rho(z_i(\mathbf{p})) \tag{5.10}$$

$$\text{where } z_i(\mathbf{p}) = \|\mathbf{R}(\mathbf{q})\mathbf{x}_i + \mathbf{t} - \mathbf{y}_i\| \tag{5.11}$$

$$\text{and } \rho(z_i) = \log(1 + \frac{1}{2}z_i^2) \tag{5.12}$$

The minimization of function E can be accomplished in a conjugate gradient search framework. Conjugate gradient search is a variation of gradient descent search; it constrains each gradient step to be conjugated to the former gradient step. This constraint avoids much of the zig-zagging that pure gradient descent will often suffer from, and consequently provides faster convergence.

In applying conjugate gradient search to our minimization problem, we need to compute the gradient of function E with respect to pose parameter $\mathbf{p}$ which can be described as equation (5.9). For the following derivations, we redefine z_i to be

$$z_i(\mathbf{p}) = \|\mathbf{R}(\mathbf{q}\mathbf{x}_i) + \mathbf{t} - \mathbf{y}_i\|^2 \tag{5.13}$$

Prior to the computation of the gradient, we pre-rotate the model points, so that the current quaternion is $\mathbf{q}_I = [0\ 0\ 0\ 1]^T$ which has the property of $\mathbf{R}(\mathbf{q}_I) = \mathbf{I}$. This allows us to take advantage of the fact that the gradient of $\mathbf{R}(\mathbf{q})\mathbf{x}$ can easily be evaluated at $\mathbf{q} = \mathbf{q}_I$:

$$\frac{\partial(\mathbf{R}\mathbf{x})}{\partial \mathbf{q}}\mathbf{x} = 2\mathbf{C}(\mathbf{x})^T b \tag{5.14}$$

where $C(x)$ is the 3×3 skew-symmetric matrix of the vector x which has the useful characteristic as follows.

$$C(x)y = x \times y \qquad (5.15)$$

where $\times$ is the cross product. With these facts, $\frac{\partial z_i}{\partial p}$ in equation (5.9) can be derived as

$$
\begin{aligned}
\frac{\partial z_i}{\partial p} &= 2(R(q)x_i + t - y_i)\frac{\partial(R(q)x_i + t - y_i)}{\partial p} \\
&= \begin{bmatrix} 2(x_i + t - y_i) \\ 4C(x)^T(x_i + t - y_i) \end{bmatrix} \\
&= \begin{bmatrix} 2(x_i + t - y_i) \\ 4x_i \times (t - y_i) \end{bmatrix} \qquad (5.16)
\end{aligned}
$$

With the gradient computed in the above manner, line minimization is accomplished with a golden section search. Line minimization methods using interpolation are not adopted, since it is easy to imagine the base function to be highly non-linear.

5.   Results

5.1   Noisy Range Images

To examine its robustness against noise, we applied the proposed method to a noisy range image sequence. We built a light stripe range finder [24], and scanned a ceramic cat. By setting the threshold of the light stripe range finder to include quite an amount of background and not to eliminate ill triangle patches (triangle patches that have large aspect ratios), we obtained three range images including a lot of noise. To compare the proposed method with the registration method proposed in [22] [2], the range images were initially aligned with each other manually as depicted in Figure 5.4. [3] After iterating both methods until convergence, we eliminated all 3D points and triangle patches that did not belong to the ceramic cat and measured the errors by using a point-plane distance metric. Table 5.1 shows the results and Figure 5.5 depicts the histograms of errors for both methods. Our method converged robustly, while the method of [22] converged into a local minima, leaving a gap as can be seen in Figure 5.6.

5.2   Preserving Cultural Heritage Objects

We have applied the proposed method to register real data, the Great Buddha in Kamakura (Figure 5.7): a 13m tall statue sitting in open air. The Great Buddha was scanned from fourteen different directions using Cyrax 2400 [8], a time-of-flight laser range scanner that can scan up to 100m with ±6mm error

Figure 5.4. Initial positions of the Noisy Cat sequence.

	Average Error	Max. Error	Min. Error
Our method	0.84	2.55	5.35×10^{-7}
[22]	1.29	2.57	3.21×10^{-5}

Table 5.1. Comparison of errors in mm.

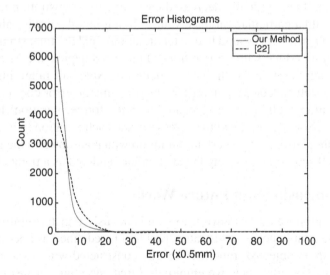

Figure 5.5. Histogram of errors.

at 50m distance. Each point cloud image consists of approximately three to four million vertices. Since registering all range images with full resolution

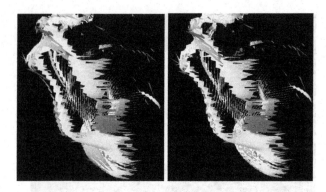

Figure 5.6. Left: Registered with [22] Right: Registered with our method.(Viewing from the top left of the cat.)

requires massive computational resource and time, we registered those range images in $1/25$ resolution as a preliminary experiment.

First the input range images were registered in a pairwise manner with occasional manual operation for initial alignment; they were then registered simultaneously. The variance of Lorentz's function was set at a large value in the beginning and then gradually decreased each time the registration procedure converged with a particular variance value. Rough initial pairwise alignment was accomplished with around five to ten iterations, and the final simultaneous registration was done with 25 iterations. Figure 5.8 depicts the M-estimator error for each iteration for the last 25 iteration. Since all range images are treated to be static inside each iteration, the M-estimator error does not always get smaller after each iteration compared with the former iteration. However, because the error is guaranteed to decrease inside each iteration, it is clear that the algorithm converges to a certain minimum which is shown in the graph.

Figure 5.9 shows the resulting Great Buddha rendered as a point cloud.

6.   Conclusion and Future Work

We have proposed a framework to simultaneously register multiple range images. The simultaneous registration problem is redefined as a least- square problem with an objective function globally constructed with respect to each range image. For efficiency, we employ k-d tree structure for fast point correspondence search and apply conjugate gradient search in minimizing the least-square problem for faster convergence. For robustness, we employ the laser reflectance strength as an additional attribute of the 3D points and search for "better" point mates based on their distance. Also, M-estimator is used for robust outlier rejection.

Figure 5.7. A photograph of the Great Buddha in Kamakura City.

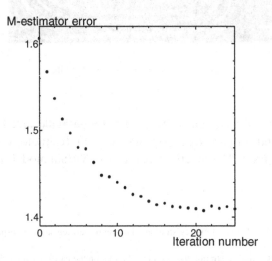

Figure 5.8. M-estimator error v.s. iteration number

For future work, we plan to automate initial estimation of the rigid transformations to pass to the simultaneous registration program, which is currently done manually.

Acknowledgments

This research was supported, in part, by Ministry of Education, Culture, Sports, Science and Technology under the Leading Project, "Development

Figure 5.9.   Registered Great Buddha.

of High Fidelity Digitization Software for Large-Scale and Intangible Cultural Assets," and, in part, by Japan Science and Technology Agency, under the CREST program, "Automatic generation of virtual models of cultural heritage."

Notes

1. Commonly referred to as "global registration" and "multi-view registration", especially in the graphics community

2. We implemented the registration method in [22] based on the paper, meaning the comparison may not be fair.

3. With more rough initial hand alignment, the other registration method did not converge.

References

[1] R. Benjemaa and F. Schmitt. Fast global registration of 3d sampled surfaces using a multi-z-buffer technique. In *Proc. Int. Conf. On Recent Advances in 3-D Digital Imaging and Modeling*, pages 113–120, May 1997.

[2] R. Bergevin, M. Soucy, H. Gagnon, and D. Laurendeau. Towards a general multi-view registration technique. *IEEE Trans. Patt. Anal. Machine*

Intell., 18(5):540–547, May 1996.

[3] R. Bernardini and H. Rushmeier. The 3d model acquisition pipeline. In *Eurographics 2000 State of the Art Report (STAR)*, Aug. 2000.

[4] P.J. Besl and N.D. McKay. A method for registration of 3-d shapes. *IEEE Trans. Patt. Anal. Machine Intell.*, 14(2):239–256, Feb 1992.

[5] G. Blais and M.D. Levine. Registering multiview range data to create 3d computer objects. *IEEE Trans. Patt. Anal. Machine Intell.*, 17(8):820–824, Aug 1995.

[6] Y. Chen and G. Medioni. Object modeling by registration of multiple range images. *Image and Vision Computing*, 10(3):145–155, Apr 1992.

[7] Cyberware. http://www.cyberware.com.

[8] Cyra. http://www.cyra.com.

[9] C. Dorai, G. Wang, A.K. Jain, and C. Mercer. From images to models: Automatic 3d object model construction from multiple views. In *Proc. of the 13th IAPR International Conference on Pattern Recognition*, pages 770–774, 1996.

[10] D.W. Eggert, A.W. Fitzgibbon, and R.B. Fisher. Simultaneous registration of multiple range views for use in reverse engineering. Technical Report 804, Dept. of Artificial Intelligence, University of Edinburgh, 1996.

[11] O.D. Faugeras and M. Hebert. The representation, recognition, and locating of 3-d objects. *International Journal of Robotic Research*, 5(3):27–52, Fall 1986.

[12] J.H. Friedman, J.L. Bentley, and R.A. Finkel. An algorithm for finding best matches in logarithmic expected time. *ACM Trans. On Mathematical Software*, 3(3):209–226, 1997.

[13] G. Godin, M. Rioux, and R. Baribeau. Three-dimensional registration using range and intensity information. In *Proc. SPIE vol.2350: Visionmetrics III*, pages 279–290, 1994.

[14] H. Jin, T. Duchamp, H. Hoppe, J.A. McDonald, K. Pulli, and W. Stuetzle. Surface reconstruction from misregistered data. In *Proc. SPIE vol.2573: Vision Geometry IV*, pages 324–328, 1995.

[15] A. Johnson. *Spin-Images: A Representation for 3-D Surface Matching*. PhD thesis, Robotics Institute, Carnegie Mellon University, Pittsburgh, PA, Aug 1997.

[16] A. Johnson and M. Hebert. Surface registration by matching oriented points. In *Proc. Int. Conf. On Recent Advances in 3-D Digital Imaging and Modeling*, pages 121–128, May 1997.

[17] A. Johnson and S.B. Kang. Registration and integration of textured 3-d data. In *Proc. Int. Conf. On Recent Advances in 3-D Digital Imaging and Modeling*, pages 234–241, May 1997.

[18] M. Levoy, K. Pulli, B. Curless, S. Rusinkiewicz, D. Koller, L. Pereira, M. Ginzton, S. Anderson, J. Davis, J. Ginsberg, J. Shade, and Duane Fulk. The Digital Michelangelo Project: 3D Scanning of Large Statues. In *Computer Graphics Proceedings, ACM SIGGRAPH 00*, pages 131–144, Jul. 2000.

[19] T. Masuda, K. Sakaue, and N. Yokoya. Registration and integration of multiple range images for 3-d models construction. In *Proc. IEEE Conf. on Computer Vision and Pattern Recognition*, pages 879–883, Jun 1996.

[20] Minolta. *Vivid 900*, 2001. http://www.minolta-rio.com/vivid/.

[21] D. Miyazaki, T. Oishi, T. Nishikawa, R. Sagawa, K. Nishino, T. Tomomatsu, Y. Takase, and K. Ikeuchi. The Great Buddha Project: Modelling Cultural Heritage through Observation. In *6th International Conference on Virtual Systems and MultiMedia VSMM2000*, pages 138–145, Oct. 2000.

[22] P. Neugebauer. Geometrical cloning of 3d objects via simultaneous registration of multiple range images. In *Proc. Int. Conf. on Shape Modeling and Application*, pages 130–139, Mar 1997.

[23] K. Pulli. Multiview registration for large data sets. In *Second Int. Conf. on 3D Digital Imaging and Modeling*, pages 160–168, Oct 1999.

[24] K. Sato and S. Inokuchi. Range-imaging system utilizing nematic liquid crystal mask. In *First International Conference on Computer Vision*, pages 657–661, 1987.

[25] G. Turk and M. Levoy. Zippered polygon meshes from range images. In *SIGGRAPH 94*, pages 311–318, Jul 1994.

[26] M.D. Wheeler. *Automatic modeling and localization for object recognition*. PhD thesis, Robotics Institute, Carnegie Mellon University, Pittsburgh, PA, Oct 1996.

[27] M.D. Wheeler and K. Ikeuchi. Sensor modeling, probablistic hypothesis generation, and robust localization for object recognition. *IEEE Trans. Pattern Analysis and Machine Intelligence*, 17(3):252–265, 1995.

[28] Z. Zhang. Iterative point matching for registration of free form curves and surfaces. *International Journal of Computer Vision*, 12(2):119–152, 1994.

Chapter 6

A FAST SIMULTANEOUS ALIGNMENT OF MULTIPLE RANGE IMAGES

Takeshi Oishi, Atsushi Nakazawa, Ryo Kurazume, and Katsushi Ikeuchi

Abstract   This chapter describes a fast, simultaneous alignment method for a large number of range images. Generally the most time-consuming task in aligning range images is searching corresponding points. The fastest searching method is the "Inverse Calibration" method. However, this method requires pre-computed look-up tables and precise sensor parameters. We propose a fast searching method using "index images," which work as look-up tables and are rapidly created without any sensor parameters by using graphics hardware. To accelerate the computation to estimate rigid transformations, we employed a linear error evaluation method. When the number of range images increases, the computation time for solving the linear equations becomes too long because of the large size of the coefficient matrix. On the other hand, the coefficient matrix has the characteristic of becoming sparser as the number of range images increases. Thus, we applied the Incomplete Cholesky Conjugate Gradient (ICCG) method to solve the equations and found that the ICCG greatly accelerates the matrix operation by pre-conditioning the coefficient matrix. Some experimental results in which a large number of range images are aligned demonstrate the effectiveness of our method.

1.   Introduction

In the last quarter-century, quite a lot of algorithms for aligning range images have been proposed. Many of these algorithms are based on the iterative closest point (ICP) proposed by Besl [1] and are adapted from the method proposed by Chen [2]. With ICP, corresponding points are searched for as the closest points between two range images, and a transformation matrix is computed so that the mean square error of the corresponding points is minimized. The computation is iterated until the mean square error falls below the threshold value. In Chen's method, the relative positions of range images are calculated so that the distance between vertices and the corresponding patches is minimized. In addition, there is a method to search for correspondences by projecting the points along with the ray direction [3, 4]. Since the ICP algorithm tends to be affected by false matching and noise, Masuda et al. proposed a robust method that uses random sampling and the Least Median Squares Estimation method (LMedS) [5].

When the number of range images is very large, a method that simultaneously aligns range images is required. The algorithms described above align two range images; when using these algorithms, error accumulation increases as the number of range images increases. In such cases, a method that simultaneously aligns range images is useful. Neugebauer et al. proposed a simultaneous registration method that adopted projection search of correspondences and point-plane error metric [6]. Benjamaa et al. extended the method proposed by Bergevin et al. [7] and implemented a simultaneous alignment method while accelerating the pair-wise alignment algorithm by using multi z-buffers [8].

Although various methods have been proposed, the problem for every method is the computation cost of correspondence search. If the number of vertices of two range images is equally assumed to be N by the original ICP, their complexity is $O(N^2)$ since correspondences are searched for in all vertices. In order to accelerate ICP, there are techniques [9, 10] that use *Kd-trees* and that narrow the search range by using data cache [11–13]. However, the complexity of *Kd-tree* search is $O(NlogN)$. That is, sufficient acceleration cannot be achieved by these algorithms. The computational complexity of the inverse calibration method proposed by Blais is $O(N)$ [3, 14]. However, this method requires precise sensor parameters (intrinsic parameters of CCD camera, parameters of scanning mechanism) and pre-computed look-up tables. In addition, the creation of the look-up tables is very time consuming because Euclidian distances between each element of a table and every ray of sampled points have to be calculated.

Another problem in aligning a large number of range images is the computation cost of matrix operations in which rigid transformations of range images are computed. To directly solve a non-linear least squares problem is very time consuming [10]. In this case, the linearized algorithm is effective in dealing with a large data set [4]. However, the computation time to solve the linear equations with conventional solvers (SVD, Cholesky decomposition, etc.) rapidly increases as the number of range images increases because the coefficient matrix becomes very large.

We propose a fast method to align a large number of range images simultaneously. Our method has three characteristics. 1) The process of searching corresponding points is accelerated by using index images, which are rapidly created without sensor parameters. 2) The method employs the point-plane error metric and linearized error evaluation. 3) An iterative solver (incomplete Cholesky conjugate gradient method) is applied in order to accelerate the computation of the rigid transformations. In Section 2, the details of our algorithm are described. Some experimental results that demonstrate the effectiveness of our method are shown in Section 3. Our conclusions are described in Section 4.

2. Alignment Algorithm

In this section, the details of our alignment algorithm are explained. We assume that all range images have been converted to mesh models. The algorithm is applied in the following steps:

1. Compute, for all pairs of partial meshes,
(a) search all correspondence of vertices
(b) evaluate error terms of all correspondence pairs
2. Compute transformation matrices of all pairs for immunizing all errors
3. Iterate steps 1 and 2 until the termination condition is satisfied

First, we explain the fast method to search corresponding points. Then, the details of error evaluation and the computation of rigid transformations are described.

2.1 Correspondence Search

Our algorithm employs points and planes to evaluate relative distance as the Chen and Medioni method [2]. The corresponding pairs are searched along the line of sight (Fig. 6.1). Here, the line of sight is defined as the optical axis of a range sensor. Let us denote one mesh as the base mesh and its corresponding mesh as the target mesh. An extension of the line of sight, from a vertex of the base mesh, crosses a triangle patch of the target mesh and creates the intersecting point. In order to eliminate false correspondences, if the distance between the vertex and the corresponding point is larger than a certain threshold value, the correspondence is removed. This correspondence search is computed for all pairs of mesh models.

Though the threshold distance is given empirically as l_{given}, it is compared with the average distance of all corresponding points $\hat{r}$, and the smaller value is selected as l_{th}.

$$l_{th} = \begin{cases} l_{given} & (if : l_{given} < \hat{r}) \\ \hat{r} & (otherwize) \end{cases} \qquad (6.1)$$

$$\hat{r} = \frac{1}{N} \sum_i^N \|\mathbf{y}_i - \mathbf{x}_i\| \qquad (6.2)$$

N is the number of vertices included in the base mesh.

To search correspondences quickly, our method uses *index images*. Though the complexity of this process is $O(N,)$,the same as that of the inverse calibration method, sensor parameters are not required. Furthermore, the searching

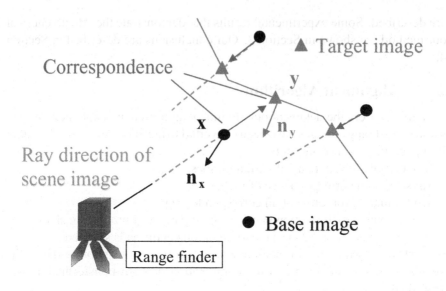

Figure 6.1.   Searching corresponding points

process can be accelerated by graphics hardware. The details of correspondence search using index images are described below.

2.1.1   Creation of Index Images

An index image works as a look-up table to retrieve the index of corresponding patches. Here, we describe the procedures for creating an index image as follows:

1. A unique index number is assigned to each triangle patch of a target mesh.

2. Index numbers are converted to unique colors.

3. Triangle patches of the target mesh are rendered on an image plane with the index colors.

First, a unique integer value is assigned to each triangle patch. Since the assigned value can be any integer number, 0 to n-1 are assigned sequentially, where n is the number of triangle patches.

Next, the assigned index values are converted to unique colors. If the precision of index values is the same as that of rendering colors, the index values are converted directly. Assume that the precision of each color channel is expressed by $q$bits. [0 q-1] bits of an index value are assigned to *Red*, and [q 2q-1]

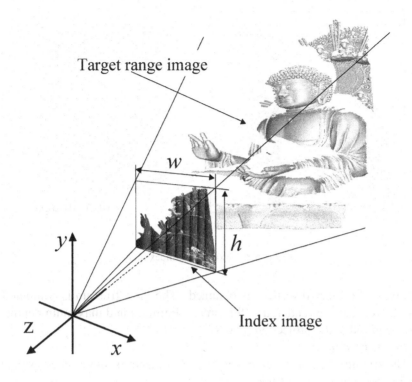

Figure 6.2.   Rendering of index image

bits to *Green*, and the next to *Blue*, and highest q bits are assigned to *Alpha*. If the precision is not the same, the indices have to be converted carefully.

All triangle patches are rendered onto an image plane using the index colors (Fig. 6.2). The pixels in which the triangle patches are not rendered are filled with an exceptional color like white. The target mesh is assumed to be described in its measured coordinate system.

Projection method

Generally, perspective projection is used for rendering the index images. Perspective projection works well for the range images that are measured by sensors that adopt a method like light sectioning. On the other hand, in the case of range images taken by sensors with scanning mechanisms using mirrors, the spherical projection is better because the angles between sampled points are equal (or nearly equal) to each other.

View frustum

To obtain a sufficient number of corresponding points, rendering areas have to be determined properly. All vertices of a target mesh are projected onto the index image plane. Then, the rectangular area $(u_{min}, v_{min}, u_{max}, v_{max})$ that

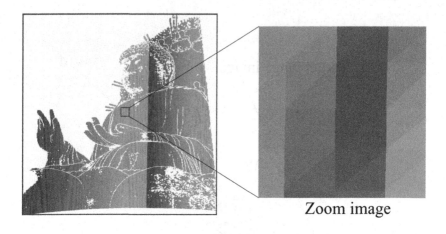

Zoom image

Figure 6.3.   Example of index images

involves all projected vertices is obtained. The view frustum is computed so that all vertices are rendered in this area. Minimum and maximum depths are also acquired at the projection process.

Image resolution

The resolution of an index image (L_u, L_v) has to be determined as the following conditions are fulfilled.

$$L_u \geq 2 \times w/\Delta w_{\text{min}} \tag{6.3}$$

$$L_v \geq 2 \times h/\Delta h_{\text{min}} \tag{6.4}$$

$$w = u_{\text{max}} - u_{\text{min}} \tag{6.5}$$

$$h = v_{\text{max}} - v_{\text{min}} \tag{6.6}$$

Variables w and h represent the height and width of the rendering area respectively (Fig. 6.2). Δw_{min} and Δh_{min} represent the minimum height and minimum width of all triangles projected onto the index image plane.

The image resolution (L_u, L_v) can be roughly determined so that the conditions described in inequality 4 and inequality 5 are satisfied. Although the parameters $(w, h, \Delta w_{\text{min}}, \Delta h_{\text{min}})$ are different in each partial mesh, a unique resolution that satisfies the conditions of all mesh models works well for all index images.

The rendering process is accelerated by using graphics hardware. The rendering time becomes small enough to ignore even if the images are rendered at each iterative step. A large memory space for storing look-up tables is not required. The memory space for only one index image can be shared by all mesh models. Figure 6.3 shows an example of index images.

2.1.2   Acquisition of Corresponding Points

By using the index image, corresponding points are rapidly searched. The procedure for this process is the reverse of that used to make an index image. Here, we assume that all vertices of the base mesh are previously converted to the local coordinate system of the target mesh. The following steps are applied to all vertices of the base mesh:

1. A vertex is projected onto the index image plane by the same projection method as is used for the index image.

2. A color is obtained from the projected pixel.

3. The obtained color is converted to the index value of a patch of the target mesh.

4. The vertex is projected onto the corresponding patch; a corresponding point is acquired.

The procedures are depicted in Fig. 6.4. A vertex of the base image is projected onto the index image plane. Then, a color is acquired from the projected pixel and is converted to the index of a corresponding patch. Since a correct index value may not be obtained because of round-off errors, the vertex is reprojected onto a corresponding patch, and the crossing point is checked to see whether it is inside the patch or not. If the crossing point is inside the patch, the accurate corresponding point is computed. Until the correct corresponding point is obtained, steps 2-4 are applied to 3×3 pixels around the projected pixel. The computational complexity of this process is also $O(N)$.

2.2   Error Metric

The error measure between corresponding points is the cosine distance between the point and the plane. Let the vertex of the base mesh and the corresponding crossing point in the target mesh be $\vec{x}$ and $\vec{y}$, respectively. The error measure of a pair k is written as

$$e_k = \vec{n} \cdot (\vec{y} - \vec{x}) \tag{6.7}$$

$$\vec{n} = \frac{\vec{n}_x + \vec{n}_y}{\|\vec{n}_x + \vec{n}_y\|}, \tag{6.8}$$

where $\vec{n}_x$ and $\vec{n}_y$ are the normal vectors of $\vec{x}$ and $\vec{y}$ defined around the vertices respectively. Since normal vectors tend to be greatly influenced by measurement errors, we used the average normal vectors for error evaluation.

The transformation matrices of the base and target mesh models are computed so that this error measure is minimized. The error evaluation function is

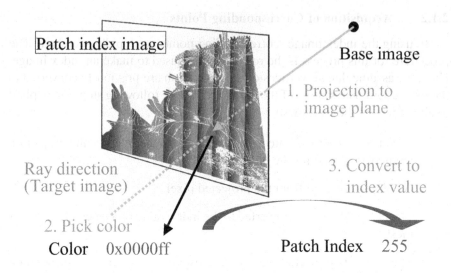

rewritten as

$$\varepsilon = R_B \vec{n} \cdot \{(R_T \vec{y} + \vec{t}_T) - (R_B \vec{x} + \vec{t}_B)\} \tag{6.9}$$

Here, the rotation matrix and the translation vector of the base and target mesh are R_M, $R_S, \vec{t}_M, \vec{t}_S$ respectively. To make the function simple, the average normal $\vec{n}$ is assumed to be rotated by the matrix of base range image $\boldsymbol{R}_B$. The distance between the base and the target mesh is expressed as

$$\bar{\varepsilon} = \min_{\mathbf{R}, \vec{t}} \sum_{i,j,k} \left(R_i \vec{n}_{ik} \cdot \{(R_j \vec{y}_{ijk} + \vec{t}_j) - (R_i \vec{x}_{ik} + \vec{t}_i)\} \right)^2 \tag{6.10}$$

If it is assumed that the angles of rotation are minute, the rotation matrix $\boldsymbol{R}$ is written as

$$\mathbf{R} = \begin{pmatrix} 1 & -c_3 & c_2 \\ c_3 & 1 & -c_1 \\ -c_2 & c_1 & 1 \end{pmatrix} \tag{6.11}$$

The translation vector is expressed as

$$\vec{t} = \begin{pmatrix} t_x & t_y & t_z \end{pmatrix}^T \tag{6.12}$$

After some algebraic manipulations [5], equation 4 is rewritten as

$$\bar{\varepsilon} = \min_{\vec{\delta}} \sum_{i \neq j} \left\| \vec{A}_{ijk} \cdot \vec{\delta} - s_{ijk} \right\|^2 \tag{6.13}$$

$$s_{ijk} = \vec{n}_{ik} \cdot (\vec{x}_{ik} - \vec{y}_{ijk}) \tag{6.14}$$

$$\vec{A}_{ijk} = \left\{ \left(\underbrace{0...0}_{6i\times1}\ \vec{C}_{ijk}^{\mathrm{T}}\ \underbrace{0...0}_{6(l-i-1)\times1} \right) + \left(\underbrace{0...0}_{6j\times1}\ -\vec{C}_{ijk}^{\mathrm{T}}\ \underbrace{0...0}_{6(l-j-1)\times1} \right) \right\}^{\mathrm{T}} \quad (6.15)$$

$$\vec{C}_{ijk} = \left(\begin{array}{c} \vec{n}_{ik} \times \vec{y}_{ijk} \\ -\vec{n}_{ik} \end{array} \right) \quad (6.16)$$

$$\vec{\delta} = (\vec{m}_0...\vec{m}_{n-1})^{\mathrm{T}} \quad (6.17)$$

$$\vec{m}_i = \left(\begin{array}{cccccc} c_{1i} & c_{2i} & c_{3i} & t_{xi} & t_{yi} & t_{zi} \end{array} \right)^{\mathrm{T}}, \quad (6.18)$$

where the number of mesh models is n. By (6.13) $\vec{\delta}$ is written as

$$\left(\sum_{i \neq j} \vec{A}_{ijk}^{\mathrm{T}} \vec{A}_{ijk} \right) \vec{\delta} = \sum_{i \neq j} \vec{A}_{ijk}^{\mathrm{T}} s_{ijk} \quad (6.19)$$

2.3   Solving Linear Equations

From Eq. 13, $\vec{\delta}$ is computed as the solution of linear equations that include $n \times 6$ arguments. However, ambiguity remains in the equation. Then, the first mesh model is assumed not to be moved. That is, as shown in Fig. 6.5, the linear equations with $((n-1)\times6) \times ((n-1)\times6)$ coefficient matrix are solved. If all mesh models are connected to the first mesh, the coefficient matrix is symmetric positive definite. Also, the matrix becomes larger and sparser as the number of mesh models increases and has 6×6 non-zero patterns as shown in Fig. 6.5.

Since the computational complexity of direct solvers is too high, we applied an iterative solver to this problem. The computational complexity of Cholesky decomposition that is the most popular direct solver for a symmetric positive definite matrix is $O(n^3)$. Then, we employed the pre-conditioned conjugate gradient method (PCG). Though the complexity of PCG is $O(n^3)$, the same as Cholesky decomposition, the number of iterations can be drastically reduced by pre-conditioning. We employed incomplete Cholesky decomposition as the pre-conditioner. Since it is known that the coefficient matrix has 6×6 non-zero patterns, we implemented the incomplete Cholesky conjugate gradient method (ICCG) specialized for the matrix pattern.

Assume that the matrix $\boldsymbol{M}$ is the $((n-1)\times6) \times ((n-1)\times6)$ coefficient matrix shown in Fig. 6.5. $\vec{\beta}$ is the $(n-1)\times6$ vector that is a part of the right side of Eq. 13. $\vec{\beta}$ does not include the transformations of the first mesh model. Equation 13 is re-written as follows.

$$\boldsymbol{M}\vec{\alpha} = \vec{\beta} \quad (6.20)$$

$$\vec{\alpha} = (\vec{m}_1...\vec{m}_{n-1})^{\mathrm{T}} \quad (6.21)$$

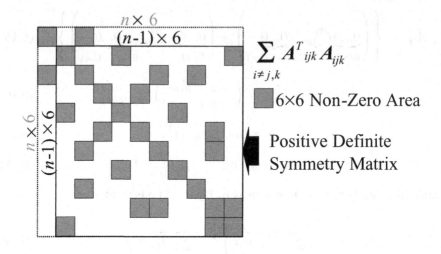

Figure 6.5. Characteristics of coefficient matrix

A matrix C is assumed to be a regular $((n-1)\times6)\times((n-1)\times6)$ matrix. Equation 14 is written as follows:

$$C^{-1}\mathbf{M}(\mathbf{C}^{\mathrm{T}})^{-1}\mathbf{C}^{\mathrm{T}}\vec{\alpha} = \mathbf{C}^{-1}\vec{\beta} \qquad (6.22)$$

To simplify the equation, we define the matrix $\tilde{\mathbf{M}}$ and the vector $\vec{\beta}'$ as follows.

$$\tilde{\mathbf{M}} = \mathbf{C}^{-1}\mathbf{M}(\mathbf{C}^{\mathrm{T}})^{-1} \qquad (6.23)$$

$$\vec{\beta}' = \mathbf{C}^{-1}\vec{\beta} \qquad (6.24)$$

Equation 16 is redefined by using the variables above.

$$\tilde{\mathbf{M}}\vec{\alpha}' = \vec{\beta}' \qquad (6.25)$$

$$\mathbf{C}^{\mathrm{T}}\vec{\alpha} = \vec{\alpha}' \qquad (6.26)$$

If the coefficient matrix $\tilde{\mathbf{M}}$ is near the identity matrix, solving Eq. 19 is drastically accelerated by the conjugate gradient method. That is, the $C^{T}C$ has to be nearly equal to the original coefficient matrix M.

$$\mathbf{M} \cong \mathbf{C}^{\mathrm{T}}\mathbf{C} \qquad (6.27)$$

But the computation cost to decompose the matrix is very high. The matrix M is incompletely decomposed by the Cholesky decomposition. In this process, only non-zero areas are computed: other elements are filled with zero[15].

$$\mathbf{M} = \mathbf{UD} \qquad (6.28)$$

Since the matrix M is sparse, the decomposition process is performed very quickly. Then, matrix C is given as follows:

$$C = UD^{1/2} \qquad (6.29)$$

Once matrix C has been computed, rigid transformations are calculated from Eq. 19 and Eq. 20 by the conventional conjugate gradient method.

3.   Experimental Results

In this section, the effectiveness of our method is demonstrated by some experimental results. Two data sets are used for the experiments. Target objects are the face of Deva in Cambodia (Fig. 6.6(a)) and the Nara Great Buddha statue in Japan (Fig. 6.6(b)). The face of Deva was measured by VIVID900. The resolution of VIVID900 was fixed to 640×480, and the view angle depended on mounted lenses. We used a wide lens for scanning the face of Deva. The Great Buddha statue was measured by Cyrax2400. The resolution and view angle of the sensor were flexible: users could change them arbitrarily. In the scanning of Nara Great Buddha, we adjusted the parameters according to measurement environments. Generally, 800×800 was used as the measurement resolution. The details of these data sets are shown in Table 1 and Table 2 respectively.

Table 6.1.   Data set 1: The face of Deva

Sensor	VIVID900
Images	45
Vertices	Max: 76612, Min: 38190, Ave: 67674
Triangles	Max: 150786, Min: 71526, Ave: 130437

Table 6.2.   Data set 2: The Nara Great Buddha

Sensor	Cyrax2500
Images	114
Vertices	Max: 155434, Min: 11231, Ave: 81107
Triangles	Max: 300920, Min: 18927, Ave: 148281

Vertices that measured outside the objects had been removed previously. Obtained point crowds had been converted into triangle mesh models. Since the original data sets were too large to deal with using one PC, the sizes of the data were reduced to 1 / 4.

Our method is evaluated according to the following three criteria:

(a)   (b)

Figure 6.6.   Target objects (a : the face of Deva, b : the Nara Great Buddha)

1 Number of corresponding points with respect to the resolution of index images

2 Computation time of matrix operations with respect to the number of mesh models

3 Computation time of alignment with respect to the number of vertices

The PC used for the experiments had Athlon MP 2400+ processor, 2Gbyte memory, and a GeForce4Ti4600 graphics card.

3.1   Number of Corresponding Points with the Resolution of the Index Image

The number of corresponding points is evaluated with respect to the resolution of the index image. As described above, if enough resolution cannot be assigned to the index image, all triangle patches are not rendered: all the corresponding points cannot be acquired. Here, the relation between the resolution of index images and the number of corresponding points is verified.

Corresponding points were searched for several pairs of mesh models by gradually changing the resolution of index images. We selected a set of mesh models that have minimum and maximum number of triangle patches from each data set as target meshes. Base meshes were arbitrarily selected. Experimental results are shown in Fig. 6.7. The vertical axis represents the ratio of the number of corresponding points acquired by our method v'_c to the ground truth v_c. The resolutions of index images are represented in the horizontal axis as the square root of total pixels.

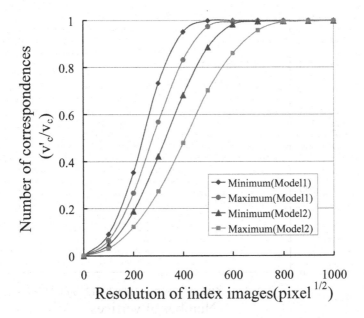

Figure 6.7. Number of corresponding points with resolution of index images

As shown in Fig. 6.7, when the resolution of the index image becomes larger than a certain size (800×800), almost all of the corresponding points are obtained. Furthermore, the resolution required for obtaining enough corresponding points becomes larger as the number of triangle patches of target mesh increases. In fact, instead of the number of triangle patches, the measurement resolution is concerned with the required index image resolution. However, in this case, it can be said that the number of triangle patches has the similar characteristics with the measurement resolution because the sampled points are distributed densely and uniformly in both vertical and horizontal directions.

It is not required to estimate the image resolution for each mesh model. Even if, due to any problems, for example the limitation of graphics memory space, a large enough resolution cannot be assigned to the index image, several corresponding points are acquired in compliance with the image resolution.

3.2   Time to Solve the Linear Equations

The computation time to solve the linear equations is evaluated. As described above, the computation time to solve the linear system is greatly influenced by the number of mesh models. Thus, the relation between the computation time and the number of mesh models is evaluated here. Data set 2 is

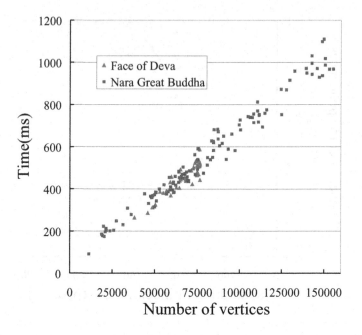

Figure 6.8.   Time to solve linear equations

used for this experiment. The computation time of the matrix operations only is sequentially measured by changing the number of mesh models.

The experimental results are shown in Fig. 6.8. The horizontal axis represents the number of mesh models, and the vertical axis represents the computation time. The results with usual Cholesky decomposition are also shown in this figure in comparison with our method. The threshold value of the ICCG was set to 1.0×10^{-6}.

In the case that the number of mesh models is lower than 60, Cholesky decomposition is faster than our method. On the other hand, the computation time of our method increases at a slow rate and becomes smaller than that of Cholesky decomposition when the number of mesh models is higher than 70. Moreover, the differences between Cholesky decomposition and our method become larger as the number of mesh models increases. That is, it can be said that ICCG is effective for aligning a large number of mesh models simultaneously.

3.3   Computation Time with Number of Vertices

The computation time is evaluated with respect to the number of vertices included in the mesh models. In this experiment, it is proven that the compu-

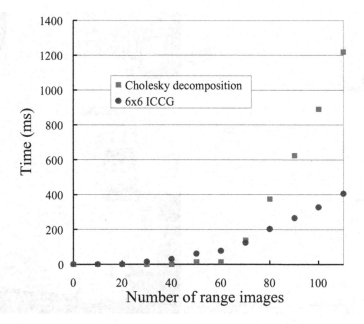

Figure 6.9. Computation time with number of vertices

tational complexity of aligning a pair of mesh models is $O(N)$, where N is the number of vertices. It can be also said that the complexity of searching corresponding points is $O(N)$ because it can be assumed that the computation time of another task is small enough to ignore.

Each mesh model was aligned to itself so that the number of vertices of base model and target model were equal to each other. Since the number of corresponding points also affects the computation time, all mesh models were not moved. That is, the amount of movement is infinitely zero; the number of corresponding points is nearly equal to the number of vertices. Index images were rendered at each iterative step. The image resolution was fixed to 800×800. The computation time was evaluated according to the average time taken for 20 iterations.

Experimental results are shown in Fig. 6.9. The horizontal axis represents the number of vertices, and the vertical axis represents the computation time. It is clear that the computation time is increasing linearly with the number of vertices. Moreover, there are no differences between two data sets though these data were taken by different sensors. That is, the efficiency of our method does not depend on the sensors used for measurements.

Figure 6.10.   Alignment results (the face of Deva)

3.4   Alignment Results

The alignment results of these data sets are shown in Fig. 6.10 and Fig. 6.11. Previously, we had aligned all mesh models one by one. Then we applied the simultaneous alignment method to these models. Figure 6.10 shows the alignment results of data set 1. The total computation time was 1738 seconds after 20 iterations. Figure 6.11 shows the results of data set 2. The number of iterations was 20, the same as for data set 1. Total computation time was 7832 seconds. The figures show that all mesh models were correctly aligned.

4.   Conclusion

In this chapter, we proposed a fast, simultaneous alignment method for a large number of range images. In order to accelerate the task of searching corresponding points, we utilized index images that are rapidly rendered using graphics hardware and are used as look-up tables. Instead of sensor parameters, only an approximate resolution of index images is required for this search. In order to accelerate the computation of rigid transformations, we employed a linearized error function. Since the computation time to solve the linear system becomes large as the number of range images increases, we applied the incomplete Cholesky conjugate gradient (ICCG) method. Experimental

Figure 6.11.   Alignment results (Nara Great Buddha)

results showed the effectiveness of our method. One of our future works will be to improve the accuracy of alignment results.

Acknowledgments

This research was supported, in part, by Ministry of Education, Culture, Sports, Science and Technology under the Leading Project, "Development of High Fidelity Digitization Software for Large-Scale and Intangible Cultural Assets," and, in part, by Japan Science and Technology Agency, under the CREST program, "Automatic generation of virtual models of cultural heritage." The author would like to thank the staffs of the Todaiji Temple in Nara, Japan. The Bayon temple in Cambodia was digitized with the cooperation of JSA (Japanese Government Team for Safeguarding Angkor).

References

[1] P. J. Besl and N. D. McKay, "A method for registration of 3-D shapes," *IEEE Trans. on Pattern Analysis and Machine Intelligence*, 14(2), 239-256, 1992.

[2] Y. Chen and G. Medioni, "Object modeling by registration of multiple range images," *Image and Vision Computing,* 10(3), pp. 145-155, 1992.

[3] G. Blais and M. Levine, "Registering Multiview Range Data to Create 3D Computer Objects," *IEEE Trans. Pattern Analysis and Machine Intelligence*, Vol. 17, No. 8, 1995.

[4] S. Rusinkiewicz, O. Hall-Holt and M. Levoy, "Real-Time 3D Model Acquisition," *ACM Transactions on Graphics.* 21(3): 438-446, July 2002.

[5] T. Masuda, K. Sakaue and N. Yokoya, "Registration and Integration of Multiple Range Images for 3-D Model Construction," *Proc. IEEE Conf. Computer Vision and Pattern Recognition*, 1996.

[6] P. J. Neugebauer. "Reconstruction of Real-World Objects via Simultaneous Registration and Robust Combination of Multiple Range Images." *Int'l J. Shape Modeling*, 3(1&2):71-90, 1997.

[7] R. Bergevin, M. Soucy, H. Gagnon, and D. Laurendeau. To-wards a general multi-view registration technique. *IEEE Trans. on Pattern Analysis and Machine Intelligence*, 18(5):540-547, May 1996.

[8] R. Benjemaa and F. Schmitt. "Fast global registration of 3d sampled surfaces using a multi-z-buffer technique," *Proc. Int'l Conf. Recent Advances in 3-D Digital Imaging and Modeling*, May 1997, pp. 113-120.

[9] Z. Zhang, "Iterative point matching for registration of free-form curves and surfaces," *Int'l J. Computer Vision*, 13(2):119-152, 1994.

[10] K. Nishino and K. Ikeuchi, "Robust Simultaneous Registration of Multiple Range Images," *Proc. Fifth Asian Conf. Computer Vision*, Jan. 2002, pp. 454-461.

[11] D. A. Simon, M. Hebert and T. Kanade, "Realtime 3-D pose estimation using a high-speed range sensor," *Proc. IEEE Int'l Conf. Robotics and Automation*, May 1994, pp. 2235-2241.

[12] M. Greenspan and G. Godin, "A Nearest Neighbor Method for Efficient ICP," *Proc. Int'l Conf. 3D Digital Imaging and Modeling (3DIM)*, 2001, pp. 161-168.

[13] R. Sagawa, T. Masuda and K. Ikeuchi, "Effective Nearest Neighbor Search for Aligning and Merging Range Images," *Proc. Int'l Conf. 3-D Digital Imaging and Modeling (3DIM)*, 2003, pp. 79-86.

[14] S. Rusinkiewicz and M. Levoy, "Efficient variants of the IPC algorithm," *Proc. Int'l Conf. 3-D Digital Imaging and Modeling (3DIM)*, May 2001, pp. 145-152.

[15] Y. Saad, *Iterative methods for sparse linear system Series*, Computer Science, PWS, 1996.

Chapter 7

PARALLEL ALIGNMENT OF A LARGE NUMBER OF RANGE IMAGES

Takeshi Oishi, Ryusuke Sagawa, Atsushi Nakazawa, Ryo Kurazume, and Katsushi Ikeuchi

Abstract This chapter describes a method for parallel alignment of multiple range images. There are problems of computational time and memory space in aligning a large number of range images simultaneously. We developed a parallel method to address the problems. Searching for corresponding points between two range images is time-consuming and requires considerable memory space when performed independently. However, this process can be preformed in parallel, with each corresponding pair of range images assigned to a node. Because the computation time is approximately proportional to the number of vertices, by assigning the pairs so that the number of vertices computed is equal on each node, the load on each node is effectively distributed. In order to reduce the amount of memory required on each node, a hypergraph that represents the correspondences of range images is created, and heuristic graph partitioning algorithms are applied to determine the optimal assignment of the pairs. Moreover, by rejecting redundant dependencies, it becomes possible to accelerate computation time and reduce the amount of memory required on each node. The method was tested on a 16-processor PC cluster, where it demonstrated high extendibility and improved performance.

1. Introduction

As described in the previous chapters, various alignment methods have been proposed in the last quarter century [1–4]. These methods are based on the Besl's ICP (Iterative Closest Point) [5] and the Chen's registration method [6]. Since the problem for every method is the computation cost of correspondence search, *Kd-trees* and the other data structures are used for the correspondence search to improve the computational efficiency [7–11]. When a large number of range images are aligned, simultaneous algorithms are employed in order to avoid error accumulation [12–14].

Despite the many alignment algorithms, it is difficult to align the large number of range images that our activities involve. When such algorithms are used, the computation time increases exponentially with the number of range images, and it is necessary to read all range images into memory. Although a method in which all range images are not required to be kept in memory has been proposed [15], completely correct correspondences between all pairs of range images have to be previously computed in this method. The method also requires many interactive operations and is very time consuming. The parallel ICP algorithm [16] which is implemented on a PC cluster accelerates the correspondence search by parallel processing. However, the method does not consider the memory requirements.

Therefore, we need a method in which the computation time is short, the amount of memory used is small, and the extendibility is high. It is also thought that the amount of data will increase along with the development of measurement technology. In addition to the computational time and memory requirements, extendibility of the alignment system is one of the important factors.

In this chapter, we propose a parallel simultaneous alignment method that improves both the computational efficiency and the memory usage. The method is implemented on a PC cluster that is cheap and highly extendible. In Section 2, the fundamental alignment algorithm is described. In Section 3, we present the algorithm of parallel computation. Sections 4 and 5 contain the evaluations of this algorithm and the alignment results of a large number of range images, respectively. Our conclusions are presented in Section 6.

2.   Simultaneous Alignment Algorithm

In this section, the outline of the fundamental alignment algorithm is explained. We assume that all range images have been converted to mesh models. The algorithm is applied in the following steps:

1. Compute, for all pairs of partial meshes,
   (a) search all correspondence of vertices
   (b) evaluate error terms of all correspondence pairs
2. Compute transformation matrices of all pairs for immunizing all errors
3. Iterate steps 1 and 2 until the termination condition is satisfied

Our algorithm employs points and planes to evaluate relative distance as the Chen and Medioni method [6]. The corresponding pairs are searched along the line of sight. Here, the line of sight is defined as the optical axis of a range sensor. Let us denote one mesh as the base mesh and its corresponding mesh as the target mesh. An extension of the line of sight, from a vertex of the base mesh, crosses a triangle patch of the target mesh and creates the intersecting point. In order to eliminate false correspondences, if the distance between the vertex and the corresponding point is larger than a certain threshold value, the correspondence is removed. This correspondence search is computed for every pairs of mesh models.

The error measure between corresponding points is the cosine distance between the point and the plane. Let the vertex of the base mesh and the corresponding crossing point in the target mesh be $\vec{x}$ and $\vec{y}$, respectively. The error measure between the pairs is written as

$$\vec{n} \cdot (\vec{y} - \vec{x}) \tag{7.1}$$

where $\vec{n}$ is the normal of $\vec{x}$ defined around the vertex.

The transformation matrices of the base and target mesh models are computed so that this error measure is minimized. The error evaluation function is rewritten as

$$\varepsilon = R_B \vec{n} \cdot \{(R_T \vec{y} + \vec{t}_T) - (R_B \vec{x} + \vec{t}_B)\} \tag{7.2}$$

Here, the rotation matrix and the translation vector of the base and target mesh are $R_M, R_S, \vec{t}_M, \vec{t}_S$ respectively. The distance between the base and the target mesh is expressed as

$$\bar{\varepsilon} = \min_{\mathbf{R}, \vec{t}} \sum_{i,j,k} \left(R_i \vec{n}_{ik} \cdot \{(R_j \vec{y}_{ijk} + \vec{t}_j) - (R_i \vec{x}_{ik} + \vec{t}_i)\} \right)^2 \tag{7.3}$$

If it is assumed that the angles of rotation are minute, the rotation matrix $\mathbf{R}$ is written as

$$\mathbf{R} = \begin{pmatrix} 1 & -c_3 & c_2 \\ c_3 & 1 & -c_1 \\ -c_2 & c_1 & 1 \end{pmatrix} \tag{7.4}$$

The translation vector is expressed as

$$\vec{t} = \begin{pmatrix} t_x & t_y & t_z \end{pmatrix}^{\mathrm{T}} \tag{7.5}$$

After some algebraic manipulations [12], (7.3) is rewritten as

$$\bar{\varepsilon} = \min_{\vec{\delta}} \sum_{i \neq j,k} \left\| \vec{A}_{ijk} \cdot \vec{\delta} - s_{ijk} \right\|^2 \tag{7.6}$$

$$s_{ijk} = \vec{n}_{ik} \cdot (\vec{x}_{ik} - \vec{y}_{ijk}) \tag{7.7}$$

$$\vec{A}_{ijk} = \left\{ \begin{pmatrix} \underbrace{0...0}_{6i \times 1} & \vec{C}_{ijk}^{\mathrm{T}} & \underbrace{0...0}_{6(l-i-1) \times 1} \end{pmatrix} + \begin{pmatrix} \underbrace{0...0}_{6j \times 1} & -\vec{C}_{ijk}^{\mathrm{T}} & \underbrace{0...0}_{6(l-j-1) \times 1} \end{pmatrix} \right\}^{\mathrm{T}} \tag{7.8}$$

$$\vec{C}_{ijk} = \begin{pmatrix} \vec{n}_{ik} \times \vec{y}_{ijk} \\ -\vec{n}_{ik} \end{pmatrix} \tag{7.9}$$

$$\vec{\delta} = (\vec{m}_0 ... \vec{m}_{n-1})^{\mathrm{T}} \tag{7.10}$$

$$\vec{m}_i = \left(\begin{array}{cccccc} c_{1i} & c_{2i} & c_{3i} & t_{xi} & t_{yi} & t_{zi} \end{array} \right)^{\mathrm{T}} \tag{7.11}$$

where the number of mesh models is n. By (7.6) $\vec{\delta}$ is written as

$$\left(\sum_{i,j,k} \vec{A}_{ijk}^{\mathrm{T}} \vec{A}_{ijk} \right) \vec{\delta} = \sum_{i,j,k} \vec{A}_{ijk}^{\mathrm{T}} s_{ijk} \tag{7.12}$$

3.   Parallel Alignment Based on a PC Cluster

In the simultaneous alignment operations described in Section 2, 1(a) correspondence search and 1(b) error evaluation require a large amount of computational time. They also require data space to read in data of all vertices. On the other hand, these two operations can be conducted independently in each pair of partial mesh models. Computation of transformation in step 2 does not require much computational time or memory space. Thus, we designed correspondence search and error evaluation in step 1 to be conducted in slave PCs in a PC cluster, and computation of transformation in step 2 to be conducted in a master PC.

3.1   Graph Simplification

We remove redundant or weak data dependency relations of partial mesh models for the sake of efficiency in parallel computation. Figure 7.1 shows overlapping data-dependency relations. Each node in the graph represents one mesh model, and each arc represents an overlapping dependency relation among mesh models. The left graph shows the original state in which all the mesh models overlap each other. If we conduct alignment of one mesh as is, we would have to read into a PC's memory all the remaining mesh models. By removing some of redundant overlapping dependencies, we can transform the original graph into a simpler one as shown in the right figure. By using this simpler relational graph, we only need adjacent data with respect to a vertex for alignment of a vertex, and we can reduce the necessary memory space.

We will remove the dependency relation between the two mesh models if any of the mesh pairs does not satisfy any one of the following four conditions:

1. The bounding-boxes of two mesh models overlap each other.

A sufficient overlapped region exists between two mesh models, provided that initial positions of two meshes are accurately estimated.

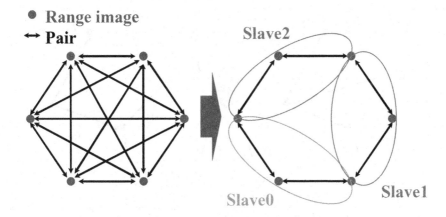

Figure 7.1. Data dependency relations

2. The angle θ between ray directions of two mesh models is less than a threshold value.

Two observation directions of the meshes are relatively near. This condition also reduces the possibility of false correspondences between front- and back-side meshes, by setting the threshold, as $\theta=90^{\circ}$. We could use a more accurately estimated value for this threshold, but since this value is used as a constraint to reduce the possibility described above, we use this $\theta=90^{\circ}$ for the sake of safety and simplicity.

3. The overlapping area of two meshes is larger than a threshold value.

Overlapping area is expressed as the ratio of the number of vertices included in one mesh model and the number of corresponding points between two meshes. Corresponding points are searched for a few vertices selected randomly. We used 10% of the vertices for this search. A pair whose overlapping area is less than threshold value will be removed as weak data dependency. We set the threshold value as 0.03 to 0.05. Since the computation of overlapping areas can be performed independently and sequentially for each pair, the computations are performed easily in parallel without the problem of memory usage.

4. Two range images are adjacent to each other.

This condition removes non-adjacent relations sequentially. For example, as shown in Fig. 7.2, if the length from I_0 to I_3 is larger than the length from I_1 to I_3 ($l_{01} < l_{03}$), the arc between I_0 and I_3 is removed. Here, the distance is evaluated from the center of a mesh model.

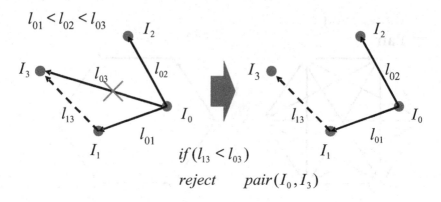

Figure 7.2. Non-adjacency relation

3.2   Parallelization by Graph Partitioning Algorithms

The problem of load balancing with a minimum amount of required memory is an NP-hard problem. It is difficult to obtain an optimal solution in a reasonable time. Alternatively, we employ an approximation method to solve this problem by applying heuristic graph-partitioning algorithms.

3.2.1   Pair-Node Hyper-Graph

First, we define the pair-node hyper-graph. The left image of Fig. 7.3 shows a graph that expresses the relations of partial meshes I_n. The graph is converted to the hyper-graph in which each node expresses pairs $P_{i,j}$ of two partial meshes i and j, and networks represent meshes, as shown in the right figure of Fig. 7.3. We refer to it as a "pair-node hyper-graph."

The weight of the network W_i^{net} is defined as the number of vertices v_i in the partial mesh, i; the weight of the node $W_{i,j}^{node}$ is defined as the sum of the number of vertices v_i and v_j.

$$W_i^{net} = v_i \tag{7.13}$$

$$W_{i,j}^{node} = v_i + v_j \tag{7.14}$$

A pair-node hyper-graph is partitioned so that the sum of the node weights in each subset is roughly equal for computational load balance, and summation of all the net-weight in each subset is minimized for efficiency of memory usage.

It is necessary to consider both node weights and net weights in optimization, even though they are related to each other, and using them seems to be redundant. Reducing the computational load requires each sub-group to have equal values in the node-weights. On the other hand, even when a hyper-graph

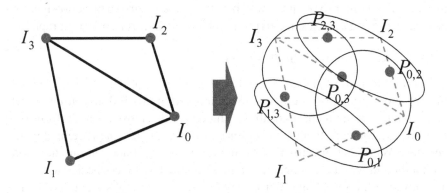

Figure 7.3. Pair node hyper-graph

is portioned equally in terms of node-weight, depending on the method, each sub-group has different memory usage. Let us consider the example, shown in Fig. 7.3, to divide the hyper-graph into two sub-graphs. For the sake of simplicity, we assume that all node-weights and net-weights are the same in all the nodes and all the networks. When the hyper-graph is divided into two groups, $\{P_{0,2}, P_{1,3}, P_{2,3}\}$ and $\{P_{0,1}, P_{0,3}\}$, the node balance is achieved in two sub-graphs. The first sub-graph needs to load in all the data $\{I_0, I_1, I_2, I_3\}$. The maximum value in sums of net-weights is four units. When the hyper-graph is divided into two groups, $\{P_{0,2}, P_{0,3}, P_{2,3}\}$ and $\{P_{1,3}, P_{0,1}\}$, each sub-group needs only to load in three data sets. The maximum value in the sum of net-weights is three units. In these two cases, both portioning methods have roughly equal load balance in terms of node-weights, but have different memory usage. When we divide the graph by considering only memory usage, it is not guaranteed that each sub-graph has equal load balance. Thus, we will consider both node-weights and net-weights in the optimization procedure.

3.2.2   Initial Partitioning

The pair-node hyper-graph is initially partitioned so that the sum of the node-weights in each subset is roughly equal. Spectral bisection methods [17, 18] that minimize the edge-cut by using second eigenvector are widely available, but it is difficult to apply the method to our problem. Intelligent graph growth algorithm [19] can obtain a fairly optimal solution in a small computation time. However, this method tends to be trapped in a poor partitioning [20]. We used the random seeded breadth first search method for initial partitioning. Since the sum of net-weight included in each subset is greatly influenced by the selection of the seed, we created initial partitions for multiple seeds and adopted the partition in which the sum of net-weight included is minimized. In order to obtain k-way partitions, the recursive bisection method is used. After $\log k$ phases, the hyper-graph is partitioned into k sub-graphs.

3.2.3   Refinement of the Partition

The partitioned graphs are refined so that the sum of net-weights included in each subset graph is minimized. We improved the KLFM algorithm, which is an iterative refinement algorithm. The algorithm moves a node from one partition to another so that the operation causes the greatest improvement in the cut-size. While the original KLFM algorithm moves a node at one iteration, our method moves a net at one iteration. That is, all nodes connected to the net are moved at the same time. For k-way refinement, the subset graph of which the sum of net-weight is maximum weight is computed with all other subsets. The refinement process is reiterated until there is no more improvement.

The net gain is computed for all nets along the boundary of two subset graphs. Now, we consider the kth net at the boundary between the subset graphs, G_i and G_j. In the case where the net $N_{(i,j),k}$ is moved to G_i, the gain $g_{i,j,k}$ is expressed using two values: $D_{i,j,k}^{int}$, the variation of the sum of net weight of G_i, and $D_{i,jk}^{ext}$, the variation of the sum of net-weight of G_j.

$$g_{i,j,k} = D_{i,j,k}^{ext} - D_{i,j,k}^{int}. \qquad (7.15)$$

On the other hand, in the case where $N_{(i,j),k}$ is moved to G_j, the gain $g_{j,i,k}$ is expressed in the similar way as

$$g_{j,i,k} = D_{j,i,k}^{ext} - D_{j,i,k}^{int}. \qquad (7.16)$$

The two lists, L_i, L_j, , consisting of all gains of the all nets at the boundary, are created. The list with the larger sum of the total node-weight (computational time) is selected for consideration of the movement, and the components, candidate nets in the list, are processed one by one in descending order of the gain. At each movement of one net, all nets and nodes concerned with the net are updated, and the moved net is locked in order to avoid thrashing. The sum of the net-weight (memory usage) and the moved net's ID are also recorded at each movement. After all nets are moved, the minimum value of the sum of the net-weight (memory usage) is compared with the value at the starting stage. If the minimum value is smaller than that of the starting state, the corresponding movement-sequence is performed, and the next iteration begins. If not, the refinement process is terminated. See Fig. 7.4 for the flow chart of the refinement process.

3.3   Implementation

We implemented our method as a master/slave system. The procedures of the computation is are as follows

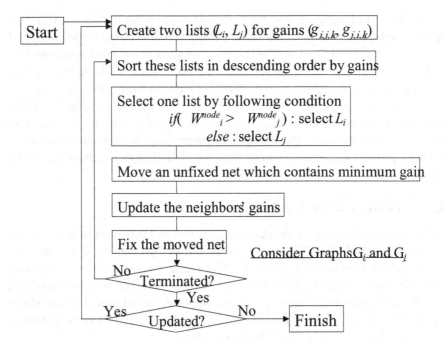

Figure 7.4. Flowchart of refinement process

Algorithm Procedure of Parallel Alignment

```
/* Check correspondence of all pairs of the partial meshes */
Create-Pair-Table();
/* Create the lists of the files for each processor */
Create-File-Lists():
while(error > threshold){
 /* Slave Process*/
 for(i = 0; i < nmeshes; ++i)
  for(j = 0; j < nmeshes; ++j)
   Whether-i-and-j-overlap-each-other?{
    Correspondence-Search(i, j);
    Calculation-Each-Matrix(i, j);
   }
 /* Master Process */
 CalculationMatrix(all);
 /* Master & Slave process */
 UpdatePosition();
 }
```

The master program holds bounding-boxes and transformation matrices from initial position to current position of all partial meshes, checks all pairs, and creates the list of computations for each node. The pairs list for each slave is computed at the beginning of the entire iteration process based on the relational table using the algorithm described above. The slave programs receive the lists and read the required partial meshes into memory. Then, each slave computes the matrices $A_{ijk}^T A_{ijk}$ and $A_{ijk}^T s_{ijk}$ in (7.12) independently, and sends the matrices to the master program. The master program computes the transformation matrices of all range images from the matrices $A_{ijk}^T A_{ijk}$ and $A_{ijk}^T s_{ijk}$ received from the slave programs. The results are applied to all master/slave data. Each iteration process is continued until the error falls below a certain threshold value.

4.   Performance Evaluation

This method was implemented on a PC cluster that consisted of 8 PCs. Each PC had dual AthlonMP2400+ processors and 4Gbytes of memory, and was connected by 100Base-TX ethernet. The range images used for evaluation were 50 images created artificially from the complete 3D model of the Great Buddha of Kamakura. Figure 7.5 shows the original 3D model of the statue and the partial mesh models created artificially. These mesh models contain an average of 83,288 vertices and 158,376 patches.

In this section, our method is evaluated from the viewpoints of convergence and accuracy, computation time, and memory usage.

(a) Original model   (b) Created mesh models

Figure 7.5.   Partial mesh models for evaluations

4.1 Convergence and Accuracy

Because our method rejects redundant dependencies, the influence of the rejection on convergence and accuracy has to be evaluated. In this case, the number of all pairs is 2,450, but it is reduced to 160 by the rejection process. We needed to verify whether accurate convergence is performed even when the number of pairs becomes very small. Virtually created mesh models have accurate positions of measured points, so convergence and accuracy can be evaluated by the distance between an accurately aligned mesh model and the target mesh model. The distance between two meshes is defined as an average of the Euclidean length of all vertices. Each mesh model added Gaussian noise along the line of sight at maximum length 10mm. All mesh models were moved at random in the maximum length of 100mm in the directions of x, y, and z, respectively, and rotated at random in the maximum angle of 0.05 radians to the x-axis, y-axis, and z-axis, respectively.

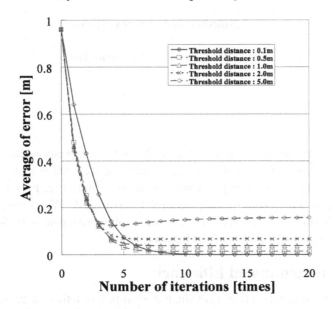

Figure 7.6. Convergence with original method

The results of the original method and our method are shown in Figures 7.6 and 7.7, respectively. The threshold distance for rejecting outliers while searching for correspondences is changed gradually. Although both the original method and our method do not converge at the correct positions when the threshold distance is 5m, our method converges at a better position than the position of the original method. Although the convergence speed of our method is slower than that of the original method, our method tends to converge at a better position than the position of the original method. It is thought that this is

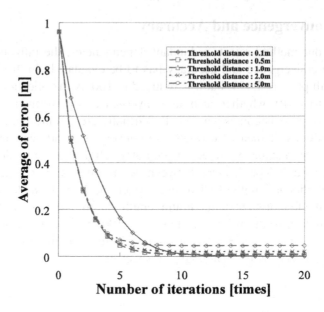

Figure 7.7. Convergence with our method

because the rejection of redundant pairs reduces false correspondence of mesh models. A feature of the alignment algorithm that we used is that it tends to be influenced by false correspondence and noise. Therefore, by rejecting redundant pairs, transformations are accurately estimated. When the threshold values are 0.1m and 0.5m, the error converges at approximately 0. So we see that accurate estimation is acquired by our method.

4.2   Computational Efficiency

Here, the computation time is evaluated. Computation time is defined as the time taken for one iteration, and an average of time of all iterations is used for the evaluation. Figure 7.8 shows the time ratio with the number of processors. Computation time T_n is expressed as the ratio to the computation time with one processor T_0. This figure shows that the computation time is linearly improved as the number of processors increases. Moreover, our method improves computation time in a predictable way unlike the sequential method in which the mesh models are assigned in arbitrary selected order. The actual computation time with one processor averages 20560ms, and the computation time with 16 processors averages 1784ms. Thus, the computation time with 16 processors is approximately 11.5 times faster than that with 1 processor.

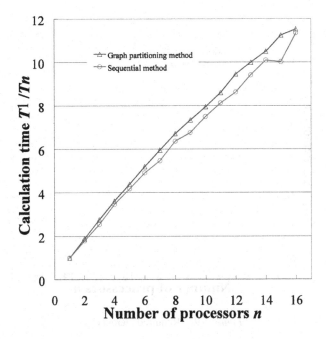

Figure 7.8. Computational Efficiency

4.3 Amount of Required Memory

Next, the evaluation of memory performance is shown. The amount of memory usage is shown in Fig. 7.9 with the number of processors. Each value shows the ratio of the amount of memory used with a single processor. It appears that the amount of required memory decreases as the number of processors increases. Compared with the sequential method, the performance is highly improved by our method. An actual maximum size of required memory with a single processor is 269Mbytes and that with 16 processors is 48Mbytes. Therefore, our method could reduce the amount of memory used by approximately 17% for these mesh models.

5. Experimental Results

In this section, we will show the result of parallel alignment of a large number of range images that could not be aligned by one PC because of limitation of memory space. We used the following two sets of partial mesh models.

Model-1. 114 mesh models that measured the Great Buddha of Nara by Cyrax2400. These models contain an average of 327,470 vertices and 606,072 meshes.

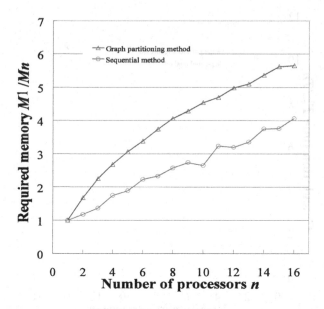

Figure 7.9.   Required memory

Figure 7.10.   Alignment result (Nara Buddha)

Figure 7.11. Alignment result (Bayon)

Model-2. 210 mesh models that measured the Bayon Temple in Cambodia by Cyrax2500. These models contain an average of 433,785 vertices and 798,890 meshes.

Due to the limitation of memory space, the minimum numbers of processors required for aligning these data sets were 2 and 4 for Model-1 and Model-2, respectively. The alignment results computed by the minimum and maximum numbers of processors are shown in Table 1 and Table 2. These tables show the average computation time, the maximum amount of memory usage, and the minimum amount of memory usage.

Table 7.1. Total performance (Nara)

Processors	Ave. Time(s)	Max. Mem(MB)	Min. Mem(MB)
2	76	1287	1275
16	13.2	292	254

Table 7.2. Total performance (Bayon)

Processors	Ave. Time(s)	Max. Mem(MB)	Min. Mem(MB)
4	103.9	1608	1456
16	40.2	559	472

In the case of Model-1, the computation time with 16 processors is 5.75 times faster than that with 2 processors, and the amount of required memory is reduced by 22.6%. For Model-2, the computation time with 16 processors is 2.58 times faster than that with 4 processors, and required memory is reduced by 34.8%. As for the size of required memory, these results show an improvement better than that described in the previous section (30% for 2-16 and 47 % for 4-16). On the other hand, in the case of Model-2, although the number of processors is quadrupled, the reason the computation time is not greatly improved (2.58 times) is that the time taken for calculation of the transformation matrix, which is not parallelized and is performed on the server program, is lengthened. An actual computation time taken by the server program is an average of 14 seconds, and is 35% of the total time taken for one iteration.

Figures 7.10 and 7.11 show the alignment results of the Great Buddha of Nara and the Bayon Temple in Cambodia, respectively. Alignment takes approximately 5 minutes for 20 iterations for Model-1 and approximately 15 minutes for Model-2.

6.   Conclusion

In this chapter, we have proposed the parallel method for simultaneous alignment of multiple range images. In considering time performance and memory performance, we parallelized the alignment algorithm. Then, we implemented this method on a PC cluster, and showed its validity by aligning a large number of range images simultaneously. Future work will deal with accelerating the computation of transformation matrices.

Acknowledgments

This research was supported, in part, by Ministry of Education, Culture, Sports, Science and Technology under the Leading Project, "Development of High Fidelity Digitization Software for Large-Scale and Intangible Cultural Assets," and, in part, by Japan Science and Technology Agency, under the CREST program, "Automatic generation of virtual models of cultural heritage." The authors would like to thank the staffs of the Todaiji Temple in Nara, Japan, and the Koutokuin Temple in Kamakura, Japan. The Bayon Temple in Cambodia was digitized with the cooperation of the Japanese Government Team for Safeguarding Angkor (JSA).

References

[1] T. Masuda, K. Sakaue and N. Yokoya, "Registration and Integration of Multiple Range Images for 3-D Model Construction," *Proc. IEEE Conf. Computer Vision and Pattern Recognition*, 1996.

[2] M. Greenspan and G. Godin, "A Nearest Neighbor Method for Efficient ICP," *Proc. Int'l Conf. 3D Digital Imaging and Modeling (3DIM)*, 2001, pp. 161-168.

[3] G. Blais and M. Levine, "Registering Multiview Range Data to Create 3D Computer Objects," *IEEE Trans. Pattern Analysis and Machine Intelligence*, Vol. 17, No. 8, 1995.

[4] H. Gagnon, M. Soucy, R. Bergevin and D. Laurendeau, "Registeration of multiple range views for automatic 3-D model building," *Proc. IEEE Conf. Computer Vision and Pattern Recognition*, 1994, pp.581-586.

[5] P. J. Besl and N. D. McKay, "A method for registration of 3-D shapes," *IEEE Trans. Pattern Analysis and Machine Intelligence*, 14(2): 239-256, 1992.

[6] Y. Chen and G. Medioni, "Object modeling by registration of multiple range images," *Image and Vision Computing* 10(3), 145-155, 1992.

[7] Z. Zhang, "Iterative point matching for registration of free-form curves and surfaces," *Int'l J. Computer Vision*, 13(2):119–152, 1994.

[8] D. A. Simon, M. Hebert and T. Kanade, "Realtime 3-D pose estimation using a high-speed range sensor," *Proc. IEEE Int'l Conf. Robotics and Automation*, 1994, pp. 2235-2241.

[9] K. Nishino and K. Ikeuchi, "Robust Simultaneous Registration of Multiple Range Images," *Proc. Fifth Asian Conf. Computer Vision*, Jan. 2002, pp. 454-461.

[10] M. Greenspan and G. Godin, "A Nearest Neighbor Method for Efficient ICP," *Proc. Int'l Conf. 3D Digital Imaging and Modeling (3DIM)*, 2001, pp. 161-168.

[11] R. Sagawa, T. Masuda and K. Ikeuchi, "Effective Nearest Neighbor Search for Aligning and Merging Range Images," *Proc. Int'l Conf. 3-D Digital Imaging and Modeling (3DIM)*, 2003, pp. 79-86.

[12] P. J. Neugebauer, "Reconstruction of Real-World Objects via Simultaneous Registration and Robust Combination of Multiple Range Images," *Int'l J. Shape Modeling*, 3(1&2):71-90, 1997.

[13] R. Bergevin, M. Soucy, H. Gagnon, and D. Laurendeau, "Towards a general multi-view registration technique," *IEEE Trans. Pattern Analysis and Machine Intelligence*, 18(5):540–547, May 1996.

[14] R. Benjemaa and F. Schmitt, "Fast global registration of 3d sampled surfaces using a multi-z-buffer technique," *Proc. Int'l Conf. Recent Advances in 3-D Digital Imaging and Modeling*, May 1997, pp. 113-120.

[15] K. Pulli, "Multiview Registration for Large Data Sets," *Proc. Int'l Conf. 3D Digital Imaging and Modeling (3DIM)*, pp. 160-168, Oct. 1999.

[16] C. Langis, M. Greenspan and G. Godin, "The parallel iterative closest point algorithm," *Proc. Int'l Conf. 3D Digital Imaging and Modeling (3DIM)*, 2001.

[17] A. Pothen, H. D. Simon and K.-P. Liou, "Partitioning sparse matrices with eigenvectors of graphs," *SIAM J. Matrix Analysis and Applications*, 11(3):430-452, 1990.

[18] L. Hagen and A. B. Kahng, "New Spectral Methods for Ratio Cut Partitioning and Clustering," *IEEE Trans. Computer-Aided Design*, Vol. 11, No. 9, pp. 1074-1085, Sep. 1992.

[19] G. Karypis and V. Kumar, "A fast and high quality multilevel scheme for partitioning irregular graphs," *SIAM J. Scientific Computing*, 20(1):359-392, 1998.

[20] S. Hauck and G. Borriello, "An Evaluation of Bipartitioning Techniques," *IEEE Trans. ComputerAided Design of Integrated Circuits and Systems*, Vol. 16, No. 8, pp. 849-866, Aug. 1997.

Chapter 8

SIMULTANEOUS DETERMINATION OF REGISTRATION AND DEFORMATION PARAMETERS AMONG 3D RANGE IMAGES

Tomohito Masuda, Yuichiro Hirota, Ko Nishino, and Katsushi Ikeuchi

Abstract   The conventional registration algorithms are mostly concerned with the rigid-body transformation parameters between a pair of 3D range images. Our proposed framework aims to determine, in a unified manner, not only such rigid transformation parameters but also various deformation parameters, assuming that the deformation we handle here is strictly defined by some parameterized formulation derived from the deformation mechanism. In this point, our proposed framework is different from the deformation researched in such field as the medical imaging.

Similar to other conventional registration algorithms, our algorithm is formulated as a minimization problem of the squared distance sum between the corresponding points among a pair of range images. While the conventional registration algorithms mainly minimize this sum concerned about 6 parameters (3 translation and 3 rotation parameters), the evaluation function in our proposed algorithm includes those deformation parameters as well. Our proposed algorithm can be applied to a wide range of application areas of computer vision, in particular, shape modelling and shape analysis. In this chapter, we describe how we formulated such an algorithm, implemented it, and evaluated its performance.

1.   Introduction

A 3D data registration algorithm determines the translation and rotation parameters between a pair of the corresponding 3D range images. The algorithm solves the nonlinear equation to minimize the distance between a pair of corresponding 3D range image with respect to the 6 unknown parameters (3 translation and 3 rotation parameters).

3D data registration has wide application areas. In the research of modeling objects in the real world, it is necessary to have multiple observations of the object in order to cover the whole surface of the object. Aligning these partial

3D data using the registration algorithm is one of the crucial steps to completing the 3D surface model of the object. The registration algorithms are also used to compare the shape difference between similar objects for the industrial inspection of manufacturing accuracy. In archeological applications, there is a need to observe the shape deformation, e.g. the deterioration process over time. Due to these reasons, many registration algorithms have been proposed.

Some applications, however, require determining more parameters than just the 6 translation and rotation parameters. For simple example, when comparing 3D data of two objects with the same shape but different size, we have to determine the scaling parameter in addition to the six translation and rotation parameters. It is also the case when aligning the data of a deformable object. When we replace a part of the range data, such as the cylinder, with a CAD primitive model in order to reduce the data amount or refine its shape, the parameter of the CAD primitive shape, the diameter and the height in cylinder case, should be determined from the measured data by fitting the primitive to the range data. The conventional registration algorithm cannot solve these problems because it formulates the registration only as a rigid-body transformation.

In this chapter, we propose the extended framework of the conventional registration algorithm to overcome these difficulties. This kinds of registration, namely, deformation registrations have been researched in such field as the medical imaging [1–5], and the target object for the registration is mainly the soft tissues. They adopt similarity, affine, quadric/superquadric, and displacement-field-based transformation so that their deformation works well for any kind of target shape.

These methods can be generally adopted in shape modelling and fitting. However, if the deformation is strictly defined by some parameterized formulation derived form the deformation mechanism, the deformation is much more accurate when using its formulation and their methods are no other than the approximated ones. The parameters obtained from the strict formulation have the essential meaning concerned about the cause and origination of the deformation. So our framework pays as much attention to the obtained parameters as to the appearance result of the deformation. In this point, our aim is different from theirs. So in our assumption that the shape changes are strictly represented with a mathematical formula including some variable parameters and its formula is known a priori, we formulate the generally extended registration which allows the 3D data to be deformed and determines both deformation and translation and rotation parameters.

The remainder of this chapter is organized as follows. Section 2 reviews the conventional registration in terms of their robustness. Our proposed formulation need to be robust because our algorithm becomes sensitive to incorrect matching correspondence due to the parameter incrementation. Section 3 describes the design and implementation of the robust rigid-body transformation as a basis of our extended framework. Section 4 presents how we extend the basic algorithm in order to be able to handle the deformation parameters. Section 5 and 6 describe how to apply our proposed algorithm to the actual applications. In particular, we determine the shape parameters of a plaster function model made in 19th century for mathematical education . Another example of our registration algorithm is to align two range images obtained from a stably set laser range sensor and a floating laser range sensor, referred to as a Flying Laser Range Sensor (FLRS). Due to the floating characteristics, the second sensor causes data distortion. Our algorithm can determine both translation and rotation and distortion parameters. We also evaluate the accuracy of these algorithms. Finally, Section 7 summarises this chapter with the conclusion and the future work.

2.   Related Work

One of the most fundamental algorithms for 3D data registration is the Iterative Closest Point (ICP) algorithm proposed by Besl and McKay [6]. This algorithm framework reduces the registration to the minimization problem of the distance sum between the corresponding data by the iterative calculation. The function minimization with respect to the transformation parameter leads the optimal one which represents the plausible transformation between the aligning data pieces, for example, 3 translation and 3 rotation parameters in case of the rigid-body transformation. This framework is extended in various way, and we can classify them from the viewpoint of the registration ordering, matching unit, and error metric.

2.1   Registration Ordering

In the registration of multiple sets of 3D data, its ordering affects the convergence of the final result. The sequential ordering chooses a corresponding pair of data piece at each iteration for the registration, and repeats this process until all the data pieces are aligned [7]. Its computation cost is lower because only two data pieces are handled at each registration. However, it is susceptible to registration failure since the registration errors are locally accumulated and this causes the local discrepancy of the registration result.

In contrast, the simultaneous ordering aligns all the data together at each iteration. Although its computation cost is higher, it enables more accurate registration because the registration error is distributed globally.

2.2   Matching Unit

There are two kinds of matching units in the ICP algorithm: the geometric feature points and all the points in the range images. Assuming that one-to-one

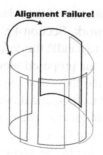

Figure 8.1. Illustration of registration failure in sequential strategy. The data are sequentially aligned counterclockwise in order from the red data and the black data, and the accumulated error prevented the black and red data from the correct registration.

correspondence is taken among all the feature points, the feature point matching doesn't change its correspondence at any iteration [8] [9]. So it cannot achieve the accurate registration in case that the correspondence cannot be taken precisely. The all point matching updates the correspondence so that it can be more plausible as the iteration proceeds [10] [11], and therefore can achieve more accurate registration as Rusinkiewicz et. al. reported [12].

2.3   Error Metric

As the error metric, the point-to-point or point-to-plain distance of the matching unit is mainly used [13] [14]. Some of other algorithm adopt such additional information as the reflectance(the reflection ratio of the laser ray) and color of the captured point as the error metric [15].

3.   Robust Determination of Translation and Rotation Parameters

Our basic registration algorithm is designed to robustly determine translation and rotation parameters as accurately as possible even by sacrificing its convergence speed. The accurate convergence is more important factor to be considered than the rapid convergence because our final objective is to determine the deformation parameters in addition to the translation and rotation parameters.

3D data, obtained by the laser range sensor, generally has considerable measurement noise , such metric as normals cannot be estimated from the point cloud with acceptable reliability. Therefore, the closest point-to-point distance should be employed as the error metric as described in [12]. To cope with erroneous measurement, the simultaneous ordering is adopted.

Again, our basic registration algorithm aligns the closest points together with all data pieces simultaneously so as to minimize the sum of distance of point-to-point distance. The minimization of the error function is represented as follows:

$$E(\mathbf{p}) = \sum_i \sum_j \rho(z_{ij}(\mathbf{p})), \qquad (8.1)$$

where

$$\mathbf{p} = (\mathbf{t}, \mathbf{q}), \qquad (8.2)$$

$$z_{ij}(\mathbf{p}) = \|\mathbf{R}(\mathbf{q})\mathbf{x}_i + \mathbf{t} - \mathbf{y}_{ji}\|^2, \qquad (8.3)$$

$$\rho(z_{ij}(\mathbf{p})) = \log(1 + \frac{1}{2\sigma^2}z_{ij}(\mathbf{p})), \qquad (8.4)$$

$\mathbf{t}$	:	translation vector,
$\mathbf{R}(\mathbf{q})$	:	rotation matrix corresponding to quaternion q,
$\mathbf{x}_i$	:	ith point in the data set of interest,
$\mathbf{y}_{ji}$	:	the corresponding point of x_i,
		in the jth measured data,
$\rho(z_{ij}(\mathbf{p}))$	:	Lorentz function as the M-estimator.

This equation shows that the weight is added to the straightforward least-square objective function.

The range images are aligned iteratively by moving (translating/rotating) the measured data according to the estimated parameters. The movement is determined such that the total sum of distance between the corresponding points is minimized. As for the rotation matrix, we use the quaternion representation with 3 degree of freedom. Finally, we solve the 6-dimensional vector $\mathbf{p}$ in order to minimize the sum of $z_{ij}(\mathbf{p})$ for all i, j.

In the direct square sum error function, considerable noise leads to the imprecise registration of 3D data because the exact correspondences between the noisy data in the initial step is unavailable. The erroneous correspondences must be removed before registration. In this algorithm, M-estimation is used for noise elimination (Function 8.4) by considering the probability distribution of the error. Lorentz function is used here since it yields the best result as written in [16].

On this error metric $E(\mathbf{p})$, we compute the parameters $\mathbf{p}$ which fulfill the following equation:

$$\mathbf{p}_{opt} = \arg\min_{\mathbf{p}} E(\mathbf{p}). \qquad (8.5)$$

For the gradient-based solution of the non-linear optimization, The descent gradient is computed as follows:

$$\frac{\partial E}{\partial \mathbf{p}} = \sum_i \sum_j \frac{\partial \rho(z_{ij})}{\partial z_{ij}} \cdot \frac{\partial z_{ij}}{\partial \mathbf{p}}$$

$$= \sum_i \sum_j \frac{1}{2\sigma^2 + z_{ij}(\mathbf{p})} \frac{\partial z_{ij}}{\partial \mathbf{p}}. \qquad (8.6)$$

If we evaluate $\partial z_{ij}/\partial \mathbf{p}$ by identifying quaternion q_I, we can represent $\partial z_{ij}/\partial \mathbf{p}$ as

$$
\begin{aligned}
\frac{\partial z_{ij}(\mathbf{p})}{\partial \mathbf{p}} &= 2(\mathbf{R}(\mathbf{q})\mathbf{x}_i + \mathbf{t} - \mathbf{y}_{ji}) \frac{\partial(\mathbf{R}(\mathbf{q})\mathbf{x}_i + \mathbf{t} - \mathbf{y}_{ji})}{\partial \mathbf{p}}\bigg|_{q_I} \\
&= \left[\begin{array}{c} 2(\mathbf{x}_i + \mathbf{t} - \mathbf{y}_{ji}) \\ -4\mathbf{x}_i \times (\mathbf{t} - \mathbf{y}_{ji}) \end{array} \right].
\end{aligned}
\qquad (8.7)
$$

4.   Simultaneous Determination of Deformation Parameters

Our proposal assume that the deformation can be represented by some parameterised mathematical formula, and is known a priori, but that its parameter is unknown.

Our goal is to simultaneously determine these deformation, translation, and rotation parameters by comparing the target data to transform with its corresponding data. The translation and rotation parameters are determined in a minimization paradigm described in the previous section. If we fix these parameters, the determination of deformation parameter becomes a shape matching problem at an iterative minimization step. Thus, we can handle both parameter determination in a unified minimization framework.

We extend the parameter estimation of the registration formulation to add the shape parameter by extending the error function in Equation (8.3). Therefore, $z_{ij}(\mathbf{p})$ in Equation (8.3) is transformed into:

$$z_{ij}(\mathbf{p}) = \sum_{i,j} ||\mathbf{R}(\mathbf{q})\mathbf{g}(\mathbf{x}_i, \mathbf{k}) + \mathbf{t} - \mathbf{y}_{ji}||^2, \qquad (8.8)$$

$$
\begin{aligned}
\textit{where} \quad \mathbf{p} &= \quad (\mathbf{t}, \mathbf{q}, \mathbf{k}), \\
\mathbf{g}(\mathbf{x}_i, \mathbf{k}) &: \quad \text{deformation function of point } \mathbf{x}_i \\
&\quad \text{with respect to parameter } \mathbf{k}.
\end{aligned}
$$

And the gradient described in Equation 8.7 is extended as:

$$\frac{\partial z_{ij}(\mathbf{p})}{\partial \mathbf{p}} = 2(\mathbf{R}(\mathbf{q})\mathbf{g}(\mathbf{x}_i, \mathbf{k}) + \mathbf{t} - \mathbf{y}_{ji}) \frac{\partial(\mathbf{R}(\mathbf{q})\mathbf{g}(\mathbf{x}_i, \mathbf{k}) + \mathbf{t} - \mathbf{y}_{ji})}{\partial \mathbf{p}}\bigg|_{q_I} \qquad (8.9)$$

$$
= \left[\begin{array}{c} 2(\mathbf{g}(\mathbf{x}_i, \mathbf{k}) + \mathbf{t} - \mathbf{y}_{ji}) \\ -4\mathbf{g}(\mathbf{x}_i, \mathbf{k}) \times (\mathbf{t} - \mathbf{y}_{ji}) \\ 2(\mathbf{g}(\mathbf{x}_i, \mathbf{k}) + \mathbf{t} - \mathbf{y}_{ji}) \frac{\partial(\mathbf{g}(\mathbf{x}_i, \mathbf{k}))}{\partial \mathbf{k}} \end{array} \right] \qquad (8.10)
$$

This straightforward extension causes the unstable convergence of the deformation registration. The obtained translation, rotation, and deformation parameters overreach the optimum if every parameter is applied simultaneously to the deformation, though each parameter can be estimated with enough accuracy if applied independently. Namely, every parameter interferes each other.

In order to prevent this interference, we design our extended formulation again to remove the translation and rotation effect caused only by deformation. The basic idea is to recover the position and posture which changes due to the deformation. This is implemented by the "preliminary" rigid-body transformation which determines only the deformation parameter. First, Every parameter is acquired by Equation 8.6 and 8.10. Then the preliminary rigid-body transformation is determined only by the deformation parameter as follows:

$$\mathbf{g}'(\mathbf{x}_i, \mathbf{k}) = \mathbf{R}_o \mathbf{g}(\mathbf{x}_i, \mathbf{k}) + \mathbf{t}_o, \tag{8.11}$$

where

$$(\mathbf{R}_o, \mathbf{t}_o) = (\mathbf{R}(\mathbf{q}_o), \mathbf{t}_o),$$

such that

$$(\mathbf{q}_o, \mathbf{t}_o) = \arg \min_{\mathbf{q}, \mathbf{t}} \sum_i ||\mathbf{R}(\mathbf{q})\mathbf{g}(\mathbf{x}_i, \mathbf{k}) + \mathbf{t} - \mathbf{x}_i||^2. \tag{8.12}$$

$\mathbf{R}_o, \mathbf{t}_o$ can be derived from the following equation:

$$\frac{\partial \sum_i \epsilon_i^2}{\partial \mathbf{t}_o} = \sum_i 2\epsilon_i \cdot \frac{\partial \epsilon_i}{\partial \mathbf{t}_o} = \mathbf{0}, \tag{8.13}$$

where

$$\epsilon_i = \mathbf{g}(\mathbf{x}_i, \mathbf{k}) + \mathbf{t}_o - \mathbf{x}_i$$

This is a conventional registration problem, but it is unnecessary to strictly solve the above equation. In fact, $\mathbf{R}_o$ doesn't affect the stable convergence so much as $\mathbf{t}_o$. If $\mathbf{R}_o$ is ignored, $\mathbf{t}_o$ in Equation 8.13 is concretely derived as follows:

$$\sum_i (\mathbf{g}(\mathbf{x}_i, \mathbf{k}) + \mathbf{t} - \mathbf{x}_i) = \mathbf{0}$$

$$\therefore \mathbf{t}_o = -\frac{\sum_i (\mathbf{g}(\mathbf{x}_i, \mathbf{k}) - \mathbf{x}_i)}{N}. \tag{8.14}$$

Finally, Equation 8.8 is replaced with:

$$z_{ij}(\mathbf{p}) = \sum_{i,j} ||\mathbf{R}(\mathbf{q})\{\mathbf{R}_o \mathbf{g}(\mathbf{x}_i, \mathbf{k}) + \mathbf{t}_o\} + \mathbf{t} - \mathbf{y}_{ji}||^2. \tag{8.15}$$

In the ICP based registration algorithm, the acquisition of the good initial parameter is significant for the optimal registration result. In our implementation, the initial transformation parameter is set manually by GUI with accuracy enough to reach the optimum. we investigate the registration behavior according to the difference of the optimum and the initial parameter in each experiment after this section.

5.   Unknown Parameter Estimation of Mathematical Model

We have examined manufacturing accuracy of mathematical models made of plaster (Figure 8.2-(1)). This model is a kind of cultural asset, and was manufactured in Germany at the end of the 19th century for educational purposes and has been exhibited in our university museum. This model visually represents the following mathematical formula:

$$X(u, v) = (l\phi(v) \cos u, l\phi(v) \sin u, l\psi(v)), \tag{8.16}$$

$$where \qquad 0 \le u \le 2\pi,$$
$$-a \cdot \sinh^{-1}\left(\tfrac{a}{b}\right) \le v \le a \cdot \sinh^{-1}\left(\tfrac{a}{b}\right),$$
$$\phi(v) = b \cosh\left(\tfrac{v}{a}\right),$$
$$\psi(v) = \int_0^v \sqrt{1 - \tfrac{b^2}{a^2}\sinh^{-1}\left(\tfrac{t}{a}\right)}\,dt.$$

This surface is generated by rotating a 2D catenary (Figure 8.2-(2)) according to the concerning documentation. The surface by revolution always has the azimuthal symmetry. Besides scale parameter (l), 2 parameters (a, b) are involved in the deformation of the revolutional surfaces. Our motivation here, because there are no documentation to identify the three deformation parameters when manufacturing the model, was to estimate the deformation parameter by applying our proposed framework to its range image and the data computed from Equation 8.16, to evaluate the manufacturing accuracy of the plaster model under the estimated parameter, and to remake the accurate model since historians and mathematicians are interested in the manufacturer's skill in those days.

We have to estimate these parameters in order to compare the range image of the model and the computed data from Equation 8.16 under the estimated parameters. In this case, our proposed method can be applied by replacing the deformation function like this:

$$\mathbf{g}(\mathbf{x}_i, \mathbf{k}) \;=\; (l\phi(v_i) \cos u_i, l\phi(v_i) \sin u_i, l\psi(v_i)),$$
$$where \qquad \mathbf{k} = (l, a, b).$$

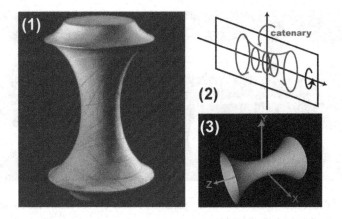

Figure 8.2. Mathematical model used in our experiment.

The descent gradient is in the following:

$$\frac{\partial z_{ij}(\mathbf{p})}{\partial \mathbf{p}} = \begin{bmatrix} 2(\mathbf{g}(\mathbf{x}_i, \mathbf{k}) + \mathbf{t} - \mathbf{y}_{ji}) \\ -4\mathbf{g}(\mathbf{x}_i, \mathbf{k}) \times (\mathbf{t} - \mathbf{y}_{ji}) \\ 2(\mathbf{g}(\mathbf{x}_i, \mathbf{k}) + \mathbf{t} - \mathbf{y}_{ji})\frac{\partial \mathbf{g}(\mathbf{x}_i,\mathbf{k})}{\partial \mathbf{k}} \end{bmatrix}, \tag{8.17}$$

where

$$\frac{\partial(\mathbf{g}(\mathbf{x}_i, \mathbf{k}))}{\partial \mathbf{v}} = \begin{bmatrix} \left((l\cos u)\frac{\partial \phi}{\partial a}, (l\sin u)\frac{\partial \phi}{\partial a}, l\frac{\partial \psi}{\partial a}\right)^T \\ \left((l\cos u)\frac{\partial \phi}{\partial b}, (l\sin u)\frac{\partial \phi}{\partial b}, l\frac{\partial \psi}{\partial b}\right)^T \\ (\phi(v_i)\cos u_i, \phi(v_i)\sin u_i, \psi(v_i))^T \end{bmatrix}. \tag{8.18}$$

Such that

$$\frac{\partial \phi}{\partial a} = -\frac{bv}{a^2}\sinh\frac{v}{a},$$

$$\frac{\partial \psi}{\partial a} = \frac{vb^2}{2a^3}\left(-\frac{1}{2a^2}\sinh^{-1}\frac{v}{a} + \frac{1}{\sqrt{v^2 + a^2}}\right),$$

$$\frac{\partial \phi}{\partial b} = \cosh\frac{v}{a},$$

$$\frac{\partial \psi}{\partial b} = -\frac{b}{a^2}\sinh^{-1}\frac{v}{a}.$$

5.1 Experiment

The 3D shape of the model was captured by the MINOLTA VIVID 900. The data was initially aligned by the manual process via GUI. The initial shape

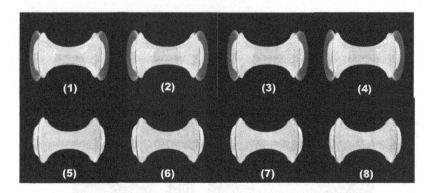

Figure 8.3. The registration process of the parametric data. (1)-(8) shows the convergence of both the measured and computed data.

parameters were also manually estimated. Figure 8.3 shows the registration process. It indicates that the computed data is transformed to fit the actual one. Estimated parameters are: $a = 0.0568, \quad b = 0.0237, \quad l = 0.996$.

5.2   Evaluation

The estimation is affected by various kinds of errors: measurement error; initial registration error; and error in initial parameters. So we investigated how the accuracy of estimated parameters depend on such errors by using the synthesized data which was computed under the known parameters with Gaussian noise added to form the noisy data. The accuracy of the estimation could be evaluated as the difference between the known parameters (ground truth) and the obtained parameters. The deformation parameters were set as $a = 0.05, b = 0.02$ and $l = 1.00$.

The first error to consider in the estimation is the measurement error of the range sensor. We first investigate how much noise is caused according to the pose of the actual object by using the measured data of the white Lambertian plane at the different poses. The system is shown in Figure 8.4. The white board was set on the turntable. The pose was changed by rotating and translating the turntable. We denote l and θ as the distance from the white board to the laser range finder and the angle between the normal of white board and the ray of the laser, respectively. Five data were obtained at each pose. Principal component analysis (PCA) was applied to estimate the most plausible plane composed by the point cloud and to obtain the standard deviation of the measurement error of the plane data. The standard deviation change of the plane data are shown in Figure 8.5.

We investigated the influence of the measurement noise by using the computed data from Equation 8.16 and its synthesized data. Noise with different standard deviation was added to its computed data. Standard deviation was set at 0.01, 0.1, 1.0, 10.0 in this experiment. Ten synthesized data were created for each standard deviation as the synthesized data. The initial translation, rotation and deformation parameter of the synthesized data were the same as the one of the computed data. The red line in Figure 8.6 show the range of the maximum and minimum of estimated parameter, a, b and l, respectively, the blue line shows the average of each estimated parameters, and the green dotted line is the ground truth.

Effects of the noise standard deviation to the estimated parameters were similar in all parameters: the larger the standard deviation was, the more different from the ground truth the estimate was and the larger the range of the maximum and minimum parameters was. However, noise added in this experiment was far higher than the observed noise. Even though noise with the standard deviation of 0.01 was added, the difference from the ground truth was almost none, and parameters were stably estimated. The maximum standard deviation of the measurement noise in MINOLTA VIVID 900 was detected at less than 0.002, so the result indicated the robustness of our estimation method against the sensor noise.

Next error is the initial registration error of translation and rotation. In the same manner, we added the noise to the computed data to create its synthesized data. The standard deviation of the noise (σ) was set to 0.0004 according to the measurement error as observed above. Each initial parameter was set to the same one of the computed data. The coordinate of the model is shown in Figure8.2-(3).

Effects of translation and rotation were investigated separately. For the initial translation, synthesized data were translated 0.01, 0.02 and 0.03 $[m]$ along x or z axis, respectively. For the initial rotation, three synthesized data were rotated 10, 20 and 30 $[degrees]$ around x axis. Since revolutional surface of catenary has the x, y and z symmetry,these translation and rotation were sufficient for the evaluation.

The results of estimation were shown in Figure 8.7. In the figure, the left, middle and right graphs show the estimation result in the case where the synthesized data is translated along x, z axis and rotated around x axis, respectively, as the difference between the ground truth and the estimated parameters. When the initial translation/rotation amount is set as shown in the translation/rotation axis (e.g. 0.01 x-t, 0.02 x-t, 0.03 x-t in the left graph), the difference between each estimated parameter in the parameter axis (a, b, scale) and its ground truth is shown in vertical axis (e.g. 0.00, $\pm$ 0.02, $\pm$ 0.04 in the left graph).

Z axis for this surface is the direction of expanding/contracting. The translation along z axis results in the ambiguity of the parameter estimation. In contrast, the translation along x axis is not directly related to the expansion

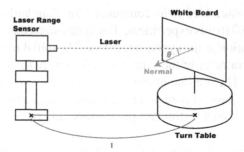

Figure 8.4.   System to evaluate measurement error. In this system, the surface normal and the
distance from the white board to the laser range sensor are changeable.

and contraction. The translation along z axis simultaneously affects the trans-
lation/rotation and deformation parameters. In fact, more iteration was needed
for good estimation in the case of translation along z axis than in the case of
translation along and rotation around x axis.

Final error is the result of the initial deformation parameter. The synthesized data were made in the same manner, and the standard deviation of the
noise (σ) was set to 0.0004. The initial pose and position of the synthesized
data were set to the same one of the computed data. Effects of each initial deformation parameter was investigated, and each initial parameter was changed
incrementally from the ground truth.

The results of estimation were shown in Figure 8.8. In the figure, the left,
middle and right graphs show the estimation results in the case where the a, b
and l are set to each value shown in the horizontal axis of the graph, respectively, as the difference between the ground truth and the estimated parameters.
When the initial deformation parameter is set as shown in the registration axis
(e.g. $0.07, 0.06, 0.04, 0.03$ in the left graph), the difference between each estimated parameter in the parameter axis (a, b, scale) and its ground truth is
shown in the vertical axis (e.g. $0.000, \pm0.005$, ..., in the left graph). Figure
8.8 indicated that the effect of incorrect initial value on each parameter was
different. It is difficult to recognize the accuracy of our algorithm via the numerical result, but the registration result is visually almost the same as shown
in Figure 8.3.

6.   Inter-and-Intra Scanning Registration

In order to measure the large-scale objects effectively, we have developed
a novel 3D measurement system: the Flying Laser Range Sensor (FLRS).
FLRS digitizes objects from the air while being suspended beneath a balloon
platform.

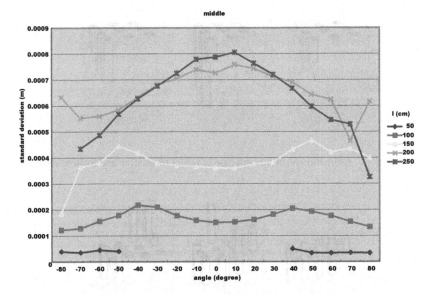

Figure 8.5. The relationship between surface normal and standard deviation. Each curve showed the data at different distance from white board to the finder.

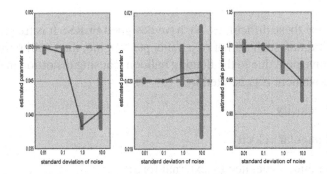

Figure 8.6. The maximum and the minimum of estimated parameter.

Concerning areal measurement systems, some techniques have been proposed so far. For example, aerial 3D measurements are achieved with a laser range sensor installed on a helicopter platform [17, 18]. High frequency vibration of the platform, however, must be considered to obtain highly accurate results. Another technique is aerial stereo photography with a digital camera that is attached to a balloon [19]; however, this stereo method cannot achieve a satisfactory level of precision in the restored data.

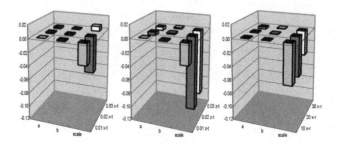

Figure 8.7.   Estimation result in each case of initial translation and rotation error.

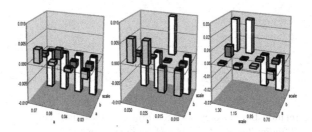

Figure 8.8.   Estimation result in each case of an initially set deformation parameter.

To overcome these difficulties, we have designed FLRS. It is free from high frequency vibration such as that of a helicopter engine; there still remains low frequency movement due to the floating balloon, causing distortion in obtained data. This movement is generated by

- Initial velocity

- Initial angular velocity

- Acceleration generated by external force

- Angular acceleration generated by external moment

We can ignore the influence of translation and angular acceleration because for scanning, FLRS needs only one second per frame. And insignificant rotation can be approximated to translation movement. Hence we consider only constant velocity movement. Under this assumption, we set up the deformation equation in Equation 8.8.

In this case, the geometrical function $g(x_i, k)$ is represented only by constant velocity vector v of FLRS movement, and Equation 8.8 is replaced with:

$$g(x_i, v) = x_i - \tau_i v, \qquad (8.19)$$

where τ_i is the time from the start of the scanning until the capture of the ith point. The descent gradient is represented in this case as follows.

$$\frac{\partial z_{ij}(\mathbf{p})}{\partial \mathbf{p}} = \left[\begin{array}{c} 2(\mathbf{g}(\mathbf{x}_i, \mathbf{v}) + \mathbf{t} - \mathbf{y}_{ji}) \\ -4\mathbf{g}(\mathbf{x}_i, \mathbf{v}) \times (\mathbf{t} - \mathbf{y}_{ji}) \\ 2(\mathbf{g}(\mathbf{x}_i, \mathbf{v}) + \mathbf{t} - \mathbf{y}_{ji})\frac{\partial \mathbf{g}(\mathbf{x}_i, \mathbf{v})}{\partial \mathbf{v}} \end{array} \right], \qquad (8.20)$$

$$where \qquad \mathbf{p} = \quad (\mathbf{t}, \mathbf{q}, \mathbf{v}),$$

$$\frac{\partial \mathbf{g}(\mathbf{x}_i, \mathbf{v})}{\partial \mathbf{v}} = \left[\begin{array}{c} (\tau_i \quad 0 \quad 0)^T \\ (0 \quad \tau_i \quad 0)^T \\ (0 \quad 0 \quad \tau_i)^T \end{array} \right].$$

While translation and rotation registration is due to the sensor movement among multiple views, the shape deformation registration is due to the sensor movement during one scan. Thus, we refer to this registration as "inter-and-intra scanning registration".

6.1 Experiment

As an experiment on actual case, we executed our algorithm on the data of the Bayon temple. In this experiment, we aligned the corresponding data captured by FLRS and Cyrax 2500. The latter data was scanned from the stable ground, namely without movement during scanning, and we assume that it is sufficiently reliable. The result is shown in Figure 8.9. You can see that our algorithm aligned and fitted the FLRS's data well onto the Cyrax2500's data.

6.2 Evaluation

To evaluate the accuracy of the algorithm, we aligned the original and synthesized data through our algorithm. The synthesized data translates, rotates, and distorts the original data with known parameters. The optimal deformation registration parameter of two data is the known parameters. We investigate how close the parameter obtained through our algorithm is to the known parameter. The synthesized data are created from a range image by removing points randomly to make them sparser and not have any of the same points to be included in both data, in order to make more actual condition in the registration of the images at the different sight. Similar to the conventional registration, each initial parameter is set via GUI, and then our algorithm is executed. We investigate the difference between the parameter obtained by our algorithm and the known parameter according to the change of $\mathbf{v}$ in the condition shown in Figure 8.1. The deformation registration is executed five times at each setting parameter of $\mathbf{v}$ in order to remove the outlier, and the difference is calculated as the average. The result is shown in Figure 8.11.

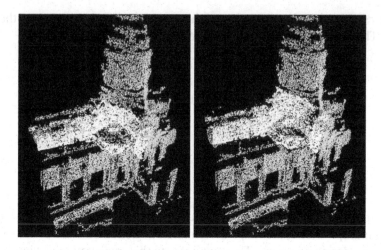

Figure 8.9. Range images before and after our registration process: The left image shows the data under the initially set translation, rotation, and deformation parameters. A range image of FLRS (yellow) is aligned and fitted onto the corresponding range image of Cyrax 2500 (purple) simultaneously as shown in the right image. These range images are the partial shape of the Bayon temple in Cambodia.

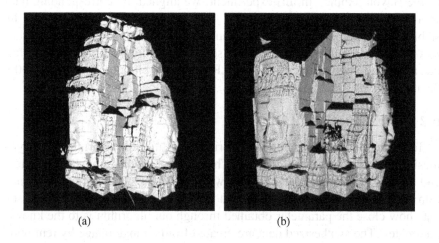

(a)　　　　　　　　　　　　　　　　(b)

Figure 8.10. Sample range images for evaluation experiments.

First, we pay attention to the stable acquisition limitation of the accurate parameter in our algorithm. The difference is stably constant in each parameter in the condition where the setting velocity is within $1.6[m/s]$, but is drastically oscillated otherwise. This result concludes that our algorithm can obtain the accurate deformation parameter for distortion correction as long as the sensor velocity is within $1.6[m/s]$.

Table 8.1.   The setting difference between the original and the transformed in each parameter for the accuracy evaluation of the deformation registration.

parameter	setting difference
$R(q)$	3 [deg] around X axis
t	0.1 [m] along X axis
v	0.00-3.00 [m/s] along X axis (every 0.01 [m/s] increment)

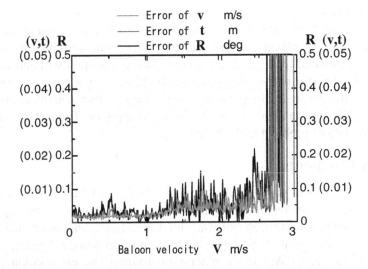

Figure 8.11.   The difference from the optimum $(\mathbf{v}, \mathbf{t}, \mathbf{R})$

Next, we also focus on the estimation accuracy of the obtained parameter under the sensor velocity of $1.6[m/s]$. The average differences of $\mathbf{t}$, $\mathbf{R}$, and $\mathbf{v}$ are $0.005[m]$, $0.1[deg]$, and $0.008[m/s]$ respectively. Note that size of faces in the images is over 1 meter.

7.   Conclusion and Future Work

We proposed an extended registration framework which allows the 3D data to be deformed. Our proposed method assumes that the deformation is strictly defined by some parameterized formulation derived from the deformation mechanism. The deformation registration reduces to the minimization problem of the error function which is the squared sum of distance between the corresponding point in the data. While the conventional registration minimizing this error function concerned 6 parameters (3 translation parameters and 3 rotation parameters for rotation), the error function in our proposed framework includes the deformation parameters as well.

We introduced two application in this chapter. One is the shape parameter estimation, and the other is the shape rectification. In the first application, the accurate shape parameters for the mathematical model could be estimated. The other application rectified the distorted data obtained from the Flying Laser Range Sensor (FLRS) which is suspended under a balloon platform. And the estimation accuracy was also shown in each application. The deformation parameter estimation is a method for 3D data fitting, and also a way to understand the cause and origination of the deformation, so can be used for the system feedback.

Our applications are only a few of the possible applications, and we are trying to develop an application to generate the CAD primitives under the shape parameter estimated from the range image. This application will convert the range images into the properly approximated CAD data. The benefit of this application is the ability to compress the range images which usually consist of numerous 3D points and polygons. We intend to apply our framework widely to various class of problem in the future.

Acknowledgments

This research was supported, in part, by Ministry of Education, Culture, Sports, Science and Technology under the Leading Project, "Development of High Fidelity Digitization Software for Large-Scale and Intangible Cultural Assets," and, in part, by Japan Science and Technology Agency, under the CREST program, "Automatic generation of virtual models of cultural heritage."

References

[1] C. V. Stewart, C. L. Tsai, and A. Perera. A view-based approach to registration: Theory and application to vascular image regisrtaion. In *Proceedings of International Conference on Information Processing in Medical Imaging (IPMI)*, pages 475–486, 2003.

[2] J. and N. Ayache. Rigid and affine registration of smooth surfaces using differential properties. In *Proceedings of Third European Conference on Computer Vision (ECCV'94)*, pages 397–406, 1994.

[3] A. Guéziec, X. Pennec, and N. Ayache. Medical image registration using geometric hashing. 4(4):29–41, 1997.

[4] Eric Bardinet, Laurent D. Cohen, and Nicholas Ayache. A parametric deformable model to fit unstructured 3d data. 71(1):39–54, 1998.

[5] P. R. Andresen and M. Nielsen. Non-rigid registration by geometrycon-strained diffusion. In *Proceedings of Medical Image Computing and Computer-Assisted Intervention (MICCAI'99)*, pages 533–543, 1999.

[6] P.J. Besl and N.D. McKay. A method for registration of 3-d shapes. *IEEE Transactions on Pattern Analysis and Machine Intelligence*, 14(2):239–256, February 1992.

[7] G. Turk and M. Levoy. Zipped polygon meshes from range images. In *ACM SIGGRAPH Proceedings*, pages 311–318, July 1994.

[8] K. Higuchi, M. Herbert, and K. Ikeuchi. Building 3-d models from un-registered range images. In *Graphical Models and Image Processing*, volume 57, pages 315–333, July 1995.

[9] A.E. Johnson and M. Herbert. Surface matching for object recogni-tion in complex 3-dimensional scenes. *Image and Vision Computing*, 16(9/10):635–651, July 1998.

[10] P.J. Besl and N.D. McKay. A method for registration of 3-d shapes. *IEEE Transactions on Pattern Analysis and Machine Intelligence*, 14(2):239–256, February 1992.

[11] David Simon. *Fast and Accurate Shape-Based Registration*. PhD thesis, School of Computer Science, Carnegie Mellon University, 1996.

[12] Szymon Rusinkiewicz and Marc Levoy. Efficient varinats of the icp algo-rithm. In *Proceedings of the 3rd International Conference on 3D Digital Imaging and Modeling*, pages 145–152, May 2001.

[13] Y. Chen and G.G. Medioni. Object modeling by registration of multiple range images. *Image and Vision Computing*, 10(3):145–155, 1992.

[14] P. Neugebauer. Geometrical cloning of 3d objects via simultaneous regis-tration of multiple range images. In *Proceedings of International Confer-ence on Shape Modeling and Application*, pages 130–139, March 1997.

[15] A.E. Johnson and S. Kang. Registration and integration of textured 3-d data. In *Proceedings of International Conference on 3D Digital Imaging and Modeling*, pages 234–241, May 1997.

[16] Mark D. Wheeler. *Automatic Modeling and Localization for Object Recognition*. PhD thesis, School of Computer Science, Carnegie Mel-lon University, 1996.

[17] Mark Daniel Sebastian Thrun and Dirk H ahnel. Scan alignment and 3-d surface modelling with a helicopter platform. In *The 4th Int. Conf. on Field and Service Robotics, July 14-16*, 2003.

[18] Ryan Miller and Omead Amidi. 3-d site mapping with the cmu au-tonomous helicopter. June 1998.

[19] Jana Visnovcova, Li Zhang, and Armin Gruen. Generating a 3d model of a bayon tower using non-metric imagery. In *Proc. of Int. Workshop Recreating the Past -Visualization and Animation of Cultural Heritage*, 2001.

Chapter 9

PARALLEL PROCESSING OF RANGE DATA MERGING

Ryusuke Sagawa, Ko Nishino, Mark D. Wheeler, and Katsushi Ikeuchi

Abstract   This chapter describes a volumetric view-merging algorithm that generates a consensus surface of an object from its range images. Our original method merges a set of range images into a volumetric implicit-surface representation, which is converted to a surface mesh by using a variant of the marching-cubes algorithm. We propose a method that increases the computation and memory efficiency for computing signed distances and the method of parallel computing on a PC cluster. Since our method permits a reduction in the data amount allocated in memory, the closest point is searched efficiently; this allows us to increase the number of parallel traversals and to reduce the computation time.

In this chapter, we describe the following two algorithms which are complementary in terms of the efficiency of CPUs and memory usage: distributed allocation of range data and parallel traversal of partial octrees. By adjusting them according to the system specifications, we can build the model efficiently by a PC cluster. We have implemented this system and evaluated its performance.

1.   Introduction

Integration of multiple range images is important to enable the use of 3D data acquired from stereo systems, laser range finders, etc. It is also fundamental and essential for any algorithms which utilize the generated 3D models, for example, tracking, object recognition and so on.

We have been developing techniques for automatically creating virtual reality models through observation of real objects; we refer to these techniques as modeling-from-reality (MFR). In order to explore unforeseen technical difficulties and to further extend our MFR techniques by solving these difficulties, we have begun a project to model Japanese cultural heritage objects through the use of these MFR techniques[9].

Some Japanese cultural heritage objects are large and their shapes may be intricate. Thus, the models of these objects' shapes must contain huge amounts of data. In our previous experiments in modeling small, indoor objects, we did not have to consider the computation and memory requirements to build those models. However, building a model of a huge amount of data necessitates our taking these requirements into account. In this chapter, we describe our proposed method for modeling the shape of huge, possibly intricate, objects.

After scanning the shape of an object by using a range sensor and then aligning all range images into the same coordinate system, our original method[13] converts a set of range images into a volumetric implicit-surface representation, It then obtains a surface mesh using a variant of the marching-cubes algorithm[6]. Unlike previous techniques[5, 2, 4] based on implicit-surface representations, our method estimates the signed distance to the object surface by finding a consensus of locally coherent observations of the surface.

Several approaches which are not based on implicit-surface representation have been proposed [11, 10, 12]. These algorithms perform poorly if the surfaces are slightly misaligned or if there is significant noise in the data.

There are some previous researches which implement the marching-cubes algorithm in a parallel manner [1, 7]. To reduce the computation time for merging range images, the signed distance should be also computed in a parallel manner.

The most costly part of the computation of our method is finding the consensus surface to compute the signed distance. To increase the computation and memory efficiency, we propose a method which reduces the amount of data to be searched, around which point the signed distance is computed.

We utilize octrees to represent volumetric implicit surfaces for effectively reducing the computation and memory requirements of the volumetric representation without sacrificing the accuracy of the resulting surface.

To further ease this size problem, we have developed parallel software that runs on a PC cluster to handle the huge amount of data. The parallel software consists of the following two components: 1. Distributed allocation of range data. 2. Parallel traversal of partial octrees.

In the following sections, 2 describes our original merging algorithm. 3 explains the method for increasing the computation and memory efficiency. In 4, the parallel merging algorithm is shown. Finally, the performance evaluation is shown in 5.

2.   Data Merging

2.1   Volumetric Modeling and Marching Cubes

Recently, the marching-cubes algorithm[6] has propelled volumetric modeling beyond the confines of "blocky" occupancy grids. Instead of storing a binary value in each voxel to indicate whether the voxel is empty or full, the marching-cubes algorithm requires that the data in the volume grid are sam-

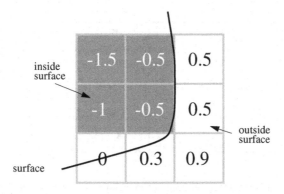

Figure 9.1. Zero-crossing interpolation from the grid sampling of an implicit surface

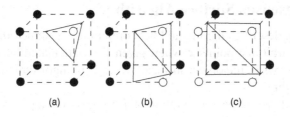

Figure 9.2. Marching Cubes: An implicit surface is approximated of by triangles. ○: voxels of outside surface. ●: voxels of inside surface.

ples of an implicit surface. In each voxel, we store the signed distance, $f(x)$, from the center point of the voxel, x, to the closest point on the object's surface. The sign indicates whether the point is outside, $f(x) > 0$, or inside, $f(x) < 0$, the object's surface, while $f(x) = 0$ indicates that x lies on the surface of the object(See **Figure 9.1**).

The marching-cubes algorithm constructs a surface mesh by "marching" around the cubes while following the zero crossings of the implicit surface $f(x) = 0$. The resulting surfaces are relatively smooth and their accuracy can be greater than the resolution of the volume grid due to sub-voxel interpolation (See **Figure 9.2**).

Now we focus on a more easily solved problem: How do we compute $f(x)$? The real problem underlying our simple question is that we do not have a single surface; instead, we have many surfaces. Some elements of those surfaces do not belong to the object of interest but rather are artifacts of the image acquisition process or background surfaces. In the next subsection, we present an algorithm that answers the question and does so reliably in spite of the presence of noisy and extraneous surfaces in our data.

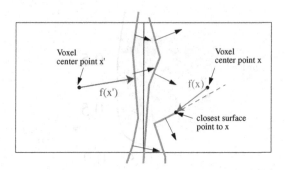

Figure 9.3.   Naive algorithm: An example of inferring the incorrect sign of a voxel's value, $f(x)$, due to a single noisy triangle.

2.2   Consensus Surface Algorithm

This section describes the method for computing the signed distance function $f(x)$ for arbitrary points x when given N triangulated surface patches from various views of the object surface. We call our algorithm the consensus-surface algorithm.

We can break down the computation of $f(x)$ into two steps:

- Compute the magnitude: compute the distance, $|f(x)|$, to the nearest object surface from x

- Compute the sign: determine whether the point is inside or outside of the object

The previous naive algorithm finds the nearest triangle from all views and uses the distance to that triangle as the magnitude $|f(x)|$. If the normal of the closest surface point is directed toward x, then x must be outside the object surface. In **Figure 9.3**, the point chosen as the closest point from x does not belong to the real surface. Thus, based on the normal information from the closest point, the algorithm incorrectly considers that x is inside the surface.

Our solution to these problems is to estimate the surface locally by averaging the observations of the same surface. The trick is to specify a method for identifying and collecting all observations of the same surface.

Nearby observations are compared using their location and surface normal. If the location and normal are within a predefined error tolerance (determined empirically), we can consider them to be observations of the same surface. Given a point on one of the observed triangle surfaces, we can search that region of 3D space for other nearby observations from other views which are potentially observations of the same surface. These searches are efficiently implemented using k-d trees[3].

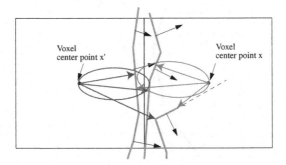

Figure 9.4. Consensus surface algorithm: The signed distance is chosen from circled consensus surfaces.

The consensus-surface algorithm examines the closest point in each image's triangle set. If there are sufficient surfaces of other triangle sets which are regarded as the same surfaces of each closest point, the closest point is a consensus surface. The algorithm which determines whether two surface observations are sufficiently close in terms of location and normal direction is as follows:

$$\text{SameSurface}(\langle p_0, n_0 \rangle, \langle p_1, n_1 \rangle) =$$
$$\begin{cases} \text{True} & (\| p_0 - p_1 \| \leq \delta_d) \wedge (n_0 \cdot n_1 \geq \cos \theta_n) \\ \text{False} & \text{otherwise} \end{cases} \tag{9.1}$$

where δ_d is the maximum allowed distance and θ_n is the maximum allowed difference in normal directions.

For example, consensus surfaces are circled in **Figure 9.4**. The algorithm chooses the closest one of them as the signed distance. In this case, it is correctly determined that x is the outside surface and x' is the inside surface.

2.3 Adaptive Resolution by Octree Representation

Volumetric modeling involves a tradeoff between accuracy and efficiency. The octree representation[8] balances this problem while keeping the algorithm implementation simple. Instead of iterating over all elements of the voxel grid, we can apply a recursive algorithm on an octree that samples the volume more finely only when near the surface of the object (See **Figure 9.5**).

To interpolate the zero crossings properly, we will need the implicit distance for the voxel containing the surface (the zero crossing) and all voxels neighboring this voxel; these voxels must all be represented at the finest level of precision. This constraint means that, if we have a surface at one corner of an octant, the longest possible distance to the center of a neighboring octant is

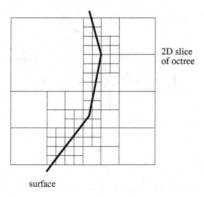

2D slice
of octree

surface

Figure 9.5.   The adaptive resolution is high around the surface and low elsewhere

one and one-half diagonals of the voxel cube, which is a distance of $\frac{3\sqrt{3}}{2}$ cube units.

Given the current octant, we can compute the signed distance. If the magnitude of the signed distance, $|f(x)|$, is larger than $\frac{3\sqrt{3}}{2}$ of the octant width, then it is not possible for the surface to lie in the current or neighboring octant. If the surface is not in the current or neighboring octant, we do not care to further subdivide the current octant.

3.   Increase the computation and memory efficiency

If the size of mesh data to be merged is huge, it is difficult to allocate all of that data to memory, Also, the computation time of the signed distance cannot be ignored. We propose the following method to increase the computation and memory efficiency by reducing the data allocated in the memory.

When the algorithm traverses a part of the octree, the data searched for finding the closest surface is only the local area around the voxel. The data of the other area are never used for computing signed distances while traversing the sub-octree.   Moreover, a closest surface is effectively searched using a k-d tree. However, it is inefficient when the k-d tree contains unnecessary data.

As described in Section 2.3, a octant is subdivided when its signed distance is less than $\frac{3\sqrt{3}}{2}$ cube units. Thus, the data farther than $\frac{3\sqrt{3}}{2}$ cube units is not necessary for finding the closest point of the voxel.

To load the necessary data into memory, we must read all of the data files. Since the overhead of reading files for the every finest octant is too costly, we read the data files for an ancestor octant. Where the width of an ancestor octant is W_0 and the width of the finest octant is W, the area of the mesh data to be loaded is inside the rectangle of a dotted line in **Figure 9.6**.

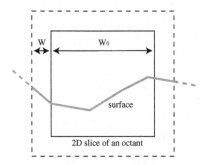

Figure 9.6. Load only the mesh data within the dotted rectangle into memory

4. Parallel Computing of Signed Distances

In this section, we describe the algorithm for parallel computing of signed distances. There are two motivations for parallel computing signed distances. We now propose the parallel computing method for each motivation:

1 Handling range data of huge size: We distribute the allocation of range data to multiple PCs.

2 Fast merging: We divide the octree into sub-octrees and assign traversal of a sub-octree to each CPU.

4.1 Distributed Allocation of Range Data

Calculating a signed distance from a point requires consideration of all range data with respect to this point. When the number of the measurement increases, more data should be considered. It becomes difficult to allocate all the range data in a single processor.

We distribute that range data to multiple PCs and compute signed distances in a parallel manner. For example, in **Figure 9.7**, Data 1,2,3 are allocated to PCs 1,2,3, respectively. Signed distances from the point, x, to Data 1 are computed by PC1. In the same manner, signed distances to Data 2 are computed by PC2, and so on. Since finding the closest point of a mesh data is independent of the others, we can compute signed distances in a parallel manner.

However, the computation times are different among CPUs; After finding the closest points of all data, we have to choose the smallest magnitude of the signed distances. To synchronize, until the remaining CPUs finish computing the signed distances.

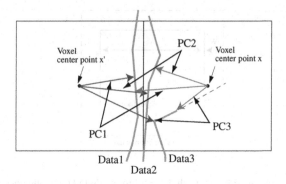

Figure 9.7.   Parallel computation of signed-distances

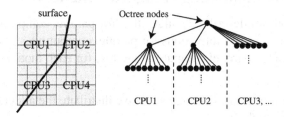

Figure 9.8.   Assignment of partial space of the octree to each CPU and parallel traversal of partial trees

4.2   Parallel Traversal of an Octree

Dividing an octree into partial trees enables us to traverse the partial trees. We assign the partial space of an octree to each CPU and traverse partial trees in a parallel manner (See **Figure 9.8**). Since the traversals of partial trees are independent of one another, a traversal does not have to synchronize with others, and the computation time can be reduced according to the number of CPUs.

By the method described in 3, the area of range data which each process owns is only inside the voxel and its peripheral area. Thus, each process owns only the range data of the local area which it takes charge of in a traversal of a partial octree.

However, each machine must cache range data files in memory to read them efficiently and repeatedly. Since a PC cluster cannot share data as a shared-memory machine can, range data files have to be allocated redundantly; therefore, memory efficiency dwindles as this parallel traversal method is used.

Figure 9.9. Merging result of Kamakura Great Buddha

Table 9.1. Results of different parameters of the number of traversals and machines of each traversal.

	Number of traversals	Number of machines in each traversal	Average required memory of each machine	Computation Time
A	1	1	200MB	468 min.
B	4	1	200MB	117 min.
C	1	4	50MB	215 min.
D	8	1	200MB	58 min.
E	1	8	20MB	256 min.
F	8	2	200MB	44 min.
G	16	1	250MB	23 min.

4.3 Combination of Parallel Methods

The above two methods are complementary in terms of the efficiency of CPUs and memory usage. In practice, they should be adjusted according to the system specification by combining those two methods with an appropriate condition. Two methods can be combined by allocating range data distributed in each parallel traversal.

The maximum number of traversals is determined by the system memory size. Thus, the combination strategy maximizes the number of traversals to deal with the memory. If the system has more CPUs than the parallel traversals, each traversal uses multiple CPUs by the method of distributed allocation.

5. Performance Evaluation

We have implemented these algorithms, and constructed one integrated digital Great Buddha of Kamakura. For this project, we have built a PC cluster that consists of eight PCs of dual PentiumIII 800MHz processors with 1GB memory for each PC. The machines are connected by 100BASE-TX Ethernet. **Figure 9.9** shows the obtained geometric model of the Great Buddha; the model contains 3 million points and 5.5 million triangles.

We tested the merging program by changing parameters of the number of traversals and machines of each traversal. Raw data consists of 12 files; of those files, the average contains about 300 thousand points and 600 thousand triangles. The total size is about 150M bytes. The result is shown in **Table 9.1**.

Without reducing the data allocated in the memory, the maximum number of the traversals is four because of the system memory size. It takes 59 hours to build the model where it is computed by 4 traversals that are allocated and distributed to 4 PCs. It has been proven that the method of reducing the data allocated in the memory increases the computation and memory efficiency. After reducing data, we can compute the signed distances by a single machine; the computation time is 468 minutes.

The algorithm without parallel processing is equal to computing by one traversal using a machine (row A). If the system computes signed distances with the distributed allocation of memory (row C,E,F), the required memory for each machine is less than row A. The reciprocal of required memory of each machine is proportional to the number of machines in each traversal (See **Figure 9.11**). Next, if the system computes with parallel traversals (row B,D,F,G), the computation time is less than row A. The reciprocal of computation time is almost proportional to the number of parallel traversals(See **Figure 9.10**).

When the memory allocation is distributed to a small number of machines, it computes faster as the number increases. In this case, row C computes faster than row A, also row F faster than row D. However, when the memory allocation is distributed to a large number of machines, the computation becomes slower because of waiting synchronization. In this case, row E is slower than row C.

According to the combination strategy, the signed distances are computed by 16 parallel traversals that are allocated to each PC to minimize the computation time for our PC cluster. Now we consider the combination of systems of different memory size for computing signed distances of the Kamakura Buddha model: First, if the memory of each PC is less than 200MB, the number of distributed allocation must be larger than 2 machines, like row C and E. When each traversals is distributed to 4 machines, the number of traversals is determined to be 4 to minimize the computation time. Next, if the memory of each PC is 200-256MB, each traversal should be distributed to 2 machines. Then, the number of traversals is determined to be 2.

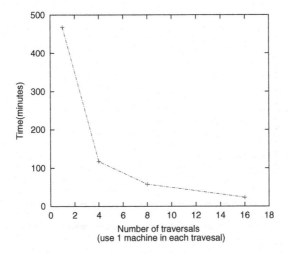

Figure 9.10. The reciprocal of computation time is proportional to the number of parallel traversals.

6. Conclusion

In this chapter, we have proposed a method which increases the computation and memory efficiency of computing signed distances, along with a method for parallel computing using a PC cluster. First, since we reduce the data allocated in the memory, the closest point is searched efficiently. Thus, we can increase the number of the parallel traversals and reduce the computation time.

In addition, we have described two algorithms which are complementary in terms of the efficiency of CPUs and memory usage. By adjusting them according to the system specifications, we can build the model efficiently by using a PC cluster.

Now we can build models of huge size. In the future, we plan to scan more Japanese cultural heritage objects and build fine models with photometric attributes.

Acknowledgments

This research was supported, in part, by Ministry of Education, Culture, Sports, Science and Technology under the Leading Project, "Development of High Fidelity Digitization Software for Large-Scale and Intangible Cultural Assets," and, in part, by Japan Science and Technology Agency, under the CREST program, "Automatic generation of virtual models of cultural heritage."

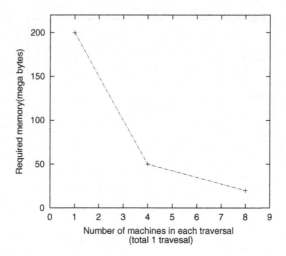

Figure 9.11. The reciprocal of required memory of each machine is proportional to the number of machines in each traversals.

References

[1] D. Bartz and W. Straer. Parallel construction and isosurface extraction of recursive tree structures. In *Proceedings of WSCG'98*, Vol. III, Plzen, 1998.

[2] Brian Curless and Marc Levoy. A volumetric method for building complex models from range images. In *Proc. SIGGRAPH'96*, pp. 303–312. ACM, 1996.

[3] Jerome H. Friedman, Jon Bentley, and Raphael Finkel. An algorithm for finding best matches in logarithmic expected time. *ACM Transactions on Mathematical Software*, Vol. 3, No. 3, pp. 209–226, 1977.

[4] A. Hilton, A.J. Stoddart, J. Illingworth, and T. Windeatt. Reliable surface reconstruction from multiple range images. In *Proceedings of European Conference on Computer Vision*, pp. 117–126, Springer-Verlag, 1996.

[5] H. Hoppe, T. DeRose, T. Duchamp, J.A. McDonald, and W. Stuetzle. Surface reconstruction from unorganized points. In *Proc. SIGGRAPH'92*, pp. 71–78. ACM, 1992.

[6] W. Lorensen and H. Cline. Marching cubes: a high resolution 3d surface construction algorithm. In *Proc. SIGGRAPH'87*, pp. 163–170. ACM, 1987.

[7] P. Mackerras. A fast parallel marching-cubes implementation on the fujitsu ap1000. Technical report, Australian National University, TR-CS-92-10, 1992.

[8] D. J. R. Meagher. *The octree encoding method for efficient solid modeling*. PhD thesis, Rensselaer Polytechnic Institute, 1980.

[9] Daisuke Miyazaki, Takeshi Ooishi, Taku Nishikawa, Ryusuke Sagawa, Ko Nishino, Takashi Tomomatsu, Yutaka Takase, and Katsushi Ikeuchi. The great buddha project: Modelling cultural heritage through observation. In *Proceedings of 6th International Conference on Virtual Systems and MultiMedia*, pp. 138–145, Gifu, 2000.

[10] M. Rutishauser, M. Stricker, and M. Trobina. Merging range images of arbitararily shaped objects. In *Proceedings of 1994 IEEE Computer Society Conference on Computer Vision and Pattern Recognition*, pp. 573–580, June 1994.

[11] M. Soucy and D. Laurendeau. A general surface approach to the integration of a set of range views. *IEEE Transactions on Pattern Analysis and Machine Intelligence*, Vol. 17, No. 4, pp. 344–358, April 1995.

[12] Greg Turk and Marc Levoy. Zippered polygon meshes from range images. In *Proceedings of SIGGRAPH'94*, pp. 311–318. ACM, 1994.

[13] M.D. Wheeler, Y. Sato, and K. Ikeuchi. Consensus surfaces for modeling 3d objects from multiple range images. In *Proc. International Conference on Computer Vision*, January 1998.

Chapter 10

ADAPTIVELY MERGING LARGE-SCALE RANGE DATA WITH REFLECTANCE PROPERTIES

Ryusuke Sagawa, Ko Nishino, and Katsushi Ikeuchi

Abstract   In this chapter, we tackle the problem of geometric and photometric modeling of large intricately-shaped objects. Typical target objects we consider are cultural heritage objects. When constructing models of such objects, we are faced with several important issues that have not been addressed in the past – issues that mainly arise due to the large amount of data that has to be handled. We propose two novel approaches to efficiently handle such large amounts of data: a highly adaptive algorithm for merging range images and an adaptive nearest neighbor search to be used with the algorithm. We construct an integrated mesh model of the target object in adaptive resolution, taking into account the geometric and/or photometric attributes associated with the range images. We use surface curvature for the geometric attributes and (laser) reflectance values for the photometric attributes. This adaptive merging framework leads to a significant reduction in the necessary amount of computational resources. Furthermore, the resulting adaptive mesh models can be of great use for applications such as texture mapping, as we will briefly demonstrate. Additionally, we propose an additional test for the k-d tree nearest neighbor search algorithm. Our approach successfully omits back-tracking, which is controlled adaptively depending on the distance to the nearest neighbor. Since the main consumption of computational cost lies in the nearest neighbor search, the proposed algorithm leads to a significant speed-up of the whole merging process. In this chapter, we present the theories and algorithms of our approaches with pseudo code and apply them to several real objects, including large-scale cultural assets.

1.   Introduction

Modeling the shape and appearance of objects in the real world are important issues in computer vision. Cultural heritage objects are one of the worthiest candidates for modeling of their shape and appearance. There are several advantages to modeling these objects, for example, presentation, preservation, and restoration. Many cultural assets are large in scale and, at the same time, their shapes consist of delicate and intricately-curved surfaces. In this study, our target objects were mainly intricately-shaped objects, such as statues of the Great Buddha and ancient temple buildings. High resolution and high precision are required for modeling these objects, just as when modeling small objects.

To acquire the 3D coordinates of the surface points of objects, we use range sensing systems. As most range sensing systems, e.g., stereo, structured light, and laser range finders return range images obtained from particular viewing points, each output range image covers only a small portion of the target object surface. To ensure that the entire surface of the target is captured, multiple range images of the same object have to be acquired while changing the viewpoint. Thus, the main issue of modeling real objects is creating the entire model of an object from multiple range images. The "integration" of multiple observations into a unified model is the main issue tackled in this chapter.

1.1   Previous Work

1.1.1   Geometric Modeling

So far, due to the recent development of range finders, several researchers [1–5] have studied the modeling of cultural heritage objects using such powerful sensors. Fig. 10.1 shows the modeling steps using a range finder. The 3D modeling of the shape of the object is accomplished by performing the following three steps:

1 Acquiring the range images (scanning).

2 Aligning of those acquired range images from different viewpoints (aligning).

3 Reconstructing the unified 3D mesh model (merging).

In the first step, a target object is observed from various viewpoints. If it is a small object, it is mounted on a turntable or a robot arm.

In the second step, multiple range images are aligned into a common coordinate system. If an object is mounted on a turntable or a robot arm, the aligning step is accomplished by recording each local coordinate system a priori. Otherwise, range images are aligned by using registration algorithms which establish point correspondences and minimize the total distance between those points, e.g., feature-based methods [6, 7], ICP-based methods [8, 9], etc. Besl and McKay [8] proposed a point-based matching method, while Chen's method [10] is based on the distance evaluation between the point and the polygons. Wheeler and Ikeuchi [11] introduced M-estimator to the ICP scheme for discarding outliers as wrong correspondences. Neugebauer [12] proposed the idea of 'simultaneous registration' that aligns range images simultaneously to avoid the error accumulation of the pairwise alignment methods. Several other

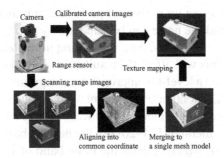

Figure 10.1. Steps of geometric and photometric modeling of a small object.

variants of simultaneous alignment have been developed [13–16]. Huber and Hebert [17] proposed a method of automatic aligning range images without any knowledge about initial positions of range images, while other methods require a rough estimation of their positions.

For merging multiple pre-aligned range images, the third step of the pipeline in Fig. 10.1, several approaches have been proposed. Turk and Levoy [18] proposed a method to "zipper" two range images at a time, by first removing overlapping portions of the meshes, clipping one mesh against another, and then re-triangulating the mesh on the boundary. Although integrating two range images is an intuitive process, pairwise merging does not remove errors well when merging multiple range images and is very sensitive to noise in the range images. Soucy and Laurendeau [19] also proposed a merging algorithm based on mesh representation, which is also sensitive to noise of mesh boundary. Given a number of range images overlapping each other, a merging procedure which extracts the isosurface is suitable, e.g., a merging method that makes use of volumetric, implicit-surface representation and then extracts the mesh surface by using the marching-cubes algorithm [20] (We will abbreviate that algorithm as MC throughout the rest of this chapter). Hoppe et al. [21] constructed 3D surface models by applying MC to a discrete, implicit-surface function generated from a set of range images. After inferring local surface approximations from clouds of points based on tangent plane estimations, a local search was accomplished to compute the signed distance from each voxel to the surface of the point set. Curless and Levoy [22] enhanced Hoppe's algorithm in a few significant ways by developing a method to compute signed distances from multiple range images. Their method efficiently traverses the volume by resampling range images along scanlines of voxels; since it finds corresponding points on the screen space by projecting both voxels and a range image, and, in effect, updates only a narrow band of voxels on either side of the zero level, it does not go through all voxels. However, none of these methods, including [23], compensate for outliers of point data; it is assumed that the data is part of the object and the noise can be removed by averaging. Each of these methods suffers from inaccuracy, e.g., integrating unrelated observations, and these accuracy problems will affect the result even when the data is noise-free. Whitaker [24] proposed a level-set approach for integrating range images; this approach introduced a smoothness constraint using a Bayesian formulation for averaging observations. This method removes outliers of range images by smoothing. Level-set methods [24–26] use the narrow-band method to reduce the computational cost, which updates the finite band of voxels on either side of zero level. Wheeler et al. [27, 28] addressed these important problems by designing a consensus surface algorithm. The consensus surface algorithm attempts to justify the selection of observations used to produce the average by finding a quorum or consensus of locally coherent observations. This process successfully eliminates many troublesome effects of noise and extraneous surface observations, and also provides desirable results with noise-free data. We developed a new method based on this method to merge large amounts of data. The methods proposed in [27, 29] use an octree as the data structure to reduce the computational cost of converting range images to a volumetric representation.

In our merging algorithm, we search the nearest neighbor points of range images. The nearest neighbor problem in multidimensional space itself is a major issue in many applications. Many methods have been developed to search for the nearest neighbor of a query. A simple exhaustive search computes the distance from a query to every point. Its computational cost is $O(n)$. This approach is clearly inefficient. Hashing and indexing [30, 31] finish a search in constant time; however, they require a large space in which to store the index table. For accessing multidimensional data, some hierarchical structures have been proposed, e.g., k-d tree [32], quadtree [33], R-tree [34], and octree spline [35]. These trees differ in structure, but their search algorithms are similar. The k-d tree [32] is one of the most widely used structures for searching nearest neighbors. It is a variant of binary tree that partitions space using hyperplanes that are perpendicular to the coordinate axes. If a k-d tree consists of n records, the k-d tree requires $O(n \log_2 n)$ operations to construct and $O(\log_2 n)$ to search. Zhang [36] proposed a method which prunes traversing branches of a k-d tree when their records are farther than a threshold. This method does not find any candidate if the nearest neighbor is farther than the threshold. Greenspan and Yurick [37] proposed an Ak-d tree for searching the nearest neighbor points approximately to speed up aligning range images by omitting back-tracking. It does not guarantee to find the correct nearest neighbor. This method is similar to our idea [38]. However, the nearest neighbor may not be accurate if it is farther than the bin size. In this chapter, we introduce a new thresholding method to the k-d tree search. This method efficiently reduces the search cost of merging large data sets of range images. The difference between ours and Zhang's method is that our method always finds a candidate of the nearest neighbor, since we need a rough estimation even if it is far from a query for hole filling [39].

1.1.2   Photometric Modeling

Modeling appearance is known as photometric modeling and typically involves registration of color images with a geometric model so that the images can be texture mapped onto the geometric model (Fig. 10.1). Several methods of aligning color images with range images [27, 40–42] have been proposed. Neugebauer and Klein [42] proposed simultaneous registration of multiple texture images. Wheeler [27] uses occluding edges extracted from the 3D model for aligning with a 2D color image. If a range image is obtained by a laser range finder, laser reflectance strength (LRS) image can be obtained. Reflectance edges are more robust than occluding edges for the change of viewpoint. Kurazume et al. [40] thus extended a technique for aligning a 2D color image and a range image of an object by comparing the edges of the color image and the edges of LRS values attached to the range image. To align a color image with a merged mesh model by this method, we propose a new method to merge range images with LRS values.

1.2   Overview of This chapter

In order to model large-scale and intricately-shaped objects, we propose the following techniques in this chapter:

1 Adaptive merging of range images according to geometric characteristics

2 Adaptive merging of photometric attributes of range images

3 Adaptive searching of the nearest neighbor points in a huge amount of range images

We first describe our merging algorithm, which is based on Wheeler's method [28] in Section 2. Then, we propose two approaches to handle a huge amount of range images in merging range images. Section 3 describes a new method to merge range images in adaptive resolution. Then, we propose a new method to merge LRS values of range images in our merging framework in Section 4. Section 5 explains an adaptive neighbor search in finding the closest point of a range image.

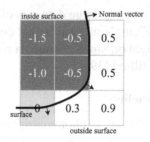

Figure 10.2.   An example of implicit surface function computed from an explicit surface.

2.   Consensus Surface Algorithm

2.1   Signed Distance Field

Using all range images, this method first constructs a volumetric representation, which is called a signed distance field (SDF). Those range images are assumed to be already aligned into a common coordinate frame. In this volumetric representation, 3D space is partitioned into three dimensional voxels. A voxel has a signed distance $f(\mathbf{x})$ from its center $\mathbf{x}$ to the nearest surface. The sign of $f(\mathbf{x})$ is positive if the center $\mathbf{x}$ is outside the object; it is negative if the center $\mathbf{x}$ is inside the object. Because the surface of the object is represented implicitly by $f(\mathbf{x}) = 0$, $f(\mathbf{x})$ is called the implicit surface function. Fig. 10.2 shows a 2D slice view of an example of SDF, which is composed of 9 voxels. If the surface is converted to SDF, the $f(\mathbf{x})$ of each voxel is computed as shown. The voxels inside the object are dark gray, and the ones outside the object are white.

2.2   Marching-Cubes Algorithm

Though a volumetric representation such as SDF can be visualized by volume rendering [43], a mesh model is suitable for our goal, which is geometric modeling and the analysis of objects. Lorensen and Cline [20] proposed the marching-cubes algorithm, which converts the volumetric representation to a mesh model. MC constructs a surface mesh by "marching" around the cubes which contain the zero level of the implicit surface $f(\mathbf{x}) = 0$. MC generates surface triangles to intersect voxels which have positive signed distances and voxels which have negative signed distances. Since the original algorithm has ambiguity in the algorithm of generating triangles, Nielson and Hamann [44] proposed a method to resolve ambiguous cases.

2.3   Taking a Consensus of Range Images

To compute signed distances from multiple range images, our approach is based on the consensus surface algorithm proposed by Wheeler et al. [28]. It computes the implicit surface function $f(\mathbf{x})$ of each voxel using multiple range images.   Fig. 10.3 shows an example in which there are three range images which are intersecting between two neighboring voxels. The centers of the two voxels are $\mathbf{x}$ and $\mathbf{x}'$. After this, the definition of a range image is a mesh model which consists of 3D vertices and triangles that connect the neighboring vertices. If there is a large discontinuity between vertices, we do not connect them in the same manner with [18, 23]. The normal vectors of the range images in Fig. 10.3 are facing outwards of the object. The normal vector of each vertex is computed by averaging the normal vectors of triangles which share the vertex.

To compute the signed distance value $f(\mathbf{x})$, the algorithm finds the nearest point to the center of the voxel in each range image. Since the nearest point is not always on a vertex of the triangles, the algorithm finds the nearest vertex of a range image, and computes the nearest point in the triangles which include the nearest vertex. We assume that true nearest point is in the neighborhood of the vertex. Although it is a heuristic that can fail, it works well in practice. In this example, there are three nearest points A, B and C.

If the positions of the nearest points are close and their normal vectors are similar directions, we regard those points as having consensus. The consensus surface algorithm computes a reliable point by taking an average of the points which have consensus. If there are some reliable points, the algorithm chooses the reliable nearest points from them. In this case, because C is isolated, the method discards C and takes an average of A and B, and computes the magnitude of $f(\mathbf{x})$ by the distance between $\mathbf{x}$ and the averaged point. Since the inner product $(\mathbf{x} - \mathbf{p}) \cdot \mathbf{n} > 0$, where the averaged nearest point is $\mathbf{p}$ and its normal vector is $\mathbf{n}$, $\mathbf{x}$ is outside and the sign is determined as $f(\mathbf{x}) > 0$. Similarly, $\mathbf{x}'$ is inside and $f(\mathbf{x}') < 0$. Because the algorithm discards outliers, it is not simply averaging the distance together as [22].

Though the original algorithm [28] uses a weighting scheme for computing consensus, we simply count the number of overlapping range images. If the number is more than a consensus threshold, the overlapping range images are valid and we take average of them. Otherwise, they are discarded from averaging. The consensus threshold depends on the accuracy of the range finder. In our experiment, the value is 2; thus, we can discard outliers if three range images are acquired at a point and one of them is an outlier as Fig. 10.3. On this assumption, we do not have to handle the boundary of range images in a special manner.

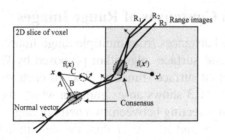

Figure 10.3. Consensus surface algorithm: The signed distance is chosen from the consensus surfaces inside the gray circle.

2.4   Subdividing Voxels Based on Octree

To determine where the implicit surface is, we have to compute the signed distances of all voxels around the zero level of the implicit function. It is costly to compute the signed distances of all voxels, since the computational cost is $O(n^3)$ if the volume of interest is uniformly divided into $n \times n \times n$ voxels along each axis.

Wheeler [28] proposed the strategy of computing signed distances by subdividing the volume of interest recursively in an octree manner. It starts with the entire volume being a single voxel for computing the signed distance; it subdivides the voxel if the signed distance satisfies the following inequality,

$$|f(\mathbf{x})| < \frac{3\sqrt{3}}{2}w, \qquad (10.1)$$

where w is the width of the voxel of interest. If Eq. (10.1) is satisfied, the implicit surface can exist inside the voxel or the neighbor voxels. It stops subdividing if the voxel becomes the user-defined finest resolution. Since the width of voxels that contain the implicit surface is the same, MC [20] is applied to the voxels of the same size which are subdivided in an octree manner. Subdividing voxels in an octree manner practically reduces the computational cost to $O(n^2)$, because the finest resolution voxels exist only near the surface.

3.   Adaptive Merging Algorithm

Wheeler's algorithm produces a mesh model of the finest resolution everywhere; however, the dense sampling is not necessary where the shape of the object is nearly planar. Thus, we propose an algorithm to construct the 3D model in an efficient representation. By taking the surface curvature into account when splitting the voxels recursively in an octree manner, the resulting 3D surface will be subdivided more in high curvature areas and less in surface areas that are nearly planar. Therefore, the resulting geometric model will require fewer triangular patches to represent the object surface.

This is similar to research on mesh model simplification algorithms based on surfaces [45–47]. On the other hand, we reconstruct a simplified 3D model through a range image merging process based on implicit surface representation. Our approach is more reasonable than generating a dense mesh model of constant resolution and simplifying it. The adaptive mesh model created by our method can be used for the input of simplification algorithms for further mesh optimization. The simplification is done when splitting voxels recursively, enabling better preservation of the topology and mass of the object compared with the results of other volume-based simplification methods [48, 49]. Frisken et al. [50] proposed adaptive sampling of the signed distance field. They generate surface meshes based on the surface nets approach [51]. For converting the volumetric representation of the 3D model to a triangle-based mesh model, we propose an extended version of the marching-cube algorithm; this version handles voxels at different resolutions. However, the aim of their paper is not merging range images. Thus, we propose a method for adaptively merging range images.

3.1   Subdividing Voxels Based on the Geometric Attributes of Range Images

We determine the sampling interval of the signed distance, depending on the variation of geometric attributes to efficiently represent the final mesh model. Depending on the change in surface curvature, the proposed method coarsely samples in planar areas, consequently reducing the amount of data and computation, while creating a finer model of an intricately-shaped object by efficiently utilizing computation power.

Our method determines the variation of surface curvature by comparing surface normals of range images. We compare the normal $\mathbf{n}_i$ of each 3D point of all range images inside the voxel in interest and the normal $\bar{\mathbf{n}}$ of the approximated plane (see Fig. 10.4), which can be estimated by applying principal component analysis (PCA) to all point data in the voxel. If the angle between the data point normals $\mathbf{n}_i$ and approximate normal $\bar{\mathbf{n}}$ satisfies

$$\max_i(\arccos(\mathbf{n}_i \cdot \bar{\mathbf{n}})) < \delta_n, \qquad (10.2)$$

where δ_n is the threshold of the angle, the sampling interval is fine enough, and no further voxel splitting is required.

To avoid erroneous subdivisions of voxels by the influence of noise included in each range image, our method takes a consensus between range images on the decision of voxel subdivision. Now, N_n is the number of range images which satisfies Eq. (10.2), and N_{all} is that of consensus range images. Our

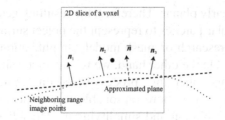

Figure 10.4. Comparison of the normal vector of each vertex and the approximate normal $\bar{n}$ by PCA

method does not subdivide the voxel if

$$\frac{N_n}{N_{all}} > T_n, \tag{10.3}$$

where T_n is the threshold of consensus for normal vectors.

If a range image is not smooth, the computation of normal vectors becomes unstable, especially in the case that it contains zigzag noise, which has high spatial frequency. It often occurs with a laser range finder when range images are acquired under inappropriate conditions. In such a case, the algorithm of computing consensus does not work well, and neither does the subdivision based on geometric attributes, because their criteria are based on normal vectors. Thus, we proposed another method for taking consensus of range images [52], which does not depend on normal vectors. If range images contain zigzag noise, we refine those range images by [52] before merging them. Since the refined range images have reliable normal vectors, we can avoid erroneous subdivisions of voxels by the influence of noise included in each range image. We therefore assume that the normal vector is reliable for subdividing voxels.

The algorithm of traversing an octree with adaptive voxel subdivision is represented as Algorithm 1. In this algorithm, **ConsensusSurface**(x, R_{set}) computes the nearest point **p** and its normal vector **n** from the point **x**. The changes from the original algorithm are indicated by gray boxes. To determine whether to subdivide the current voxel N, we consider the curvature of range images inside the voxel by **LocalCurvature**(N, R_{set}). **LocalCurvature** returns the percentage of range images which satisfies Eq. (10.2). Moreover, since we subdivide the voxels adaptively, the voxels attain sufficient resolution even if the threshold value of the magnitude of a signed distance is reduced to $\frac{\sqrt{3}}{2}w$. If voxels are at a fixed resolution, a voxel should be subdivided if one of the neighboring voxels contains vertices of range images. However, in the case of adaptive resolution, it is enough to subdivide voxels which contains vertices in order to attain the sufficient resolution of a merged mesh model.

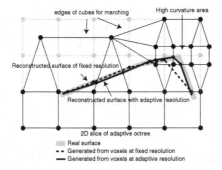

Figure 10.5. Edges connecting adjacent voxels in an adaptive octree and the generated mesh model by MC

Algorithm 1 AdaptiveTraverseOctree($N, d_{\max}, R_{\text{set}}$)

Input: Current Node of Octree: N
Input: Maximum Depth of Octree: $d_{\max}$
Input: Set of Range Images: R_{set}
Local: Center of N: $\mathbf{x}$
Local: Octree Depth of N: d
Local: Width of N: w
Local: Tuple of Point, Normal: $\langle \mathbf{p}, \mathbf{n} \rangle$
Output: Signed Distance of N: v
$\langle \mathbf{p}, \mathbf{n} \rangle \leftarrow \mathbf{ConsensusSurface}(\mathbf{x}, R_{\text{set}})$
if $(\mathbf{x} - \mathbf{p}) \cdot \mathbf{n} > 0$ **then**
    $v \leftarrow \| \mathbf{x} - \mathbf{p} \|$
else
    $v \leftarrow - \| \mathbf{x} - \mathbf{p} \|$
end if
if $|v| < \frac{\sqrt{3}}{2} w \wedge d < d_{\max}$
    $\wedge$ **LocalCurvature**$(N, R_{\text{set}}) > T_n$ **then**
    for all children $N_i (i = 0, \ldots, 7)$ of N **do**
        AdaptiveTraverseOctree$(N_i, d_{\max}, R_{\text{set}})$
    end for
end if

3.2   Marching Cubes for Adaptive Octree

The original marching-cubes algorithm can be applied only to voxels that have the same resolution (size of voxels). We extend the algorithm to triangulate voxels at different resolutions as generated in our method.

For voxels that are surrounded by voxels with the same resolution, the vertices of a cube to march are the centers of 8 adjacent voxels. In a similar manner, voxels surrounded by different size voxels will have a set of adjacent

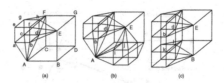

Figure 10.6.   Partially subdivided cubes

voxels, which are no longer cube-shaped as shown in Fig. 10.5. When we use voxels of fixed resolution (grids of gray lines), a mesh model of the dotted line is generated, and its vertices are on the edges of cubes. When we use adaptively subdivided voxels up to a resolution one level higher (grids of black lines), the mesh model of a solid line is generated, and its vertices are on the edges of transformed cubes. If we subdivide the high curvature area into small voxels, the generated mesh model gets closer to the real surface (gray thick lines) without increasing unnecessary vertices in planar areas. Since a transformed cube becomes a skewed rectangle or a triangle in a 2D slice of the volume, as shown in Fig. 10.5, the vertices of the mesh model generated by MC are on those edges.

Fig. 10.6 shows three partially subdivided cubes, whose vertices are the centers of voxels. One of 8 voxels which compose a cube is subdivided in Fig. 10.6(a). Similarly, two voxels are subdivided in Fig. 10.6(b) and (c). After subdivision, a cube is partitioned into several forms: for example, in (a), the number of forms is seven and their vertices are {ABCDdEFG}, {Aabcd}, {ABbdE}, {Ebdfh}, {dEhFG}, {Fcdgh}, and {abcdefgh}. The form composed by {abcdefgh} is a cube, and {Aabcd} is a quadratic pyramid, while {ABbdE} is not a polyhedron. Since MC interpolates points of zero level on the edges, the form to which MC is applied is not necessarily a cube, nor even a polyhedron.

Fig. 10.7 shows examples of a transformed cube. Fig. 10.7(b) is a pyramid, such as {Aabcd} in Fig. 10.6(a). We can regard that Fig. 10.7(b) is equal to Fig. 10.7(a) whose upper four vertices have the same signed distance with the top vertex of (b), and they gather to the position of top vertex of (b). Thus, we can generate the isosurface of (b) by applying MC to the transformed cube from (a). By regarding the irregular forms as degenerated and transformed cubes, MC can be applied to them without creating new tables of mesh generation for the irregular forms.

Fig. 10.7(c) is {AijbdE} in Fig. 10.6(b) and Fig. 10.7(d) is {BklbdE} in Fig. 10.6(c). In the case of Fig. 10.7(b) and (c), two triangles are generated. However, the number of triangles is reduced in the case of Fig. 10.7(d), because the number of edges of the transformed cube is reduced. We therefore removed the redundant vertices of the mesh model after generation by MC.

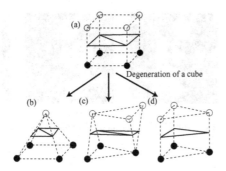

Figure 10.7.   Examples of degenerated cubes and the surfaces generated by MC

4.   Adaptive Merging with Reflectance Properties

With regard to applications that utilize geometric models, for instance, 3D object recognition and localization tasks, it is desirable to construct 3D models with additional attributes such as color and intensity. With the additional information provided by photometric attributes, higher accuracy and robustness can be expected from those applications. Thus, it is necessary to efficiently create a model with photometric attributes. In this section, we consider an adaptive merging method which subdivides voxels based on photometric attributes.

When we acquire a range image using a laser range finder, we can obtain a LRS value of the surface for each vertex of the range image. Thus, our proposed method takes a consensus of the reflectance parameters of the target object from multiple range images. It reconstructs the 3D model with reflectance parameters attached per vertex, discarding outliers due to noise and specular reflection produced in the image-capturing process.

4.1   Laser Reflectance Strength Attached to Range Images

Laser range finders measure distance by shooting a laser and receiving its reflection from the target object. The distance to a particular point on the target object is computed by measuring the time duration between the time laser was shot and the time it was received back in time-of-flight range finders by measuring the phase difference in phase-transition based range finders, or by optical triangulation of the illuminant, surface, and optical sensors. In either case, an LRS value, which is the ratio of the discharged laser strength and the reflected laser strength, can be obtained per each 3D point. If we assume the dichromatic reflection model, as the laser can be considered to be light with a very narrow wavelength distribution, almost a single value, the behavior of the reflected laser on the target surface can be considered to be the same as the general light reflection. Namely, almost isotropic reflection analogous to diffuse

Figure 10.8. Range images of the Great Buddha of Kamakura using LRS values as pixel values.

reflection and sharp reflection distributed around the perfect mirror direction analogous to specular reflection occurs. Since the specular reflection is observed only if the laser is almost parallel to the normal direction of the object surface, the observed laser is usually caused by the diffusive reflection. Thus, it is exceptional to observe the specular reflection, which can be regarded as an outlier. Fig. 10.8 depicts four images using the LRS values attached to each 3D point as pixel values, rendered from the view point of the laser range finder Cyrax2400 [53].

LRS values are considered to depend on the characteristics of the surface, the incident angle of laser light, and the distance from the sensor. The LRS value which we obtain by a laser range finder is the ratio of the discharged laser strength and the reflected laser strength. If we assume that the LRS value depends only on the diffuse reflection, the relationship of the LRS value and the other parameters are represented by the following equation:

$$I_1 = I_0 e^{-\alpha x} \tag{10.4}$$

$$I_2 = r I_1 e^{-\alpha x} \cos \theta, \tag{10.5}$$

where I_0 is the discharged laser strength, I_1 is the incident laser strength on the surface, and I_2 is the reflected laser strength. As for the other parameters, x is the distance from the laser range finder; α is the absorption coefficient of the laser in the air; r is the reflectance parameter of the surface; and θ is the incident angle of the laser (see Fig. 10.9). Since I_0 is a given value and I_2 is measured by the sensor, while I_1 is unknown, Eq. (10.4) and Eq. (10.5) become

$$\frac{I_2}{I_0} = r e^{-2\alpha x} \cos \theta. \tag{10.6}$$

Since the reflectance parameter r is a characteristic value to the surface, we want to obtain r by using several observations from various viewpoints.

Since we can obtain I_2/I_0, x and θ for each vertex of range images, the unknown variables are r and α. The logarithm of Eq. (10.6) becomes

$$\log \frac{I_2}{I_0} = \log r - 2\alpha x + \log \cos \theta. \tag{10.7}$$

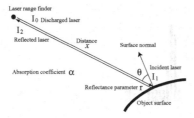

Figure 10.9.   Reflection model of a laser light

Thus, the system becomes a linear equation with two unknowns. Since we find corresponding points of the range images in taking a consensus of range images, as shown in Fig. 10.3, we can solve the system if more than two corresponding points are found. If we have more than three equations, we can solve the system by the least square method.

Another method to estimate the reflectance parameter r is calibrating the absorption coefficient α before scanning a target. Since the absorption coefficient α depends on the atmosphere around the environment of the target, α can be assumed to be constant for all points in the range images which are acquired at roughly the same time. If we measure the same point from a fixed direction with varying distances, we can estimate α by fitting α to the following equation:

$$y = -2\alpha x + c, \tag{10.8}$$

where $y = \log I_2/I_0$ and $c = \log r + \log \cos \theta$. Once α is determined, the reflectance parameter r can be computed by Eq. (10.6); however, the reflectance parameters of the corresponding points, which are found in the merging process, vary because of the specular reflection. Thus, in the merging process, we take a consensus of r of the corresponding points of the range images.

The reflectance variation of the corresponding points should have a DC component because of the invariant diffuse reflection with a sharp peak caused by specular reflection added to it, which can be observed from a narrow viewing direction. Thus, if the point is observed from a sufficient number of viewing directions, the histogram of the reflectance parameters should have a sharp peak at the diffuse reflection value, with some distribution around it due to specular reflection. Fig. 10.10 depicts an example of the LRS values of the corresponding points for a voxel. Based on this consideration, we take the median value of the corresponding points as a consensus value of the reflectance parameter.

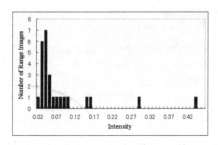

Figure 10.10.   An example of the histogram of the reflectance parameter of corresponding points. Some outliers due to specular reflection are observed. In this case, the median value is 0.04.

4.2   Subdividing Voxels Based on the Reflectance of Range Images

We have introduced a new criterion of voxel subdivision based on the geometric attributes of the surface for the adaptive merging method in Section 3.1. As the second criterion of voxel subdivision, we propose the voxel subdivision based on the variation of the reflectance parameters. Photometric attributes are used for the criterion of mesh simplification in [45, 47]. We estimate reflectance parameters in addition to geometric attributes. For further applications, such as texture mapping, we subdivide voxels, which are not subdivided by geometric attributes, from the viewpoint of reflectance parameters. It can be accomplished in a similar manner as with geometric attributes.

If we subdivide voxels around the drastic variation of reflectance parameters, each triangular patch contains almost the same reflectance parameters. Since the LRS image and color/intensity image of an object are highly correlated, those 3D models tessellated with regard to the reflectance variation of the models are useful to accomplish further texture analysis and synthesis. For instance, the registration of a 2D image and a 3D model of an object can be considered. Kurazume et al. [40] used the edges of LRS values attached to a range image.   If we apply this method to our merged 3D model, the subdivision based on the reflectance parameters is desirable to extract fine edges of reflectance parameters, and we can directly extract 3D reflectance edges from range images.   Moreover, when a texture image is mapped on the adaptive model subdivided based on the reflectance parameters, view-dependent texture mapping like [54] can achieve higher compression, since global texture compression stacking triangular patches with a similar texture can be applied.

In a similar manner to subdividing by the curvature of the surface, our method computes the variation of reflectance parameters of 3D points inside the voxel of interest. Now, r_i, r_j are the reflectance parameters of neighbor points included in a range image. If the maximum difference satisfies

$$\max_{i,j}(\text{Distance}(r_i, r_j)) < \delta_r, \tag{10.9}$$

where δ_r is the threshold and $\text{Distance}(r_i, r_j)$ is the function which computes the difference of two reflectance parameters, the sampling interval is fine enough for the range image.

Our method also takes a consensus while considering the reflectance parameters. Similar to Eq. (10.3), our method does not subdivide the voxel if

$$\frac{N_r}{N_{all}} > T_r, \tag{10.10}$$

where N_r is the number of range images which satisfy Eq. (10.9), and T_r is the threshold of consensus for the reflectance parameters.

5. Adaptive Nearest Neighbor Search

In the previous section, we described algorithms for constructing 3D models that efficiently represent the object by adaptively merging a large amount of range images. When the number of range images and the number of points in those range images is very large, it is also crucial to speed up the merging process. The speed of the whole process depends on how efficiently one can search the nearest neighbor points. In many cases of merging a lot of range images simultaneously, most of the vertices of the range images can be discarded from searching the nearest neighbor points, since the portion of range images which are overlapped at a position is quite small compared with the total range images.

We introduce an additional test that takes place when traversing the k-d tree. This test compares the distance from a query to the nearest neighbor with a threshold defined by the user. Since this method improves the locality of reference, we can reduce not only the computational cost for searching the nearest neighbor but also the required memory to traverse a k-d tree. At the same time with reducing the search cost, this method roughly estimates the nearest neighbor even if it is far from a query. The signed distance is used when we fill holes of a model [39]. Since the hole filling works well even if we do not find the true nearest neighbor, our adaptive nearest neighbor search is effective.

5.1 Basic Search Algorithm using k-d Tree

First, we explain the basic algorithm by which the k-d tree searches for the nearest neighbor. Fig. 10.11 shows a 2-D example of a k-d tree that consists of four leaf nodes labeled A, B, C and D. We do not describe how to construct a k-d tree in this chapter; for details, please refer to [32].

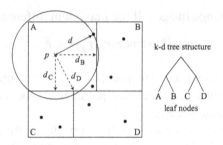

Figure 10.11. A 2-D example of a k-d tree

Now we describe how to find the nearest neighbor point from a query point **p**. In the search algorithm, we start at the root node and traverse down to the leaf node that contains the query point. In Fig. 10.11, the leaf node A contains **p**, and we compute the distances from **p** to the records of A.

To avoid examining all leaf nodes, the algorithm prunes branches by the Bounds-Overlap-Ball (BOB) test [32]. After node A is examined, the distance from **p** to the nearest neighbor is d. We examine B if d satisfies the following BOB test:

$$d > d_B, \qquad\qquad (10.11)$$

where d_B is the distance from the query point **p** to the boundary of A and B. Similarly, we compare d with d_C and d_D to decide whether or not we will examine C and D. In this case, d satisfies Eq. (10.11) for B, C and D. Thus, we have to examine all nodes. If the hypersphere of radius d is completely inside of a node after examining the node, the algorithm finishes the search. (This is called the Ball-Within-Bounds (BWB) test.)

5.2   Bounds-Overlap-Threshold Test

In this section, we introduce the Bounds-Overlap-Threshold (BOT) test to the search algorithm. BOT test prunes branches which are farther than a threshold δ in the similar manner to BOB test. In Fig. 10.12, the node B and D are pruned. Though this method is same as the thresholding technique proposed by Zhang [36], his method discards all records farther than the threshold from the result. In this situation, since the records even in node A are discarded, it finds no records. On the other hand, our method chooses the nearest one from all the records which are examined while traversing a tree. Thus, it finds at least a record even if all records are far away from the query. In Fig. 10.12, the nearest neighbor is the record in node A, to which the distance from the query is d. The pseudo code is shown in the Appendix.

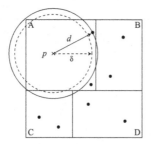

Figure 10.12.   The Bounds-Overlap-Threshold (BOT) test

When we apply the BOT test to the consensus surface algorithm, if the distance from a voxel to the range images is larger than $\frac{\sqrt{3}}{2}w$, where w is the interval of voxels, there is no surface around the voxel. Thus, it is enough for us to find that no point in the k-d tree is closer than $\frac{\sqrt{3}}{2}w$, and we set $\delta = \frac{\sqrt{3}}{2}w$. Our merging method reduces the computation of the SDF in an octree manner; therefore, the voxel width w varies according to the depth of octree subdivision to which the current voxel belongs; we adaptively change the threshold δ as well as the voxel width w.

6.   Experiments

For evaluation of our method, we have built a PC cluster that consists of eight PCs, each equipped with dual PentiumIII 800MHz processors with 1GB memory, connected by 100BASE-TX Ethernet. Since consensus surfaces can be computed independently requiring only adjacent voxels, we have proposed a parallel merging algorithm [55, 56] by splitting the whole volume into pieces and parallel searching the nearest neighbors. With this parallel implementation, we are able to handle a huge amount of range image data. In our experiments, we use the Cyrax 2400 and 2500 [53] to measure distances.

6.1   Preliminary Experiment of Estimation of Reflectance Parameter

First, we verify the reflection model of Eq. (10.7). We measure the same point several times from different distances. Since the incident angles are constant in this experiment, the reflectance parameters are considered to satisfy Eq. (10.8). Fig. 10.13 shows the logarithm of the LRS value ($\log(I_2/I_0)$) at each distance. At far distance ($> 20\text{m}$), the logarithm of the LRS values becomes almost linear. Thus, it indicates that our model is appropriate and α is estimated to be 1.7×10^{-3}.

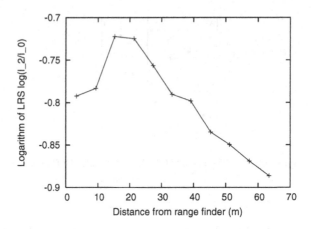

Figure 10.13.   Ratio of discharged and reflected laser

However, at near distance (< 20m), the logarithm of LRS values becomes nonlinear. One of the reasons is the focus of the laser beam. Since laser range finders use lenses to detect the light, the lasers are focused in the expected range. If the distance of the object is in the unfocused range, a part of the reflected laser does not land on the receiver. Thus, the reflected laser is clipped by the receiver and the power of light becomes less than expected. Though this result occurs in the case of Cyrax, similar effects are expected to occur with other laser range finders.

Nevertheless, our model works well in the focused range of a laser range finder; however, we have to take the focus/clipping effects into account when the object is in the unfocused range. In the following experiments, we measured objects in the focused range, and the reflectance parameters were computed by Eq. (10.7) with the estimated α. If we use range images acquired in the unfocused range, a look-up table, which is created from the result shown in Fig. 10.13, is utilized to estimate the reflectance parameters.

6.2   Adaptive Merging of Range Images

We first apply our method to a standard model from Stanford University [57]. Fig. 10.14 shows the merged results of the bunny from 10 range images. The upper row (model (a)) is the result without adaptive subdivision, and the lower (model (b)) is the result with adaptive subdivision based on the geometric attributes. When we merge range images without adaptive integration, the volume is divided to $128 \times 128 \times 128$ voxels in the finest resolution. We used $\delta_n = 37°$ and $T_n = 0.5$ for Eq. (10.2) and Eq. (10.3) for generating the model (b), which is chosen manually. The model (a) contains 34,667 ver-

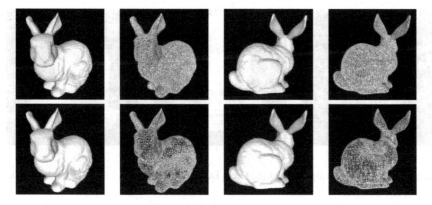

Figure 10.14.   Merged models of Stanford bunny. Upper (a): without adaptive subdivision. Lower (b): with adaptive subdivision based on geometric attributes.

tices and 69,463 triangles, while the model (b) contains 23,671 vertices and 47,338 triangles. The computational times are 10 minutes and 4.8 minutes, respectively. We computed the difference of (a) and (b) using Metro [58]. The mean/RMS/max differences are 0.096%/0.23%/2.7% of the longest edge of bounding box. Therefore, our method effectively reduced the amount of data and the computational time.

6.3   Adaptive Merging of Range-Reflectance Images

Next, we applied our algorithm to the Great Buddha of Kamakura, whose height is about 11.3m. We acquired 16 range images with LRS values attached to each 3D point; about 0.3 million vertices and 0.6 million triangles were contained in each range image. Fig. 10.8 shows four of the range images with reflectance parameters, and Fig. 10.15 shows the merging result with reflectance parameters. Fig. 10.16 shows three different results of our method. Column (A) contains the models created without adaptive integration, column (B) contains those created by adaptive subdivision only based on the curvature of the surface, and column (C) contains those with adaptive subdivision by the estimation of curvature and reflectance. Row (1) contains wire-frame representations and Row (2) has polygonal representations of these models. Row (3) shows the images rendered with reflectance. The far upper and far lower rows are zoom-ups of the forehead of the Buddha. We used $\delta_n = 18°$, $\delta_r = 0.1$ and $T_n = T_r = 0.5$.

When we merge range images without adaptive integration, the volume is divided to $1024 \times 1024 \times 1024(= 2^{10})$ voxels in the finest resolution, and the width of the finest voxel is about 1.4cm. The merged model consists of 3.0 million vertices and 6.0 million triangles. The mean difference between the

Figure 10.15. The merging result of the Great Buddha of Kamakura with reflectance parameters.

merged model and a range image is 2.7mm. It is appropriate compared with the maximum error of the Cyrax2400, which is about 7-8mm.

The figures in row (2) are rendered using triangular faces. The result of the adaptive merging (B-2) seems completely the same as the result of the fixed resolution (A-2). However, if they are rendered by a wire frame, as shown in Row (1), we can see that our adaptive merging algorithm generates larger triangles in more or less planar areas. Thus, the size of the result of the adaptive merging is reduced to less than 50% of the result of the fixed resolution. Consequently, the time for merging is also reduced to less than 50%.

Fig. 10.16(A-3) is the result of reflectance merging without adaptive integration. The texture of reflectance of Fig. 10.16(B-3) is smoothed out compared with Fig. 10.16(A-3). However, by considering the reflectance as a criterion of voxel subdivision, the sharp edges due to the variation in reflectance are well preserved (see Fig. 10.16(C-3)).

The statistics of the merging process are described in 10.1. The adaptive merging algorithm reduces the amount of data and computation time required using the original merging method. We compared the difference between the models of column (A) and (B), the models of (A) and (C) using Metro. The mean difference (0.99mm) between (A) and (B) was quite small compared with the height of the Buddha. Our method successfully reduces the amount of data and computation time. However, the mean errors are quite small compared with the Buddha size. Also, adaptive merging based on the photometric attributes successfully reduces the amount of data and the computational time, while it preserves the edges of the reflectance well.

6.4   Evaluation of BOT test

Fig. 10.17 and Fig. 10.18 show an example of the distribution of the number of records examined during the search for a nearest neighbor point in merging

Table 10.1.   Statistics of models of the Buddha

	Number of points	Time for integration	Mean/RMS/Max difference
(A)	3.0 million	61 min.	N/A
(B)	1.2 million	25 min.	0.99/3.5/86 mm
(C)	1.4 million	30 min.	0.44/1.2/66 mm

range images.   When we search for the nearest neighbor points using the BOT test, the number of records examined gets closer to 1 at any distance from the query. This is because we adjust threshold δ according to the criterion described in Section 5.2. In this example, the total numbers of records examined are 11,844,253 without the BOT test and 2,716,475 with the BOT test.   Specifically, the computational cost of searching the nearest neighbor points is reduced to 22.9% of that of the basic search algorithm.

The performance of the BOT test depends on the distribution of distances from queries to nearest neighbor points. Our method works best when the portion of the number of nearest neighbor points that are farther than δ becomes larger. The BOT test can be applied with the variable threshold δ without re-creating the structure of a k-d tree. Thus, the BOT test works efficiently since we subdivide voxels in an octree manner.

6.5   Application: Aligning a Merged Model with a 2D Image

An example of applications utilizing a merged model with reflectance is a 2D-3D registration [40]. Fig. 10.19 shows an example of aligning a 2D image and a 3D model of the Kamakura Buddha with reflectance. Fig. 10.19(b) is the edges of the color values extracted using a Canny filter [59] from the camera image Fig. 10.19(a). Fig. 10.19(c) shows the occluding edges and reflectance edges extracted from the 3D model. In Fig. 10.19(d) and (e), the method estimates the posture of the camera by taking matching edges of 2D image (gray lines) and 3D model (white lines). Fig. 10.19(d) is the initial posture of camera before iterative computation and the posture converges to Fig. 10.19(e). Finally, texture mapping is accomplished using estimated camera parameter(Fig. 10.19(f)).

7.   Conclusion

In this chapter, we have tackled the problem of geometric and photometric modeling of large-scale and intricately-shaped objects. In modeling such objects, the following new issues occurred: creating a detailed model from a huge amount of data, and merging of reflectance parameters of range images.

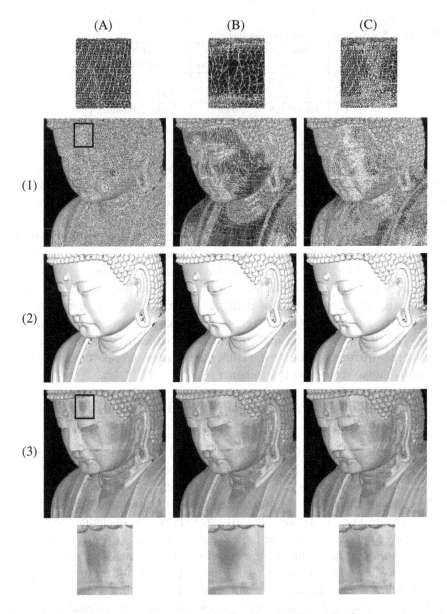

Figure 10.16. Adaptive merging results of the Kamakura Buddha with reflectance parameter.

For merging a huge amount of range images, we proposed two approaches: the adaptive algorithm of merging range images, and a new algorithm for searching for the nearest neighbor using the k-d tree. First, we developed an algorithm for constructing a 3D model in an efficient resolution. Taking into

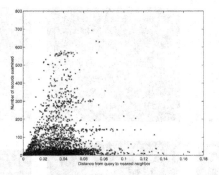

Figure 10.17. Relationship between distance from a query to the nearest neighbor and the number of records examined using the basic search algorithm for merging range images.

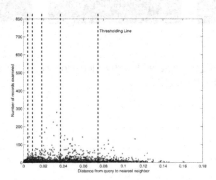

Figure 10.18. Relationship between distance from a query to the nearest neighbor and the number of records examined with the BOT test for merging range images.

account the surface curvature and the photometric attributes, we constructed 3D models that have higher detail in surface areas that contain high curvature and variety of reflectance parameters. If the nearest neighbor point is far from a query, the nearest neighbor is not used in extracting a merged mesh model. Thus, we developed the Bounds-Overlap-Threshold test, which approximately searches by pruning branches if the nearest neighbor point is beyond a threshold. This technique drastically reduces the computational cost if the nearest neighbor is far from a query.

We extended our merging framework to merge reflectance parameters which are attached with range images acquired by a laser range finder. By taking a consensus of the appearance changes of the target object from multiple range images, we reconstructed a 3D model with an appearance which discards outliers due to noise. Also, we were able to provide a model with Lambertian reflected light values by discarding specular reflections as outliers. The re-

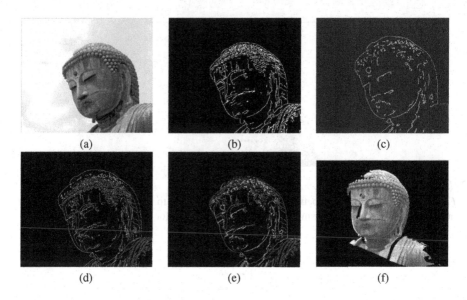

Figure 10.19. Aligning a 2D image with a 3D model of the Kamakura Buddha using the photometric attributes of the 3D model.

flectance parameters of the model can be used for aligning 2D images with the 3D model surface.

We have been able to successfully construct detailed models using these proposed methods; these models have millions of vertices and triangles. Thus, we can make full use of the power of range finders and can model large-scale and intricately-shaped objects using a huge amount of range images.

Appendix: Algorithm of BOT test

Algorithm 2 shows the algorithm of BOT test, which is written in a recursive manner. N is the node of interest. p is the query point. d is the distance of the current nearest neighbor. $\text{rightson}(N)$ and $\text{leftson}(N)$ mean the children of node N. $d_{\text{rightson}(N)}$ and $d_{\text{leftson}(N)}$ are the distance from the query to the boundary of the right/left child of N. The difference from the basic algorithm is illustrated in the gray boxes.

Algorithm 2 SearchNearestNeighborBOT(N, p)

Input: Node N
Input: Query Point p
  if N is leaf node **then**
    Examine records of N and compute the smallest d
  else
    if p is inside leftson(N) **then**
      SearchNearestNeighborBOT(leftson(N,p))
      if $d > d_{\text{rightson}(N)} \quad \wedge \quad \delta > d_{\text{rightson}(N)}$ **then**
        SearchNearestNeighborBOT(rightson(N,p))
      end if
    else
      SearchNearestNeighborBOT(rightson(N,p))
      if $d > d_{\text{leftson}(N)} \quad \wedge \quad \delta > d_{\text{leftson}(N)}$ **then**
        SearchNearestNeighborBOT(leftson(N,p))
      end if
    end if
  end if
  if ball(center p, radius d) is within N **then**
    Finish search
  end if

Acknowledgments

This research was supported, in part, by Ministry of Education, Culture, Sports, Science and Technology under the Leading Project, "Development of High Fidelity Digitization Software for Large-Scale and Intangible Cultural Assets," and, in part, by Japan Science and Technology Agency, under the CREST program, "Automatic generation of virtual models of cultural heritage."

References

[1] K. Ikeuchi, Y. Sato, K. Nishino, R. Sagawa, T. Nishikawa, T. Oishi, I. Sato, J. Takamatsu, and D. Miyazaki, "Modeling cultural heritage through observation," in *Proc. of IEEE First Pacific-Rim Conference on Multimedia*, Dec. 2000.

[2] D. Miyazaki, T. Ooishi, T. Nishikawa, R. Sagawa, K. Nishino, T. Tomomatsu, Y. Takase, and K. Ikeuchi, "The great buddha project: Modelling cultural heritage through observation," in *Proceedings of 6th International Conference on Virtual Systems and MultiMedia*, Gifu, 2000, pp. 138–145.

[3] F. Bernardini, I. Martin, J. Mittleman, H. Rushmeier, and G. Taubin, "Building a digital model of michelangelo's florentine pieta'," *IEEE Computer Graphics & Applications*, vol. 22, no. 1, pp. 59–67, Jan/Feb 2002.

[4] M. Levoy, K. Pulli, B. Curless, S. Rusinkiewicz, D. Koller, L. Pereira, M. Ginzton, S. Anderson, J. Davis, J. Ginsberg, J. Shade, and D. Fulk,

"The digital michelangelo project: 3D scanning of large statues," in *Proc. SIGGRAPH 2000*, 2000, pp. 131–144.

[5] J.-A. Beraldin, M. Picard, S. El-Hakim, G. Godin, V. Valzano, A. Bandiera, and C. Latouche, "Virtualizing a byzantine crypt by combining high-resolution textures with laser scanner 3d data," in *Proc. 8th International Conference on Virtual Systems and MultiMedia*, Korea, Sept. 2002.

[6] F. Stein and G. Medioni, "Structural indexing: efficient 3-d object recognition," *IEEE Trans. Pattern Analysis and Machine Intelligence*, vol. 14, no. 2, pp. 125–145, 1992.

[7] A. Johnson and M. Hebert, "Surface registration by matching oriented points," in *Proc. Int. Conf. On Recent Advances in 3-D Digital Imaging and Modeling*, May 1997, pp. 121–128.

[8] P. Besl and N. McKay, "A method for registration of 3-d shapes," *IEEE Trans. Patt. Anal. Machine Intell.*, vol. 14, no. 2, pp. 239–256, Feb 1992.

[9] C. Dorai, G. Wang, A. Jain, and C. Mercer, "From images to models: Automatic 3d object model construction from multiple views," in *Proc. of the 13th IAPR International Conference on Pattern Recognition*, 1996, pp. 770–774.

[10] Y. Chen and G. Medioni, "Object modeling by registration of multiple range images," *Image and Vision Computing*, vol. 10, no. 3, pp. 145–155, Apr 1992.

[11] M. D. Wheeler and K. Ikeuchi, "Sensor modeling, probabilistic hypothesis generation, and robust localization for object recognition," *IEEE Trans. Pattern Analysis and Machine Intelligence*, vol. 17, no. 3, pp. 252–265, March 1995.

[12] P. Neugebauer, "Geometrical cloning of 3d objects via simultaneous registration of multiple range images," in *Proc. Int. Conf. on Shape Modeling and Application*, Mar 1997, pp. 130–139.

[13] K. Nishino and K. Ikeuchi, "Robust simultaneous registration of multiple range images," in *Proc. Fifth Asian Conference on Computer Vision ACCV '02*, Jan. 2002, pp. 454–461.

[14] K. Pulli, "Multiview registration for large data sets," in *Second Int. Conf. on 3D Digital Imaging and Modeling*, Oct 1999, pp. 160–168.

[15] D. Eggert, A. Fitzgibbon, and R. Fisher, "Simultaneous registration of multiple range views for use in reverse engineering," Dept. of Artificial Intelligence, University of Edinburgh, Tech. Rep. 804, 1996.

[16] R. Bergevin, M. Soucy, H. Gagnon, and D. Laurendeau, "Towards a general multi-view registration technique," *IEEE Trans. Patt. Anal. Machine Intell.*, vol. 18, no. 5, pp. 540–547, May 1996.

[17] D. Huber and M. Hebert, "Fully automatic registration of multiple 3d data sets," *Image and Vision Computing*, vol. 21, no. 7, pp. 637–650, July 2003.

[18] G. Turk and M. Levoy, "Zippered polygon meshes from range images," in *Proc. SIGGRAPH'94*, Jul 1994, pp. 311–318.

[19] M. Soucy and D. Laurendeau, "A general surface approach to the integration of a set of range views," *IEEE Trans. Patt. Anal. Machine Intell.*, vol. 17, no. 4, pp. 344–358, April 1995.

[20] W. Lorensen and H. Cline, "Marching cubes: a high resolution 3d surface construction algorithm," in *Proc. SIGGRAPH'87*. ACM, 1987, pp. 163–170.

[21] H. Hoppe, T. DeRose, T. Duchamp, J. McDonald, and W. Stuetzle, "Surface reconstruction from unorganized points," in *Proc. SIGGRAPH'92*. ACM, 1992, pp. 71–78.

[22] B. Curless and M. Levoy, "A volumetric method for building complex models from range images," in *Proc. SIGGRAPH'96*. ACM, 1996, pp. 303–312.

[23] A. Hilton, A. Stoddart, J. Illingworth, and T. Windeatt, "Reliable surface reconstruction from multiple range images," in *Proceedings of European Conference on Computer Vision*, Springer-Verlag, 1996, pp. 117–126.

[24] R. Whitaker, "A level-set approach to 3d reconstruction from range data," *International Journal of Computer Vision*, vol. 29, no. 3, pp. 203–231, October 1998.

[25] H.-K. Zhao, S. Osher, and R. Fedkiw, "Fast surface reconstruction using the level set method," in *Proc. First IEEE Workshop on Variational and Level Set Methods, in conjunction with Proc. ICCV '01*. IEEE, 2001, pp. 194–202.

[26] J. Sethian, *Level Set Methods*. Cambridge University Press, 1996.

[27] M. D. Wheeler, "Automatic modeling and localization for object recognition," Ph.D. dissertation, School of Computer Science, Carnegie Mellon University, 1996.

[28] M. Wheeler, Y. Sato, and K. Ikeuchi, "Consensus surfaces for modeling 3d objects from multiple range images," in *Proc. International Conference on Computer Vision*, January 1998.

[29] K. Pulli, T. Duchamp, H. Hoppe, J. McDonald, L. Shapiro, and W. Stuetzle, "Robust meshes from range maps," in *Proc. Int. Conf. on Recent Advances in 3-D Digital Imaging and Modeling*, Ottawa, Canada, May 1997, pp. 205–211.

[30] H. J. Wolfson and I. Rigoutsos, "Geometric hashing: An overview," *IEEE Computational Science & Engineering*, vol. 4, no. 4, pp. 10–21, 1997.

[31] A. Califano and R. Mohan, "Multidimensional indexing for recognizing visual shapes," *IEEE Trans. Pattern Analysis and Machine Intelligence*, vol. 16, pp. 373–392, 1994.

[32] J. Friedman, J. Bentley, and R. Finkel, "An algorithm for finding best matches in logarithmic expected time," *ACM Transactions on Mathematical Software*, vol. 3, no. 3, pp. 209–226, 1977.

[33] H. Samet, "The quadtree and related hierarchical data structure," *ACM Computing Surveys*, vol. 16, no. 2, pp. 187–260, 1984.

[34] A. Guttman, "R-trees: A dynamic index structure for spatial searching," in *Proc. ACM SIGMOD Int. Conf. on Management of Data*, 1984, pp. 47–54.

[35] S. Lavallee and R. Szeliski, "Recovering the position and orientation of free-form objects from image contours using 3-d distance maps," *IEEE Transactions on Pattern Analysis and Machine Intelligence*, vol. 17, no. 4, pp. 378–390, April 1995.

[36] Z. Zhang, "Iterative point matching for registration of free-form curves and surfaces," *International Journal of Computer Vision*, vol. 13, no. 2, pp. 119–152, 1994.

[37] M. Greenspan and M. Yurick, "Approximate k-d tree search for efficient icp," in *Proc. 3DIM 2003*, 2003, pp. 442–448.

[38] R. Sagawa, T. Masuda, and K. Ikeuchi, "Effective nearest neighbor search for aligning and merging range images," in *Proc. 3DIM 2003*, 2003, pp. 79–86.

[39] R. Sagawa and K. Ikeuchi, "Taking consensus of signed distance field for complementing unobservable surface," in *Proc. 3DIM 2003*, 2003, pp. 410–417.

[40] R. Kurazume, K. Nishino, Z. Zhang, and K. Ikeuchi, "Simultaneous 2d images and 3d geometric model registration for texture mapping utilizing reflectance attribute," in *Proc. The 5th Asian Conference on Computer Vision*, vol. 1, January 2002, pp. 99–106.

[41] I. Stamos and P. Allen, "Registration of 3d with 2d imagery in urban environments," in *Proc. the Eighth International Conference on Computer Vision, to appear*, Vancouver, Canada, 2001.

[42] P. Neugebauer and K. Klein, "Texturing 3d models of real world objects from multiple unregistered photographic views," in *Proc. Eurographics '99*, 1999, pp. 245–256.

[43] J. Foley, A. van Dam, S. Feiner, and J. F. Hughes, *Computer Graphics: Principles and Practice in C*, 2nd ed.   Addison Wesley Professional, 1995, ISBN:0-201-84840-6.

[44] G. Nielson and B. Hamann, "The asymptotic decider: resolving the ambiguity in marching cubes," in *Proceedings of Visualization'91*.   IEEE, 1991, pp. 83–91.

[45] M. Garland and P. Heckbert, "Simplifying surfaces with color and texture using quadric error metrics," in *Proc. IEEE Visualization 1998*, 1998.

[46] H. Hoppe, "Progressive meshes," in *Computer Graphics (SIGGRAPH 1996 Proceedings)*, 1996, pp. 99–108.

[47] ——, "New quadric metric for simplifying meshes with appearance attributes," in *Proc. IEEE Visualization 1999*, 1999, pp. 59–66.

[48] R. Shekhar, E. Fayyad, R. Yagel, and J. Cornhill, "Octree-based decimation of marching cubes surfaces," in *Proc. Visualization'96*, 1996, pp. 335–342.

[49] R. Shu, Z. Chen, and M. Kankanhalli, "Adaptive marching cubes," *The Visual Computer*, vol. 11, pp. 202–217, 1995.

[50] S. Frisken, R. Perry, A. Rockwood, and T. Jones, "Adaptively sampled distance fields: A general representation of shape for computer graphics," in *Proc. SIGGRAPH2000*. ACM, July 2000, pp. 249–254.

[51] S. F. F. Gibson, "Using distance maps for accurate surface representation in sampled volumes," in *IEEE Symposium on Volume Visualization*, 1998, pp. 23–30.

[52] R. Sagawa, T. Oishi, A. Nakazawa, R. Kurazume, and K. Ikeuchi, "Iterative refinement of range images with anisotropic error distribution," in *Proc. IEEE/RSJ International Conference on Intelligent Robots and Systems*, October 2002, pp. 79–85.

[53] Cyra Technologies, Inc. [Online]. Available: http://www.cyra.com

[54] K. Nishino, Y. Sato, and K. Ikeuchi, "Eigen-texture method: Appearance compression based on 3d model," in *Proc. of Computer Vision and Pattern Recognition '99*, vol. 1, Jun. 1999, pp. 618–624.

[55] R. Sagawa, K. Nishino, M. Wheeler, and K. Ikeuchi, "Parallel processing of range data merging," in *Proc. 2001 IEEE/RSJ International Conference on Intelligent Robots and Systems*, vol. 1, Oct. 2001, pp. 577–583.

[56] R. Sagawa, "Geometric and photometric merging for large-scale objects," Ph.D. dissertation, Graduate School of Engineering, The University of Tokyo, 2003.

[57] "The Stanford 3D Scanning Repository." [Online]. Available: http://www-graphics.stanford.edu/data/3Dscanrep/

[58] P. Cignoni, C. Rocchini, and R. Scopigno, "Metro: measuring error on simplified surfaces," *Computer Graphics Forum*, vol. 17, no. 2, pp. 167–174, June 1998.

[59] F. Canny, "A computational approach to edge detection," *IEEE Trans. Pattern Anal. Machine Intell.*, vol. 8, no. 6, pp. 679–698, 1986.

Chapter 11

ITERATIVE REFINEMENT OF RANGE IMAGES WITH ANISOTROPIC ERROR DISTRIBUTION

Ryusuke Sagawa, Takeshi Oishi, Atsushi Nakazawa, Ryo Kurazume, and Katsushi Ikeuchi

Abstract   We propose a method which refines the range measurement of range finders by computing correspondences of vertices of multiple range images acquired from various viewpoints. Our method assumes that a range image acquired by a laser range finder has anisotropic error distribution which is parallel to the ray direction. Thus, we find corresponding points of range images along with the ray direction. We iteratively converge range images to minimize the distance of corresponding points. We describe the effectiveness of our method by the presenting the experimental results of artificial and real range data. Also we show that our method refines a 3D shape more accurately as opposed to that achieved by using the Gaussian filter.

1.   Introduction

Large scale 3D modeling technology has become popular and is often used for modeling industrial plants, buildings, cultural heritages and so on. Using these technologies, many project scientists are digitizing large scale cultural heritages or natural scenes.

3D object modeling is accomplished by performing the following three steps:
(1) Acquiring the range images (Scanning).
(2) Aligning of many range images acquired from different viewpoints (Alignment).
(3) Re-generating the unified meshes (Merging).
Usually, during the scanning process, some range images cover the same portion of the object surface to ensure that the whole 3D shape data is acquired.

For the alignment of the small objects, the geometrical relationship between range images can be acquired easily because the objects' motions are controlled by using rotation tables or manipulators. However, it cannot be acquired for large objects; in such cases, range image matching techniques are used for the alignment. Many studies have been devoted to achieving this purpose. Besl proposed a feature point-based matching method [1], while Chen's method is based on the evaluation between the point and the polygons. Neugebauer proposed the idea of 'simultaneous registration' that aligns range images simultaneously to avoid the error accumulation of the pairwise alignment methods [6]. A similar idea was proposed by Nishino et al. [7].

A merging procedure produces unified meshes from aligned range images . This is achieved by concatenating the polygons' borders [10], using deformable surfaces [4] or implicit functions [2, 11]. Wheeler's method uses 'signed distance' to represent the distance from 3D mesh surfaces and their consensus. As the result, the errors and outliers are eliminated.

The errors of the final 3D model come from these factors.

(1) A measurement error on the range images .

(2) A matching error on the alignment process.

(3) The quantization and equalization errors on the merging process.

The type (2) and (3) errors depend on the object shape and the algorithm, and so are solved by taking a suitable algorithm according to the objects. For the type (1) error, Taubin used the spatial smoothing filter [9], but fine features can be lost during this procedure. Basically, this kind of error cannot be avoided from one range image by any software algorithms.

Taking many range images on the same surface is one of the solutions for this problem. Generally, any range measurement system has its characteristic minimum measurement accuracy and error distributions. Wheeler's method is based on this consideration, but is weak for spatially high resolution range images . The signed distance is calculated along the normal direction of the surface. If the normal directions are not responsible because of a measurement error, then the final merging result is so not responsible.

We propose a method to avoid this weakness and improve the accuracy of the final 3D model. This reduces the measurement errors on the distance value in the overlapping areas of the aligned range images . By applying this method before the merging process, a much finer 3D model can be acquired. Unlike the existing spatial filtering method, this method is able to not only smooth the surface of the final 3D mesh model but also to extract fine features. In the following sections, 2 describes our proposed estimation and correction method. 3 shows the result of refinement of artificial and real range data. Finally, we summarize our method in 4.

2.   Proposed Method

Our method corrects errors by iterative computation similar to registration techniques like ICP[1]. Let us call the base range image the model and others

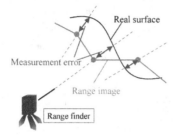

Figure 11.1.   Measurement error

the 'scenes.' We search the corresponding points on all scenes of each vertex of the model. Then, we move every vertex of the model respectively to reduce the distance of each correspondence. Our method continues this process until the distances become sufficiently small.

The following pseudo code shows the proposed algorithm:

```
Algorithm   Procedure of Correct Errors
while  (error > threshold){
    for  (i = 0; i < nImage; ++i){
        /* range image  i is model */
        for  (j = 0; j < nImage; ++j){
            /* Search corresponding points */
            /* for all vertices of the model*/
            if  (i != j) CorrespondenceSearch(i, j);
        }
        /* Compute the next position of vertices */
        MoveVertex(i);
    }
    /* Update the motion of all vertices */
    UpdateVertex(all);
}
```

2.1   Error model of Range Measurement

Laser range finders measure distance by shooting a laser and receiving its reflection from the target object. The 3D position of the point of reflection is computed by the distance and the ray vector. The error of the 3D position mainly depends on the error of the distance. The error of the vertical direction to the ray vector, which is caused by the mechanism of the range finder, is much smaller than the error of the distance. Thus, we assume the error of the range measurement by a laser range finder is anisotropic and exists only along the ray vector (**Figure 11.1**).

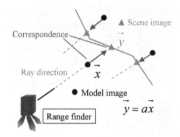

Figure 11.2.   Search correspondence

2.2   Correspondence Search

Since we assume that error exists only along the ray vector and that range images are completely aligned, our method searches corresponding points along the ray vector. Now, $\vec{x}$ is the vector from the center of the sensor to the vertex of the model and $\vec{y}$ is the vector from the center to the corresponding point of the scene. Then,

$$\vec{y} = a\vec{x} \qquad (11.1)$$

where a is the coefficient. Thus, these points are on the same line (**Figure 11.2**).

To eliminate wrong correspondences, if the distance of corresponding points is larger than a threshold, we remove the scene point from the correspondence. We use the maximum error of the range finder as the threshold. This correspondence search is computed for every combination of range images .

2.3   Error Correction

The error is corrected by moving each vertex to the new position, which is estimated from the corresponding points. Since the direction of error of each range image is different, some correspondences are not accurate. In the case that the number of overlapped range images is small, it is difficult to estimate the accurate point. Thus, we move each vertex to the weighted average point of the correspondence to gradually converge the error. The kth vertex of ith range image $\vec{x}_{ik}$ is moved to the weighted average point

$$\vec{x}'_{ik} = (1 - w) \cdot \vec{x}_{ik} + w \cdot \frac{1}{n_{ik} - 1} \sum_{i \neq j} \vec{y}_{jk} \qquad (11.2)$$

where n_{ik} is the number of the corresponding points and w is weight. In this chapter, we use $w = 0.5$. This process is applied to all vertices of each range image respectively. We reiterate it until the error of correspondence converges enough.

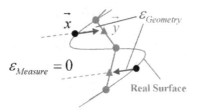

Figure 11.3. Error by resolution and geometry

2.4 Discussion

The error of corresponding points ϵ depends on the error of measurement $\epsilon_{Measure}$ and the error by sparse sampling of a range image $\epsilon_{Geometry}$.

$$\epsilon = \epsilon_{Measure} + \epsilon_{Geometry} \qquad (11.3)$$

$\epsilon_{Measure}$ is corrected by iterative computation. However, $\epsilon_{Geometry}$ is caused by the curvature of the surface and the sampling interval of a range image .

In **Figure 11.3**, the range measurement is noise-free and the vertices of range images are on the real surface (namely $\epsilon_{Measure} = 0$); however, the error exists between $\vec{x}$ and $\vec{y}$. Thus, $\epsilon = 0$ only if the surface is planar.

$$\epsilon \begin{cases} = 0 & \text{planar area} \\ > 0 & \text{otherwise} \end{cases} \qquad (11.4)$$

Figure 11.4 shows a 2D example of range images . For simplicity, we assume the new positions of x_2, y_1, y_2 after an iteration is computed as

$$\begin{aligned}
x_2' &= (1-w)x_2 + w((1-\alpha)y_1 + \alpha y_2) \\
y_1' &= (1-w)y_1 + w((1-\beta)x_1 + \beta x_2) \\
y_2' &= (1-w)y_2 + w((1-\gamma)x_2 + \gamma x_3)
\end{aligned} \qquad (11.5)$$

where w, α, β, γ are coefficients. After one more iteration, x_2' moves to

$$\begin{aligned}
x_2'' &= (1-w)x_2' + w((1-\alpha')y_1' + \alpha' y_2') \\
&= w^2(1-\alpha')(1-\beta)x_1 + w^2\alpha'\gamma x_3 + \\
&\quad ((1-w)^2 + w^2(1-\alpha')\beta + w^2\alpha'(1-\gamma))x_2 + \\
&\quad w(1-w)(2-\alpha-\alpha')y_1 + \\
&\quad w(1-w)(\alpha+\alpha')y_2
\end{aligned} \qquad (11.6)$$

where α' is a coefficient. Since the equation of x_2'' includes the neighbor vertices x_1, x_3, the smoothing effect occurs during an iteration similar to the smoothing filter. However, the weight of x_1 and x_3 in (11.6) is small compared with that of the smoothing filter, for example,

$$x_2' = \alpha x_1 + \beta x_2 + (1-\alpha-\beta)x_3, \qquad (11.7)$$

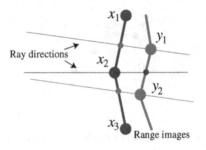

Figure 11.4.   Smoothing effect by iteration

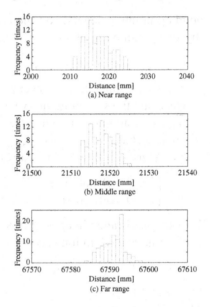

Figure 11.5.   Distribution of errors of Cyrax2500

which does not include y_1, y_2. Thus, the propagation of the smoothing effect of our method is slower than that of the smoothing filter.

3.   Experiment

3.1   Error Distribution of Laser Range Finder

Among types of laser range finders, a time-of-flight range finder is useful to measure a far object with high accuracy. We use a laser range finder of the time-of-flight type, Cyrax 2500 [3] made by Cyra Technologies, Inc. To estimate the error distribution of the Cyrax 2500, we set the range finder in front of a concrete wall and measure the distance to the wall many times. We tested three configurations of different distances, far range (67m), middle range (20m) and near range (2m) [1]. **Figure 11.5** shows the result of measurement

Table 11.1.   Distance measurement error of Cyrax 2500

Average distance $[mm]$	Var. $[mm^2]$	STD. $[mm]$
2017.2 (near)	11.0	3.3
21518.0 (middle)	9.1	3.0
67591.1 (far)	7.7	2.8

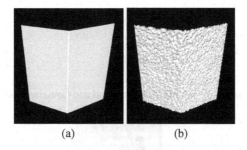

(a)   (b)

Figure 11.6.   Artificially created model

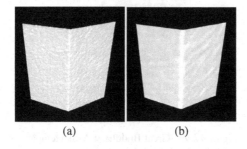

(a)   (b)

Figure 11.7.   Refined model

and the average, variance and standard deviation are shown in **Table 11.1**. The error distribution becomes wide in the near range; however, it can be regarded as a normal distribution with about 3mm standard deviation. The maximum error is about 7–8mm, which is a little larger than the 6mm (at 50m range) of the catalog specification.

We did not test the error distribution of the vertical direction to the ray vector. According to the catalog, it is 0.25mm at 50m range (0.0003 degree), which is drastically smaller than that of the ray direction. Thus, the error distribution of the range image by Cyrax 2500 depends on the ray direction.

3.2   Error Correction of Artificial Data

First, we create artificial range images with random noise and experiment with the error correction. **Figure 11.6**(a) shows the model without noise. Its

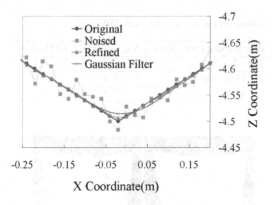

Figure 11.8.   Compare our method and Gaussian filter

Figure 11.9.   Great Buddha at Asuka temple

width and height are 40cm, its depth is 20cm and it consists of 100×100 points. The range image with noise, of which the maximum is 6mm, is **Figure 11.6**(b). We create 10 range images to which noises of different direction are added. The result of error correction is shown in **Figure 11.7**(a). **Figure 11.7**(b) is one of range images filtered by Gaussian filter. We can see that our method corrects errors sufficiently and preserves edges more accurately than the Gaussian filter. **Figure 11.8** compares these two results.

3.3   Error Correction of Real Data

Next, we experiment on the error correction of range images acquired by a laser range finder Cyrax 2400, whose accuracy is the same as that of the Cyrax 2500.

The observed object is the Nara Asuka Great Buddha, which is considered to be the oldest Buddha statue in Japan. Its height is about 2.7m. Cyrax 2400 is a range finder for long range, and not suitable for measuring objects of the

Figure 11.10.   Original range image range image

Figure 11.11.   Refined range image range image

Asuka Buddha's size. However, because of the unsuitable environment around the Buddha, we cannot use a more accurate range finder for close range. Thus, we measure the Buddha a little apart from it by Cyrax 2400.

We have acquired 9 range images of the front of the Buddha. We align these range images simultaneously by using a robust registration method [7] (see **Figure 11.10**). Since the object is relatively small and the range is near, the obvious noise can be seen in the range images .

Figure 11.11 shows the result of the error correction by our method. The noise has been removed from the model and its surface is smooth. In spite of that, the edges are well preserved because our method is not a smoothing operation such as the Gaussian filter. In **Figure 11.12**, the error converges to 0 as the number of the iteration increases.

Figure 11.13 shows the results of merging range images using the original range images and using the refined range images . We use the merging technique by Sagawa [8]. Since the method draws a consensus of range images

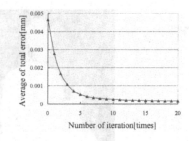

Figure 11.12. Convergence of error

Original   Refined

Figure 11.13. Results of merging

using the distance and normal direction [11], it can remove the error caused by measurement and registration. However, in this experiment, it is difficult to correct the error because the range images are too noisy and its normal direction cannot be relied on. We can see that the error remains in the merging result which uses the original range images in **Figure 11.13**. On the other hand, the accurate model is reconstructed in the merging result with the refined range images . In the area where range images are not overlapped such as the side of the head, the error is not removed.

We compare our method with the model filtered by the Gaussian filter. **Figure 11.14** shows a part of the model filtered by the Gaussian filter after merging and the model merged from refined range images . The model with Gaussian filter is smoothed out; however, our method removes noise and preserves the edge of the surface.

Finally, we consider whether our method can be applied to other range finders, for example, a stereo range finding system. We construct a multi-baseline stereo system [5], which consists of 9 cameras. **Figure 11.15** shows one of the camera images and a stereo range image . Since the multi-baseline stereo

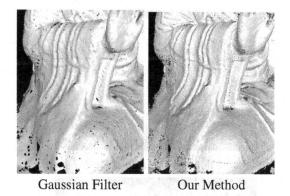

Gaussian Filter   Our Method

Figure 11.14. Compare with Gaussian filter

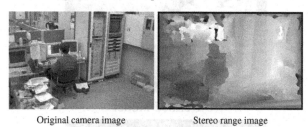

Original camera image   Stereo range image

Figure 11.15. Range measurement by stereo

generates a range image for each camera by taking matching with the other 8 cameras, we generate 9 stereo range images . These range images are pre-aligned by stereo calibration. Thus, our refining process can be applied straightforwardly to the 9 range images . In the raw stereo range image (**Figure 11.16**(a)), we can see the step-shaped error caused by quantization of images. **Figure 11.16**(b) is the refined model after 10 times of the iteration. The step-shaped error is removed after refinement . Also, **Figure 11.16**(a) contains a lot of debris due to mismatching. Since the refining process is namely an estimation of the confidence of range data, we can regard the vertices of the range image which cannot be refined as unreliable vertices. **Figure 11.16**(c) is the range image after the unreliable vertices are removed.

4.   Summary

In this chapter, we have proposed an efficient range image refinement method under the consideration of unique error distributions of multiple range images . We described how we applied this method to the modeling of the artificial test object and the actual cultural heritage object from the images acquired by the time-of-flight range sensor. Finally, we applied our method to the range images which are generated by the multi-baseline stereo system.

(a)Raw model by stereo

(b)Refined model

(c)Remove unreliable vertices

Figure 11.16.   Refinement of range image range image by stereo

The experimental result shows the validity of this method compared with that of the existing filter-based methods.

Acknowledgments

This research was supported, in part, by Ministry of Education, Culture, Sports, Science and Technology under the Leading Project, "Development of High Fidelity Digitization Software for Large-Scale and Intangible Cultural Assets," and, in part, by Japan Science and Technology Agency, under the

CREST program, "Automatic generation of virtual models of cultural heritage ."

Notes

1. The recommended range of Cyrax 2500 is 1.5–50m.

References

[1] P. J. Besl and N. D. McKay. A method for registration of 3-d shapes. *IEEE Trans. Pattern Anal. Machine Intell.*, 14(2):239–256, 1992.

[2] Brian Curless and Marc Levoy. A volumetric method for building complex models from range images. In *Proc. SIGGRAPH'96*, pages 303–312. ACM, 1996.

[3] http://www.cyra.com.

[4] Martial Hebert, Katsushi Ikeuchi, and Herve Delingette. A spherical representation for recognition of free-form surfaces. *IEEE Transactions on Pattern Analysis and Machine Intelligence*, 17(7):681–690, 1995.

[5] M.Okutomi and T.Kanade. A multiple-baseline stereo. *IEEE Trans. Pattern Analysis and Machine Intelligence*, 15(4):353–363, 1993.

[6] P. J. Neugebauer. Geometrical cloning of 3d objects via simultaneous registration of multiple range image. In *Proc. of the 1997 Int. Conf. on Shape Modeling and Application (SMA'97)*, pages 130–139, 1997.

[7] K. Nishino and K. Ikeuchi. Robust simultaneous registration of multiple range images. In *Proc. of Fifth Asian Conference on Computer Vision ACCV '02*, pages 454–461, 2002.

[8] R. Sagawa, K. Nishino, and K. Ikeuchi. Robust and adaptive integration of multiple range images with photometric attributes. In *Proc. IEEE Computer Society Conference on Computer Vision and Pattern Recognition 2001*, volume 2, pages 172–179, December 2001.

[9] Gabriel Taubin. A signal processing approach to fair surface design. *Computer Graphics*, 29(Annual Conference Series):351–358, 1995.

[10] G. Turk and M. Levoy. Zippered polygon meshes from range images. In *SIGGRAPH 94*, pages 311–318, Jul 1994.

[11] M.D. Wheeler, Y. Sato, and K. Ikeuchi. Consensus surfaces for modeling 3d objects from multiple range images. In *Proc. International Conference on Computer Vision*, January 1998.

Chapter 12

HOLE FILLING OF 3D MODEL BY FLIPPING SIGNS OF SIGNED DISTANCE FIELD IN ADAPTIVE RESOLUTION

Ryusuke Sagawa and Katsushi Ikeuchi

Abstract   When we use range finders to observe the shape of an object, many occluded areas may be found. These become holes and gaps in the model and make it undesirable for various applications. We propose a novel method to fill holes and gaps to complete this incomplete model. As an intermediate representation, we use a Signed Distance Field (SDF), which stores Euclidean signed distances from a voxel to the nearest point of the mesh model. By using an SDF, we can obtain interpolating surfaces for holes and gaps. The proposed method generates an interpolating surface that is smoothly continuous with real surfaces by minimizing the area of the interpolating surface. Since the isosurface of an SDF can be identified as being a real or interpolating surface from the magnitude of signed distances, our method computes the area of an interpolating surface in the neighborhood of a voxel both before and after flipping the sign of the signed distance of the voxel. If the area is reduced by flipping the sign, our method changes the sign for the voxel. Therefore, we minimize the area of the interpolating surface by iterating this computation until convergence. Unlike methods based on Partial Differential Equations (PDE), our method does not require any boundary condition, and the initial state that we use is automatically obtained by computing the distance to the closest point of the real surface. Moreover, because our method can be applied to an SDF of adaptive resolution, our method efficiently interpolates large holes and gaps of high curvature. We tested the proposed method with both synthesized and real objects and evaluated the interpolating surfaces.

1.   Introduction

Recently, many researchers have focused on modeling the shape of real-world objects by scanning them using three-dimensional digitizers, such as laser range finders [1, 2] and structured-light range finders [3]. These methods measure distances from the point of view to the surface of the object, which can be seen from the sensors. A range finder obtains a range image that contains the measured distances for each pixel by two-dimensional scanning. Thus, to acquire the whole shape of an object, we have to scan it from various viewpoints by using those sensors. If the object has an intricate shape, many occluded areas may occur. Consequently, there are often unobserved surfaces, even when full use is made of the various kinds of sensors. However, it is too costly to take range images from various viewpoints to cover every hole that is not observed by a full range image. In the worst case scenario, we are not able to obtain the data needed to create a complete model. However, we need to fill these holes to make use of constructed models in many different applications, such as creating a solid model and visualizing the model. Therefore, we propose a new method that enables us to complement the geometric models by estimating the neighborhood area of the holes and filling the holes and gaps.

Since filling the holes of a model is a major issue in this field, several approaches have previously been proposed. The simplest approach is interpolation by triangulating the boundary vertices of a hole. Liepa [4] fills holes by triangulation, adjusting the size of triangles. If the hole is small and the topology is simple, the triangulation works well; however, triangulation becomes difficult if the surface is intricate and the hole is large. The second approach is to fit a mesh model around the hole, that is, a three-dimensional version of snakes and related studies [5–7]. In these methods, a deformable surface moves iteratively to fit the model by satisfying the smoothness constraint. However, since they determine topology *a priori*, these methods are not suitable for intricately shaped objects. The third approach is called "space carving." Curless and Levoy [8] tag one of the states, unseen, empty, and near the surface, to each voxel during the merging process. The hole filling is accomplished by generating a surface between voxels of unseen states and those of empty states. Since space carving methods do not consider viewing objects from other viewpoints, the result of rendering from different viewpoints may be far from acceptable. The fourth approach is interpolation by volumetric representation, such as level-set approaches [9, 10] and re-computation of the implicit surface [11, 12]. Davis et al. [12] re-compute the implicit surface by diffusing the signed distance function from the vicinity of the observed surface to the whole volume. Some other volumetric-based methods are proposed, such as a PDE-based method [13] that minimizes the divergence of implicit surface, a method based on Finite Element Methods (FEM) [14] that minimizes the mean curvature of implicit surface, and a method [15] interpolating an SDF by fitting quadrics. Since the volumetric-based methods use voxels of fixed resolution, they are not efficient to fill large holes and high curvature gaps. Moreover, though the PDE-based methods requires an initial state and a boundary condition of an interpolating surface, it is difficult to give an initial state automatically, and it is not simple to implement a boundary condition because the shape of the boundary of a hole has a great deal of variation.

Our method is similar to the third and fourth approaches. In our framework, we compute the SDF using multiple real surfaces, which are the surfaces measured by sensors. Since we separate the entire volume into two manifolds by SDF, we can generate a closed surface by converting the SDF to a mesh model. In this chapter, we propose a method that obtains an interpolating surface by minimizing the curvature at the same time that the interpolating surface is smoothly continuous with the real surface. Unlike PDE-based methods, our method does not require a boundary condition, and the initial state that we use is automatically obtained by computing the distance to the closest point of the real surface. Thus, our method is very simple to implement. Moreover, since our method can be applied to an SDF of adaptive resolution, it is efficient to fill large holes and high curvature gaps by using voxels of appropriate resolution for the shape of the holes.

This chapter is organized as follows. We define an interpolating surface that is a goal for our method in 2. In 3, we briefly explain a method to compute an SDF from real surfaces to give the initial state automatically, and we also point out the problems of the interpolating surface that is generated from SDF. We propose a method to obtain a desirable interpolating surface in 4. We report the testing of our method and evaluate the interpolating surface in 5. Finally, we summarize this chapter in 6.

2. Hole Filling by Minimizing the Curvature of the Interpolating Surface

A real surface measured by a range finder has boundaries such as occluding boundaries. Since a closed surface is generated by filling holes of surfaces by our method, a hole of surface to be filled is defined by the boundaries of real surfaces. At the same time, an interpolating surface is defined as a surface that is included in a closed surface, but not in the real surface.

The surface that is suitable for filling holes depends on applications. In this chapter, we interpolate holes by minimizing the curvature of interpolating surfaces that are smoothly continuous with real surfaces. In this section, we analyze the issue and define the goal of the interpolating surfaces.

In the level set formulation [16], the surface is represented as the zero level set $f(\boldsymbol{x}) = 0$, where the implicit function $f(\boldsymbol{x})$ means the distance from the surface to the point $\boldsymbol{x}$. The zero level isosurface $f(\boldsymbol{x}) = 0$ evolves according to the following partial differential equation:

$$\frac{\partial f}{\partial t} + F|\nabla f| = 0. \qquad (12.1)$$

If we consider the curvature κ of the isosurface, which is computed by $\kappa = \nabla \cdot \frac{\nabla f}{|\nabla f|}$, the speed function $F = -\kappa$ is used in several cases, such as the heat equation. If the boundary is defined as the position of the surface, it is well known that the highly curved surface is smoothed out and the surface becomes closer to a minimal surface [17]. A minimal surface is the surface of which the mean curvature is zero at arbitrary points and the area becomes minimum by satisfying the given boundary condition.

Since our goal is generating a surface to fill a hole by minimizing the curvature of the interpolating surface, it is similar to a minimal surface. However, we must consider not only the position on the boundary of real surfaces, but the continuity with them. Thus, the boundary condition for this issue is both the position and normal vector of the surface. Therefore, a desirable surface is obtained if the change of surface is represented by the speed function, which smoothes out the curvature of the surface while at the same time keeping continuity with real surfaces.

To solve the problem based on the PDE-based method, the initial state and boundary condition are necessary. However, it is difficult to give the initial state automatically, and not simple to implement a boundary condition because the shape of the boundary of a hole has a great deal of variation and the 3D domain to be considered is unknown *a priori*. Thus, instead of a PDE-based method, we propose a method that gives the initial state automatically and iteratively computes an interpolating surface without any boundary condition.

Since our method is a volumetric approach, the topology of a hole is not necessary to be given. Our method certainly generates a closed surface and has no restriction on the shape and size of a hole unless the interpolating surface diverges out of the 3D space to be operated.

3.   Computing Initial State from Real Surfaces

In this section, we explain the computation of an SDF from real surfaces. Our method uses the SDF as an initial state to estimate an interpolating surface.

First, we explain the computation of an SDF from range images, and then we point out a problem in computing the signs of an SDF.

3.1   Computing SDF from Range Images

Since a range image can be converted to a mesh model, a range image is represented as a mesh model which consists of 3D vertices and triangles that connect the neighboring vertices. Some methods of merging range images [8, 18, 9, 19, 20] use an SDF as an intermediate representation of the surface, and there are several ways to compute a signed distance. For example, Curless and Levoy [8] used the distance between a voxel and the point of a range image along the line of sight of the range image.   Wheeler et al. [18] used the

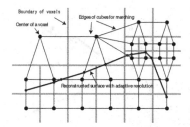

Figure 12.1. A 2D slice of an SDF of adaptive resolution: The gray lines indicates the boundaries of voxels of adaptive resolution. A mesh model is generated by interpolating the signed distances. The vertices of the mesh model exist on the edges that connect the centers of voxels.

closest point of a range image from the center of a voxel to compute the signed distance.

In this study, we assume that the magnitude of a signed distance is the Euclidean distance from the center of a voxel to the closest point of range images.

We compute an SDF by our merging algorithm [21, 22]. Since the magnitude of the signed distances of the method is Euclidean distances, we use the SDF as an initial state of the new method proposed in this chapter. Naturally, we can apply our new method to the SDF created by other methods if the SDF satisfies this assumption.

In our merging algorithm, the sign of a signed distance is determined by considering the normal vector $\boldsymbol{n}$ of the closest point, which faces outside and is computed by averaging the normal vectors of the triangles to which it belongs, and the vector $\boldsymbol{v}$ from the center of the voxel v to the closest point. Thus, the signed distance $d(v)$ is computed as

$$d(v) = \mathrm{sgn}(-\boldsymbol{n} \cdot \boldsymbol{v})|\boldsymbol{v}|, \tag{12.2}$$

where $\mathrm{sgn}(x)$ is 1 if x is positive and is -1 if x is negative.

Moreover, our merging algorithm proposed in [21] uses voxels of adaptive resolution in an octree manner. In an area that is far from range images, we sample the 3D space coarsely and use voxels of large size. If range images are nearby, we sample the 3D space more finely. The width of voxel W is determined by the magnitude of the signed distance:

$$W(v) < \frac{2}{3\sqrt{3}}|d(v)|. \tag{12.3}$$

If (12.3) is satisfied, the implicit surface can exist inside the voxel or the neighbor voxels, since the diagonal width of the voxel is $\sqrt{3}W(v)$. We start the computation of signed distances by finding the closest point of range images from the center of the largest voxel, which is the root node of the octree

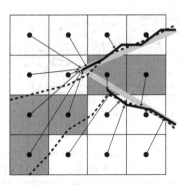

Figure 12.2. An SDF is computed for a sharp corner. The gray line denotes the true surface of the object. The black solid lines indicate the range images. Each arrow is the vector from the center of a voxel to the nearest point. The voxels that have negative signed distances are filled by gray color. Although the lower left area is obviously outside of the object, it is considered to be inside by the normal vector of the nearest point. Therefore, the generated surface corrupts, as represented by the dotted lines.

and can be set independently from range images. If the signed distance does not satisfy (12.3), we subdivide the voxel to eight voxels. Then, we compute the signed distances for the eight voxels and apply the procedure recursively to the finest voxel size, which is given by the user. Otherwise, we stop the subdivision.

Figure 12.1 shows a 2D slice of an SDF of adaptive resolution. The gray lines indicate the boundaries of voxels of adaptive resolution. A mesh model is generated by interpolating the signed distances. The vertices of the mesh model exist on the edges that connect the centers of voxels. We can change the level of detail of the mesh model by using an SDF of adaptive resolution.

If we use an SDF of adaptive resolution for hole filling, it is efficient to interpolate a large hole and a gap of high curvature.

3.2   Problem of Computing Signs of SDF

In this section, we point out the problem of computing a signed distance. Although we use the SDF computed from real surfaces as an initial state of an interpolating surface, it is far from a desirable surface in some situations.

In the computation of the initial state of an SDF, we determine the sign by using the normal vector of a point of real surfaces. The signs determine if a voxel is inside or outside a surface; however, since a normal vector is a local feature of a surface, it is not determined from a global point of view. This is a problem when computing signs of an SDF.

If a hole is much larger than the voxel size, it is difficult to determine the signs from global point of view by considering only a local feature of a sur-

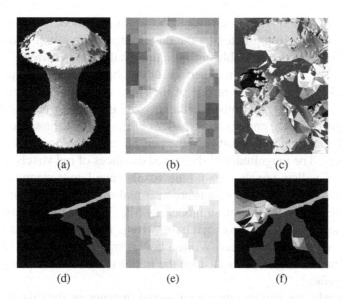

Figure 12.3. (a) shows a 3D model with holes and (d) is a zoom-up of a sharp corner of (a). There are some small holes and gaps. (b) and (e) are 2D slices of the SDF computed from (a). Yellow and red voxels indicate that they have positive signed distances, and blue voxels indicate negative ones. The magnitudes of the signed distances of red and blue voxels are larger than those of yellow and light-blue voxels respectively. And green voxels are near the surface. Though the left side of (e) is outside of the model, voxels of negative signs exist. Therefore, the generated mesh model from the SDF becomes (c) and (f).

face. The curvature is also a local feature if the voxel size is small. Moreover, since the initial surface can be very different from the desirable surface, many steps of iterative computation are required to converge it to a desirable one. Therefore, we overcome this problem by using an SDF of adaptive resolution to improve the convergence.

Even if a hole is not large, the initial surface can be far from the desirable surface when a surface of the object is highly curved. **Figure 12.2** shows an example of computing signed distances when the surface of an object has a high curvature. The gray line denotes the true surface of the object. The black solid lines indicate the range images. There is a narrow gap between two range images. Each arrow is the vector from the center of a voxel to the nearest point. If a voxel is inside the object when considering normal vectors of range images, the sign is negative, and the voxel is filled by gray color in **Figure 12.2**.

Although the lower left area is obviously outside of the object in **Figure 12.2**, the signs of those voxels are negative because they are considered to be inside by the normal vector of the nearest point. If we use the Marching Cubes algorithm (MC) [23] to convert the SDF to a mesh model, the generated surface corrupts, as represented by the dotted lines. The initial interpolating surface is far from the desirable one even though the gap is narrow.

Figure 12.3(a) shows the real surface of an object that has sharp corners. **Figure 12.3**(d) is a zoom-up of one of the sharp corners. Although the gap is narrow, it is hard to determine whether a voxel is inside or outside near the corner. **Figure 12.3**(b) and (e) are 2D slices of the SDF. Yellow and red voxels indicate that they have positive signed distances, and blue voxels indicate negative ones. The magnitudes of the signed distances of red voxels are larger than those of yellow voxels. Also, blue voxels have larger magnitudes than light-blue voxels. And green voxels are near real surfaces. Therefore, the result of converting SDF to a mesh model by MC is shown in **Figure 12.3**(c) and (f). Since the signs of some voxels are wrong, many vertices and triangles are generated outside the object. While a hole is small, it is difficult to restrict the 3D domain to be considered since the initial surface can be far from the desirable surface.

In this study, we simply compute a signed distance as the distance to the nearest neighbor point even if it is on the boundary of a real surface. The computation of a sign becomes unstable in the case of boundary; however, it is impossible to determine the sign from the global point of view by using only a single normal vector even if we use a more elaborate method such as [24]. Thus, we compute it by a simple method in the initialization and improve it by iterative computation described in 4.

4.   Hole Filling by Minimizing the Area of Interpolating Surface

Though the methods based on volumetric representation [9, 12, 13] compute an SDF during iteration, our method has already computed the SDF during merging of range images. In this section, we propose a method that generates a surface to fill a hole by iteratively updating the computed SDF while keeping continuity with range images [25]. Though (12.1) with $F = -\kappa$ minimizes the curvature of a surface, it is equal to minimizing the area of the surface in a local domain. Therefore, our method minimizes the area of a surface instead of considering the curvature of a surface. While a PDE-based method requires a boundary condition and restricts the 3D space to be considered, these restrictions are not necessary for our method. At the end of this section, we show that the proposed method approximates (12.1).

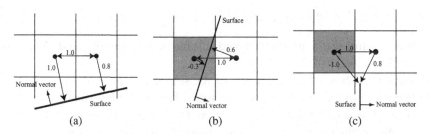

Figure 12.4. Three examples of signed distances of adjacent voxels: The width of the voxels is 1.0. (a) Both voxels are outside an object whose signed distances are 1.0 and 0.8. Since the signs of the adjacent voxels are the same, the isosurface does not exist between them. (b) The signs of the adjacent voxels are different. The signed distances are -0.3 and 0.6. The isosurface between two voxels represents a real surface. (c) The signed distances are -1.0 and 0.8. The isosurface represents an interpolating surface.

4.1   Approximation of the Area of Interpolating Surface

The area of interpolating surface A is computed by

$$A = \int_V \delta(f(x, y, z)) dx dy dz, \qquad (12.4)$$

where $\delta(f)$ is the delta function and V is the volume that includes the interpolating surface. Since we use discretized voxels to represent the SDF, (12.4) can be approximated as follows:

$$\hat{A} = \sum_{i,j} S(v_i, v_j) \qquad (12.5)$$

$$S(v_i, v_j) = \begin{cases} s & \text{the interpolating surface exists between } v_i \text{ and } v_j \\ 0 & \text{otherwise,} \end{cases}$$

where v_i and v_j are two adjacent voxels, and s is the area of surface between v_i and v_j. If $s = 1$, $\hat{A}$ equals to the number of interfaces between two voxels. Therefore, our method minimizes $\hat{A}$ instead of A. The issue of computing $\hat{A}$ is to determine which voxels are facing with the interpolating surface.

4.2   Finding Interpolating Surface between Two Adjacent Voxels

To determine which voxels are facing with the interpolating surface, we classify the signed distances of two adjacent voxels into the following three situations:

- $\text{sgn}(d(v_i)) = \text{sgn}(d(v_j))$
- $\text{sgn}(d(v_i)) \neq \text{sgn}(d(v_j))$ and $|d(v_i) - d(v_j)| \leq W(v_i)$

- $\mathrm{sgn}(d(v_i)) \neq \mathrm{sgn}(d(v_j))$ and $|d(v_i) - d(v_j)| > W(v_i)$

where $d(v_i)$ and $d(v_j)$ are their signed distances, respectively, and $W(v_i)$ is the width of a voxel.

Figure 12.4 shows three examples of the signed distances of adjacent voxels. The width of the voxels is 1.0. In **Figure 12.4**(a), both voxels are outside an object whose signed distances are 1.0 and 0.8. Since the signs of the adjacent voxels are the same, the isosurface does not exist between them.

In **Figure 12.4**(b), the signs of the adjacent voxels are different. The signed distances are -0.3 and 0.6. The gray voxel means that it has a negative signed distance. Though an isosurface exists between two voxels, it is not an interpolating surface because it represents a real surface.

In **Figure 12.4**(c), the signs of the adjacent voxels are different, as in **Figure 12.4**(b). The difference from **Figure 12.4**(b) is that the signed distances are -1.0 and 0.8. Though no real surface exists between these two voxels, there is an isosurface of the SDF between them. Thus, the isosurface is interpolating a real surface.

If a surface exists between two voxels, the sum of the magnitude of the two signed distances will be smaller than the width of the voxel as the case of **Figure 12.4**(b). On the other hand, in the case of **Figure 12.4**(c), the sum is larger than 1, which is the width of the voxel. Therefore, we find an interpolating isosurface by the following inequality:

$$\mathrm{sgn}(d(v_i)) \neq \mathrm{sgn}(d(v_j)) \quad \text{and} \quad |d(v_i) - d(v_j)| > W(v_i). \qquad (12.6)$$

Since our merging method uses voxels of adaptive resolution in an octree manner, the width of the adjacent voxel can be different. Thus, (12.6) is modified to

$$|d(v_i) - d(v_j)| > \alpha D(v_i, v_j), \qquad (12.7)$$

where $D(v_i, v_j)$ is the distance of the centers of two adjacent voxels and α is a parameter defined by the user. If $\alpha = 1.0$, the condition is equal to (12.6) except changing $W(v)$ to $D(v_i, v_j)$. Thus, we use $\alpha = 1.0$ as a default value. Moreover, the area of surface s between two voxels changes if we use voxels of adaptive resolution. The width of a voxel of the depth level $l(v)$ is $2^{-l(v)}$, when the width of the root node of an octree is 1; the area of surface s between two voxels, whose depth levels $l(v_i)$ and $l(v_j)$, is approximated by $s = 4^{-\max(l(v_i), l(v_j))}$, which is the area of the face of the smaller voxel of the two voxels. Thus, (12.5) can be rewritten as follows:

$$\hat{A} = \sum_{i,j} S(v_i, v_j) \qquad (12.8)$$

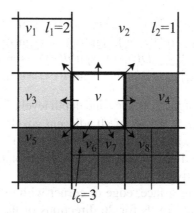

Figure 12.5. A 2D example of adjacent voxels of different sizes: An adjacent voxel shares a face, edge or corner with the voxel of interest. $v_1, \ldots, v_8$ are the adjacent voxels of the voxel of interest v. Since a voxel v_2 is larger than v, the area between v and v_2 is found twice as an adjacent voxel. On the other hand, if the resolution of adjacent voxels is finer than the voxel of interest, both v_6 and v_7 are considered as adjacent voxels.

$$
S(v_i, v_j) = \begin{cases} 4^{-\max(l(v_i), l(v_j))} & \text{if } \mathrm{sgn}(d(v_i)) \neq \mathrm{sgn}(d(v_j)) \\ & \text{and } |d(v_i) - d(v_j)| > \alpha D(v_i, v_j) \\ 0 & \text{otherwise.} \end{cases}
$$

4.3 Minimizing Surface Area by Flipping Signs

To minimize the area of interpolating surface, we propose a method that flips the signs of signed distances, because their signs are important to generate an interpolating surface. Even after flipping signs, (12.8) can be computed because the magnitudes of signed distances do not change by flipping the signs. Thus, our method iteratively updates the SDF to minimize the area. At each step, we compute the area of interpolating surface around each voxel before and after flipping the sign. If the area around a voxel decreases by flipping the sign, we update the SDF by changing the sign for the voxel.

Now, we compute the surface area around a voxel with all adjacent voxels. If the sizes of adjacent voxels are the same, the number of adjacent voxels in a 3D space is 26. If the voxel of interest is a voxel of depth level l and has a signed distance d, we compute the following four types of areas around the voxel:

$$
\hat{A}_k(v) = \sum_{v_i \in V_k} 4^{-\max(l(v), l(v_i))}, \quad k = 1, \ldots, 4 \tag{12.9}
$$

$$V_1 = \{v_i \mid |d(v)-d(v_i)| \leq \alpha D(v, v_i),\ \mathrm{sgn}(d(v)) \neq \mathrm{sgn}(d(v_i)),\ v_i \in V_{all}\}$$
$$V_2 = \{v_i \mid |d(v)-d(v_i)| > \alpha D(v, v_i),\ \mathrm{sgn}(d(v)) \neq \mathrm{sgn}(d(v_i)),\ v_i \in V_{all}\}$$
$$V_3 = \{v_i \mid |-d(v)-d(v_i)| \leq \alpha D(v, v_i),\ \mathrm{sgn}(d(v)) = \mathrm{sgn}(d(v_i)),\ v_i \in V_{all}\}$$
$$V_4 = \{v_i \mid |-d(v)-d(v_i)| > \alpha D(v, v_i),\ \mathrm{sgn}(d(v)) = \mathrm{sgn}(d(v_i)),\ v_i \in V_{all}\}$$

where $d(v_i)$ and $l(v_i)$ the signed distance and depth level of one of the adjacent voxels v_i respectively. V_{all} is the set of all adjacent voxels. $\hat{A}_1(v)$ and $\hat{A}_3(v)$ are the area of real surface before and after flipping the signed distance d respectively, while $\hat{A}_2(v)$ and $\hat{A}_4(v)$ are the area of interpolating surface before and after flipping it respectively.

An adjacent voxel shares a face, edge or corner with the voxel of interest. Thus, we find the adjacent voxels for 26 directions of the voxel of interest. **Figure 12.5** shows a 2D example of computing (12.9) with adjacent voxels of different sizes. $v_1, \ldots, v_8$ are the adjacent voxels of the voxel of interest v. In this 2D figure, we find the adjacent voxels for 8 directions in a 2D space. If an adjacent voxel is larger than the voxel of interest, the same adjacent voxel is found multiple times. The area is computed multiple times in (12.9). In this example, since a voxel v_2 is larger than v, the area between v and v_2 is computed twice. On the other hand, if the resolution of adjacent voxels is finer than the voxel of interest, the number of adjacent voxels increases. In this example, the voxels v_6, v_7 and v_8 are smaller than v. Both v_6 and v_7 are considered as adjacent voxels though they share the same face with v. Therefore, $V_{all} = \{v_1, v_2, v_2, v_3, v_4, v_5, v_6, v_7, v_8\}$ in this case.

The depth levels of the voxels are $l(v_2) = 1$, $l(v) = l(v_1) = l(v_3) = l(v_4) = l(v_5) = 2$, and $l(v_6) = l(v_7) = l(v_8) = 3$. The area of surface between v and v_3 is approximated as $1/2^2 \times 1/2^2 = 1/16$. Similarly, the area between v and v_6 is $1/2^3 \times 1/2^3 = 1/64$, and the area between v and v_2 is $2 \times 1/2^2 \times 1/2^2 = 1/8$. Now, we assume that the adjacent voxels are categorized as follows: the white voxels, v_1 and v_2, are the case 4, the light gray voxel v_3 is the case 3, the gray voxel v_4 is the case 2, and the dark gray voxels, v_5, v_6, v_7 and v_8, are the case 1 in (12.9), respectively. In this 2D example, the areas becomes as follows: $\hat{A}_1(v) = 1/4^2 + 3 \times 1/4^3 = 7/64$, $\hat{A}_2(v) = 1/4^2 = 1/16$, $\hat{A}_3(v) = 1/4^2 = 1/16$, and $\hat{A}_4(v) = 2 \times 1/4^2 + 1/4^2 = 3/16$.

If $\hat{A}_4(v) < \hat{A}_2(v)$, the area of interpolating surface decreases by flipping the sign. We extend this simple criterion as follows by considering the both real and interpolating surface:

$$\hat{A}_1(v) + \hat{A}_4(v) < \beta(\hat{A}_1(v) + \hat{A}_2(v) + \hat{A}_3(v) + \hat{A}_4(v)), \qquad (12.10)$$

where β is a parameter defined by the user. If $\beta = 0.5$ and $\hat{A}_1(v) = \hat{A}_3(v)$, the condition becomes $\hat{A}_4(v) < \hat{A}_2(v)$, which is the simplest criterion. Thus, we use $\beta = 0.5$ as a default value.

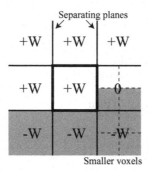

Figure 12.6. The adjacent volume of a voxel is separated to 9 parts by 6 planes which consists of the faces of the voxel. This figure shows the 2D slice of an example. Smaller voxels exist in the adjacent volume (right side). Temporary signed distances are assigned for each part as follows: if it only includes voxels of positive or negative signed distances, we assign W or $-W$ respectively, and otherwise, we assign 0, where W is the width of voxel.

If the voxel of interest satisfies (12.10), we can decrease the area of interpolating surface by flipping the sign of the signed distance $d(v)$. Our method iterates flipping the signs until no voxels satisfy (12.10). In some situations, since it is not always $|-d(v)-d(v_i)| \leq \alpha D(v, v_i)$ when $|d(v)-d(v_i)| > \alpha D(v, v_i)$, the signs of the flipping voxels may oscillate and the number of flipping voxels may not converge to 0. In such cases, we increase α or β and relax the condition during iteration if the convergence becomes slow.

After one iteration, we can restrict the voxels to examine their signs. If the signs of a voxel and its adjacent voxels did not flip in the previous iteration, we do not have to examine it in the current iteration because the result of (12.10) does not change. Thus, we record the voxels whose signs were flipped, and examine only these voxels and their adjacent ones in the next iteration.

The pseudo code of the proposed method is as follows. v and v_i are nodes (voxels) of an octree, $d(v)$ and $d(v_i)$ are their signed distances, and $l(v)$ and $l(v_i)$ are their levels in the octree, respectively. Since the structure of the octree is already determined by the process of computing the SDF, this procedure does not change the structure. α and β are parameters described above. We use a voxel of the finest resolution at each position as an adjacent voxel. $d_o(v)$ is the new signed distance, which is used in the next iteration. We start this **FlipSign** procedure from the root node, and iterate it until no voxels are flipped.

Algorithm: FlipSign(v)
  if need to examine v **then**
    $\hat{A}_1(v), \hat{A}_2(v), \hat{A}_3(v), \hat{A}_4(v) \leftarrow 0$
    for all adjacent voxels v_i of v **do**
      $D(v, v_i) \leftarrow$ the distance between v and v_i
      if $\mathrm{sgn}(d(v)) \neq \mathrm{sgn}(d(v_i))$ **then**
        if $|d(v) - d(v_i)| \leq \alpha D(v, v_i)$ **then**
          $\hat{A}_1(v) \leftarrow \hat{A}_1(v) + 4^{-\max(l(v), l(v_i))}$
        else
          $\hat{A}_2(v) \leftarrow \hat{A}_2(v) + 4^{-\max(l(v), l(v_i))}$
        end if
      else
        if $|-d(v) - d(v_i)| \leq \alpha D(v, v_i)$ **then**
          $\hat{A}_3(v) \leftarrow \hat{A}_3(v) + 4^{-\max(l(v), l(v_i))}$
        else
          $\hat{A}_4(v) \leftarrow \hat{A}_4(v) + 4^{-\max(l(v), l(v_i))}$
        end if
      end if
    end for
    if $\hat{A}_1(v) + \hat{A}_4(v) < \beta(\hat{A}_1(v) + \hat{A}_2(v) + \hat{A}_3(v) + \hat{A}_4(v))$
      $d_o(v) \leftarrow -d(v)$
    else
      $d_o(v) \leftarrow d(v)$
    end if
  end if
  if v is nonterminal **then**
    for all children v_j ($j = 0, \ldots, 7$) of v
      FlipSign(v_j)
    end for
  end if

4.4   Local Smoothing of Interpolating Surface

By flipping the signs of an SDF, we minimize the area of interpolating surface. While the resulting surface becomes a smooth surface from a global point of view, a mesh model generated by MC is not smooth from a local point of view. The reason is that MC interpolates the signed distances to generate vertices; however, it is not suitable for interpolating surfaces because the magnitudes of the signed distances for them are much larger than the width of the voxels. Therefore, we recompute the signed distances before generating interpolating surfaces by MC.

First, we separate the adjacent volume into $3 \times 3 \times 3 = 27$ parts by 6 planes which are the faces of a voxel. **Figure 12.6** shows the 2D slice of an example. The adjacent volume is separated into 9 parts in this figure. A part can include several voxels if smaller voxels exists in the octree as shown in **Figure 12.6**. Voxels that have positive and negative signed distances are indicated by white and gray voxels respectively. Second, to recompute the

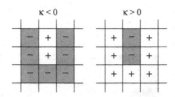

Figure 12.7. Two examples of the relationship between signed distances and curvature: the sign of the signed distance of the center voxel is opposite to that of the curvature κ.

signed distance, we assign a temporary signed distance to each part as follows: if it only includes voxels of positive or negative signed distances, we assign W or $-W$ respectively, and otherwise, we assign 0, where W is the width of the voxel. Finally, we assign a new signed distance to the center voxel by computing the average of 27 temporary signed distances. In the case of **Figure 12.6**, the new signed distance is $0.22W$. Since the scale of a new signed distance is nearly equal to the width of the voxels, a smooth mesh model can be generated by MC.

4.5 Analysis of Interpolating Surface

In this section, we analyze the surface that is obtained by generating the mesh model of an SDF after flipping the signs. The change of a signed distance updated by our method is represented as $d_{n+1} = d_n + G$, where d is a signed distance, n is the number of iterations, and G is the offset by flipping. When the algorithm flips the sign, $G = -2d_n$. If we discretize (12.1) with a time step Δt, (12.1) becomes $d_{n+1} = d_n - \Delta t |\nabla d_n| F$. By substituting these two equations, we obtain $F = \frac{2d_n}{\Delta t |\nabla d_n|}$. When the algorithm does not flip the sign, $G = F = 0$. Consequently, the speed function F is represented as follows:

$$F = \begin{cases} \frac{2d_n}{|\nabla d_n| \Delta t} & \text{if (12.10) is satisfied} \\ 0 & \text{otherwise.} \end{cases} \qquad (12.11)$$

Since $\text{sgn}(d_n) = -\text{sgn}(\kappa)$, our method smoothes out an isosurface the same way as a level set method with $F = -\kappa$ does by minimizing the curvature. **Figure 12.7** shows two examples of SDF, and $+$ and $-$ mean the sign of signed distances. If the adjacent voxels that have different signs satisfy (12.7), the center voxel of both cases in **Figure 12.7** satisfies (12.10). The signed distance of the center voxel d and the curvature κ have the opposite sign.

Because our method approximates the speed function by flipping the signs of an SDF, the smoothness of the isosurface is not taken into account from the local point of view as described in Section 4.4. However, it is guaranteed that an isosurface exists between positive and negative voxels. Therefore,

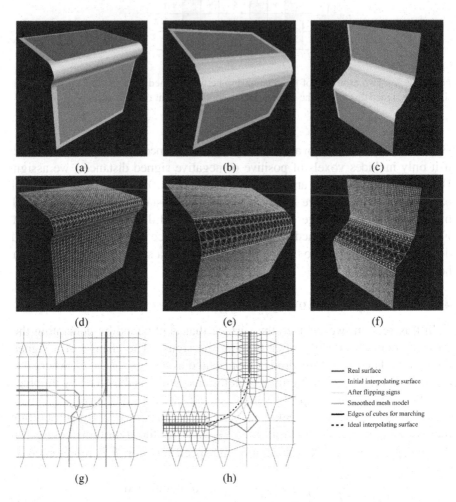

Figure 12.8.   The gap between two synthesized surfaces is filled by the proposed method: (a), (b) and (c) The real surfaces of the objects are indicated by blue planes. The white surfaces are the results of interpolating surfaces obtained by the proposed method. (d), (e) and (f) The results are represented by the wire-frame. (g) and (h) are the 2D slices of (a) and (b) respectively. The black lines are the edges of cubes for marching, which connect the centers of voxels in an octree as shown in **Figure 12.1**. The real surface is indicated by blue lines. The red lines are the initial interpolating surface computed from the real surfaces. After flipping signs to minimize the surface area, we obtain the interpolating surfaces indicated by yellow lines. Green lines indicate a smooth interpolating surface obtained by recomputing the signed distances.

the accuracy of our method is defined by voxel size. Since we use an SDF of adaptive resolution, the speed of convergence is fast where a voxel is far from the real surface. This characteristic is useful for filling gaps in the high curvature area and large holes. The resolution of interpolating mesh model is determined by the voxel size. Since the voxel size is determined by (12.3), the resolution, which is the density of vertices of a mesh model, is inversely proportional to the distance to the real surface.

Meanwhile, the convergence of our method is not guaranteed as described in Section 4.3 because our method is a discretized approximation of partial differential equations. Thus, we introduced the two parameters, α and β, to make sure of the convergence. Instead of stopping flipping by the maximum number of iteration, we relax the condition by increasing α and β to converge gradually. Since their default values are determined from their definition, we just increase them slowly to avoid a sudden convergence. If we choose the slow change of the parameters to become the convergence, it would not be a sensitive choice because the parameters just make the convergence slow. Even if we increase them more slowly, although more iterations are necessary before convergence, the computational cost does not increase so much because the voxels to be examined is restricted as described in Section 4.3.

5. Experiments

We first evaluate the proposed method with synthesized objects as shown in **Figure 12.8**. The real surfaces of the objects, which simulate the observation of a sensor, are indicated by blue planes in **Figure 12.8**(a), (b), and (c). A gap exists between two surfaces for each object. The white surfaces are the results of interpolating surfaces obtained by the proposed method. **Figure 12.8**(d), (e), and (f) show the wire-frame representations of the results. **Figure 12.8**(g) and (h) are 2D slices of (a) and (b) respectively. The black lines are the edges of cubes for marching, which connect the centers of voxels in an octree as shown in **Figure 12.1**. The real surface is indicated by the blue lines. The red lines are the initial interpolating surfaces computed from the real surfaces.

In the case of (g), though the gap is not so large compared to the voxel size, the initial surface diverges far away from the real surface. After flipping signs to minimize the surface area, we obtain the interpolating surfaces indicated by yellow lines. The interpolating surfaces smoothly connect with the real surfaces from the global point of view. Since they are not smooth from the local point of view, we recompute the signed distances and obtain a smooth interpolating surface indicated by green lines.

In the case of (h), the ideal interpolating surface becomes a circular arc indicated by a dotted line if the curvature is minimized. We estimate the error of the interpolating surface from the ideal one by computing the distance of

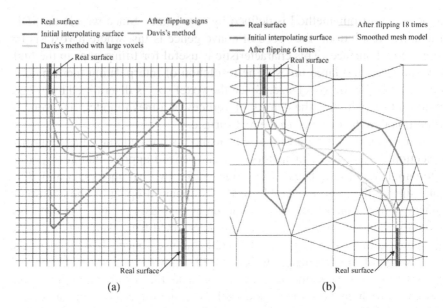

(a)   (b)

Figure 12.9. The 2D slices of the results of **Figure 12.8**(c): (a) with an SDF of fixed resolution, (b) with an SDF of adaptive resolution. In (a), the real surface is indicated by blue lines, and the red and light-blue lines are the initial and final interpolating surfaces. The orange line is the result of Davis's method after 300 iterations. The light-orange line is the result with three times larger voxels than that shown in the figure. In (b), the light-blue and yellow lines show the interpolating surface after flipping signed distances 6 and 18 times respectively. The green line indicates a smooth interpolating surface obtained by recomputing the signed distances.

the vertices of a mesh model of the surface from the circular arc. If the size of the finest voxel is 1, the mean distance is 0.27 and the maximum distance is 1.21, while the width of the gap is 25.3. If we compare the error with the voxel that generates the vertex, which becomes larger where it is far from the real surfaces, the mean and maximum distance is 6.5% and 20.0% of the voxel size respectively. Because the error is small compared to the voxel size, our method successfully obtains the interpolating surface.

Figure 12.9 shows the 2D slices of the results of **Figure 12.8**(c). The gap of **Figure 12.8**(c) is relatively large compared to the voxel size. We estimate the effectiveness of the adaptive signed distance field in the case of a large gap. **Figure 12.9**(a) shows the results with an SDF of fixed resolution. The real surface is indicated by blue lines. The red and light-blue lines are the initial and final interpolating surfaces. Since small voxels are used everywhere, the convergence stops before fully minimizing the surface area. We compare Davis's method [12] as another method that uses grids of fixed resolution. The orange line is the result of Davis's method after 300 iterations. The convergence stops before fully smoothing out. If the method is applied with large voxels, the re-

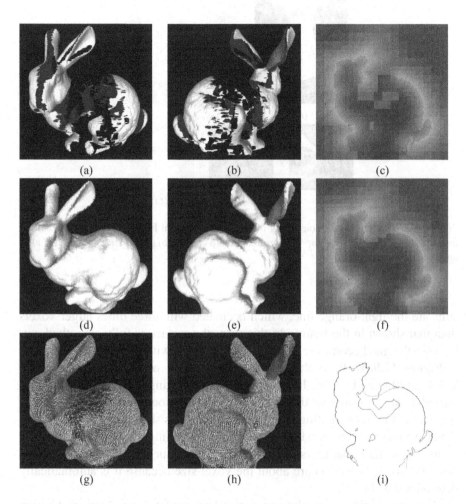

Figure 12.10. Interpolation of large holes and gaps between two range images: (a),(b) are two range images acquired from opposite viewpoints that are already aligned. (c) is a 2D slice of the initial SDF computed from the two range images. (d),(e),(g),(h) show the resulting mesh model of filling holes and gaps. (f) is a 2D slice of the SDF after flipping signs. (i) is a 2D slice of the generated mesh models.

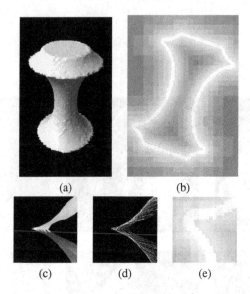

Figure 12.11. The result of hole filling of the object shown in **Figure 12.3**: (a) the resulting mesh model; (c),(d) the zoom-up view around a sharp corner; (b),(e) 2D slices of the SDF after applying the proposed method.

sults are the light-orange line, which is created with three times larger voxels than that shown in the figure. In this case, the surface is fully smoothed out, because the gap becomes relatively small compare with the voxel size.

Figure 12.9(b) shows the results with an SDF of adaptive resolution. The light-blue and yellow lines show the interpolating surface after flipping signed distances 6 and 18 times respectively. A smooth interpolating surface is obtained by recomputing the signed distances as shown by the green line. When we use an SDF of adaptive resolution for filling a gap, we successfully obtained the interpolating surface if the gap is much larger than the voxel size. We do not have to care about the voxel size because it is automatically determined by (12.3).

Next, we apply our method to a standard model from Stanford University [26]. **Figure 12.10**(a) and (b) show two range images. They are acquired from the opposite viewpoints, and the mutual positions are already aligned. There are large holes and gaps between the two range images because of occlusion. **Figure 12.10**(c) is a 2D slice of the initial SDF computed from the two range images. The meaning of the colors is the same as those in **Figure 12.3**; for example, yellow and red voxels indicate that they have positive signed distances, and blue voxels indicate negative ones. **Figure 12.10**(d) and (e) are the results of filling holes and gaps and **Figure 12.10**(g) and (h) are the wire-frame representations. **Figure 12.10**(f) is a 2D slice of the SDF after

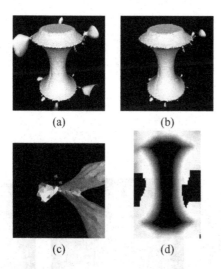

Figure 12.12. The result of hole filling by Davis's method: (a),(b) are the resulting mesh model after 100 and 300 iterations, respectively. (c) is the zoom-up view around a sharp corner. (d) is a slice of the volumetric representation of (b).

flipping signs. The isosurface becomes smooth from a global point of view. **Figure 12.10**(i) is a 2D slice of the generated mesh models. The range images are indicated by blue lines, and the red lines are the initial interpolating surfaces. The green line indicates a smooth interpolating surface obtained by recomputing the signed distances. Our method successfully interpolates the large holes by using an adaptive signed distance field.

Next, we test our algorithm using an object shown in **Figure 12.3**, which has holes around the sharp corners. **Figure 12.11** shows the result of hole filling. **Figure 12.11**(a) is the resulting mesh model, and the zoom-up view around a sharp corner is shown in (c) and (d). **Figure 12.11**(b) and (e) are 2D slices of the SDF after applying the proposed method. Since our method uses an SDF of adaptive resolution, it successfully removed the interpolating surfaces which are far from the real surface.

Now, we compare our method with Davis's method [12]. First, we converted the mesh model of this object shown in **Figure 12.3**(a) to the volumetric representation of Davis's method by a tool provided by Allen [27]. We adjusted the parameter so that the size of voxels after conversion was the same as the original size. **Figure 12.12** shows the result of hole filling by this method. **Figure 12.12**(a) and (b) are the resulting mesh model after 100 and 300 iterations, respectively. The interpolating surface still exists where it is far from the real surface. **Figure 12.12**(d) is a slice of the volumetric representation of (b). Positive and negative voxels are represented by white and black. The isosurface

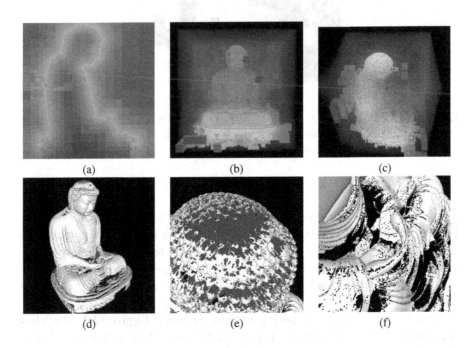

Figure 12.13.   The SDF and mesh models of the Great Buddha of Kamakura before filling holes: it is difficult to observe the top of the head and the inside of the hands, since the Buddha is a large object. (a) is a 2D slice of the SDF. (b),(c) are the rendering results of the SDF directly by volume rendering. In (d),(e),(f) the model has many holes.

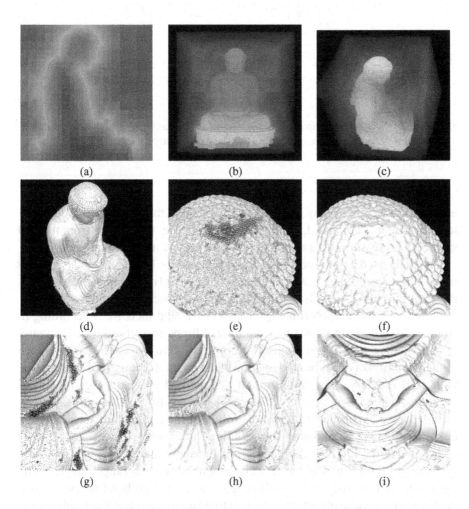

Figure 12.14. The models after flipping the signs of the SDF of the Buddha: (a) a 2D slice of the SDF; (b),(c) the results of volume rendering; (d),(f),(h) the mesh model rendered with triangles; (e),(g) the wire-frame representations; (i) the red surfaces are created by the voxels that do not converge without changing α and β.

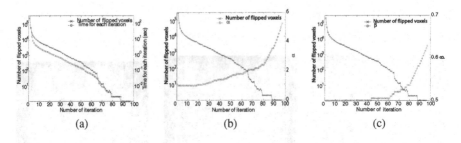

Figure 12.15. The relationship between the number of flipped voxels and the computational time, α and β. The scales of the number of voxels and computational time are logarithmic.

exists at the voxels of gray. Since it is obvious that the isosurface around the top-left corner is collapsed, the interpolating surface that are far from the real surface. The reason is that the method uses a grid of fixed resolution.

The SDF used by our method is divided into $128 \times 128 \times 128 (= 2^{21})$ voxels in the finest resolution; however, since we use voxels of adaptive resolution, the total number of voxels is 130,521. We construct the resulting SDF by 20 iterations. In this experiment, we set α to 1, and increase β according to $\beta_{n+1} = 1.01\beta_n$ at time n when the number of flipped voxels does not decrease. It starts with $\beta = 0.5$, and finally β becomes 0.52 in this case. We tested the implementation of our proposed method using an Intel Xeon 2.4GHz processor with 1GB memory. The total time of our method was 5.72 seconds for 20 iterations, while Davis's method takes 51.4 seconds for 300 iterations.

Finally, we experimented with hole filling of the unobserved surface of the Great Buddha of Kamakura. Before filling holes and gaps, we got a model shown in **Figure 12.13**. It is created from 16 range images; about 0.3 million vertices and 0.6 million triangles were contained in each range image. The merged model consists of 3.0 million vertices and 6.0 million triangles. Since the Buddha is a large object, it is difficult to observe the top of the head and the inside of the hands. **Figure 12.13**(a) is a 2D slice of the SDF, and (b) and (c) are the rendering results of the SDF directly by volume rendering [28]. The model has a great many holes, which are shown in **Figure 12.13**(d),(e) and (f).

After flipping the signs of the SDF, we obtained the model shown in **Figure 12.14**. **Figure 12.14**(a) is a 2D slice of the SDF, and (b) and (c) are the results of volume rendering. The isosurfaces that are far from the real surfaces are removed after flipping signs. **Figure 12.14**(d),(f) and (h) were rendered with triangles, and (e) and (g) are the wire-frame representations. We successfully filled holes of the model by converting the SDF to a mesh model. Because we used voxels in adaptive resolution, large triangles were generated to fill large holes using marching cubes with voxels of adaptive size.

Since the Buddha has an intricate shape, we estimated the convergence of flipping signs. If $\alpha = 1.0$ and $\beta = 0.5$ are fixed, some voxels oscillate and the number of flipped voxels does not converge to 0. The red parts in **Figure 12.14**(i) depict the surfaces created by the voxels that oscillate without changing α and β. In this experiment, we increased both α and β according to $\alpha_{n+1} = 1.05\alpha_n$ if $M_n \geq 0.95M_{n-1}$, and $\beta_{n+1} = 1.01\beta_n$ if $M_n \geq M_{n-1}$, where M_n is the number of flipped voxels at time n. They are empirically chosen to converge slowly. **Figure 12.15** shows the relationship between the number of flipped voxels and the time for each iteration, α and β; the scales of the number of voxels and computational time are logarithmic. After the first iteration, the computational time is drastically reduced because we restrict voxels to be examined by the method described in Section 4.3. The number of flipped voxels is reduced quickly at the beginning, and it is much smaller than the total number of voxels. Thus, the reduction of computation by using the database of flipped voxels works effectively. Since the number of flipped voxels finally becomes zero by changing α and β, the algorithm converges even if the object has an intricate shape.

The SDF of the Buddha model has $1024 \times 1024 \times 1024$ voxels in the finest resolution, while the actual number of voxels is 17,024,273. Flipping signs is iterated 97 times, and the total computational time was about 14 minutes. The memory used was about 550MB at maximum. The number of triangles and surface areas after filling holes was 5,383,549 and 402.75m^2, while those of the original model were 5,241,486 and 329.23m^2. (The height of the Buddha is 11.3m.) The rate of increase of the triangles was only 2.7%, while that of the area was about 22%. Thus, our algorithm efficiently filled holes with few additional triangles.

6.   Conclusion

We have proposed a novel method to fill holes of a 3D model. Though the surface that is suitable for filling holes varies with applications, our method obtains an interpolating surface by minimizing the curvature at the same time that the interpolating surface is smoothly continuous with the real surface. Our method computes a signed distance field and minimizes the area of interpolating surface by computing it in the neighborhood of a voxel both before and after flipping the sign of the signed distance of the voxel. The initial state that we use is automatically obtained by computing the distance to the closest point of the real surface. Unlike PDE-based methods, it is not necessary for our method to define both a 3D domain to be considered and a boundary condition. Moreover, in cases where a hole is much larger than the voxel size, and a gap exists on an edge of a sharp corner, the relative voxel size compared to the size of a hole is important for the convergence of iteration. Therefore, our method uses an adaptive signed distance field that consists of voxels of adaptive resolution. The efficiency of our method was validated in the experiments by using synthesized surfaces and real range images. As future work, we will improve the accuracy that is determined by the voxel size, by post-processing to obtain an optimal interpolating surface. Moreover, though the voxel size is determined by (12.3), we will estimate the optimal size of voxels in an adaptive SDF to fill holes.

Acknowledgments

This research was supported, in part, by Ministry of Education, Culture, Sports, Science and Technology under the Leading Project, "Development of High Fidelity Digitization Software for Large-Scale and Intangible Cultural Assets," and, in part, by Japan Science and Technology Agency, under the CREST program, "Automatic generation of virtual models of cultural heritage."

References

[1] Cyra Technologies, Inc., "Cyrax 2500," http://www.cyra.com.

[2] MINOLTA Co. Ltd., "Vivid 900 non-contact digitizer," http://www.minoltausa.com/vivid/.

[3] K. Sato and S. Inokuchi, "Range-imaging system utilizing nematic liquid crystal mask," in *Proc. International Conference on Computer Vision*, 1987, pp. 657–661.

[4] P. Liepa, "Filling holes in meshes," in *Symposium on Geometry Processing*, 2003, pp. 200–205.

[5] M. Kass, A. Witkin, and D. Terzopoulos, "Snakes: Active contour models," *International Journal of Computer Vision*, vol. 1, no. 4, pp. 321–331, 1988.

[6] H. Delingette, M. Hebert, and K. Ikeuchi, "Shape representation and image segmentation using deformable surfaces," *Image and vision computing*, vol. 10, no. 3, pp. 132–144, April 1992.

[7] Y. Chen and G. Medioni, "Description of complex objects from multiple range images using an inflating balloon model," *Computer Vision and Image Understanding: CVIU*, vol. 61, no. 3, pp. 325–334, 1995.

[8] B. Curless and M. Levoy, "A volumetric method for building complex models from range images," in *Proc. SIGGRAPH'96*. ACM, 1996, pp. 303–312.

[9] R. Whitaker, "A level-set approach to 3d reconstruction from range data," *International Journal of Computer Vision*, vol. 29, no. 3, pp. 203–231, October 1998.

[10] H.-K. Zhao, S. Osher, and R. Fedkiw, "Fast surface reconstruction using the level set method," in *Proc. First IEEE Workshop on Variational and Level Set Methods, in conjunction with Proc. ICCV '01.* IEEE, 2001, pp. 194–202.

[11] J. Carr, R. Beatson, J. Cherrie, T. Mitchell, W. Fright, B. McCallum, and T. Evans, "Reconstruction and representation of 3d objects with radial basis functions," in *Proc. SIGGRAPH 2001.* ACM, 2001, pp. 67–76.

[12] J. Davis, S. Marschner, M. Garr, and M. Levoy, "Filling holes in complex surfaces using volumetric diffusion," in *Proc. First International Symposium on 3D Data Processing, Visualization, and Transmission*, 2002, pp. 428–438.

[13] J. Verdera, V. Caselles, M. Bertalmio, and G. Sapiro, "Inpainting surface holes," in *Proc. 2003 International Conference on Image Processing*, vol. 2, 2003, pp. 903–906.

[14] U. Clarenz, U. Diewald, G. Dziuk, M. Rumpf, and R. Rusu, "A finite element method for surface restoration with smooth boundary conditions," *Computer Aided Geometric Design*, vol. 21, no. 5, pp. 427–445, 2004.

[15] T. Masuda, "Filling the signed distance field by fitting local quadrics," in *Proc. the 2nd International Symposium on 3D Data Processing, Visualization and Transmission (3DPVT 2004)*, 2004, pp. 1003–1010.

[16] J. Sethian, *Level Set Methods and Fast Marching Methods.* Cambridge University Press, 1999.

[17] D. Chopp, "Computing minimal surfaces via level set curvature flow," *Journal of Computational Physics*, vol. 106, no. 1, pp. 77–91, 1993.

[18] M. Wheeler, Y. Sato, and K. Ikeuchi, "Consensus surfaces for modeling 3d objects from multiple range images," in *Proc. International Conference on Computer Vision*, January 1998, pp. 917–924.

[19] H. Hoppe, T. DeRose, T. Duchamp, J. McDonald, and W. Stuetzle, "Surface reconstruction from unorganized points," in *Proc. SIGGRAPH'92.* ACM, 1992, pp. 71–78.

[20] T. Masuda, "A unified approach to volumetric registration and integration of multiple range images," in *Proc. the 14th International Conference on Pattern Recognition*, 1998, pp. 977–981.

[21] R. Sagawa, K. Nishino, and K. Ikeuchi, "Adaptively merging large-scale range data with reflectance properties," *IEEE Transactions on Pattern Analysis and Machine Intelligence*, vol. 27, no. 3, pp. 392–405, March 2005.

[22] R. Sagawa, "Geometric and photometric merging for large-scale objects," Ph.D. dissertation, Graduate School of Engineering, The University of Tokyo, 2003.

[23] W. Lorensen and H. Cline, "Marching cubes: a high resolution 3d surface construction algorithm," in *Proc. SIGGRAPH'87*. ACM, 1987, pp. 163–170.

[24] A. Hilton, A. Stoddart, J. Illingworth, and T. Windeatt, "Reliable surface reconstruction from multiple range images," in *Proceedings of European Conference on Computer Vision*, Springer-Verlag, 1996, pp. 117–126.

[25] R. Sagawa and K. Ikeuchi, "Taking consensus of signed distance field for complementing unobservable surface," in *Proc. 3DIM 2003*, 2003, pp. 410–417.

[26] "The Stanford 3D Scanning Repository." [Online]. Available: http://www-graphics.stanford.edu/data/3Dscanrep/

[27] B. Allen, http://grail.cs.washington.edu/software-data/ply2vri/, 2002.

[28] J. Foley, A. van Dam, S. Feiner, and J. F. Hughes, *Computer Graphics: Principles and Practice in C*, 2nd ed.   Addison Wesley Professional, 1995, iSBN:0-201-84840-6.

III

COLOR ANALYSIS

Chapter 13

SIMULTANEOUS REGISTRATION OF 2D IMAGES ONTO 3D MODELS FOR TEXTURE MAPPING

Ryo Ohkubo, Ryo Kurazume, and Katsushi Ikeuchi

Abstract

Recently, creation of realistic 3D contents through sensing the real world has become fundamental for many applications. To enhance 3D geometric models obtained through laser range scanners with their textures reconstructed from several photographic 2D images taken from various view points, it is necessary to determine the camera position and orientation relative to the 3D models for each of the images.

In this chapter, a registration method is proposed, which automatically and simultaneously aligns multiple 2D images onto a 3D model. For each iteration process, correspondences between 2D edge pixels and 3D edge points are automatically searched and updated. Besides these 2D-3D edge correspondences, 2D-2D edge correspondences on 3D surface model are also considered simultaneously for global optimization among all the images. Errors are minimized by using conjugate gradient search, utilizing M-estimator for robustness. From texture mapped objects, the usefulness of the proposed simultaneous registration method is shown. Also, it is applied to the creation of digital cultural assets.

1. Introduction

1.1 Background

In recent years, widespread demand for 3D contents have been greatly increased in many areas: computer graphics, entertainment, E-commerce, preservation of cultural assets, ITS(Intelligent Transportation System), etc. However, most of them are created manually by human experts using 3D modeling systems and this input process is normally very time-consuming. To simplify the process, some research have been investigated to aid designers through novel human interfaces, like SKETCH[34] and Teddy[11].

On the other hand, in many situations, to obtain 3D models by observation of real world objects is much more convenient and reasonable. One obvious example is the faithful modeling of cultural heritages. In this case, it is essential to create realistic 3D models by measuring those objects through sensors. Recently, such measuring-techniques and algorithms for processing acquired data have been rapidly developed by many researchers.

The term "3D model" can be classified into three detailed categories: geometric model, physical model and environmental model. Therefore, to acquire the complete 3D model through observation, several processes are necessary and vast numbers of studies have been made in wide fields.

A geometric model represents the shape of objects. It is usually composed of the vertex and mesh structure (or sometimes by voxels). To build these data, several steps are necessary. First, several range images are measured by laser range scanners from various viewpoints and directions. For each pixel of a range image, the distance to the object at respective direction is stored. Therefore one range image contains shape information from one direction. Next, registration calculation is applied, which aligns multiple range images from various viewpoints to obtain the whole shape [2, 4, 24, 21]. Finally, they are merged to form a unique consensus surface of the object [17, 25].

A physical model represents colors and reflectance properties of surfaces and is an essential factor for rendering. There are numbers of research for decades and various reflection models have been studied [12]. However, the pursuit of the exact analysis is significantly difficult because the radiance observed in the scene is caused by complex interactions among surface intrinsic colors, surface reflection functions, viewing position, illumination conditions, inter-reflection, etc. Recently, several novel methods have been proposed to model realistic appearances of real objects utilizing 3D geometric models [29, 22].

An environmental model includes illumination distributions and interactions between surrounding objects (like shadows and inter-reflection), and plays an important role in achieving the mixed reality. Although it is quite difficult to formulate such a model, several approaches have been investigated lately. Global illumination is measured using a fisheye lens or a mirror ball, so that virtual objects are seamlessly synthesized onto an image of a real scene with correct shadings [27, 5, 6]. High dynamic range radiance maps which are supposed to be necessary in illumination measurements, are recovered from multiple photographs [19, 7]. Imari et al. [28] have directly estimated the illumination distribution of a real scene from a radiance distribution inside shadows cast by an object in the scene.

Recently, much interest has been focused on a physical model since nowadays the geometric models can be obtained accurately, and the need for realistic rendering of these geometric objects has increased.

Although there are various algorithms to recover detailed physical properties, the texture mapping method is a good compromise between the complexity and the quality of appearance. It does not require a large number of photographs which are usually necessary to obtain more complex physical models, and makes the measurement process easier and more practical for the wide range of applications. Indeed, the restrictions at the measurement time can become a big bottle neck in practice. Another advantage of the texture mapping method is that it can be processed entirely by normal 3D graphics hardwares.

However, for the texture mapping and the other methods which acquire the photometric attributes of 3D geometric models using 2D photographic images, it is necessary to know camera positions and directions relative to the 3D geometric models. In other words, camera parameters are required to map the coordinates between the 3D world and the 2D images.

1.2   Obtaining Camera Parameters

In most researches concerning the physical models, camera parameters have been usually assumed to be known. They can be estimated using camera calibration, which is a well-studied problem [10, 32, 36, 9]. In addition, there exist some 3D scanners which can obtain both a range image and a photometric image at the same time, which means the precise camera parameters relative to the 3D geometry are always known for each measurement. However, there are several drawbacks in the use of camera calibration and these 3D scanners, and we cannot always assume camera parameters to be known. First, although camera calibration methods are practical for the experiments taken place in the laboratories, it is inconvenient and often quite difficult to use them in the outdoor environments, especially in large-scale environment. Second, in the case of 3D-2D integrated sensors, 2D capturing systems attached to such sensors are often inferior than normal digital cameras. The image captured by them has worse quality and lower resolution, and they cannot allow sufficient configurations of capturing system like shutter speed, aperture, etc. Mounting a separate high-quality digital camera on a 3D scanner and fixing their relationship completely can solve this problem. Relative camera parameters against the 3D scanner can be calculated by camera calibration beforehand and such a system can emulate 3D-2D integrated scanners. Indeed, it can become a practical solution in many cases. Even so, there are several situations where it is favorable or necessary to take photographs separately from 3D geometry. Generally, the required sampling density for 2D photometric images is often different from 3D geometry, so extra capture of 3D data may burden the capacity and the processing time. Furthermore, the measuring situation in practice often causes various constraints and may make it impossible to use such large-scale devices: e.g., the measurements of the unfavorably located objects like cultural heritages, the measurements under controlled lighting conditions, etc.

Under the condition of uncalibrated cameras, 2D-3D registration is necessary to estimate camera parameters. There have been numerous 2D-3D registration researches and their aims are not necessarily restricted to the texture mapping, e.g., for object recognition, robot navigation, medical image processing, and etc.

2D-3D registration algorithms require some kinds of information about correspondences between 2D features and 3D features. The simplest correspondence information is specified by a set of point pairs between the 2D image and the 3D geometric model. From these correspondences the camera parameters for the 2D image can be directly calculated using standard camera calibration algorithms [10, 32, 36]. However, the problem is to find these points and pairs. Without using markers, it is difficult and not robust to detect these points and pairs automatically through image processing techniques. Therefore, specifying a set of corresponding pairs manually, i.e., the pixels on the 2D image and the corresponding points in the 3D geometries, is a commonly used approach [23–1, 20]. Since the accuracy of the obtained camera parameters heavily depends on the accuracy of point-pairs specified by the user, Neugebauer et al. [20] have refined the registration results by considering the outline of the object and the intensities of images. Instead of using a set of point pairs, a set of corresponding lines is also used to derive the camera parameters of each image [31]. They extract planar regions from the range image and a 3D line is obtained by the intersection of these regions. It is manually matched to a 2D line extracted from the image.

Debevec et al. [8] have used simple predefined models like a box and a wedge, to recover both camera parameters and 3D geometries from only photographic images. By manually specifying locations of parametric primitives for each photograph, both primitive parameters and camera parameters can be obtained at the same time.

Although the methods which need 2D-3D correspondence information specified manually by the user are robust and practical in some cases, they require tedious labor and they would fail when the number of input photographs increases. For this reason, automatic algorithms to create the correspondence information are investigated. Instead of directly searching corresponding features like points and lines, which is usually not a robust and practical process, the methods which use more structured features such as contours and edges and use the error minimization framework are proposed.

Lavallée et al. [15] have proposed a registration method which use the outline of a 3D object from volumetric medical data. The pose of a 3D smooth surface is estimated by minimizing the distance between a 3D object surface and the projection of camera-contours in 2D X-ray projections.

In the field of robot vision, the pose information of the object is estimated by the edgel correspondences [33]. The edgel is the element of the edge and their correspondences are automatically searched and updated through iterative calculations. Based on this algorithm, the registration methods for texture mapping have been studied [14, 13] and this study also utilizes this technique.

Lensch et al. [16] have used the silhouette information. The silhouette of a 3D object generated by the 3D geometric model and the silhouette extracted from the 2D image are compared and their distance is minimized by using downhill simplex method. It can utilize the acceleration of graphics hardwares for a calculation speed and register the image without user intervention through multi-resolutional approach. However, extracting the exact silhouette from 2D image is very difficult in real outdoor environments.

A few works mentioned above [16, 20, 13] have also considered the global registration problem. Besides registering each 2D image respectively, they also consider a multi-view global optimization. This is because even if one 2D image is thoroughly registered to the 3D object in the error metric of that viewpoint, it does not necessarily mean it is globally optimal. Due to various errors such as the inaccuracy of 3D geometry, the resolution of pixels, lens distortions, etc., it is impossible to make exactly correct registration. Therefore, the errors always exist and they need to be distributed globally. Otherwise, when textures are mapped using multiple photographs, undesirable artifacts may be caused around the boundary where textures from different views intersect.

In [20] and [16], the points on the 3D surface which are visible from multiple images are used for the optimization of 2D-2D registration. For such points, the former method calculates a 3D euclidean distance to the nearest edge on each visible image and minimizes these differences. The latter uses the difference of colors projected from each visible image. For the color component, hue and saturation channels are used to reduce the influence of the specular element.

Kurazume et al. [13] have used the technique of epipolar geometry, instead of minimizing the differences of image attributes on the 3D surface points. It extracts the point correspondences between adjacent images using KLT method [30] and calculates the relative camera transformation and the epipolar lines of corresponding point pairs [35]. For the global registration, the sum of distance between the point and its corresponding epipolar line on each image is considered. However, finding corresponding points between two images is a very difficult task, so directly depending on these results makes the registration process not robust. Further, when epipolar lines are almost parallel, which is often the case in adjacent photographs taken closely, this method does not work along the direction of these lines.

1.3   Overview

In this chapter, a novel registration method is proposed, which automatically and simultaneously aligns multiple 2D images onto a 3D model. Throughout iterative calculations, the correspondence information between 2D edge pixels and 3D edge points are automatically searched and updated. Therefore, there is no need to specify corresponding points or lines manually. In addition, the global optimization among all the images are also executed by the simultaneous registration of 2D-2D edge correspondences on 3D surfaces. Outliers are eliminated using M-estimates and the errors are minimized by conjugate gradient search. Registration results are shown with the texture mapped objects and the usefulness of the proposed simultaneous registration method is shown. In addition, the application for the creation of digital cultural assets is also presented.

The remainder of this chapter is organized as follows. In Section 2, mathematical notations and camera parameters which are used in this thesis, are explained. In Section 3, a registration algorithm concerning the single 2D image and the 3D geometric model is presented. In Section 4, multiple 2D images are simultaneously registered to the 3D model through the global optimization. In Section 5, experiments are shown and results are examined. Finally, in Section 6, the summary and future work are mentioned.

2.   Preliminaries

2.1   Mathematical Notation

- Vectors are expressed in boldface type: $\mathbf{x}$ is a vector, x is a scalar.

- Unit vectors have the hat symbol: $\hat{\mathbf{x}}$ is a unit vector.

- Matrices are expressed by the capitalized and boldface character: $\mathbf{M}$ is a matrix, and especially, $\mathbf{I}$ is the identity matrix and $\mathbf{R}$ is a rotation matrix.

- $\mathbf{x}$ will be used to denote the 3D coordinate of the 3D geometric models.

- $\mathbf{y}$ will be used to denote the 2D coordinate of the 2D photometric images.

- $\mathbf{U}$ will be used to denote the 2D coordinate which is projected from the 3D world (note, this is the only vector that will be capitalized).

- Vectors should be assumed to be three dimensional except for the above.

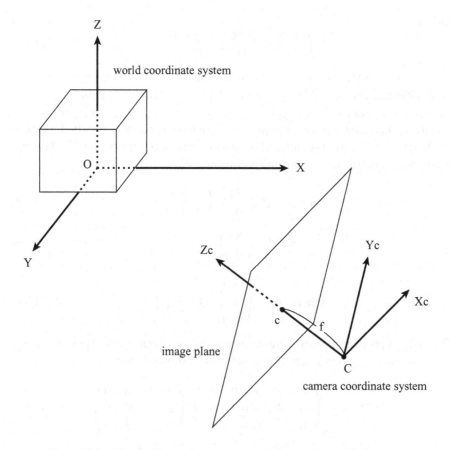

Figure 13.1.   The world coordinate system and the camera coordinate system

2.2   Camera Parameter

The 3D geometric objects are located in the world coordinate system and the camera is also located in the same world, viewing the objects. Seen from the camera, the coordinates of objects are expressed in the camera coordinate system. They are illustrated in Figure 13.1 The camera is located at C and this point is named "focal point". Z_c represents the viewing direction.

The transformation between world and camera coordinates can be described with the set of rotation and translation, $\langle \mathbf{R}, \mathbf{t} \rangle$. Since they represent the camera position and orientation, they are called "camera extrinsic parameters". Let a 3D point in the world coordinate be $\mathbf{x}_w = (x_w, y_w, z_w)$. Then, the coordinate of the point in the camera coordinate system, $\mathbf{x}_c = (x_c, y_c, z_c)$, is expressed as follows:

$$\begin{pmatrix} \mathbf{x}_c \\ 1 \end{pmatrix} = \begin{pmatrix} \mathbf{R} & \mathbf{t} \\ \mathbf{0}^\mathrm{T} & 1 \end{pmatrix} \begin{pmatrix} \mathbf{x}_w \\ 1 \end{pmatrix} \tag{13.1}$$

The photographic image can be obtained by projecting the camera-centered view onto the image plane (in Figure 13.1). The point c at which the viewing direction and the image plane intersect, is named the "principal point", and the distance between that point c and the optical point C is called the "focal length". Let the projected 2D point on the image plane be $\mathbf{U}$, then the projection equation can be written as follows:

$$\mathbf{u} = \mathbf{P} \begin{pmatrix} \mathbf{R} & \mathbf{t} \\ \mathbf{0}^\mathrm{T} & 1 \end{pmatrix} \begin{pmatrix} \mathbf{x}_w \\ 1 \end{pmatrix} \tag{13.2}$$

$$= \mathbf{P} \begin{pmatrix} \mathbf{x}_c \\ 1 \end{pmatrix} \tag{13.3}$$

$$\text{where } \mathbf{u} = \begin{pmatrix} u \\ v \\ w \end{pmatrix}, \ \mathbf{U} = \begin{pmatrix} \frac{u}{w} \\ \frac{v}{w} \end{pmatrix} \tag{13.4}$$

$\mathbf{P}$ is a 3×4 projection matrix and contains various parameters. They are called "camera intrinsic parameters", and details are shown below.

$$\mathbf{P} = \begin{pmatrix} k_u & -k_u\cot\theta & u_0 \\ 0 & k_v/\sin\theta & v_0 \\ 0 & 0 & 1 \end{pmatrix} \begin{pmatrix} f & 0 & 0 & 0 \\ 0 & f & 0 & 0 \\ 0 & 0 & 1 & 0 \end{pmatrix} \tag{13.5}$$

They consist of the focal length, principal point, aspect ratio, and skew.

As we have seen, there are two kinds of camera parameters: the intrinsic parameters and the extrinsic parameters. However, estimating both the extrinsic parameters and the intrinsic parameters simultaneously makes the registration process unstable and not robust. Therefore, only the extrinsic parameters, i.e., the camera rotation and translation $\langle \mathbf{R}, \mathbf{t} \rangle$ are optimized in this thesis. To robustly refine the focal length along with the registration process remains one of the future work.

Aside from the 2D-3D registration process, the camera intrinsic parameters need to be estimated using the camera calibration method. Among intrinsic parameters, important components are the focal length f, and the principal point (u_0, v_0). Although the precise parameters are only acquired through camera calibration, we can obtain their approximate estimates in a easy way. First, the skew and the aspect ratio can be ignored in the recent digital cameras. And often, the principal point are also presumed to be $(0, 0)$. Further, the approximate focal length can be obtained by EXIF (Exchangeable Image

File) and DCF (Design rule for Camera File system) data which are recorded in JPEG/TIFF files captured by digital cameras.

In practice, besides the camera intrinsic and extrinsic parameters, lens distortions also affect the obtained photographic image. They primarily consists of the radial distortions and the tangential distortions, which are especially outstanding when the wide-angle lenses or the small handy cameras are used. Lens distortions can be estimated by various camera calibration methods and they should be removed before any image processing.

2.3   Quaternion Representation

In the following sections, the set of camera parameters to be estimated is expressed as the vector **p**. It consists of the camera extrinsic parameters, that is, the camera position and the camera orientation. In general, it is convenient to represent them as the set of the camera rotation matrix and the camera translation vector, $\langle \mathbf{R}, \mathbf{t} \rangle$.

However, representing a rotation as the matrix form, **R**, causes a great difficulty in the computation of the optimal rotation. While a rotation in 3D space has only three degrees of freedom, a rotation matrix has nine degrees. This restricts the values of **R** in a non-linear way as follows:

$$\mathbf{R}\mathbf{R}^T = I \tag{13.6}$$

$$|\mathbf{R}| = 1 \tag{13.7}$$

R must always satisfy these constraints to represent a rotation and this makes difficult to take advantage of the linear matrix form of rotation.

The generally accepted alternative for the representation of rotation is the use of quaternion. A quaternion is a 4-vector, consisting of a 3-vector $(u, v, w)^T$ and a scalar s, that is, $\mathbf{q} = (u, v, w, s)^T$ and it can represent an arbitrary rotation in the 3D space. It has several useful characteristics.

- The constraint of rotation is easily maintained by standard vector normalization.

- The inverse rotation is obtained by simply negating first 3 components of the quaternion vector.

- It can avoid the gimbal lock problem. Roughly speaking, the continuous change of the elements always lead to the smooth change of rotation, and vice versa.

- The intermediate rotation between two quaternions can be calculated linearly.

- With the quaternion representation, the rotation between two sets of corresponding 3D points can be solved in closed form.

In addition, another important advantage of the quaternion representation is utilized in Section 3.7

Thus, the following vector is used to express the camera parameters:

$$\mathbf{p} = (\mathbf{q}^T \ \mathbf{t}^T)^T \tag{13.8}$$

where $\mathbf{p}$ is a 7-vector, $\mathbf{q}$ is a quaternion representing a camera rotation, and $\mathbf{t}$ is a 3-vector representing a camera translation. If necessary, the form of rotation matrix is also used and the rotation matrix corresponding to $\mathbf{q}$ is denoted by $\mathbf{R}(\mathbf{q})$.

3.   2D-3D Registration Algorithm

In this section, the registration method which optimizes the camera position and orientation of a 2D texture image with respect to the 3D geometric models, is described. It is accomplished through the iterative algorithms. In each stage, corresponding 2D-3D point pairs are automatically searched and the estimated camera parameters are updated. In addition, the robust estimation framework is used to eliminate the unfavorable effects of outliers.

3.1   Outline of 2D-3D Registration

Nowadays, we can capture the precise 3D geometric models through sensing the real world objects. In addition, 2D photographic images of those objects can be easily obtained with digital cameras. The 2D-3D registration shown in this chapter is the problem to estimate the camera positions and orientations from which the photograph is taken, and to make the correspondence between 3D geometries and 2D photometric attributes (colors, etc.). The camera parameters consist of the camera rotation and translation and are written as $\mathbf{p} = (\mathbf{q}^T, \ \mathbf{t}^T)^T$.

To align the 2D image with the 3D model, the edge features of the 2D image and the edge features of the 3D model are considered. The outline of the registration algorithm is shown in Figure 13.2. The "edgel" refers to the edge element (cf. pixel as the picture element). First, 2D edgels and 3D edgels are extracted from the 2D image and the 3D geometric model. Next, their correspondences are automatically searched and then, camera parameters are adjusted to minimize their distances. After that, the new 3D edgels are detected using the newly estimated camera parameters and the above processes are repeated iteratively.

Note that in this 2D-3D registration algorithm the 3D geometric model is not necessarily restricted to the one object. We can assume many objects as long as they provide the 3D edgels, so this method is applicable to the outdoor environment, too. However, in the presence of multiple objects, especially when they are located at the different distances, the small change of camera

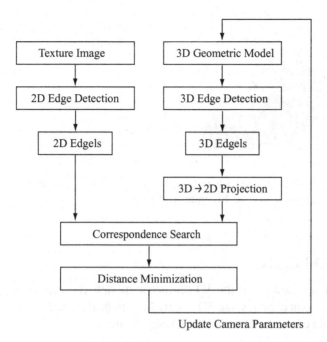

Figure 13.2.   Outline of the 2D-3D registration algorithm

parameters is likely to cause the large separate movements of objects. Therefore, the algorithm is supposed to be not so robust compared to the environment of the indoor experiments, and the importance of initial position specification grows.

3.2   2D Edgels

The detection of 2D edgels from the 2D photographic image is a very important stage in the registration algorithm. To achieve the stable and robust registration, well-structured edges are crucial. If the edges are too scattered and dense, the mismatch rate of 2D-3D correspondences will expand. Simple edge detection methods such as the Sobel operator is likely to cause such noisy edges. In out experiment, we use the Canny edge detector [3]. The example of texture image and the result of 2D edge detection are shown in Figure 13.3. Each edge pixel drawn as the black pixels in Figure 13.3(b) constructs the 2D edgel. Note that 2D edgels do not change throughout the whole registration process and they are detected only once.

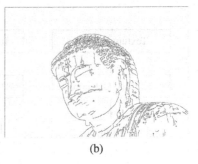

(a)   (b)

Figure 13.3.   Result of the 2D edge detection: (a) original 2D photographic image, (b) edge image of (a). Each black pixel on (b) constructs the 2D edgel.

3.3   3D Edgels

Since the appearance of the 3D geometric models changes as the estimated camera viewpoint changes, the 3D edgels have to be detected at every iteration. The desirable characteristics of the 3D edgels are

- They should have the similar edge structures as the 2D edgels (similarity).

- They should contain sufficient details to register the image precisely, while they should not have too much minor junks (density).

- They should be robustly detected from various kinds of 3D models, e.g., the models might be noisy (robustness).

Considering these conditions, the three types of 3D edgels are proposed in this chapter: occluding edgels, reflectance edgels, and rendered edgels (in Figure 13.4).

1 Occluding Edgels:
   Occluding edgels are detected around the surfaces whose normal are almost perpendicular to the viewing direction (in Figure 13.4(b)). They are supposed to cause the distance gap and can be seen as the edge. To reduce the effects of noise, surface normals are calculated by the PCA (Principal Component Analysis) method around the neighboring vertices. Although the occluding edgels can be detected robustly, they are not likely to have much information to align details.

2 Reflectance Edgels:
   Usually, in the process of measuring 3D geometric objects by using

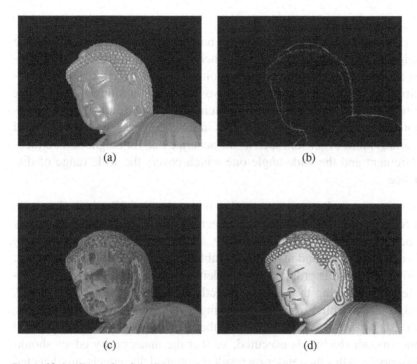

(a)   (b)

(c)   (d)

Figure 13.4.   Example of the three types of 3D edgels: (a) original 3D geometric model, (b) detected occluding edgels, (c) reflectance values of the laser range sensor and the edgels they form, (d) edgels obtained by the rendering result.

the laser range finder, the data concerning the reflectance ratio of the laser are also obtained. Since the reflectance values have already corresponded to the 3D geometries, it is reasonable to use these values for the registration. The change of reflectance ratio results from the difference of the surface material, which also causes the change of surface colors. Therefore, the edges of the reflectance values are supposed to have the similar structures as the edges of 2D photometric image and used as the 3D edgels (in Figure 13.4(c)).

3 Rendered Edgels:
   Although occluding edgels do not have much information, reflectance edgels have sufficient details and their combination works well. However, we cannot assume the 3D geometric data always contain the reflectance values. For example, if we use different kinds of laser range finders at the same time, the consistent reflectance values cannot be obtained. Such situation easily occurs in practice because we would need various kinds of sensors such as the accurate one for neighborhood measurement and the wide-angle one which covers the wide range of distance.

   Therefore, an alternative method to detect detailed 3D edgels becomes necessary. One possibility is to detect edgels using geometric features such as the curvature of the surface. However, these methods are very sensitive to noise and many undesirable junk edgels would be detected. To overcome this problem, the rendered edgels are proposed here. Instead of detecting the features directly from the 3D geometric model, edges are detected from the rendering result. In the rendering process, the 3D surface is assumed to be Lambertian (no specular highlights) and the smooth shading is executed, so that the unnecessary edges should disappear. After the rendering result is obtained, the edgels are detected by the Canny edge filter. As a result, the edge structures are supposed to be similar to the one which results from the 2D edge detection, and also they have enough density of edgels.

These three types of 3D edgels are used properly and in combination.

3.4   2D-3D Correspondence

After detecting both 2D edgels and 3D edgels, their correspondences are searched. In advance, the visibility of 3D edgels has to be checked, because only part of the 3D edgels can be observed from the camera viewpoint of the 2D image. This visibility checking stage utilizes the z-buffer resulting from the rendering process. Each 3D edgel is transformed to the camera-centered coordinate and if it is located within some threshold range from the z-value, it is marked as visible.

Then, each visible 3D edgel is projected to the 2D image coordinate using the currently estimated camera parameters. The nearest 2D edgel is searched according to the 2D Euclidean distance and the pairs of 2D-3D edgels are established.

3.5   Error Metric of Corresponding 2D-3D Pairs

Given a set of N corresponding points $\langle \mathbf{x}_i, \mathbf{y}_i \rangle$, where $i = 0, ..., N - 1$ and $\mathbf{x}_i$ is a 3D edgel and $\mathbf{y}_i$ is a 2D edgel, the registration problem is to compute the camera parameters $\mathbf{p}$, i.e., the camera rotation and translation $\langle \mathbf{R}, \mathbf{t} \rangle$, which aligns the projections of 3D edgels $\mathbf{x}_i$ with 2D edgels $\mathbf{y}_i$. The projection of $\mathbf{x}_i$ is written as

$$\mathbf{u}_i = \mathbf{P} \begin{pmatrix} \mathbf{R} & \mathbf{t} \\ \mathbf{0}^{\mathrm{T}} & 1 \end{pmatrix} \begin{pmatrix} \mathbf{x}_i \\ 1 \end{pmatrix} \tag{13.9}$$

$$\mathbf{u}_i = \begin{pmatrix} u_i \\ v_i \\ w_i \end{pmatrix}, \quad \mathbf{U}_i = \begin{pmatrix} \frac{u_i}{w_i} \\ \frac{v_i}{w_i} \end{pmatrix} \tag{13.10}$$

where $\mathbf{P}$ is a 3×4 projection matrix, and $\mathbf{U}_i$ is the coordinate of the projected point on the 2D image.

To facilitate further analysis, several assumptions are made in the following equations: the focal length is unity, the principal point lies exactly at $(0, 0)$ on the image, the aspect ratio is unity and the skew is zero. These assumptions can be done without loss of generality. Thus, the projection equation 13.9 is simplified to

$$\mathbf{u}_i = \mathbf{R}\,\mathbf{x}_i + \mathbf{t} \tag{13.11}$$

$$\mathbf{u}_i = \begin{pmatrix} u_i \\ v_i \\ w_i \end{pmatrix}, \quad \mathbf{U}_i = \begin{pmatrix} \frac{u_i}{w_i} \\ \frac{v_i}{w_i} \end{pmatrix} \tag{13.12}$$

One way of defining the error metric of corresponding 2D-3D point pairs is the squared distance on the 2D image.

$$z_i = \| \mathbf{U}_i - \mathbf{y}_i \|^2 \tag{13.13}$$

However, it does not take the distance to the 3D point $\mathbf{x}_i$ into account, and it only accounts for the direction of the 3D point. Consequently, it would favor parts of the 3D edgels that are closer to the camera.

Instead of using a 2D error metric, a similar 3D error metric can be considered. It can be expressed as the distance between a 3D edge point and a line connecting the focal point to a 2D edge point. Figure 13.5 shows an example of such a point and a line. Let $\hat{\mathbf{v}}_i$ be the unit vector of that line, i.e., the viewing direction to a 2D edge point $\mathbf{y}_i$ from the focal point. Now we can determine the closest point on that line to the 3D edge point $\mathbf{u}_i$ ($\mathbf{x}_i$ is transformed into $\mathbf{u}$ for the camera-centered coordinates).

$$\mathbf{y}'_i = (\mathbf{u}_i \cdot \hat{\mathbf{v}}_i)\, \hat{\mathbf{v}}_i \qquad (13.14)$$

Subsequently, the error z_i is expressed as follows.

$$z_i = \|\mathbf{u}_i - \mathbf{y}'_i\|^2 \qquad (13.15)$$

This error computation is now in 3D rather than 2D.

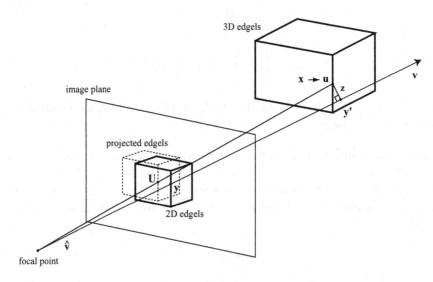

Figure 13.5. The error metric of corresponding 2D-3D edgels in 3D space. The 3D euclidean distance between the 3D edgel $\mathbf{u}$ and the line stretching to the 2D edgel $\mathbf{y}$ is used for the error metric.

3.6   Robust Estimation

In the registration process, the camera position and orientation are updated toward the direction which reduces the sum of corresponding 2D-3D errors.

$$E(\mathbf{p}) \;=\; \sum_i z_i(\mathbf{p}) \qquad (13.16)$$

$$= \sum_i \|\mathbf{u}_i - \mathbf{y}_i'\|^2 \qquad (13.17)$$

where $\mathbf{p}$ is the camera extrinsic parameters that we want to estimate, and $E(\mathbf{p})$ is the evaluation function. This form of the equation 13.17 represents the least squares estimation of parameters $\mathbf{p}$.

However, it is not practical to use the above formulation directly since the least squares method is very sensitive to the outliers and the estimated parameters tend to be strongly biased by them. This is because the least squares method is the maximum-likelihood estimator which assumes that the errors are distributed according to the normal distribution function. In the problems of computer vision, there exist much more outliers which can have fractionally large departures than expected in the normal distribution. Furthermore, much worse situation is expected in this case. Since the corresponding point pairs are automatically searched, a large part of them is supposed to be incorrectly matched, especially in the initial stage of registration.

Outlier thresholding is the simplest and commonly used technique to remove outliers. It regards the data values outside some range as outliers and simply eliminates those data points. The range is often determined by estimating the standard deviation σ of the errors in data and the value $k\sigma$ is used for thresholding, where k is typically greater than or equal to 3. Although it is computationally easy and cheap, there are significant problems. One problem is that the hard threshold is used to eliminate the outliers. This means, regardless of where the threshold is chosen, some of the valid data are rejected as the outliers and some of the outliers are classified as valid. In addition, the hard threshold makes the objective function discontinuous and causes the difficulties for the numerical optimization. The other problem is that in our case the initial correspondences are supposed to be highly incorrect. Therefore, both valid data and incorrect data may exist in the same range and distinguishing them may be meaningless.

To deal with outliers, various sorts of robust statistical estimators have been studied. The two representative classes of robust estimation are the least-median-of-squares (LMedS) method and the M-estimation.

The former class, LMedS method estimates the parameters by solving the following non-linear minimization problem.

$$E(\mathbf{p}) = \text{med}_i \; z_i(\mathbf{p}) \qquad (13.18)$$

$$\mathbf{p} = \arg\min_{\mathbf{p}} E(\mathbf{p}) \qquad (13.19)$$

The concept of LMedS is to select the median value of the errors for each observation and use that value as the error value at the current parameters. The logic behind this is that the median is almost guaranteed not to be an outlier as long as half of the data is valid. Essentially, this requires an exhaustive search of possible values **p**, by testing least-squares estimates of **p** for all possible combinations of matches between 2D-3D edgels. Although this median based technique can be very robust, its computation cost is extremely high.

The M-estimation is another representative method for robust estimation and it is used in this thesis. The "M" refers to maximum-likelihood estimation and the arbitrary error model can be used. Assuming that each error z_i is independently random and it is observed according to the probability density **P**,

$$P = \prod_i e^{\,\rho(z_i)} \tag{13.20}$$

the maximum-likelihood parameters can be obtained by minimizing the following objective function,

$$E = \sum_i \rho(z_i) \tag{13.21}$$

where $\rho(z) = -\log P(z)$.

For example, assuming that the errors z_i follow the normal distribution, they are written as follows.

$$P \propto \prod_i e^{-z_i^2}, \quad \rho(z) = z_i^2 \tag{13.22}$$

$$E = \sum_i z_i^2 \tag{13.23}$$

Notice that this is equivalent to the least-squares formulation.

Using the framework of M-estimation, our evaluation function (Equation 13.16) can be modified to

$$E(\mathbf{p}) = \sum_i \rho(z_i(\mathbf{p})) \tag{13.24}$$

By taking the derivative of E with respect to **p** and setting it to 0, the parameters **p** that minimize E can be obtained.

$$\frac{\partial E}{\partial \mathbf{p}} = \sum_i \frac{\partial \rho}{\partial z_i} \cdot \frac{\partial z_i}{\partial \mathbf{p}} = 0 \tag{13.25}$$

By substituting

$$w(z) = \frac{1}{z} \frac{\partial \rho}{\partial z} \tag{13.26}$$

we get

$$\frac{\partial E}{\partial \mathbf{p}} = \sum_i w(z_i)\, z_i\, \frac{\partial z_i}{\partial \mathbf{p}} = 0 \tag{13.27}$$

If we temporarily forget that w is a function of z, this can be interpreted as weighted-least squares minimization, which has the form $\rho(z) = w z^2$. In other words, the term $w(z)$ represents the weight of contribution of errors of magnitude z with respect to a weighted-least squares estimate.

There are many possible choices of $\rho(z)$ to reduce the sensitivity to outliers on the estimation. The famous functions are: Lorentz's, Tukey's, Andrew's, Huber's and the sigmoid function. Among them, the Lorentzian function is used in the current implementation.

In the weighted-least squares sense, the behavior of M-estimation function can be intuitively understood by analyzing the weight function $w(z)$. The Figure 13.6(a) shows the graph of weight functions. While the normal distribution (Gaussian function) has the constant weight value for all ranges of data, the Lorentzian function discounts observations with large errors, which makes this function more robust against outliers. For comparison, the simple thresholding method is also tested, with the threshold value 3σ. Figure 13.6(b) compares the error probability distribution functions. Both the Gaussian and the Lorentzian function look similar around the center, however, the Gaussian function hardly allow large errors, in particular the errors larger than 3σ. For this reason, the least-squares estimate which assumes the Gaussian distribution does not work correctly in the presence of such outliers.

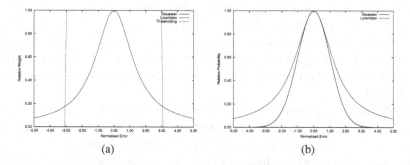

(a)   (b)

Figure 13.6.   Plots of weight and probability distribution functions. (a) shows the weight functions. While the Lorentzian function discounts observations with large errors, the Gaussian function always weighs constantly. The thresholding method is also drawn for comparison, with the threshold value 3σ. (b) compares the error probability distribution. They look similar around the center, however, the Gaussian function hardly allow the errors which are larger than 3σ.

3.7   Iterative Refinement of Camera Parameters

Now, we review the registration problem in detail. Given a set of N corresponding point pairs $\langle \mathbf{x}_i, \mathbf{y}_i \rangle$, where $i = 0, ..., N - 1$ and $\mathbf{x}_i$ is a 3D edgel point and $\mathbf{y}_i$ is a 2D edgel point, the objective function to be minimized can

Function Name	$\rho(z)$	$w(z)$
Gaussian	$\rho(z) = z^2$	$w(z) = 1$
Lorentzian	$\rho(z) = \log\left(1 + \frac{1}{2}z^2\right)$	$w(z) = \frac{1}{1+\frac{1}{2}z^2}$
Thresholding	$\rho(z) = \begin{cases} z & \lvert z \rvert \leq \theta \\ 0 & \lvert z \rvert > \theta \end{cases}$	$w(z) = \begin{cases} 1 & \lvert z \rvert \leq \theta \\ 0 & \lvert z \rvert > \theta \end{cases}$

Table 13.1. Comparison of weight functions. θ in the row "Thresholding" is the threshold value.

be written as follows:

$$E(\mathbf{p}) = \frac{1}{N} \sum_{i}^{N} \rho(z_i(\mathbf{p})) \tag{13.28}$$

$$\text{where } z_i(\mathbf{p}) = \lVert \mathbf{u}_i - \mathbf{y}'_i \rVert^2 \tag{13.29}$$

$\rho(z)$ is the M-estimate function, the Lorentzian function in this case, and the parameters $\mathbf{p}$ is a 7-vector which denotes the camera rotation and translation $(\mathbf{q}^T \ \mathbf{t}^T)^T$. Both $\mathbf{u}_i$ and $\mathbf{y}'_i$ are the function of $\mathbf{p}$ and they are shown in Equation 13.11 and 13.14. The normalization factor $1/N$ is introduced to take the average distance of corresponding point pairs, since the number of them changes through the iterative process by the automatic generation and visibility check of 3D edgels.

The difficulty in minimizing $E(\mathbf{p})$ is that the 2D edgel $\mathbf{y}_i$ corresponding to the 3D edgel $\mathbf{x}_i$ is also the function of $\mathbf{p}$, that is, the movement of $\mathbf{p}$ may cause the change of their correspondences. Although ignoring this fact can lead to inefficiency and possibility of incorrect results, it seems impossible to take these effects into account in the above mathematical formulation.

To overcome this problem, iterative minimization processes are used. In each iterative process, the current correspondences are searched using the current camera parameters. Within each minimization calculation, they are regarded as fixed and the better camera parameters are estimated under such constraints. It starts with a crude set of correspondences and gradually converge to the correct correspondences and at the same time finds the true camera parameters. An improvement in $E(\mathbf{p})$ should correspond to an improvement in $\mathbf{p}$, and that leads to an improvement in the correspondences as well.

Each minimization calculation is accomplished by the conjugate gradient search. Other non-linear optimization methods, such as the Levenberg-Marquardt method, can also be used.

To use these non-linear optimization methods, the gradient of the objective function E with respect to the camera parameters $\mathbf{p}$ must be computed:

$$\frac{\partial E}{\partial \mathbf{p}} = \frac{1}{N} \sum_{i}^{N} w(z_i) z_i \frac{\partial z_i}{\partial \mathbf{p}} \tag{13.30}$$

In particular,

$$\frac{\partial z_i}{\partial \mathbf{p}} = \frac{\partial \mathbf{u}_i}{\partial \mathbf{p}} \frac{\partial z_i}{\partial \mathbf{u}_i} \tag{13.31}$$

The former component, $\frac{\partial \mathbf{u}_i}{\partial \mathbf{p}}$, is the Jacobi matrix of the camera coordinates with respect to the camera parameters. The latter component, $\frac{\partial z_i}{\partial \mathbf{u}_i}$, tells us how we must move $\mathbf{u}_i$, the camera-centered coordinates of $\mathbf{x}_i$, to reduce z_i.

First, the former component, $\frac{\partial \mathbf{u}_i}{\partial \mathbf{p}}$, is inspected in detail.

$$\mathbf{u}_i(\mathbf{p}) = \mathbf{R}(\mathbf{q})\mathbf{x}_i + \mathbf{t} \tag{13.32}$$

The difficult point is the differentiation of $\mathbf{R}(\mathbf{q})\mathbf{x}$ with respect to the rotation quaternion $\mathbf{q}$. To simplify the computation, we pre-rotate the model points so that the current quaternion is $\mathbf{q_I} = (0, 0, 0, 1)^T$, i.e., the unit quaternion. It has the property $\mathbf{R}(\mathbf{q_I}) = \mathbf{I}$ and considering the gradient around it depends on the fact that this becomes the very simple form:

$$\left.\frac{\partial \mathbf{R}\mathbf{x}}{\partial \mathbf{q}}\right|_{\mathbf{q_I}} \mathbf{x} = 2\mathbf{C}(\mathbf{x})^T \tag{13.33}$$

where $\mathbf{C}(\mathbf{x})$ is the 3×3 skew-symmetric matrix of the vector $\mathbf{x}$. The skew-symmetric matrix is defined as follows.

$$\mathbf{x} \times \mathbf{a} = \mathbf{C}(\mathbf{x})\,\mathbf{a} = \begin{pmatrix} 0 & -z & y \\ z & 0 & -x \\ -y & x & 0 \end{pmatrix} \mathbf{a} \tag{13.34}$$

where $\mathbf{x} = (x, y, z)^T$. In other words, the cross product of the vector $\mathbf{x}$ is equivalent to the multiplication of its skew-symmetric matrix $\mathbf{C}(\mathbf{x})$. Notice that, by the skew-symmetry of $\mathbf{C}(\mathbf{x})$, $\mathbf{C}^T = -\mathbf{C}$. Therefore,

$$\frac{\partial \mathbf{u}_i}{\partial \mathbf{p}}\mathbf{a} = \left[\begin{array}{c} \mathbf{a} \\ 2\mathbf{C}(\mathbf{x_i})^T \mathbf{a} \end{array} \right] \tag{13.35}$$

can be obtained.

Next, the differentiation of z_i by $\mathbf{u}_i$ is derived. From Equation 13.29,

$$\frac{\partial z_i}{\partial \mathbf{u}_i} = \left(\mathbf{I} - \frac{\partial \mathbf{y}_i'}{\partial \mathbf{u}_i}\right) \{2(\mathbf{u}_i - \mathbf{y}_i')\} \tag{13.36}$$

where

$$\frac{\partial \mathbf{y}'_i}{\partial \mathbf{u}_i} = \frac{\partial (\mathbf{u}_i \cdot \hat{\mathbf{v}}) \hat{\mathbf{v}}}{\partial \mathbf{u}_i} \tag{13.37}$$

$$= \frac{\partial (\hat{\mathbf{v}}^T \mathbf{u}_i) \hat{\mathbf{v}}}{\partial \mathbf{u}_i} \tag{13.38}$$

$$= \hat{\mathbf{v}} \hat{\mathbf{v}}^T \tag{13.39}$$

Since $\mathbf{y}'_i$ is on the line stretched from the 3D point $\mathbf{u}_i$ and that line is perpendicular to the viewing direction $\hat{\mathbf{v}}$,

$$(\mathbf{u}_i - \mathbf{y}'_i) \cdot \hat{\mathbf{v}} = 0 \tag{13.40}$$

Consequently, we get

$$\frac{\partial z_i}{\partial \mathbf{u}_i} = \mathbf{I} \{ 2(\mathbf{u}_i - \mathbf{y}'_i) \} \tag{13.41}$$

$$= 2(\mathbf{u}_i - \mathbf{y}'_i) \tag{13.42}$$

Finally, from Equation 13.31, 13.35 and 13.42, the derivative of z_i with respect to the camera parameters $\mathbf{p}$ can be obtained.

$$\frac{\partial z_i}{\partial \mathbf{p}} = \frac{\partial \mathbf{u}_i}{\partial \mathbf{p}} \frac{\partial z_i}{\partial \mathbf{u}_i} \tag{13.43}$$

$$= \left\{ \frac{\partial (\mathbf{R}(\mathbf{q}) \mathbf{x}_i + \mathbf{t})}{\partial \mathbf{p}} \right\} \{ 2(\mathbf{u}_i - \mathbf{y}'_i) \} \tag{13.44}$$

$$= \begin{bmatrix} 2(\mathbf{u}_i - \mathbf{y}'_i) \\ 4\mathbf{C}(\mathbf{x}_i)^T (\mathbf{u}_i - \mathbf{y}'_i) \end{bmatrix} \tag{13.45}$$

$$= \begin{bmatrix} 2(\mathbf{u}_i - \mathbf{y}'_i) \\ -4\mathbf{x}_i \times (\mathbf{u}_i - \mathbf{y}'_i) \end{bmatrix} \tag{13.46}$$

Now, we can compute the gradient of E and the minimization calculation can be executed by the conjugate gradient search.

4.   Simultaneous Registration Algorithm

In the previous section, the registration method which aligns one 2D image and estimates the single viewpoint against the 3D geometric models, is described. In this section, multiple 2D images are taken into account and multiple viewpoints are simultaneously estimated.

4.1 Illustration of Simultaneous Registration

Since one photographic image taken from one viewing point is a partial view of the model, multiple images must be measured to cover the entire 3D geometric models. To obtain the whole texture-mapped model, the apparent approach is to sequentially align each 2D image with the 3D geometric model using the 2D-3D registration technique mentioned in the previous Chapter.

However, it may cause undesirable artifacts around the boundary where texture images from different views intersect, since there would be a gap between two adjacent texture images. Figure 13.7 shows the example. After registering two images separately, aligned 2D edgels are projected onto the 3D surface. We can observe lots of gaps between the edge projected from one texture image and the one projected from another texture image. These gaps lead to the discontinuity at the boundary switching from one texture image to another and result in the visual artifacts.

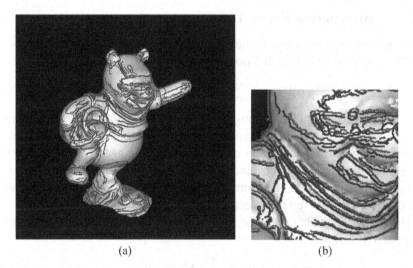

(a)   (b)

Figure 13.7. Example of the gap between two adjacent texture images. Adjacent 2D image edges which are already aligned by the single-viewpoint 2D-3D registration, are projected onto the 3D surface. (b) is a zoomed view of (a).

These gaps result from the fact that even if each 2D image is thoroughly registered to the 3D object in the error metric of respective viewpoint, it does not necessarily mean it is globally optimal. Due to various errors such as the inaccuracy of 3D geometry, the resolution of pixels, irremovable lens distortions, etc., it is impossible to seek exactly correct registration. Accordingly, we have to assume errors always exist and they need to be distributed globally. Otherwise, if they are minimized only in terms of the single-viewpoint registration, each adjacent image is aligned toward the different kind of objective function and it results in the gaps between adjacent images. Therefore, the multi-view global optimization is necessary which registers multiple images simultaneously.

The simultaneous registration method has the other good point, too. In Section 3.3, the topic of density and similarity of edge features was mentioned. The occluding edgels have less features than other kinds of edgels and the reflectance and rendered edgels might have different edge structures compared to the photometric edges. In the global registration, the gaps seen in Figure 13.7 are optimized, i.e., the 2D edgels from adjacent images are taken into account. These features have highly similar structures in the photographs taken from neighboring viewpoints, and also, they contain sufficient details. Consequently, the global registration process utilizing these features is supposed to lead to more accurate and detailed registration results.

4.2   Interactive Error Term

To minimize gaps shown in the previous section, the interactive term is introduced into the objective function $E(\mathbf{p})$:

$$E^{(t)}(\mathbf{p}^{(t)}) = E_{\text{single}}^{(t)}(\mathbf{p}^{(t)}) + E_{\text{interactive}}^{(t)}(\mathbf{p}^{(t)}) \qquad (13.47)$$

Since there are multiple 2D photographic images and multiple camera parameters to estimate in the simultaneous registration problem, the upper script (t) is used to denote that the value is related to t-th 2D image. The above formula represents that the evaluation function with respect to t-th image, $E^{(t)}(\mathbf{p}^{(t)})$, comprises two parts, i.e., the term regarding the single-viewpoint registration and the term considering the interaction among neighboring images.

The former term is the same as the one shown in Equation 13.28 and can be expressed as follows.

$$E_{\text{single}}^{(t)}(\mathbf{p}^{(t)}) = \frac{1}{N^{(t)}} \sum_i \rho(z_i^{(t)}(\mathbf{p}^{(t)})) \qquad (13.48)$$

It is slightly rewritten to distinguish multiple viewpoints, that is, the script (t) are added. $z_i^{(t)}(\mathbf{p}^{(t)})$ is the distance between i-th visible 3D edgel in the 3D geometric model and the corresponding 2D edgel on the t-th image at the camera parameter $\mathbf{p}^{(t)}$. The normalization factor $1/N^{(t)}$ is presented to obtain the average distance of corresponding points, since the number of them change through the iterative process by the automatic detection and visibility check of 3D edgels.

In addition to the term concerning the single-viewpoint registration, the interactive term which aligns the edgels among neighboring images is introduced in the simultaneous registration. It minimizes the distances of newly

generated 3D edgels on the 3D surface. These processes are explained below
and illustrated in Figure 13.8.

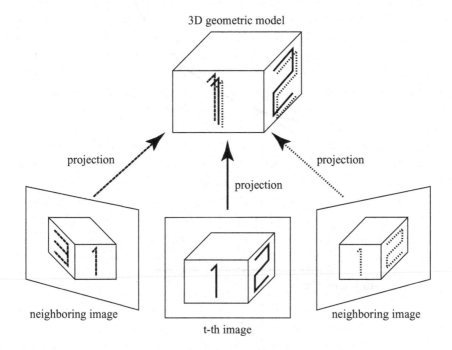

Figure 13.8. Projecting 2D edgels from neighboring images onto the 3D surface. These projected 2D edgels compose the new 3D edgels and they are aligned on the 3D surface.

1 After each image is registered to the 3D geometric model, its 2D edgels
   are projected onto the surface of the 3D geometric model.

2 Subsequently, they form the new sets of 3D edgels.

* We now consider the objective function concerning the t-th image.

3 The sets generated from neighboring images are chosen.

4 Among them, the edgels which are not visible from t-th viewpoint are
   removed.

5 Visible neighboring edgels are registered with the edgels projected from
   t-th image, that is, t-th viewpoint is modified to make them agree on the
   3D surface.

Note that at the projection stage, only the edgels projected onto the smooth
gradual surface are used, i.e., edgels projected onto the discontinuous surface
or onto the steep slope are eliminated.

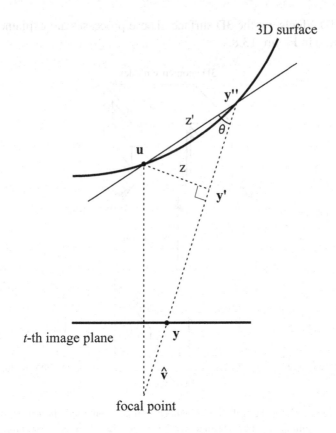

Figure 13.9. Error metric of corresponding edgel pairs on the 3D surface

The error metric of corresponding edgel pairs on the 3D surface is illustrated in Figure 13.9; $\mathbf{u}$ is the novel 3D edgel projected from the neighboring image, $\mathbf{y}$ is its corresponding 2D edgel on the t-th image, and $\hat{\mathbf{v}}$ is the viewing direction. These formulations are constructed to imitate the normal 2D-3D registration. In the 2D-3D error metric, the distance z between the 3D edgel $\mathbf{u}$ and the line connecting from the focal point to the 2D edgel $\mathbf{y}$ is considered and minimized. On the other hand, in simultaneous registration, the distance between projected edgels along the 3D surface is minimized. Let $\mathbf{y}''$ be the projected point of the 2D edgel on the t-th image. Here, we can assume that the distance of corresponding edgel pairs along the 3D surface is approximated by the Euclidean distance between $\mathbf{u}$ and $\mathbf{y}''$. This is because the projected edgels exist on the smooth surface and their neighborhood can be approximated by the tangential plane. Consequently, the error metric for the interactive term can be written as follows:

$$z'_i = \frac{z_i}{\sin \theta_i} \tag{13.49}$$

where θ is the angle between the viewing direction and the tangential plane.

Assuming that θ is fixed in one iteration step, z'_i and its gradient $\partial z'_i / \partial \mathbf{p}$ are almost the same as the 2D-3D   registration case. Therefore, this mutual registration algorithm can take advantage of the similar framework of the single-viewpoint registration between 3D edgels and 2D edgels.

Now, the formula of the interactive term is shown below.

$$E^{(t)}_{\text{interactive}}(\mathbf{p}^{(t)}) = \frac{1}{N'^{(t)}} \sum_{s \in U(t)} \sum_i \rho(z'^{(t,s)}_i(\mathbf{p}^{(t)})) \tag{13.50}$$

$U(t)$ denotes the set of neighboring images of t-th image. Among them, s-th image is chosen and $z'^{(t,s)}_i(\mathbf{p}^{(t)})$ is the distance of i-th edgel pair which comprises the edgels projected from t-th image and the edgels projected from s-th image.

Thus, the objective function regarding the t-th camera parameter $\mathbf{p}^{(t)}$ is constructed to meet both the 3D edgels   from 3D geometric model and the edgels projected from neighboring images.

4.3   Iterative and Simultaneous Refinement

In the global registration problem, we have to estimate N sets of camera parameters $\mathbf{p}^{(i)}$ $(0 \le i \le N - 1)$. First of all, separate single-viewpoint registrations need to be accomplished to approximately align all images. After that, simultaneous refinement   process starts and it is also achieved by the iterative calculations.

The outline of the simultaneous refinement algorithm is described in Figure 13.10. Since it takes advantage of the similarity to the single-viewpoint registration, there are not so many differences. However, some points are described in detail below.

1 For each iterative step, 2D texture edgels are projected onto the 3D surface using their current camera parameters and they form the new temporal 3D edgels.   At this projection stage, uncertain edgels which are projected to a steep surface or around occluding boundaries should be removed.

2 The t-th objective function consists of the single-viewpoint term and the interactive term. The latter considers the differences of projected edgels on the 3D surface. It minimizes the distance between the edgels

projected from t-th image and the edgels projected from neighboring images on the 3D surface.

3 By minimizing the t-th objective function, the update of t-th camera parameters is estimated. Minimization is executed by the conjugate gradient search.

4 The estimated update of t-th camera parameters is "not" applied at this point. Instead, it is recorded in the update list.

5 After all objective functions are minimized and all camera updates are estimated, they are finally applied to the sets of camera parameters.

6 The above loops are repeated until the objective functions converge.

Note that the camera parameters are not transformed immediately. Considering that the changes of camera parameters caused by each step will not be so large, this latency of propagation will not cause a problem. The strategy of updating every camera parameters at once is not taken because the order of processing texture images matters in that case, and further, it requires duplicated calculations of projecting 2D edgels.

5.   Experiments and Results

5.1   Implementation Details

- Rough and detailed registration:
  In the experiment, the single-viewpoint registration was divided into two separate stages: the rough registration stage and the detailed registration stage. At first, only the occluding edgels are used so that the rough position can be easily aligned without the interference of small edge structures. After that, the reflectance edgels (if available) or the rendered edgels are also considered to align the detailed structures.

  Each 2D image is registered separately as described above. Finally, the all images are simultaneously registered by the global optimization.

- σ of the Lorentzian function:
  In the M-estimation framework, the argument of the Lorentzian function must be the normalized value with respect to the proper standard deviation σ. Otherwise, reduction of outliers might be too weak or too strong. Therefore, σ is always updated by analyzing the distribution of corresponding 2D-3D errors. Every time the 2D-3D correspondences are updated, their lower quartile error is chosen as σ. Since lower quartile contains the smallest values, proper σ will be chosen as long as the quarter of the correspondences are correct.

- Selection of the neighboring images:
  In the simultaneous registration, 2D edgels are projected onto the 3D surface and they are registered among the neighboring images. In the experiment, only two adjacent images, i.e., the left and the right neighbors, are used as the neighborhood since the texture images are captured on the circular position surrounding the target object. However, in practice, the neighborhood within some range should be automatically chosen.

- Selection of the texture image:
  For each mesh, the texture image which minimizes the inner product of the mesh normal and the viewing direction, is chosen. To avoid too much fragmentation, the mesh normal is averaged around the neighborhood.

5.2   Results

Proposed registration method is applied to a plastic bear object (In Figure 13.11). Range images are measured with a Minolta VIVID 900, and the 3D geometric model has been constructed using these alignment and merging methods [21, 25]. The obtained geometry has 31300 vertices and 62277 meshes. 2D photographic images are taken with a NIKON D1x digital camera which yields an image of 3008x1960 resolution. Lens distortions are eliminated using the camera calibration method [36], and at the same time, the camera focal length is also obtained. Other camera intrinsic parameters are assumed to be idealized value, i.e., the principal point is $(0, 0)$, the aspect ratio is unity and the skew is zero. Registration calculations are carried out on the PC which has the AMD Athlon processor of 1400MHz and 512MB memory.

To begin with, the single-viewpoint 2D-3D registration method is examined. Figure 13.12 shows detected 2D and 3D edgels. In this experiment, the occluding edgels and the rendered edgels are used as the 3D edgels. The process of the iterative calculation is illustrated in Figure 13.13. The camera extrinsic parameters have been refined to align corresponding 2D edgels and 3D edgels and the proper camera viewpoint is estimated. This registration took approximately 30 seconds. More than half of them is consumed in the process of the 2D edge detection using Canny method which is executed several times to obtain 3D rendered edgels. Other time consuming processes are: the rendering process of 3D geometries using OpenGL which is necessary to obtain the z-buffer for visibility checking, and the calculation of the objective function which is evaluated many times in the conjugate gradient search.

Thus, 11 photographs taken from different viewpoints can be separately registered to the 3D geometric model. However, the set of images which are registered separately is not necessarily consistent around the boundary where images from different views intersect. Since there always remain some registration errors due to the inaccuracy of 3D geometries, irremovable lens distortions, incorrect camera intrinsic parameters, etc., the perfectly correct registration cannot be achieved, and such errors must be distributed globally. Therefore, the simultaneous registration is applied after the separate single-viewpoint registrations, and the effects are examined. 2D edgels of two adjacent texture images are projected onto the 3D surface and their gaps before and after the simultaneous refinement are compared in Figure 13.14. Here, we can see that these gaps undoubtedly shrank, thanks to the simultaneous registration. For this simultaneous refinement, 20 iterations were necessary and it took roughly 10 minutes.

In the simultaneous registration, the objective function consists of two parts, i.e., the single-viewpoint error terms relating to the separate 2D-3D registration and the interactive error terms concerning the global errors.

$$E(\mathbf{p}) = E_{\text{single}}(\mathbf{p}) + E_{\text{interactive}}(\mathbf{p}) \tag{13.51}$$

The behavior of these two kinds of components is examined in Figure 13.15. This graph contains two experiments: one is the separate single-viewpoint registration of 40 iterations, and the other is also the single-viewpoint registration for first 20 iterations but the simultaneous registration follows for successive 20 iterations. Although the interactive error terms do not exist in the single-viewpoint registration, they are temporarily evaluated at each iteration to observe the global errors. While the first half of the plots are exactly the same, we can observe the interesting difference after the simultaneous registration starts in one experiment. It is plainly seen in the zoomed views around the simultaneous registration (in Figure 13.16). Although the single-viewpoint registration reduces the single error terms slightly better than the simultaneous registration, the interactive errors do not necessarily decrease. Indeed, further single-viewpoint registration tries to reduce the single error terms too much at the expense of the global errors.

The quality of the texture-mapped object is also compared in Figure 13.17. Since the registration errors are absorbed globally, visual artifacts are reduced in simultaneously registered results. However, when examined carefully, there still remain some defects and we can consider two major reasons: registration errors and color inconsistency. The former means that although the simultaneous registration distributes errors globally, there should remain excessive errors. The latter is the more serious problem. Even if the images are perfectly aligned, there might exist the color gaps between adjacent images. This is because the observed color in the photograph changes due to various factors: illumination conditions, viewing positions, specular highlights, etc. Note that, to avoid such problems, many researches concerning the texture mapping adopt the blending strategy of textures from neighboring images.

Recently, our laboratory has been conducting the project of creating digital cultural assets through observation, and the precise 3D geometric models of such objects have been constructed using accurate laser scanners [18, 21, 25, 26]. Thus, the proposed registration method is applied to one of them, the Great Buddha of Kamakura (in Figure 13.18(a)) and its texture-mapped model is created. The Great Buddha of Kamakura is a 13m tall statue sitting in an open air. It was scanned using a Cyrax 2400 sensor and the fine geometric model has been reconstructed, which has approximately 0.7 million vertices and 1.3 million meshes (in Figure 13.18(b)). Since registering 2D images to such high resolutional data requires massive computational time, the simplified model was used, which has approximately 100 thousand vertices and 200 thousand meshes.

18 photographs are taken with D1x digital camera and they are registered to the geometric model. Results of the textured model are shown in Figure 13.19. Although the registration process is almost the same as the previous bear example, reconstructed Great Buddha has several visual artifacts. This is because there exist excess difficulties in this case due to the outdoor environment and the size of the object. First, the illumination condition should easily change in the outdoor environment. Although all measurements of photographs are carried out within only a few minutes, the observed colors are slightly changed. This would be caused by the imperceptible movement of the sun and the clouds. Second, a 17mm wide lens was necessary to capture the unoccluded whole image of the Great Buddha. The wide lens leads to larger lens distortions particularly in the periphery of the image, and indeed, the camera calibration could not remove part of the distortions around the leg of the Great Buddha (in Figure 13.18(a)). As a result, the simultaneous registration did not perform well especially in the lower half of the Great Buddha and this leads to the alignment gaps around that region.

6. Conclusions

6.1 Summary

In this chapter, a novel registration method is introduced and described, which automatically and simultaneously aligns multiple 2D images onto 3D geometric models. Usually, corresponding features between the 2D image and the 3D model have to be specified to estimate the camera position and orientation. However, in the proposed method, the correspondence information between 2D edge pixels and 3D edge points are automatically searched and updated throughout the iterative calculations. Considering the robustness and the density of edge features, three types of 3D edge features are proposed and used in combination. Further, the global optimization among all the 2D images is also achieved by the simultaneous registration which considers the 2D-2D edge correspondences on 3D surfaces. To make the algorithm robust against the outliers, the framework of M-estimates is employed. Registration results are examined with the texture mapped objects and the meaningful importance of the simultaneous registration is presented. Also, this method is applied to the creation of digital cultural assets and the issues concerning the measurement in large-scale outdoor environments are revealed.

6.2   Future Work

To achieve accurate texture mapping, lens distortions must be removed. Therefore, the practical camera calibration is needed, which can be easily performed at the measurement time even in the large-scale outdoor environments.

To improve the quality of texture-mapped objects, the intrinsic color of the object surface must be estimated. Since the observed texture image contains various factors at the measurement time: illumination conditions, shadows, specular highlights, etc., the colors of the corresponding points from different viewpoints are not consistent. Therefore, in order to reconstruct the precise 3D models, such factors must be canceled out and the intrinsic color of the surface needs to be estimated.

Acknowledgments

This research was supported, in part, by Ministry of Education, Culture, Sports, Science and Technology under the Leading Project, "Development of High Fidelity Digitization Software for Large-Scale and Intangible Cultural Assets," and, in part, by Japan Science and Technology Agency, under the CREST program, "Automatic generation of virtual models of cultural heritage."

References

[1] P. K. Allen, I. Stamos, A. Troccoli, B. Smith, M. Leordeanu, and Y. C. Hsu. 3D modeling of historic sites using range and image data. *submitted to the International Conference of Robotics and Automation*, 2003.

[2] P. Besl and N. McKay. A method for registration of 3-D shapes. *IEEE Trans. on Pattern Analysis and Machine Intelligence*, Vol. 14, No. 2, pp. 239–256, February 1992.

[3] J. Canny. A computational approach to edge detection. *IEEE Trans. on Pattern Analysis and Machine Intelligence*, Vol. 8, No. 6, pp. 679–698, 1986.

[4] Y. Chen and G. Medioni. Object modeling by registration of multiple range images. *Image and Vision Computing*, Vol. 10, No. 3, pp. 145–155, 1992.

[5] P. E. Debevec. Rendering synthetic objects into real scenes: Bridging traditional and image-based graphics with global illumination and high dynamic range photography. *Computer Graphics*, pp. 189–198, 1998. Proc. of SIGGRAPH '98 (July 1998, Orlando, Florida).

[6] P. E. Debevec. A tutorial on image-based lighting. *IEEE Computer Graphics and Applications*, pp. 26–34, 2002.

[7] P. E. Debevec and Jitendra Malik. Recovering high dynamic range radiance maps from photographs. *Computer Graphics*, pp. 369–378, 1997. Proc. of SIGGRAPH '97 (August 1997, Los Angeles, California).

[8] P. E. Debevec, C. J. Taylor, and J. Malik. Modeling and rendering architecture from photographs: A hybrid geometry- and image-based approach. *Computer Graphics*, pp. 11–20, 1996. In Proc. of SIGGRAPH '96 (August 1996, New Orleans, Louisiana).

[9] K. Deguchi and T. Okatani. Calibration of multi-view cameras for 3D scene understanding (in japanese). *CVIM*, January 2002.

[10] O. Faugeras. *Three-Dimensional Computer Vision: A Geometric Viewpoint*. The MIT Press, 1993.

[11] T. Igarashi, S. Matsuoka, and H. Tanaka. Teddy: A sketching interface for 3D freeform design. *Computer Graphics*, pp. 409–416, 1999. In Proc. of SIGGRAPH '99 (Los Angels, 1999).

[12] B. Klaus and P. Horn. *Robot Vision*. The MIT Press, McGraw-Hill Book Company, 1986.

[13] R. Kurazume, K. Nishino, Z. Zhang, and K. Ikeuchi. Simultaneous 2D images and 3D geometric model registration for texture mapping utilizing reflectance attribute. In *Proc. 5th Asian Conf. on Computer Vision*, January 2002.

[14] R. Kurazume, M. D. Wheeler, and K. Ikeuchi. Mapping textures on 3D geometric model using reflectance image. *Data Fusion Workshop in IEEE Int. Conf. on Robotics and Automation*, May 2001.

[15] S. Lavallée and R. Szeliski. Recovering the position and orientation of free-form objects from image contours using 3D distance maps. *IEEE Trans. on Pattern Analysis and Machine Intelligence*, Vol. 17, No. 4, pp. 378–390, April 1995.

[16] H. P. A. Lensch, W. Heidrich, and H. Seidel. Automated texture registration and stitching for real world models. In *Proc. Pacific Graphics '00*, pp. 317–326, October 2000.

[17] W. E. Lorensen and H. E. Cline. Marching cubes: A high resolution 3D surface construction algorithm. *Computer Graphics*, Vol. 21, No. 4, pp. 163–169, July 1987. In Proc. SIGGRAPH '87.

[18] D. Miyazaki, T. Ooishi, T. Nishikawa, R. Sagawa, K. Nishino, T. Tomomatsu, Y. Takase, and K. Ikeuchi. The great buddha project: Modelling cultural heritage through observation. In *Proc. 6th Inter. Conf. on Virtual Systems and MultiMedia (VSMM 2000)*, pp. 138–145, 2000.

[19] S. K. Nayar and T. Mitsunaga. High dynamic range imaging: Spatially varying pixel exposures. In *Proc. IEEE Inter. Conf. on Computer Vision and Pattern Recognition*, Hilton Head Island, South Carolina, June 2000.

[20] P. J. Neugebauer and K. Klein. Texturing 3D models of real world objects from multiple unregistered photograpihic views. In *Proc. Eurographics '99*, pp. 245–256, Milan, September 1999.

[21] K. Nishino and K. Ikeuchi. Robust simultaneous registration of multiple range images. In *Proc. 5th Asian Conf. on Computer Vision*, pp. 454–461, Melbourne, Australia, January 2002.

[22] K. Nishino, Y. Sato, and K. Ikeuchi. Eigen-texture method: Appearance compression and synthesis based on a 3D model. *IEEE Trans. on Pattern Analysis and Machine Intelligence*, Vol. 23, No. 11, pp. 1257–1265, 2001.

[23] C. Rocchini, P. Cignoni, and C. Montani. Multiple textures stitching and blending on 3D objects. In *10th Eurographics Workshop on Rendering*, pp. 127–138, June 1999.

[24] S. Rusinkiewicz and M. Levoy. Efficient variants of the ICP algorithm. *3DIM*, 2001.

[25] R. Sagawa, K. Nishino, and K. Ikeuchi. Robust and adaptive integration of multiple range images with photometric attributes. In *Proc. IEEE Computer Society Conf. on Computer Vision and Pattern Recognition*, pp. 172–179, December 2001.

[26] R. Sagawa, T. Oishi, A. Nakazawa, R. Kurazume, and K. Ikeuchi. Iterative refinement of range images with anisotropic error distribution. In *Proc. of 2002 IEEE/RSJ International Conference on Intelligent Robots and Systems*, pp. 79–85, October 2002.

[27] I. Sato, Y. Sato, and K. Ikeuchi. Acquiring a radiance distribution to superimpose virtual objects onto a real scene. *IEEE Trans. Visualization and Computer Graphics*, Vol. 5, No. 1, pp. 1–12, 1999.

[28] I. Sato, Y. Sato, and K. Ikeuchi. Illumination distribution from brightness in shadows: adaptive estimation of illumination distribution with unknown reflectance properties in shadow regions. In *Proc. IEEE Inter. Conf. Computer Vision*, pp. 875–882, September 1999.

[29] Y. Sato, M. D. Wheeler, and K. Ikeuchi. Object shape and reflectance modeling from observation. *Computer Graphics*, pp. 379–387, August 1997. In Proc. SIGGRAPH '97.

[30] J. Shi and C. Tomasi. Good features to track. In *Proc. IEEE Inter. Conf. on Computer Vision and Pattern Recognition*, pp. 593–600, 6 1994.

[31] I. Stamos and P. K. Allen. 3-D model construction using range and image data. In *Proc. IEEE Inter. Conf. on Computer Vision and Pattern Recognition*, Vol. 1, pp. 531–536, South Carolina, June 2000.

[32] R. Tsai. A versatile camera calibration technique for high-accuracy 3D machine vision metrology using off-the-shelf tv cameras and lenses. *IEEE Journal of Robotics and Automation*, Vol. 3, No. 4, pp. 323–344, August 1987.

[33] M. D. Wheeler. *Automatic Modeling and Localization for Object Recognition*. PhD thesis, Robotics Institute, Carnegie Mellon University, Pittsburgh, PA, October 1996.

[34] R. C. Zeleznik, K. P. Herndon, and J. F. Hughes. Sketch: An interface for sketching 3D scenes. *Computer Graphics*, pp. 163–170, 1996. In Proc. of SIGGRAPH '96 (New Orleans, 1996).

[35] Z. Zhang. Determining the epipolar geometry and its uncertainty: A review. *International Journal of Computer Vision*, 1997.

[36] Z. Zhang. A flexible new technique for camera calibration. *IEEE Trans. on Pattern Analysis and Machine Intelligence*, Vol. 22, No. 11, pp. 1330–1334, 2000.

```
// separate single-viewpoint registration stage
foreach t in AllTextureImages {
   do {
      Model3DEdgel[t] = GetVisibleEdgel(GeometricModel, Camera[t]);
      PointPairs = [];
      foreach i in PointsOf(Model3DEdgel[t])
         PointPairs += CorrespondenceSearch(i, Texture2DEdgel[t]);
      UpdateList[t] = EstimateCameraUpdate(PointPairs);
      TransformSingle(Camera[t], UpdateList[t]);
   } until converge
}


// simultaneous registration stage
do {
   foreach t in AllTextureImages {
      Model3DEdgel[t] = GetVisibleEdgel(GeometricModel, Camera[t]);
      Projected3DEdgel[t] = Project2DEdgel(GeometricModel, Camera[t], Texture2DEdgel[t]);
   }

   foreach t in AllTextureImages {
      PointPairs = [];
      PointPairs2 = [];

      // single-viewpoint term
      foreach i in PointsOf(Model3DEdgel[t])
         PointPairs += CorrespondenceSearch(i, Texture2DEdgel[t]);

      // interactive term
      foreach s in NeighboringImages
         foreach i in PointsOf(Projected3DEdgel[s])
            PointPairs2 += CorrespondenceSearch(i, Texture2DEdgel[t]);

      UpdateList[t] = EstimateCameraUpdate(PointPairs, PointPairs2);
   }

   // update all camera parameters at this point
   TransformAll(Camera, UpdateList);
} until converge
```

Figure 13.10.   Outline of simultaneous registration algorithm

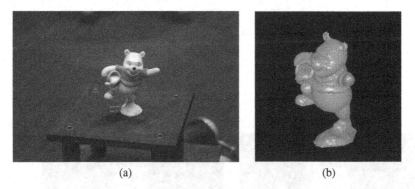

Figure 13.11.   Plastic bear object: (a) photographic image, (b) 3D geometric model.

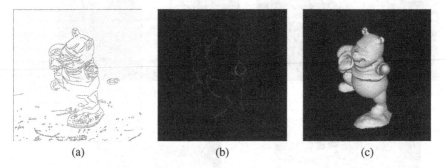

Figure 13.12.   Detected 2D and 3D edgels: (a) 2D edgels, (b) 3D occluding edgels, and (c) 3D rendered edgels.

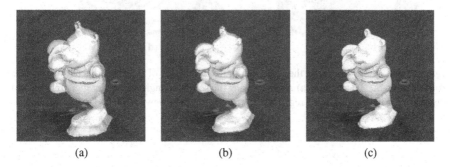

Figure 13.13.   2D-3D registration: (a) initial position, (b) after 8 iterations, and (c) after registration calculation. The 3D geometry and 3D edgels are overlaid on the photographic image; red pixels are the 2D edgels, green pixels are the occluding edgels, and blue pixels are the rendered edgels.

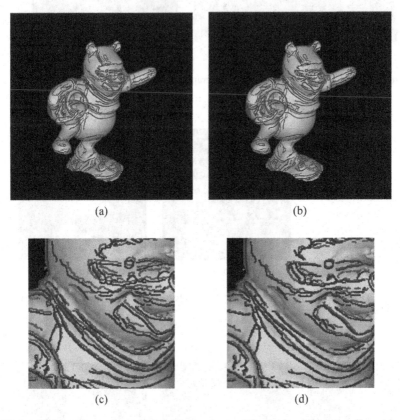

Figure 13.14. Comparison of the alignment gap: 2D edgels of the two adjacent images are projected onto the 3D surface. (a) Aligned using the separate single-viewpoint registrations. (b) Aligned using the simultaneous registration. (c), (d) Zoomed views of (a) and (b), respectively.

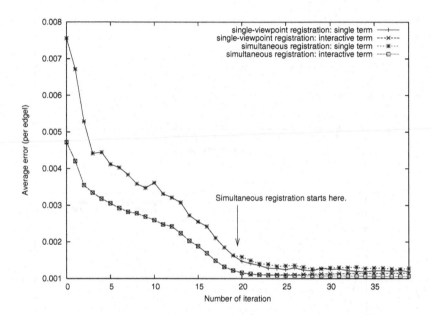

Figure 13.15.   Plotting two kinds of error terms: the single error terms relating to the single-viewpoint errors, and the interactive error terms concerning the global errors.

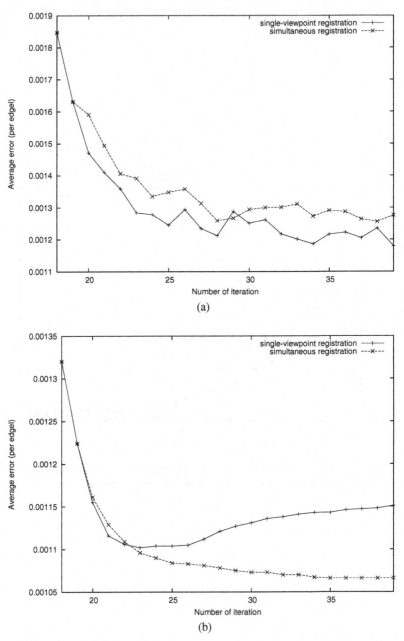

Figure 13.16. Behavior of the single error terms (a) and the interactive error terms (b). These are the zoomed views of Figure 13.15.

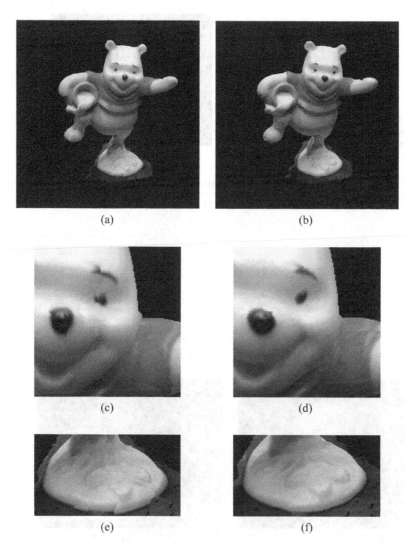

Figure 13.17.   Comparison of the texture-mapped model: (a) Separate single-viewpoint registrations. (b) Simultaneous registration. (c), (d), (e), (f) Zoomed views of the top images.

(a)   (b)

Figure 13.18.   The Great Buddha of Kamakura: (a) a photograph taken with the 17mm wide lens, (b) the high resolutional geometric model.

(a)   (b)

Figure 13.19.   Textured Great Buddha. (a) one image is mapped, (b) 18 images are mapped.

Chapter 14

CONSISTENT SURFACE COLOR FOR TEXTURING LARGE OBJECTS IN OUTDOOR SCENES

Rei Kawakami, Robby T. Tan, and Katsushi Ikeuchi

Abstract   Color appearance of an object is significantly influenced by the color of the illumination. When the illumination color changes, the color appearance of the object will change accordingly, causing its appearance to be inconsistent. To arrive at color constancy, we have developed a physics-based method of estimating and removing the illumination color. In this chapter, we focus on the use of this method to deal with outdoor scenes, since very few physics-based methods have successfully handled outdoor color constancy. Our method is principally based on shadowed and non-shadowed regions. Previously researchers have discovered that shadowed regions are illuminated by sky light, while non-shadowed regions are illuminated by a combination of sky light and sunlight. Based on this difference of illumination, we estimate the illumination colors (both the sunlight and the sky light) and then remove them. To reliably estimate the illumination colors in outdoor scenes, we include the analysis of noise, since the presence of noise is inevitable in natural images. As a result, compared to existing methods, the proposed method is more effective and robust in handling outdoor scenes. In addition, the proposed method requires only a single input image, making it useful for many applications of computer vision.

Figure 14.1.   The texture of the Bayon Temple in Angkor, Cambodia. The color of the objects varies due to the use of textures taken at different times.

1.   Introduction

Reflected light from an object is the product of surface spectral reflectance and illumination spectral power distribution. Consequently, illumination color significantly determines the object's color appearance. When the illumination color changes, the object color appearance changes accordingly. This leads to many problems in algorithms of computer vision. For example, Figure 14.1 shows that the illumination change in creating a realistic model causes the color appearance of an object to be inconsistent. Recovering the surface's actual color requires a method of color constancy that discounts the inconsistencies caused by variations in illumination.

Color constancy is one important aspect of the field of computer vision. Many algorithms in this field, such as color-based object recognition, image retrieval, reflection component separation, and real object rendering, require recovery of the actual color of objects. Many methods have been proposed for this recovery [3, 9, 18, 5, 7, 11, 15, 16, 10, 12, 17]. Based on their input, we can categorize these methods into dichromatic-based methods and diffuse-based methods [17]. Dichromatic-based methods [5, 7, 11, 15, 16, 10, 17] require the presence of highlighting, while diffuse-based methods [3, 9, 18] require body-only reflection.

Most diffuse-based methods use a single input image of objects lit by a uniformly colored surface. Usually these methods require strong constraints in surface colors domain, such as a prior surface color database, and cannot accurately estimate images with few surface colors [18]. A few researchers alternatively introduce color constancy methods based on varying or changing illumination color [4, 8, 2]. They have found that, despite creating the problem of color constancy, the change of illuminations could be a crucial constraint to solving the color constancy problem itself. D'Zmura [4] proposed a method using approximated linear basis functions to form a closed-form equation. One drawback of the method is that it fails to provide robust estimations for real images. Finlayson et al. [8] introduced a method that uses a single surface color illuminated by two different illumination colors. Barnard et al. [2] utilized the retinex algorithm [14] to automatically obtain a surface color with different illumination colors, and then applied the method of Finlayson et al. [8] to estimate varying illumination colors in a scene.

In this chapter, our goal is to estimate and to remove the illumination color of outdoor scenes by using a single image. To accomplish this goal, we utilize shadowed and non-shadowed regions. Previously researchers (for example, [7]) have discovered that shadowed regions are illuminated by sky light, while non-shadowed regions are illuminated by a combination of sky light and sunlight. Note that sunlight is due to the direct rays from the sun, and sky light is due to the scattered light rays from the atmosphere. Based on this difference of illumination in shadowed and non-shadowed regions, we have developed a method to estimate the illumination colors (both the sunlight and the sky light) and then remove them. To reliably estimate the illumination colors in outdoor scenes, we include the analysis of noise, since the presence of noise is inevitable in natural images, due to the sensors, the medium, or noise inherent in the objects, such as dust and imperfect painting.

Our basic idea of using shadowed and non-shadowed regions is similar to the idea of using varying illumination [8, 2], and our method is principally based on a method proposed by Finlayson et al. [8]. However, unlike the method of Finlayson et al., we take into account the presence of noise, which is inevitable in real images. Finlayson et al. did not include noise in their analyses, which makes their method unreliable for natural images, particularly outdoor scenes. Moreover, instead of using a discrete illumination model, we employ a continuous model that is computed from the Planck Formula.

To estimate the actual color of the surface successfully, we made the following assumptions: (1) The illumination chromaticity forms a straight line in a two-dimensional inverse-chromaticity space. (2) The camera sensitivity function is narrowband and known. (3) The output of camera response is linear to the flux of incoming light intensity. The last two assumptions are common assumptions used in many color constancy algorithms.

The rest of the chapter is organized as follows: in Section 2, we describe image color formation and the definition of chromaticity. In Section 3, we discuss constraints used in our method. In Section 4, we introduce our approach to make the estimation more robust and accurate. We provide the implementation of our approach and experimental results for real images in Section 5. Finally, in Section 6, we conclude this chapter.

2. Reflection Model

Image Formation. According to general image formation, an image of a diffuse object taken by a digital color camera can be described as:

$$I_c = \int_\Omega S(\lambda)E(\lambda)q_c(\lambda)d\lambda \tag{14.1}$$

where I_c is the sensor response (RGB pixel values), $S(\lambda)$ is the surface spectral reflectance and $E(\lambda)$ is the illumination spectral power distribution, q_c is the three-element vector of sensor sensitivity, and index c represents the type of sensors (r, g and b). Integration is done over the visible spectrum (Ω). In this model we ignore camera noise and gain. By assuming narrowband sensitivity that follows the Dirac delta function, Equation (14.1) can be simply written as:

$$I_c = S_c E_c \tag{14.2}$$

where $S_c = S(\lambda_c)$ and $E_c = E(\lambda_c)$. If camera sensitivity cannot be approximated by the Dirac delta function (narrowband sensor), we could apply camera sharpening algorithms proposed by [6, 1].

Chromaticity Following Finlayson et al. [8], in this chapter we define chromaticity (or specifically *image* chromaticity) as:

$$\sigma_c = \frac{I_c}{I_b} \tag{14.3}$$

where index $c = \{r, g\}$. Equation (14.2) still holds in this chromaticity space:

$$\sigma_c = s_c e_c \tag{14.4}$$

where s_c and e_c correspond to the chromaticities of S_c and E_c, which we call surface and illumination chromaticity, respectively.

Planck Formula In this study, as in many existing color constancy methods, we assume that natural (outdoor) illumination can be approximated by a blackbody radiator, which is modeled by the Planck formula.

The Planck formula is expressed as:

$$M(\lambda) = c_1 \lambda^{-5} [exp(c_2/\lambda T) - 1]^{-1} \tag{14.5}$$

where $c_1 = 3.7418 \times 10^{-16}$ Wm^2, $c_2 = 1.4388 \times 10^{-2}$ mK, λ is wavelength (m), and T is temperature in Kelvin. By combining with known sensor sensitivity, we can obtain a camera response of the Planck formula:

$$I_c = \int_\Omega M(\lambda, T) q_c(\lambda) d\lambda \tag{14.6}$$

The last equation is the combination of image formation and the Planck formula.

3.   Estimating Surface Chromaticity

From Equation (14.4), the problem of color constancy can be described as the problem of estimating the values of e_c and s_c given the value of σ_c, where index is $c = \{r, g\}$. However, to estimate four unknown values (e_r, e_g, s_r, s_g) from two known values (σ_r, σ_g) is mathematically ill-posed. To solve the problem, we should add more constraints, which we do in this chapter by increasing the number of the image chromaticities: σ_c^1 and σ_c^2 that are taken from the same surface chromaticity (s_c) but different illumination chromaticities (e_c):

$$\sigma_c^1 = s_c e_c^1 \tag{14.7}$$
$$\sigma_c^2 = s_c e_c^2 \tag{14.8}$$

From the last two equations, we can have four knowns $(\sigma_r^1, \sigma_g^1, \sigma_r^2, \sigma_g^2)$, and six unknowns $(s_r, s_g, e_r^1, e_g^1, e_r^2, e_g^2)$, which is mathematically still ill-posed.

Fortunately, from Section 2, we know that natural (outdoor) illumination can be approximately modeled by the Planck formula, implying that by using the formula we can have the correlation of e_r^i and e_g^i, namely, $e_g^i = f(e_r^i)$ where f is a function derived from the Planck formula and index $i = \{1, 2\}$. As a result, we can have four unknowns: (s_r, s_g, e_r^1, e_r^2), and thus the problem has the possibility to be well-posed. In the subsequent section, we will discuss the correlation of e_g and e_r, and then explain how we can automatically have two image chromaticities with the same surface chromaticity but different illumination chromaticity (pixels from shadowed and non-shadowed regions).

3.1   Illumination Constraints and Shadows

Illumination Constraints.   Based on Planck formula (Equation (14.5)), Marchant et al. [19] derived the correlation of e_g and e_r as follows:

$$e_r = m e_g^A \tag{14.9}$$

where: $A = \left(\frac{1}{\lambda_r} - \frac{1}{\lambda_b}\right) / \left(\frac{1}{\lambda_g} - \frac{1}{\lambda_b}\right)$, $m = \frac{\lambda_g^{5A}/\lambda_b^{5A}}{\lambda_r^5/\lambda_b^5}$ and $\{e_r, e_g\}$ is the chromaticity of the illumination. A and m are constant numbers characterizing the camera. λ_c (where index $c = \{r, g, b\}$) is the center wavelength of the camera sensitivity. If we plot this correlation into two-dimensional chromaticity rg-space, we can find that all illumination colors form a curved line, which is usually called a Planckian locus.

We have mentioned in the beginning of this section that by knowing the correlation of e_g and e_r, we can probably have a well-posed color constancy problem from two different illuminations, since we have four knowns $(\sigma_r^1, \sigma_g^1, \sigma_r^2, \sigma_g^2)$ and four unknowns (s_r, s_g, e_r^1, e_r^2). Unfortunately, by further derivation from Equation (14.7), (14.8) and (14.9), we obtain the following equations:

$$\sigma_r^1 = \frac{s_r}{(s_g)^A}(\sigma_g^1)^A \tag{14.10}$$

$$\sigma_r^2 = \frac{s_r}{(s_g)^A}(\sigma_g^2)^A \tag{14.11}$$

The last two equations show that we cannot determine the absolute values of s_r and s_g, since having the same surface chromaticity means that $(\sigma_r^1/(\sigma_g^1)^A = \sigma_r^2/(\sigma_g^2)^A)$. Thus, to solve the problem, we should add more constraints, which will be discussed further in Section 3.2.

Two Image Chromaticities with the Same Surface Chromaticity While Equation (14.10) shows that we cannot have absolute values of s_r and s_g, the

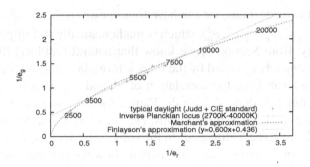

Figure 14.2. Illumination Models: typical daylight, Planckian locus, Finlayson et al.'s straight-line approximation.

equation is useful to determine whether two or more image chromaticities (σ_c) have the same surface chromaticity (s_c) but different illumination chromaticity (e_c). The equation shows that $(s_r/(s_g)^A)$ can be the same, implying the same s_c, for different values of image chromaticities (σ_c), implying different e_c. Particularly in outdoor scenes, the equation can be used to detect whether the shadowed and non-shadowed regions are part of the same surface color [19].

3.2   Straight-Line Constraint

In the previous section we have shown that solely increasing the number of the inputs (σ_1 and σ_2) and having exponential correlation of e_g and e_r described in Equation (14.9) are not sufficient to solve the color constancy problem. Following Finlayson et al. [8], we further assume that in two-dimensional inverse-chromaticity $(1/e_r, 1/e_g)$ space, the illumination can be approximated by a straight line:

$$\frac{1}{e_g} = m\frac{1}{e_r} + c \tag{14.12}$$

where in Finlayson et al.'s method the values of m and c are constant (not equal to zero), and are computed beforehand. Figure 14.2 shows a red line that represents the straight line approximation. Based on Equation (14.12), we have that:

$$\sigma_r^i = s_r e_r^i \tag{14.13}$$

$$\sigma_g^i = s_g \frac{1}{\frac{m}{e_r^i} + c} \tag{14.14}$$

where $i = \{1, 2\}$. By deriving the last two equations further, we can obtain the following linear correlation:

$$s_g = (m \frac{\sigma_g^i}{\sigma_r^i}) s_r + \sigma_g^i c \tag{14.15}$$

The last equation means that in chromaticity space, the image chromaticity (σ_c) can form a straight line. This implies that if we have two image chromaticities with the same surface chromaticity (s_c), then their straight lines will intersect at a certain location that is identical to the value of s_c.

Note that the straight line assumption prevails only for the limited range of e_c^1 and e_c^2. For instance, we cannot use the assumption when the temperature of e_c^1 equals $2500K$ and the temperature of e_c^2 equals $8000K$, since, instead of forming a straight line, the illumination chromaticity forms a curved line as shown in Figure 14.2.

4. Robust Framework for Outdoor Scenes

4.1 Problems

While Finlayson et al's method elegantly solves the problem of color constancy from varying illumination, we discovered that it is significantly sensitive to noise.

We have investigated the effects of noise to estimate surface chromaticity in Finlayson et al.'s method quantitatively. Assuming that we have image chromaticity σ_r^1 with noise $\Delta\sigma_r$, where $\Delta\sigma_r/\sigma_r^1 \ll 1$, then the estimated surface chromaticity will deviate from the correct value, described as $s_c + \Delta s_c$, with Δs_c representing the error of the estimation. Mathematically, we found that the error ratio of the estimated surface chromaticity can be expressed as by the equation (see Appendix A for detailed derivation):

$$\frac{\Delta s_r}{s_r} \approx \frac{\Delta\sigma_r}{\sigma_r^1} \frac{1}{\left(1 - \frac{e_r^1/e_g^1}{e_r^2/e_g^2}\right)} \tag{14.16}$$

(As can be seen in the last equation, the error ratio of surface chromaticity ($\Delta s_r/s_r$) will be large if the two illumination colors e_c^1 and e_c^2 are similar. The same analysis can also be done for the green channel. To investigate this further, we simulated the error ratio described in the last equation, and we present the results in Figure 14.3. The y-axis of the figure represents the error ratio and the x-axis represents the temperature of the second illumination in Kelvin. The first simulation is shown in red points when the temperature of the first illumination is $3000K$. As can be observed, when the second illumination's temperature near $3000K$, the error becomes large. Other simulations using different temperatures of σ_c^1 can be observed in the blue and green lines. In this simulation we set $\Delta\sigma_r/\sigma_r = 0.01$.

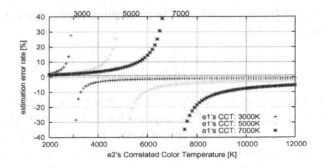

Figure 14.3.   Simulating the effect of noise in estimating the surface chromaticity.

Thus, if we intend to have relatively accurate results by using Finlayson et al.'s method, the difference between illuminations (e_c^1 and e_c^2) should be relatively large. However, a large difference would violate the straight line assumption explained in Section 3.2. We therefore conclude that because of the presence of noise, and because Finlayson et al.'s method is restricted to certain conditions of illumination, the method is unreliable in general conditions of outdoor illumination.

4.2   Basic Outline

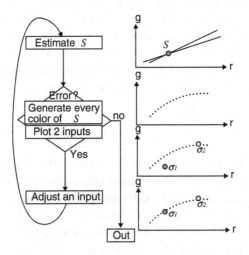

Figure 14.4.   The outline of noise reduction and thus of our robust framework.

In principle, to solve the problems in Finlayson et al.'s method, our idea is, first, to reduce the effect of noise $\Delta\sigma_c$ as much as possible so that the final

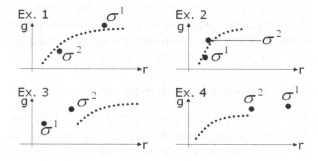

Figure 14.5. Examples of the distance between the two image chromaticities and the generated possible image chromaticities based on the Planckian locus.

estimation has a relatively small deviation from the ground truth, even if the difference of illumination chromaticity is relatively small.

The outline of our noise reduction and thus our robust framework is shown in Figure 14.4. First, from two image chromaticities (σ_c^1, σ_c^2), where σ_c^1 is taken from a non-shadowed pixel and σ_c^2 is taken from a shadowed pixel, we estimate the surface chromaticity (s_c) by solving Equation (14.15), as shown in the top rg-space in Figure 14.4.

Second, we generate all possible image chromaticities based on the estimated surface chromaticity and all possible illumination chromaticities, and then plot them into the rg-space. The curved dash-line in Figure 14.4 represents the generated image chromaticities. Mathematically, generating the image chromaticities can be described as:

$$\sigma_c^{planck} = s_c e_c^{planck} \tag{14.17}$$

where e_c^{planck} is the chromaticity of Planckian locus, i.e., the colors of all natural illumination, s_c is the estimated result, and σ_c^{planck} is the generated image chromaticity.

Third, we examine the correctness of our estimated surface chromaticity by the following rule: If the estimated surface chromaticity is correct then the two image chromaticities (σ_c^1, σ_c^2) must lie on the generated curved line; otherwise, σ_c^1, σ_c^2 do not lie on the curved line. Examples of inputs that largely lie on the curved line and that do not lie in the curved line are shown in Figure 14.5. Ex. 1 and Ex. 2 are examples of inputs that largely lie on the curved line, and Ex. 3 and Ex. 4 are examples of inputs that do not lie on the curved line.

Fourth, if the inputs largely lie on the curved line, then the process terminates and we can have a relatively correct result. Otherwise, we consider that one or two of the input chromaticities have noise. To reduce this noise, we change the position by adjusting the value of the image chromaticity slightly.

After the adjustment, we estimate the value of s_c once again and then detect whether the inputs largely lie on the curved line. The process is done iteratively until the inputs largely lie on the curved line. In practice we use Euclidean distance to determine whether the inputs lie on the curved line.

4.3 Image-chromaticity Adjustment

There are two issues in adjusting the values of image chromaticity that has noise. First, from two image chromaticities $(\sigma_c^1$ and $\sigma_c^2)$, we should choose which chromaticity has more noise than the other. This becomes an issue because we intend to adjust one image chromaticity instead of two. We found that if we adjust both image chromaticities, ambiguity will result. Consider Equations (14.10) and (14.11) and assume that both σ_c^1 and σ_c^1 have noise ($\Delta\sigma_c^1$ and $\Delta\sigma_c^2$), where at first their values are different ($\Delta\sigma_c^1 \neq \Delta\sigma_c^2$), meaning the values of $s_r/(s_g)^A$ will be different. Then we adjust both of them. This adjustment could lead to a certain condition where the values of $(s_r/(s_g)^A)$ are the same, but it does not guarantee that $\Delta\sigma_c^1 = \Delta\sigma_c^2 = 0$.

Therefore, we decided to choose only one of the inputs to be modified to reduce the error. This constraint brings us two benefits. First, the processing time becomes fast. Second, we are sure that the processing always terminates. In our implementation, we chose the pixel from a shadowed region to be adjusted, since the darker pixels in general have much noise than brighter pixels.

Second, upon choosing the image chromaticity to be adjusted, we have to decide in which direction the adjustment has to be done. This issue is due to the random value of noise, which could be positive and negative. To solve the problem, first we adjust the input in either vertical direction (green-channel) or horizontal direction (red-channel), which we determine by using following equation (see Appendix B for the detailed derivation):

$$\frac{\left(\sigma_r^B - \sigma_r^A\right)}{\left(\sigma_g^B - \sigma_g^A\right)} \frac{\sigma_g^B}{\sigma_r^B} > 1 \tag{14.18}$$

If the left side of the last equation is larger than 1, then $\Delta\sigma_g/\sigma_g$ has a greater effect on the estimation. Thus, we move the image chromaticity in parallel with the green channel (vertical direction). Second, to determine whether the adjustment should be upward or downward (in the case of vertical direction, or right or left in the case of horizontal direction), we use the iteration procedure we have explained in Section 4.2, namely, at first we apply positive adjustment. If the distance between the adjusted image chromaticity and the generated curved line is larger than that without adjustment then we should apply negative adjustment, or vice-versa.

5. Implementation and Experimental Results

5.1 Implementation

The implementation of our method is as follows. First, from an input image that has shadows (as an example see Figure 14.6.a), we compute its image chromaticity by using Equation (14.3). Then, we find pixels from a shadowed region and a non-shadowed region that have the same surface chromaticity or the same value of $(s_r/(s_g)^A)$. Figure 14.6.b shows an image representing the values of $(s_r/(s_g)^A)$. If we plot this value in chromaticity space, then we can obtain clustered points, as shown in Figure 14.7.a. The blue line represents the same value of $(s_r/(s_g)^A)$, implying the same value of surface chromaticity.

Upon knowing the values of $(s_r/(s_g)^A)$, we can obtain two or more pixels that have the same value of $(s_r/(s_g)^A)$ but different values of image chromaticity (σ_c), namely, pixels from shadowed and non-shadowed regions, by analyzing the points that lie on the blue line shown in Figure 14.7.a. If we compute the histogram of points lying on the blue line, we will obtain a distribution shown in Figure 14.7.b (the red lines). As shown in the figure, we have two peaks. The left peak represents the first illumination chromaticity (non-shadowed region), and the right peak represents the second illumination chromaticity (shadowed region). By finding the two peaks, we can have pixels representing different illumination chromaticity but the same surface chromaticity. From those pixels, we can use the algorithm explained in Section 4 to estimate the illumination chromaticities.

Then, having estimated the illumination chromaticities, we intend to obtain the surface chromaticities of all pixels in the input image. To do this we use a simple approach. From Figure 14.7.b, we can have two peaks representing the shadowed and non-shadowed regions. If we cluster the pixels according to the peaks, we can have all pixels representing the shadowed region and all pixels representing the non-shadowed region. The result can be seen in Figure 14.6.c, where blue pixels represent the shadowed region and red pixels represent the non-shadowed region. Then, we can compute the surface chromaticity simply by dividing the image chromaticity by the estimated illumination chromaticity.

The result of removing one of the illumination colors can be seen in the distribution of the green lines in 14.7.b. Unlike the red lines, the green lines only have one peak.

5.2 Experimental Result

Conditions. We conducted several experiments on real images, taken using SONY DXC-9000 and Nikon-D1 progressive 3 CCD digital cameras, by setting their gamma correction off. To ensure that the outputs of the cameras were linear to the flux of incident light, we used the Macbeth color chart. We

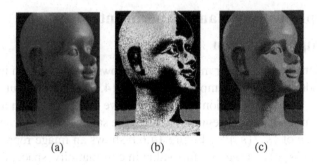

(a)   (b)   (c)

Figure 14.6.   Result of indoor experiment, by using artificial lights.

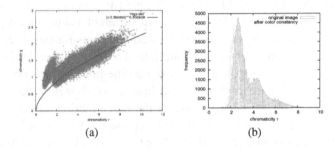

(a)   (b)

Figure 14.7.   (a) Points that have the same value of (s_r/s_g^A) plotted in rg-space. (b) Comparison results between the histogram of input image chromaticities and that of output image chromaticities in the red channel

used planar and convex objects to avoid inter-reflection, and excluded saturated pixels and pixels below the camera dark from the computation. For evaluation, we compared the results with the average values of image chromaticity of a white reference image (Photo Research Reflectance Standard model SRS-3), captured by the same cameras.

Evaluation We have conducted a number of experiments using the Macbeth color chart under outdoor illumination. One of the experiments was done by using a green surface taken under cloudy daylight conditions at 16:30 and 17:30. The illumination chromaticities taken from the white reference were (0.403,0.310) and (0.456,0.305). Using Finlayson et al.'s method, the estimations were (0.525,0.288) and (0.533,0.285), while using our method, the estimations were (0.401,0.324) and (0.409,0.322). We also calculated the average error and the maximum error of our method compared with Finlayson et al.'s method, as shown in Table14.1. The total number of images in our experiments was 30. As shown in Table, our method produced more accurate and robust results. The error in the table was computed based on chromaticity defined by standard CIE.

Table 14.1.   Comparison of estimated illumination chromaticities resulting from our method and from Finlayson et al.'s method.

	Average Error	Maximum Error
Our Estimation	0.063	0.16
Finlayson et al.'s Estimation	0.11	0.32

Outdoor Scenes The input of our experiment is shown in Figure 14.8.a, and the image chromaticity of the input is shown in Figure 14.8.b. Figure 14.8.c shows the values of $(s_r/(s_g)^A)$. The same values of $(s_r/(s_g)^A)$ represent the same surface chromaticity. From the input chromaticity (Figure 14.8.b.) and Figure 14.8.c, we determine pixels that correspond to shadowed regions and non-shadowed regions of the same surface chromaticity. Figure 14.8.d shows the shadowed region (blue pixels) and non-shadowed region (red pixels). Note that, in this study, we do not intend to detect or segment the shadowed region; the red and blue pixels only represent two image chromaticities we used for color constancy (thus we do not need to precisely cluster the pixels). Figure 14.8.e shows the result of color constancy, and Figure 14.8.f shows its image chromaticity. Notice that compared with Figure 14.8.b which has different image chromaticity in the shadowed area, Figure 14.8.f shows that there is no longer any difference in illumination color.

Besides using shadows from a single image to evaluate the robustness of our method, we also conducted experiments by using two images taken at different times, and thus having different colors of illumination. Figure 14.9.a and 14.9.b show the input images. By using 3D geometrical data (provided by a laser range sensor), we obtained the corresponding location of each surface point. For the two different pixels taken from the same point, we estimated the illumination and then removed the illumination color. Figure 14.9.c shows our estimated surface color, while Figure 14.9.d shows the result by using the white reference.

6.   Conclusion

We have proposed a method to estimate surface color from shadows. Our main contribution is to develop a method that is robust and accurate even for outdoor objects, where conditions are less controllable compared with conditions for indoor objects. The underlying idea of our approach is to reduce noise and to find the most appropriate parameters of the straight-line assumption. The experimental results for outdoor scene show the effectiveness of our method.

Figure 14.8. Results of outdoor experiment: (a) input image (b) input chromaticity (c) the image of the values of $(s_r/(s_g)^A)$ (d) the shadowed (blue) and non-shadowed (red) pixels of the same surface chromaticity (e) the result of color constancy (f) the result in chromaticity.

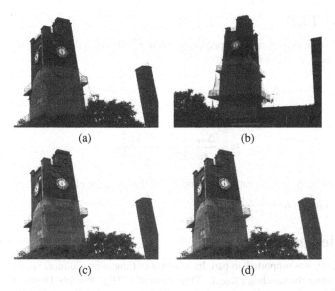

Figure 14.9. (a) One of the two input scenes, illuminated by cloudy daylight at 18:00. (b) The other input, illuminated by cloudy daylight at 18:00 on another day. (c) The estimated scene's actual color of the image shown in (a) computed using our proposed method. (d) The estimated scene's actual color using the standard white reference.

Appendix

The surface chromaticity s_r can be derived as:

$$s_r = \frac{\sigma_r^1 \sigma_r^2 (\sigma_g^2 - \sigma_g^1)}{\sigma_r^2 \sigma_g^1 - \sigma_r^1 \sigma_g^2} \frac{c}{m} \tag{14.A.1}$$

If input σ_r^1 has noise $\Delta\sigma_r^1$, then the estimated surface chromaticity becomes $s_r + \Delta s_{rr}$:

$$s_r + \Delta s_{rr} = \frac{(\sigma_r^1 + \Delta\sigma_r^1)\sigma_r^2(\sigma_g^2 - \sigma_g^1)}{\sigma_r^2 \sigma_g^1 - (\sigma_r^1 + \Delta\sigma_r^1)\sigma_g^2} \frac{c}{m} \tag{14.A.2}$$

Thus, the error ratio $\Delta s_{rr}/s_r$ can be calculated as:

$$\frac{\Delta s_{rr}}{s_r} = \frac{\Delta\sigma_r^1}{\sigma_r^1} \frac{1}{1 - \frac{\sigma_r^1/\sigma_g^1}{\sigma_r^2/\sigma_g^2} - \frac{\Delta\sigma_r^1}{\sigma_r^1}\frac{\sigma_r^1/\sigma_g^1}{\sigma_r^2/\sigma_g^2}} \tag{14.A.3}$$

Since we assume $\Delta\sigma_r^1/\sigma_r^1 \ll 1$, the equation becomes:

$$\frac{\Delta s_{rr}}{s_r} \approx \frac{\Delta\sigma_r^1}{\sigma_r^1} \frac{1}{1 - \frac{\sigma_r^1/\sigma_g^1}{\sigma_r^2/\sigma_g^2}} \tag{14.A.4}$$

Appendix 14.B

Using the same derivation in Appendix A, when σ_g^1 has noise $\Delta\sigma_g^1$, then the error ratio of estimated surface chromaticity becomes:

$$\frac{\Delta s_{rg}}{s_r} \approx -\frac{\Delta\sigma_g^1}{\sigma_g^1}\frac{1}{1-\frac{\sigma_r^1/\sigma_g^1}{\sigma_r^2/\sigma_g^2}}\frac{\left(\sigma_r^2-\sigma_r^1\right)\sigma_g^2}{\left(\sigma_g^2-\sigma_g^1\right)\sigma_r^2} \qquad (14.B.1)$$

$$\approx \frac{\Delta s_{rr}}{s_r}\frac{\left(\sigma_r^2-\sigma_r^1\right)\sigma_g^2}{\left(\sigma_g^2-\sigma_g^1\right)\sigma_r^2} \qquad (14.B.2)$$

This shows that even the error ratio of σ_r^1 and σ_g^1 are the same, the effect on the estimation error ratio depends on the factor $\frac{(\sigma_r^2-\sigma_r^1)\sigma_g^2}{(\sigma_g^2-\sigma_g^1)\sigma_r^2}$.

Acknowledgments

This research was supported, in part, by Ministry of Education, Culture, Sports, Science and Technology under the Leading Project, "Development of High Fidelity Digitization Software for Large-Scale and Intangible Cultural Assets," and, in part, by Japan Science and Technology Agency, under the CREST program, "Automatic generation of virtual models of cultural heritage."

References

[1] K. Barnard, F. Ciurea, and B. Funt. Sensor sharpening for computational color constancy. *Journal of Optics Society of America A.*, 18(11):2728–2743, 2001.

[2] K. Barnard, G. Finlayson, and B. Funt. Color constancy for scenes with varying illumination. *Computer Vision and Image Understanding*, 65(2):311–321, 1997.

[3] D.H. Brainard and W.T. Freeman. Bayesian color constancy. *Journal of Optics Society of America A.*, 14(7):1393–1411, 1997.

[4] M. D'Zmura. Color constancy: surface color from changing illumination. *Journal of Optics Society of America A.*, 9(3):490–493, 1992.

[5] M. D'Zmura and P. Lennie. Mechanism of color constancy. *Journal of Optics Society of America A.*, 3(10):1162–1672, 1986.

[6] G.D. Finlayson, M.S. Drew, and B.V. Funt. Spectral sharpening sensor transformations for improved color constancy. *Journal of Optics Society of America A.*, 11(10):1162–1672, 1994.

[7] G.D. Finlayson and B.V. Funt. Color constancy using shadows. *Perception*, 23:89–90, 1994.

[8] G.D. Finlayson, B.V. Funt, and K. Barnard. Color constancy under varying illumination. *in proceeding of IEEE International Conference on Computer Vision*, pages 720–725, 1995.

[9] G.D. Finlayson, S.D. Hordley, and P.M. Hubel. Color by correlation: a simple, unifying, framework for color constancy. *IEEE Trans. on Pattern Analysis and Machine Intelligence*, 23(11):1209–1221, 2001.

[10] G.D. Finlayson and S.D.Hordley. Color constancy at a pixel. *Journal of Optics Society of America A.*, 18(2):253–264, 2001.

[11] B.V. Funt, M. Drew, and J. Ho. Color constancy from mutual reflection. *International Journal of Computer Vision*, 6(1):5–24, 1991.

[12] J.M. Geusebroek, R. Boomgaard, S. Smeulders, and T. Gevers. A physical basis for color constancy. In *The First European Conference on Colour in Graphics, Image and Vision*, pages 3–6, 2002.

[13] D.B. Judd, D.L. MacAdam, and G. Wyszecky. Spectral distribution of typical daylight as a function of correlated color temperature. *Journal of Optics Society of America*, 54(8):1031–1040, 1964.

[14] E.H. Land and J.J. McCann. Lightness and retinex theory. *Journal of Optics Society of America*, 61(1):1–11, 1971.

[15] H.C. Lee. Method for computing the scene-illuminant from specular highlights. *Journal of Optics Society of America A.*, 3(10):1694–1699, 1986.

[16] H.C. Lee. Illuminant color from shading. In *Perceiving, Measuring and Using Color*, page 1250, 1990.

[17] R. T. Tan, K. Nishino, and K. Ikeuchi. Color constancy through inverse intensity-chromaticity space. *Journal of the Optical Society of America A (JOSA A)*, 21(3):321-334, 2004.

[18] S. Tominaga and B.A. Wandell. Natural scene-illuminant estimation using the sensor correlation. *Proceedings of the IEEE*, 90(1):42–56, 2002.

[19] J.A. Marchant and C.M. Onyango. *Shadow-invariant classification for scenes illuminated by daylight. Journal of Optics Society of America A.* 17(11):1952–1961, 2000.

Chapter 15

SEPARATING ILLUMINATION AND SURFACE SPECTRAL FROM MULTIPLE COLOR SIGNALS

Akifumi Ikari, Rei Kawakami, Robby T. Tan, and Katsushi Ikeuchi

Abstract   A number of methods have been proposed to separate a color signal into its components: illumination spectral power distribution and surface spectral reflectance. Most of these methods usually use a minimization technique from a single color signal. However, we found that this technique is not effective for real data, because of insufficiency of the constraints. To resolve this problem, we propose a minimization technique that, unlike the existing methods, uses multiple color signals. We present three methods for recovering surface and illumination spectrums which differ in obtaining color signals: first, from two different surface reflectances lit by a single illumination spectral power distribution; second, from identical surface reflectances lit by different illumination spectral power distributions; and third, from a single surface reflectance with two types of reflection components, diffuse and specular, lit by a single illumination spectral power distribution. Practically we applied our method to deal with the color signals of a scene taken by the interference filter, and we separated its illumination spectral power distribution and surface spectral reflectance.

1.   Introduction

Observed color signal of a cultural heritage is a product of two components: illumination spectral power distribution and surface spectral reflectance. To separate the spectral reflectance from the illumination spectrum is an important issue in computer vision and color science, since many applications in those fields, such as color-based object recognition, reflection component separation, real object rendering, etc., require the reflectance information of the target object. The color signal separation technique is part of a color constancy algorithm [9, 6, 8, 7], which is commonly done in a three-color channel (RGB) operation instead of in a spectral operation.

In three-color channels (Red, Green, Blue, or RGB), various color constancy methods have been proposed. For instance, Finlayson et al. [6] showed that illumination change that causes the problem of color constancy can be turned into a crucial constraint to solve the problem of color constancy itself. Using a straight-line approximation model of illumination in diagonal matrix components space, they proposed an intersection approach of two pixels with the same surface color but lit by different illumination. Tan et al. [21] introduced a method focusing on highlighted regions that could be applied for both single and multi-colored surface.

While the aforementioned methods are applicable for separating three-color channel data, unfortunately, most of them cannot be applied to spectral (color signal) separation, since spectral data cannot be converted into chromaticity values, on which most methods are based, without losing spectral information (the metamerism problem). Hence, for color signals, a different technique is required.

Tominaga et al. [25] have shown that, by using the dichromatic reflectance model, illumination distribution can obtained using both highlighted (specular) regions and diffuse regions of two different surface colors. By using this method, high performance results are obtained. Marchant et al. [14] introduced spectral constancy under daylight, by assuming that illumination could be approximated with a blackbody radiator. This method can detect whether a surface has the same surface spectral reflectance, yet it is not intended to separate illumination spectral power distribution and surface spectral reflectance.

Ho et al. [11] showed that, by considering illumination spectral power distribution and surface spectral reflectance to be the sums of linear basis functions[3, 12, 16, 19], the color signal separation can be done by minimizing the square difference of a color signal and product of the sums of linear illumination basis functions and surface spectral reflectance basis functions.

While theoretically this method can separate a color signal into its components, a few problems exist. First, some parts of the separated signal in certain cases become negative, which infringes on the physical reality of the spectral components since, in reality, those components are always positive. Second, in cases where the constraints are insufficient, the minimization algorithm could be trapped in the local minimum, thereby producing incorrect separation.

Chang et al. [1] improved the method of Ho et al. by putting additional constraints on the illumination and surface reflection components, as well as using a simulated annealing algorithm and a hit-and-run algorithm to increase the efficiency and stability. Their method gives a more robust result compared with that of Ho et al.; however, their separation still suffers from the same drawbacks as those of Ho et al.'s method. Their main problem is that a single color signal has such limited constraints that no current algorithm can avoid the trap of the local minimum.

In this chapter, our goal is to describe how to separate color signals into illumination spectral power distribution and surface spectral reflectance components by giving more constraints in the input data, and separate a spectral image into illumination spectral power distribution and reflectance spectral images. We propose a minimization technique that, unlike the existing methods, uses multiple color signals. These multiple color signals can improve the robustness of the estimation because, by using them, we can obtain more constraints in the input data. In our implementation of using multiple color signals, we introduce three different approaches: first, color signals obtained from two different surface reflectances lit by a single illumination spectral power distribution; second, color signals from identical surface reflectances lit by different illumination spectral power distributions; and third, color signals from identical surface reflectances but different types of reflection components (diffuse and specular pixels) lit by a single illumination spectral power distribution. By using these three conditions of color signals, a better solution can be obtained, and the stability of the separation increases.

To obtain spectral images, Schechner[18] shows that by using an interference filter and performing a mosaicing algorithm[20, 15, 27, 2], we can obtain spectral images. But their approach cannot obtain the exact spectral distribution because they use the gray world assumption. To measure a correct spectral distribution, we have to know the conversion function that includes a camera sensitivity and the filter's absorptance. So we show how to obtain the conversion function correctly. And then, we apply a separation algorithm to these spectral images.

The rest of the chapter is organized as follows. In Section 2, we discuss the theoretical background of the proposed method. In Section 3, we explain our method of dealing with multiple color signals. The method to obtain a color signal is shown in Section 4. The implementation of our algorithm and the experimental results are provided in Sections 5 and Section 6. And finally, in Section 7 we conclude this chapter.

2.   Theoretical Background

2.1   Linear Basis Functions

Reflected light from an object is the product of illumination spectral power distribution (SPD) and surface spectral reflectance. Let $I(\lambda)$ be the reflected color signal at a wavelength λ, $E(\lambda)$ be the illumination SPD and $S(\lambda)$ be the surface spectral reflectance. Then, the color signal $I(\lambda)$ can be expressed as follows.

$$I(\lambda) = E(\lambda)S(\lambda) \qquad (15.1)$$

This study aims to separate the color signal $I(\lambda)$ into those two components $E(\lambda)$ and $S(\lambda)$.

A number of researchers have asserted that the natural illumination spectrum $E(\lambda)$ can be approximated by the linear combination of a small number of basis functions[12, 19].

$$E(\lambda) \simeq \sum_{i=1}^{m} e_i E_i(\lambda) \tag{15.2}$$

where $E_i(\lambda)$ are the basis functions and e_i are the corresponding coefficients. Judd at el.[12] confirmed that the last equation approximates the SPD of daylight and indoor light sources that emit lights by heat. They also reported that three basis functions are sufficient to cover the entire SPDs of natural illumination ($m = 3$). Judd et al.'s three illumination basis functions are shown in Fig.1.a. Slater et al. [19] argued that more sophisticated approximation needs eight basis functions. Yet, they also admitted that the first three dominantly cover the whole SPDs. Three basis functions were used by Ho et al. [11] and Chang et al. [1] in their estimation process.

Similar to illumination SPDs, several researchers [3, 16] have shown that the surface spectral reflectance can be expressed by the basis functions:

$$S(\lambda) \simeq \sum_{j=1}^{n} s_j S_j(\lambda) \tag{15.3}$$

where $S_j(\lambda)$ are the basis functions and s_j are the coefficients. Fig.1.b shows Parkkinen et al.'s four reflectance basis functions[16]. Parkkinen et al. examined various surface colors and concluded that eight basis functions could completely cover all the existing surface color database. They also showed that the first three basis functions cover 99% of the database within an error of 10 %. Cohen et al. [3] determined the basis functions by investigating Munsell chips. Ho et al. [11] and Chang et al. [1] used three basis functions for surface spectral reflectance. As the number of basis functions increases, the approximation becomes accurate.

2.2   Separation Model

A color signal can be resolved into illumination SPD and surface spectral reflectance using the minimization technique;

$$F(\mathbf{u}) = \sum_{\lambda} \left(\sum_{i=1}^{m} e_i E_i(\lambda) \sum_{j=1}^{n} s_j S_j(\lambda) - I(\lambda) \right)^2 \tag{15.4}$$

where the wavelength λ ranges over the visible spectrum from 400nm to 700nm. The last equation is derived from Equations (15.1), (15.2), and (15.3). By searching the coefficients $\mathbf{u} = [e_1, e_2, \cdots, e_m, s_1, s_2, \cdots, s_n]^t$ which minimize the objective function F, the original illumination SPD $E(\lambda)$ and the surface spectral reflectance $S(\lambda)$ can be recovered.

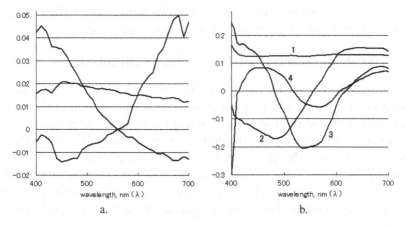

Figure 15.1. a. Judd's [12] three basis functions of illumination distribution. b. Parkkinen's [16] first four basis functions of surface spectral reflectance.

In order to obtain realistic results, the following constraints proposed by Chang et al. [1] should be added.

$$I(\lambda) \leq \sum_{i=1}^{m} e_i E_i(\lambda) \leq \text{maxlimit} \qquad (15.5)$$

$$0 \leq \sum_{j=1}^{n} s_j S_j(\lambda) \leq 1 \qquad (15.6)$$

The two equations represent the physical reality of illumination and surface spectral reflectance. Equation (15.5) means that the illumination SPD is always larger than the input color signal. The upper limitation has no physical meaning but it is important for computation. Equation (15.6) limits surface spectral reflectance to be between zero and one. It avoids scale ambiguity. Chang et al. [1] applied those constraints to the minimization algorithm of Equation (15.4) using the hit-and-run algorithm and the simulated annealing algorithm.

3. Proposed Method: Separation using Multiple Color Signals

This chapter proposes a new method that uses multiple signals to estimate illumination SPDs and surface reflectances. The conventional methods only use a single color signal. However, a real scene has an abundance of available color signals. Three types of constraints are introduced in our method: (1) Multiple surfaces with identical illumination. (2) Identical surfaces with multiple illumination. (3) Signals from specular and diffuse surfaces. Each includes two strategies and corresponding error functions. The more spectrals are used, the more constraints are obtained. Hence, this constrained separation can produce more accurate results compared to the conventional one. The system to acquire the spectrums of the entire scene are described in Section 4.

3.1 Multiple Surfaces with Identical Illumination

Constrained signal separation is expected when multiple color signals are obtained from multiple surfaces illuminated by identical illumination. The condition is illustrated in Figure 15.2. Here, two strategies for separation calculation can be considered using the minimization technique. (1) We minimize the difference between the input signals and the estimated signals. (2) Since the illumination is identical, we minimize the difference between the illumination calculated from one surface and the other. For efficient and stable decomposition, it is important to choose surface points chromatically as different as possible.

3.1.1 Strategy (1)

We minimize the sum of Equation (15.4) at each surface under the constraint that the illumination SPDs are common. The error function can be expressed as follows:

$$F(\mathbf{u}) = \sum_{p=1}^{\text{points}} \sum_{\lambda} \left(\sum_{i=1}^{m} e_i E_i(\lambda) \sum_{j=1}^{n} s_{p,j} S_j(\lambda) - I_p(\lambda) \right)^2 \qquad (15.7)$$

where $E_i(\lambda)$ and $S_j(\lambda)$ are the basis functions of illumination and surface spectral reflectance, e_i and $s_{p,j}$ are the coefficients of the corresponding basis functions, and $I_p(\lambda)$ are the input signals. $I_p(\lambda)$ and $s_{p,j}$ have suffix p to express each surface point. The coefficients $\mathbf{u} = [\cdots, e_i, \cdots, s_{p,j}, \cdots]^t$ are optimized so that they minimize the error function.

The constraints that represent physical reality, which have been described in Equations (15.5) and (15.6), can be combined to the above minimization. Though Equation (15.5) can be directly used, Equation (15.6) should be modified as follows:

$$0 \leq \sum_{j=1}^{n} s_{p,j} S_j(\lambda) \leq 1 \qquad (p = 1, 2, \cdots, \text{points}) \qquad (15.8)$$

3.1.2 Strategy (2)

Suppose that two color signals $I_1(\lambda)$, $I_2(\lambda)$ are obtained from two surfaces $S_1(\lambda)$, $S_2(\lambda)$ illuminated by an identical illumination $E(\lambda)$. Since the illumination is identical, the following constraint can be obtained using Equation (15.1).

$$I_1(\lambda)/S_1(\lambda) - I_2(\lambda)/S_2(\lambda) = 0 \qquad (15.9)$$

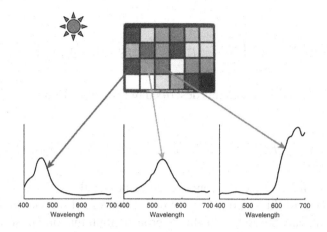

Figure 15.2.   Example of multiple surfaces with identical illumination

By plugging Equation (15.3) into the last equation, we could derive the following error function to be minimized.

$$F(\mathbf{u}) = \sum_{\lambda} \left(I_1(\lambda) \sum_{i=1}^{m} s_{2,i} S_i(\lambda) - I_2(\lambda) \sum_{i=1}^{m} s_{1,i} S_i(\lambda) \right)^2 \qquad (15.10)$$

Each surface spectral reflectance $S_1(\lambda, S_2(\lambda)$ can be estimated by optimizing the coefficients $\mathbf{u} = [\cdots, s_{1,i}, \cdots, s_{2,i}, \cdots]^t$ in the last equation so that the difference becomes the minimum. The same constraints for physical reality as in the previous subsubsection 3.1.1 can be combined with the minimizing function.

3.2   Identical Surfaces with Multiple Illumination

Another constrained separation can be considered using spectrums from identical surfaces illuminated by multiple light sources. Figure 15.3 illustrates the condition. Similar to the case of multiple surfaces, two strategies will be presented for the decomposition. (1) We minimize the difference between the input signals and the estimated signals. (2) Since the surfaces are identical, we minimize the difference between the surfaces' spectral reflectances calculated from each color signal.

3.2.1   Strategy (1)

The separation can be resolved by minimizing the sum of Equation (15.4) of each color signal under the constraint that the surface spectral reflectance is common:

$$F(\mathbf{u}) = \sum_{p=1}^{\text{points}} \sum_{\lambda} \left(\sum_{i=1}^{m} e_{p,i} E_i(\lambda) \sum_{j=1}^{n} s_j S_j(\lambda) - I_p(\lambda) \right)^2 \quad (15.11)$$

and using the physical constraints described in Equation (15.6) and the following equation:

$$I(\lambda) \leq \sum_{i=1}^{m} e_{p,i} E_i(\lambda) \leq \text{maxlimit} \quad (p = 1, 2, \cdots, \text{points}) \quad (15.12)$$

$I_p(\lambda)$ and $e_{p,j}$ have suffix p to denote each color signal.

The problem of this approach is similar to that of subsubsection 3.1.1, but the constraints are different. In this approach, illumination constraints play a dominant role, which theoretically gives more constraints compared to the approach in 3.1.1 because of the lower dimensionality of illumination SPDs.

3.2.2   Strategy (2)

Given two color signals $I_1(\lambda)$, $I_2(\lambda)$ obtained from a common point $S(\lambda)$ but with different illuminations $E_1(\lambda)$, $E_2(\lambda)$, the following error function can be derived using a derivation similar to subsubsection 3.1.2 where Equation (15.10) is introduced.

$$F(\mathbf{u}) = \sum_{\lambda} \left(I_1(\lambda) \sum_{i=1}^{m} e_{2,i} E_i(\lambda) - I_2(\lambda) \sum_{i=1}^{m} e_{1,i} E_i(\lambda) \right)^2 \quad (15.13)$$

By minimizing the last equation, we can obtain the illumination SPDs and then the surface spectral reflectance. The constraints for physical reality are Equations (15.6) and (15.12).

3.3   Specular and Diffuse Points

Dielectric inhomogeneous material exhibits specular and diffuse reflections. By targeting this material, we can take advantage of the color signals of specular and diffuse points illuminated by the same illumination. Figure 15.4 illustrates this situation. In this subsection, we show the relationship between diffuse and specular points and explain two algorithms to utilize them for color signal separation.

The specular reflection can be modeled by the well-known dichromatic reflection model. It describes the observing light of a specular point as follows:

$$I(\lambda) = C_s E(\lambda) S_s(\lambda) + C_b E(\lambda) S_b(\lambda) \quad (15.14)$$

where $S_s(\lambda)$ is the specular spectral reflectance function, and $S_b(\lambda)$ is the diffuse spectral reflectance function. (The suffix b stands for the body reflection.)

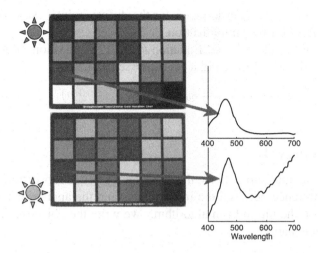

Figure 15.3.   Example of identical surfaces, different illuminations

The geometric factors C_s and C_b are constant over the wavelengths. $S_b(\lambda)$ can be rewritten as $\sum_{j=1}^{n} s_j S_j(\lambda)$ using the basis functions. Further, we introduce the Neutral Interface Reflection (NIR) assumption named by Lee et al. [13] According to this assumption, the reflectance of specular component $S_s(\lambda)$ can be assumed to be constant over the wavelengths. This is because the SPD of reflected light of a specular component solely is almost identical to that of the incident light for most dielectric inhomogeneous objects. Parkkinen et al. [16] showed the first basis function $S_1(\lambda)$ can be considered to be a constant (Fig.1.b, line 1). Therefore, $S_s(\lambda)$ can be rewritten as $kS_1(\lambda)$ where k is a constant scalar.

By combining the dichromatic reflection model with the NIR assumption and the linear basis functions, the light of a specular point can be expressed as follows:

$$I_s(\lambda) \simeq C_s E(\lambda) k S_1(\lambda) + C_b E(\lambda) \sum_{j=1}^{n} s_j S_j(\lambda) \qquad (15.15)$$

$$= E(\lambda) \sum_{j=1}^{n} s_{s,j} S_j(\lambda) \qquad (15.16)$$

where new coefficients $s_{s,j}$ is introduced to simplify the equation.

After modeling the light of a specular point, we now consider the light of a diffuse point. We assume that it has the same surface spectral reflectance as the specular point. Therefore, the light of a diffuse point can be expressed as follows:

$$I_b(\lambda) = C_b' E(\lambda) S_b(\lambda) \simeq C_b' E(\lambda) \sum_{j=1}^{n} s_j S_j(\lambda) \qquad (15.17)$$

$$= E(\lambda) \sum_{j=1}^{n} s_{b,j} S_j(\lambda) \qquad (15.18)$$

where C_b' is another geometric factor for the diffuse point. New coefficients $s_{b,j}$ is introduced for the simplification.

From Equations (15.15) and Equation (15.17), the relation of coefficients between specular and diffuse point is expressed as follows.

$$s_{s,2} : s_{s,j} = s_{b,2} : s_{b,j} \quad (j = 3 \sim n) \tag{15.19}$$

3.3.1 Strategy (1)

As in the previous subsections, the first strategy in this subsection is to minimize the difference between the input signals and the approximated signals. In order to use the hit-and-run algorithm, we write the objective function as the following equations:

$$F(\mathbf{u}) = \sum_{p=\{s,b\}} \sum_{\lambda} \left(\alpha_p \sum_{i=1}^{m} e_i E_i(\lambda) \sum_{j=1}^{n} s_{p,j} S_j(\lambda) - I_p(\lambda) \right)^2 \tag{15.20}$$

$$s_{s,j} = s_{b,j} \quad (j = 2 \sim n) \tag{15.21}$$

where α_p is the ratio between $s_{s,2}$ and $s_{b,2}$ in Equation (15.19). The equation can generate a new state efficiently when using the hit-and-run algorithm.

3.3.2 Strategy (2)

We can utilize the fact that the surface spectral reflectance of body reflection component $S_b(\lambda)$ is common in both diffuse and specular points. By canceling out $S_b(\lambda)$ from Equations (15.14) and (15.17), the following relation is derived:

$$C_b' I_s(\lambda) - C_b I_b(\lambda) = C_b' C_s E(\lambda) S_s(\lambda) \tag{15.22}$$

where $I_s(\lambda)$ is the light from the specular point and $I_b(\lambda)$ is the light from the diffuse point. Using the last equation, we can linearly solve the unknown coefficients.

The details of solving the unknowns are as follows. Let us divide the last equation by C_b', then

$$I_s(\lambda) - g I_b(\lambda) = h E(\lambda) \tag{15.23}$$

where we replaced C_b/C_b' by g, and $C_s S_s(\lambda)$ by h. Note that h is also a constant number since we assume the NIR assumption. $hE(\lambda)$ can be rewritten as $\sum_{i=1}^{m} h e_i E_i(\lambda)$ using the basis functions of illumination SPDs. Let us redefine the coefficients e_i so that it means $h e_i$. Then, Equation (15.23) becomes

$$I_s(\lambda) - g I_b(\lambda) = \sum_{i=1}^{m} e_i E_i(\lambda) \tag{15.24}$$

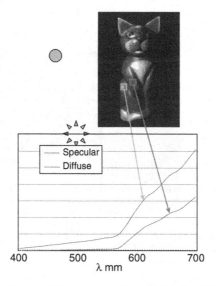

Figure 15.4. Example of a specular color signal and a diffuse color signal

which can be transformed into the linear equation as follows;

$$\left(\begin{array}{cccc} E_1(\lambda) & \dots & E_m(\lambda) & I_b(\lambda) \end{array} \right) \left(\begin{array}{c} e_1 \\ \vdots \\ e_m \\ g \end{array} \right) = I_s(\lambda) \qquad (15.25)$$

Using the last equation, we can linearly solve the unknown coefficients e_i, g.

4.   Acquiring Scene Spectrums

This section describes a system to measure the spectrums of an entire scene. Conventional equipment, such as a spectrometer or a line spectral scanner, only measures spectrums of a point or a line. The following system has a wide field of view, which is a great advantage for the proposed method because it needs spectrums from multiple points. The system, originally proposed by Yoav et al.[18], consists of an interference filter and a monochrome camera. First, we briefly explain the interference filter and the method by Yoav et al. Second, we present two types of camera motion: parallel translation and pan rotation. Pan rotation is important to measure the spectrum of a specular point. Then, we describe a method to convert images to spectrums and to estimate the sensitivity of a camera and the filter itself, which is necessary to obtain accurate data.

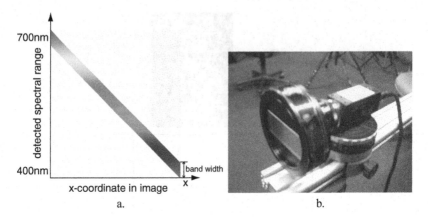

Figure 15.5.   a. The range of penetrating lights of an interference filter. b. An interference filter and a monochrome camera (SONY XC55)

4.1   Interference Filter

An interference filter is a prism filter whose spectral sensitivity is linearly spatially varying. A particular wavelength that the filter passes varies linearly from 400 nm to 700 nm across the filter (horizontally). Fig.15.5.a illustrates this characteristic. Yoav et al.[18] attached the filter to an 8-bit monochrome camera as Fig.15.5.b. shows.

The mechanism of how the system captures spectrums can be explained using Fig.15.6. Let us consider a three-dimensional space formed by an image plane (x, y) and a wavelength (λ). In this space, the system captures a plane where x and λ are linearly correspondent. Therefore, by moving the camera continuously, the entire three-dimensional data can be obtained. Unified image can be produced by mosaicing the images[20, 15, 27, 2] using a smoothing algorithm and an edge detection algorithm.

4.2   Camera motion

Two types of camera motion can be considered: parallel translation and pan rotation. Both motions are illustrated in Fig.15.6.a. and b. In our implementation, a camera is usually set either on a positioning stage that moves parallel to the horizontal axis x of the image plane, or on a rotation stage so that the plane of rotation becomes parallel to the x axis of the image plane.

These two motions have their advantages and disadvantages. Parallel translation enables a camera to move a long distance, but it cannot capture a spectrum of a specular point, because the position of a specular point changes as a camera changes its viewing position. It also causes azimuth difference depending on the distance from the camera to the target points. Unlike paral-

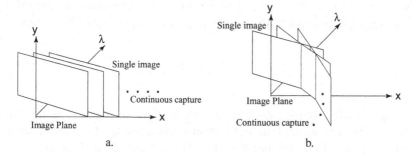

Figure 15.6. Capturing scene spectrums using an interference filter. a. Parallel translation. b. Pan rotation.

lel translation, pan rotation does not cause those problems though it fixes a camera on a certain viewing position.

4.3 Conversion of Input RGB to Spectrum

Spectral data is converted from image data as follows. First, we find the corresponding points between the collected images. This can be achieved by the mosaicing technique or calibrating the camera position. Owing to the characteristic of an interference filter, the image intensity $I(x, y)$ implies the spectral intensity of a certain wavelength λ of the point (x, y);

$$I_{\text{Spec}}(x, y, \lambda) = I(x, y) \qquad \text{where} \quad \lambda = ax + b$$

By tracking the image coordinates (x, y) of a certain point through the captured images, the spectral intensity of the point can be calculated.

Second, we have to consider the light energy absorption by the interference filter and the camera sensor. The obtained spectral intensity is affected by those factors.

$$I_{\text{Spec}}(x, y, \lambda) = E(x, y, \lambda)S(x, y, \lambda)F(\lambda)C(\lambda)$$

where $E(x, y, \lambda)$ is the illumination SPD at (x, y), $S(x, y, \lambda)$ is the surface spectral reflectance, $F(\lambda)$ is the transmissivity of an interference filter, and $C(\lambda)$ is the sensitivity of a camera sensor. Therefore, the real spectral intensity of an incoming light ray is expressed as follows.

$$I_{\text{Real}}(x, y, \lambda) \quad = \quad E(x, y, \lambda)S(x, y, \lambda) = I(x, y)/F(\lambda)C(\lambda) \quad (15.26)$$
$$\text{where} \quad \lambda = ax + b$$

The parameters a, b, and $F(\lambda)C(\lambda)$ must be clarified before we use the system. a and b were calculated by taking images under single-wavelength laser lights. $F(\lambda)C(\lambda) \equiv H(\lambda)$ should be the function that minimizes the difference between the real spectrum and the spectrum captured by the system.

$$\sum_{p=1}^{18}\sum_{\lambda}\Big(I_{\text{Spec},p}(\lambda) - H(\lambda)I_{\text{Real},p}(\lambda)\Big)^2 \qquad (15.27)$$

In our experiments, we measured the spectrum of eighteen colors of the Macbeth Color Checker under blue lights with a spectrometer ($I_{\text{Real}}(\lambda)$) and the system ($I_{\text{Spec}}(\lambda)$). From the last equation, $H(\lambda)$ should be as follows.

$$H(\lambda) = \sum_{p=1}^{18} I_{\text{Spec},p}(\lambda)I_{\text{Real},p}(\lambda) \,/\, \sum_{p=1}^{18} I_{\text{Real},p}(\lambda)^2 \qquad (15.28)$$

5.   Implementation

Our implementation is based on the simulated annealing algorithm with the hit-and-run algorithm [1]. The simulated annealing algorithm enables us to avoid local minima in solving a non-linear optimization problem. While using the hit-and-run algorithm, we can obtain a good performance in searching the interior point as a new state.

The simulated annealing algorithm is expressed as follows.

1 Decide an initial state for a variable $\mathbf{u} = [e_1, ..., e_m, s_1, ..., s_n, \alpha]^t$

2 Generate a new state $\mathbf{u}''$ by the hit-and-run algorithm. Details are described below.

3 If $\Delta F = F(\mathbf{u}) - F(\mathbf{u}'') < 0$, or $\exp(-\Delta F/T_e(t)) > \text{Random}(0, 1)$, then $\mathbf{u} = \mathbf{u}''$ and go to 2. Otherwise, go directly to 2.

where F is the minimizing function and T_e is called the cooling function, which controls the size of the searching space. T_e varies according to t, which reflects the current number of the iteration. We used $T_e(t) = \text{Const}/(1 + t)^2$. The function $\text{Random}(0, 1)$ returns a uniformly random number between 0 and 1. The vector $\mathbf{u}$ that minimizes $F(\mathbf{u})$ can be obtained by repeating the above process until convergence.

The hit-and-run alogrithm is used to make a good performance in searching an interior point in a convex space. The process is as follows:

1 Given an interior point $\mathbf{u}$,

2 Generate a vector $\mathbf{u}'$ whose probability is equal to that of $\mathbf{u}$, randomly.

3 Decide the maximum and minimum range r^+, r^- by the next calculation.

$$k_{1,\lambda} = \frac{\text{maxlim} - \sum_{i=1}^{m} e_i E_i(\lambda)}{\sum_{i=1}^{m} e_i' E_i(\lambda)}, \qquad k_{2,\lambda} = \frac{-\sum_{i=1}^{m} e_i E_i(\lambda)}{\sum_{i=1}^{m} e_i' E_i(\lambda)},$$

$$k_{3,\lambda} = \frac{1 - \sum_{j=1}^{n} s_j S_j(\lambda)}{\sum_{j=1}^{n} s_j' S_j(\lambda)}, \qquad k_{4,\lambda} = \frac{-\sum_{j=1}^{n} s_j S_j(\lambda)}{\sum_{j=1}^{n} s_j' S_j(\lambda)}$$

$$r^+ = \arg \min k_{l,\lambda} \qquad r^- = \arg \max k_{l,\lambda} \qquad (l = \{1, ..., 4\})$$

4 $\mathbf{u}'' = \mathbf{u} + (\text{Random}(0,1)r^+ + (1 - \text{Random}(0,1))r^-)\,\mathbf{u}'$

The calculated vector $\mathbf{u}''$ will be the new state in the simulated annealing algorithm.

6.   Experimental Results

6.1   Experiments using Point Spectrums

To confirm the performance of the separation algorithm, we performed experiments using some samples. We measured color signal spectrums using the Spectrascan PR650. By using Spectrascan PR650, we can measure a color signal from 380nm to 780nm by 4nm. We resampled color signals from 400nm to 700nm by 5nm. We used the Macbeth Color Checker as our target object. For the basis functions, we used Judd's [12] three illumination basis functions and Parkkinen's [16] reflectance basis functions.

Fig.15.7 shows the result of estimation using multiple surfaces. Two illuminations were tested: outdoor illumination and incandescent light at 2800K. In those experiments, three reflectance basis functions were used. The top row in Fig.15.7 shows the results using the outdoor illumination. Estimated illumination SPD by using one, two, and three points of the Macbeth Color Checker's (red, green and blue colors), are shown. Better results were obtained when the number of points increased. The bottom row in Fig.15.7 shows the results using the incandescent light at 2800K. As in the first experiment, one, two and three points of the Macbeth Color Checker (red, green and blue colors), are used. Using incandescent light, our algorithm provided good separation results with multiple color signals. As shown in Fig.15.7.d, the results using the red and blue points' spectrals, or the red and green and blue points' spectrals are quite satisfactory.

Fig.15.8 also shows the result of estimation using multiple surfaces. This time, eighteen points' spectrals of the Macbeth Color Checker were used.

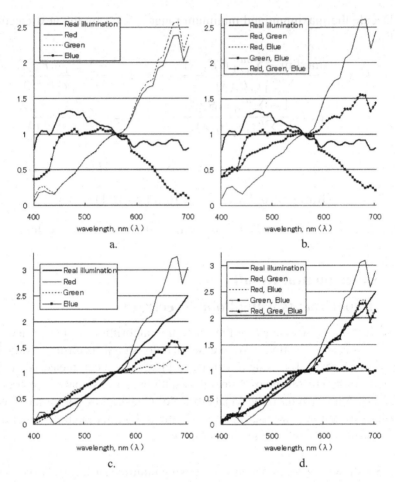

Figure 15.7. Experimental results using multiple surfaces. Top row: Measured outdoor illumination SPD, and the estimated illumination by the separation algorithm using a: one point, and b: multi points. Bottom row: Measured illumination SPD of incandescent light at 2800K, and the estimated illumination using c: one point, and d: multi points.

Furthermore, three, four, six, and eight reflectance basis functions were tested, respectively. Outdoor illumination SPD was used.

Fig.15.9 shows the result of estimation using multiple illuminations. Two illuminations were outdoor illumination and incandescent light at 2800K. Three points of the Macbeth Color Checker (red, green and blue colors) were used. Here, two strategies described in 3.2.1 and 3.2.2 were tested. The top row shows the result of strategy (1) in 3.2.1. Fig.15.9.a shows the estimated illumination using the blue surface, and Fig.15.9.b shows the estimated illumination

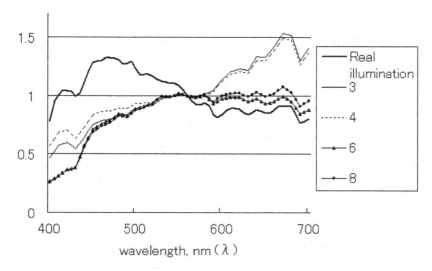

Figure 15.8. Measured outdoor illumination SPD and the estimated illumination by the separation algorithm with three, four, six, and eight reflectance basis functions using all eighteen colors of the Macbeth Color Checker.

using the green. Eight reflectance basis functions were used for the experiments. As shown in Fig.15.9.a, a blue surface lit by the outdoor illumination and incandescent light at 2800K provided a good result. The bottom row shows the separation results by the strategy (2) in 3.2.2. The estimated illuminations are shown in Fig.15.9.c and d. Fig.15.9.c shows the result using the red surface, and Fig.15.9.d shows the result using the blue surface. As shown in Fig.15.9.d, a red point lit by the outdoor illumination and incandescent light at 2800K provided an especially good result.

Fig.15.10 shows the result of estimation using specular and diffuse points. We tested two illuminations: outdoor illumination and incandescent light at 2800K. Red, green, and blue points' diffuse and specular spectrals were used. Here, we tested two strategies described in 3.3.1 and 3.3.2. The top row shows the results of strategy (1) in 3.3.1. The estimated illuminations are shown in Fig.15.10.a and b. Fig.15.10.a shows the results using incandescent light at 2800K, and Fig.15.10.b shows the results using outdoor illumination. The bottom row shows the results of strategy (2) in 3.3.2. Fig.15.10.c shows the results using incandescent light at 2800K, and Fig.15.10.d shows the results using outdoor illumination. As can be observed in Fig.15.10, utilizing diffuse and specular points using strategy (2) produces excellent results.

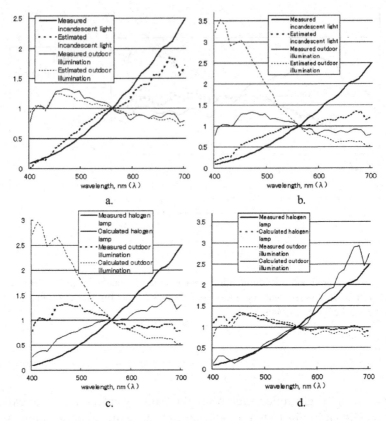

Figure 15.9. Experimental results using multiple illuminations. Top row: Measured outdoor illumination SPD and incandescent light at 2800K, and the estimated illuminations by the separation algorithm (strategy (1)) using a surface (a: blue, b: green) under those illuminations. Bottom row: Measured outdoor illumination SPD and incandescent light at 2800K, and the estimated illuminations by the separation algorithm (strategy (2)) using a surface (c: blue, d: red) under those illuminations.

Table 15.1. The error value of one point algorithm and our algorithms, using all combinations of eighteen colors of the Macbeth Color Checker.

Light source	Single point	Multiple surfaces	Multiple illuminations	Specular-diffuse strategy (1)	strategy (2)
outdoor	34.55	11.39	28.10	13.01	0.76
incandescent	11.22	0.79	26.16	3.18	0.54

Table.1 shows the overall error value of each algorithm. By using the multiple-point algorithm, especially using specular-diffuse points,   a great performance can be achieved.

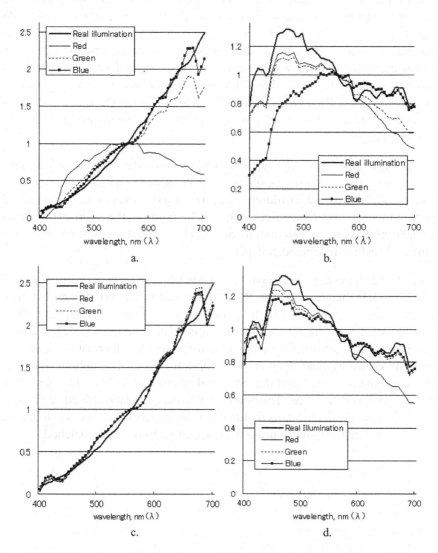

Figure 15.10. Experimental results using specular and diffuse spectrums. Top row: Measured SPD of a: halogen lamp b: outdoor illumination, and the estimated SPD by the separation algorithm (strategy (1)), using red, green, and blue diffuse-specular points. Bottom row: Measured SPD of c: halogen lamp and d: outdoor illumination, and the estimated SPD by the separation algorithm (strategy (2)), using red, green, and blue diffuse-specular points.

6.2   Experiments using Scene Spectrums

We used the system described in Section 4 to acquire scene spectrums. An interference filter was attached to a SONY XC-55, monochrome camera. We took images by moving the camera continuously with both parallel translation and pan rotation. The conversion function, $H(\lambda)$ in Equation (15.28), was calculated by the method described in 4.3. First, we took the Macbeth Color Checker continuously under blue illumination, by moving a camera with parallel translation. Then we mosaiced the images. Using the spectrums from the system and a spectrometer, we calculated the conversion function with Equation (15.28).

Fig.15.11 shows the scene separation result using the multiple-points algorithm. We took scenes with parallel translation under two lights: incandescent light at 2800K and outdoor illumination. The top two images are the obtained spectral images under each light source. The figure in the middle row shows the measured and estimated illumination SPD. The bottom two images are the estimated surface-reflectance images.

Fig.15.12 shows the scene separation result using specular and diffuse points. The top left image shows the RGB image that is converted from obtained spectral images. Each pixel in the top left image contains spectral data. They were obtained with pan rotation under an incandescent light source. The top right image shows obtained specular and diffuse spectral distribution, from two positions shown by blue squares in the top left image. The bottom right image shows the measured and the estimated illumination SPD. The algorithm shows a good performance. The bottom left is the estimated reflectance image. Highly precise mosaicing was required for this experiment. The specular data tend to have large amount of noise if the specular point is mismatched.

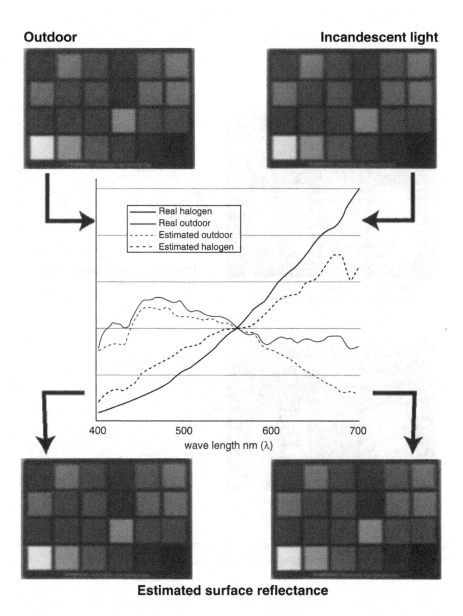

Figure 15.11. Scene separation result using algorithm (26). This was achieved by taking a scene moving a camera in parallel translation under incandescent light at 2800K and outdoor illumination, using red, green, and blue points of the Macbeth Color Checker.

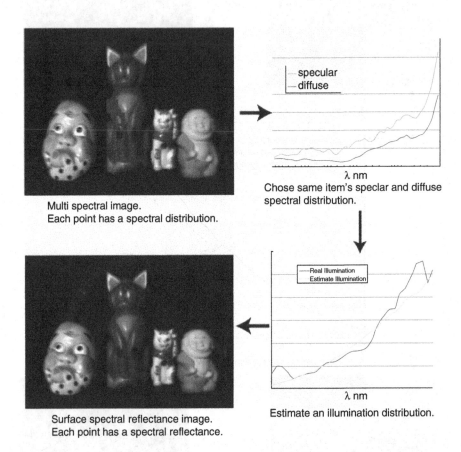

Multi spectral image.
Each point has a spectral distribution.

Chose same item's speclar and diffuse
spectral distribution.

Surface spectral reflectance image.
Each point has a spectral reflectance.

Estimate an illumination distribution.

Figure 15.12.   Scene separation result using specular and diffuse points. This was achieved by taking a scene moving a monochrome camera pan rotated under outdoor illumination.

7.   Conclusion

In this chapter, we have evaluated a spectrum separation method under three different conditions, as follows: 1) points with different color spectrum distributions illuminated by the same light source, 2) the same point under different illumination sources of different spectrum color distributions, 3) diffuse and specular points under the same illumination source. We found that using multi-point spectrum distributions significantly increases reliability in separating scene spectrum distribution into illumination and reflectance spectrum distribution.

Acknowledgments

This research was supported, in part, by Ministry of Education, Culture, Sports, Science and Technology under the Leading Project, "Development of High Fidelity Digitization Software for Large-Scale and Intangible Cultural Assets," and, in part, by Japan Science and Technology Agency, under the CREST program, "Automatic generation of virtual models of cultural heritage."

References

[1] P.-R. Chang and T.-H. Hsieh, "Constrained nonlinear optimization approaches to color-signal separation," *IEEE Transactions on Image Processing*, Vol. 4, No. 1, pp. 81-94, 1995.

[2] N. Chiba, H. Kano, M. Minoh, and M. Yasuda, "Feature-based image mosaicing," *Transactions of IEICE*, Vol. J82-D-II, No. 10, pp. 1581-1589, 1999 (in Japanese).

[3] J. Cohen, "Dependency of the spectral reflectance curves of the Munsell color chips," *Psychonomical Science*, Vol. 1, pp. 369-370, 1964.

[4] M. D'Zmura and P. Lennie, "Mechanisms of color constancy," *Journal of the Optical Society of America A*, Vol. 3, No. 10, pp. 1662-1672, 1986.

[5] M. D'Zmura, "Color constancy: surface color from changing illumination," *Journal of the Optical Society of America A*, Vol. 9, No. 3, pp. 490-493, 1992.

[6] G.D. Finlayson, B.V. Funt, and K. Barnard, "Color constancy under varying illumination," *Proceedings of the Fifth International Conference on Computer Vision*, pp. 720-725, 1995.

[7] G.D. Finlayson, S.D. Hordley, and P.M. Hubel, "Color by correlation: A simple, unifying framework for color constancy," *IEEE Transactions on Pattern Analysis and Machine Intelligence*, Vol. 23, No. 11, pp. 1209-1221, 2001.

[8] G.D. Finlayson and G. Schaefer, "Solving for colour constancy using a constrained dichromatic reflection model," *International Journal of Computer Vision*, Vol. 42, No. 3, pp. 127-144, 2001.

[9] G.D. Finlayson and S.D. Hordley, "Color constancy at a pixel," *Journal of the Optical Society of America A*, Vol. 18, No. 2, pp. 253-264, 2001.

[10] Th. Gevers, H.M.G. Stockman, and J. van de Weijer, "Color constancy from hyper-spectral data," *Proceedings of The Eleventh British Machine Vision Conference*, 2000.

[11] J. Ho, B.V. Funt, and M.S. Drew, "Separating a color signal into illumination and surface reflectance components: Theory and applications," *IEEE Transactions on Pattern Analysis and Machine Intelligence*, Vol. 12, No. 10, pp. 966-977, 1990.

[12] D.B. Judd, D.L. MacAdam, and G. Wyszecki, "Spectral distribution of typical daylight as a function of correlated color temperature," *Journal of the Optical Society of America*, Vol. 54, No. 8, pp. 1031-1040, 1964.

[13] H.C. Lee, E.J. Breneman, and C.P. Schulte, "Modeling light reflection for computer color vision," *IEEE Transactions on Pattern Analysis and Machine Intelligence*, Vol. 12, No. 4, pp. 402-409, 1990.

[14] J.A. Marchant and C.M. Onyango, "Spectral invariance under daylight illumination changes," *Journal of the Optical Society of America A*, Vol. 19, No. 5, pp. 840-848, 2002.

[15] Y. Nakatani and M. Okutomi, "Image mosaicing using an active camera," *The Journal of the Institute of Image Electronics Engineers of Japan*, Vol. 29, No. 5, pp. 462-470, 2000 (in Japanese).

[16] J.P.S. Parkkinen, J. Hallikainen, and T. Jaaskelainen, "Characteristic spectra of Munsell colors," *Journal of the Optical Society of America A*, Vol. 6, No. 2, pp. 318-322, 1989.

[17] R. Lenz, P. Meer, M. Hauta-Kasari, "Spectral-based illumination estimation and color correction," *COLOR Research and Application*, Vol. 24, No. 2, pp. 98-111, 1999.

[18] Y.Y. Schechner and S.K. Nayar, "Generalized mosaicing: Wide field of view multispectral imaging," *IEEE Transactions on Pattern Analysis and Machine Intelligence*, Vol. 24, No. 10, pp. 1334-1348, 2002.

[19] D. Slater and G. Healey, "What is the spectral dimensionality of illumination functions in outdoor scenes?," *Proceedings of IEEE Computer Society Conference on Computer Vision and Pattern Recognition*, pp. 105-110, 1998.

[20] R. Szeliski and H.-Y. Shum, "Creating full view panoramic image mosaics and environment maps," *Proceedings of SIGGRAPH 97*, pp. 251-258, 1997.

[21] R.T. Tan, K. Nishino, and K. Ikeuchi, "Illumination chromaticity estimation using inverse-intensity chromaticity space," *Proceedings of IEEE Computer Society Conference on Computer Vision and Pattern Recognition*, pp. 673-680, 2003.

[22] S. Tominaga, "Multichannel vision system for estimating surface and illuminat functions," *Journal of the Optical Society of America A*, Vol. 13, No. 11, pp. 2163-2173, 1996.

[23] S. Tominaga, S. Ebisui, and B.A. Wandell, "Scene illuminant classification -brighter is better-," *Journal of the Optical Society of America A*, Vol. 18, No. 1, pp. 55-64, 2001.

[24] S. Tominaga, "Surface identification using the dichromatic reflection model," *IEEE Transactions on Pattern Analysis and Machine Intelligence*, Vol. 13, No. 7, pp. 658-670, 1991.

[25] S. Tominaga and B.A. Wandell, "Standard surface-reflectance model and illuminant estimation," *Journal of the Optical Society of America A*, Vol. 6, No. 4, pp. 576-584, 1989.

[26] S. Tominaga and B.A. Wandell, "Natural scene illuminant estimation using the sensor correlation," *Proceedings of The IEEE*, Vol. 90, No. 1, pp. 42-56, 2002.

[27] Y. Xiong and K. Turkowski, "Registration, calibration and blending in creating high quality panoramas," *Proceedings of the 4th IEEE Workshop on Applications of Computer Vision*, pp. 69-74, 1998.

[28] J.Y. Hardeberg, "On the spectral dimensionality of object colours," *Proceedings of IS&T First European Conference on Colour in Graphics, Image and Vision*, pp. 480-485, 2002.

Chapter 16

COLOR CONSTANCY THROUGH INVERSE-INTENSITY CHROMATICITY SPACE

Robby T. Tan, Ko Nishino, and Katsushi Ikeuchi

Abstract   Existing color constancy methods cannot handle both uniformly colored surfaces
and highly textured surfaces in a single integrated framework. Statistics-based
methods require many surface colors, and become error prone when there are
only a few surface colors. In contrast, dichromatic-based methods can successfully handle uniformly colored surfaces, but cannot be applied to highly textured surfaces since they require precise color segmentation. In this chapter, we
present a single integrated method to estimate illumination chromaticity from
single-colored and multi-colored surfaces. Unlike existing dichromatic-based
methods, our proposed method requires only rough highlight regions, without
segmenting the colors inside them. We show that, by analyzing highlights,
a direct correlation between illumination chromaticity and image chromaticity
can be obtained. This correlation is clearly described in "inverse-intensity chromaticity space", a novel two-dimensional space we introduce. In addition, by
utilizing the Hough transform and histogram analysis in this space, illumination
chromaticity can be estimated robustly, even for a highly textured surface.

1.   Introduction

The spectral energy distribution of light reflected from an object is the product of illumination spectral energy distribution and surface spectral reflectance.
As a result, the color of an object observed in an image is not the actual color of
the object's surface. Recovering the actual surface color requires the capability
to discount the color of illumination. A computational approach to recover the
actual color of objects is referred to as a color constancy algorithm .

Human perception inherently has the capability of color constancy. This capability plays an important role in object recognition processes. Unfortunately,
up to now, the mechanism of human perception color constancy has not been
well understood. For machine vision, color constancy is essential for various
applications such as color-based object recognition, color reproduction, image

retrieval, reflection components separation, etc. This has motivated researchers in the field of machine vision to develop various color constancy methods.

Previous Work.   Finlayson *et al.* [6] categorized color constancy methods into two classes: statistics-based and physics-based methods. Statistics-based methods utilize the relationship between color distributions and statistical knowledge of common lights and surfaces [2, 4, 9, 21, 25, 27]. One drawback of these methods is that they require that many colors be observed on the target surfaces. On the other hand, physics-based methods [3, 5, 10, 17, 18], whose algorithms are based on understanding the physical process of reflected light, can successfully deal with fewer surface colors, even to the extreme of a single surface color [6, 7]. In addition, based on the surface type of the input image, physics-based methods can be divided into two groups: diffuse-based and dichromatic-based methods. Diffuse-based methods assume that input images have only diffuse reflection, while dichromatic-based methods assume both diffuse and specular reflections occur in the images. Geusebroek *et al.* [12, 11] proposed a physical basis of color constancy by considering the spectral and spatial derivatives of the Lambertian image formation model. Andersen *et al.* [1] provided an analysis on image chromaticity under two illumination colors for dichromatic surfaces. Since our aim is to develop an algorithm that is able to handle both a single and multiple surface colors, in this section, we will concentrate our discussion on existing physics-based methods, particularly dichromatic-based methods.

Methods in dichromatic-based color constancy rely on the dichromatic reflection model proposed by Shafer [23]. Klinker *et al.* [14] introduced a method to estimate illumination color from a uniform colored surface, by extracting a T-shape color distribution in the RGB space. However, in real images, it becomes quite difficult to extract the T-shape due to noise, thereby making the final estimate unreliable.

Lee [17] introduced a method to estimate illumination chromaticity using highlights of at least two surface colors. The estimation is accomplished by finding an intersection of two or more dichromatic lines in the chromaticity space. While this simple approach based on the physics of reflected light provides a handy method for color constancy, it suffers from a few drawbacks. First, to create the dichromatic line for each surface color from highlights, one needs to segment the surface colors beneath the highlights. This color segmentation is difficult when the target object is highly textured. Second, nearly parallel dichromatic lines caused by similar surface colors can make the intersection sensitive to noise. Consequently, for real images, which usually suffer from noise, the estimation for similar surface colors becomes unstable. Third, the method does not deal with uniformly colored surfaces. Parallel to this, several methods have been proposed in the literature [3, 24, 26].

Recently, three methods which extend Lee's algorithm have been proposed [17]: Lehmann *et al.* [20] developed a more robust technique to identify the dichromatic lines in the chromaticity space. The success of this technique depends on an assumption that, in each highlight region, the surface color is uniform. As a consequence, the technique fails when dealing with complex textured surfaces, which usually have more than one surface color in their highlighted regions. Finlayson *et al.* [8], proposed imposing a constraint on the colors of illumination. This constraint is based on the statistics of natural illumination colors, and improves the stability in obtaining the intersection, i.e., it addresses the second drawback of Lee's method. Furthermore, Finlayson *et al.* [6] proposed the use of the Planckian locus as a constraint to accomplish illumination estimation from uniformly colored surfaces. This Planckian constraint on the illumination chromaticity makes the estimation more robust, especially for natural scene images. However, the method still has a few drawbacks. First, the position and the shape of the Planckian locus in the chromaticity space make the estimation error prone for certain surface colors, such as blue or yellow. Second, since they include diffuse regions in obtaining dichromatic lines, the result could become inaccurate. While the fact that their method does not require reflection separation is one of the advantages, the diffuse cluster, due to noise, usually has a different direction from the specular cluster; as a result, the dichromatic line can be shifted from the correct one. Third, like other previous methods, for multicolored surfaces, color segmentation is required.

Contributions.   In this chapter, our goal is to accomplish illumination chromaticity estimation for single- and multi-colored surfaces based on a dichromatic reflection model. Briefly, the method is as follows. Given a single colored image, we estimate rough highlight regions by thresholding on brightness and saturation values. We transform the pixels of the estimated highlight regions into inverse-intensity chromaticity space, a novel space which we introduce. In this space, the correlation between image chromaticity and illumination chromaticity becomes linear. As a result, based on this linear correlation, we are able to estimate illumination chromaticity for both single- and multi-colored surfaces without segmenting the color beneath the highlights. In addition, we use the Hough transform and histogram analysis for accurate and robust estimation.

In comparison with Lee's method [17], our method has two advantages: first, it does not require multicolored surfaces, and second, it does not suffer from the problem of similar surface colors. The method also advances Lehmann *et al.*'s method [20], since it does not assume that the surface color underneath a highlight region is uniform, and it is feasible even for uniformly colored surfaces. Moreover, unlike Finlayson's dichromatic method [6], the method does not require known camera sensitivity and a strong constraint on illumination such as blackbody radiator. Basically, this chapter provides two main contributions. First, it presents a single integrated method that can be applied for both uniformly colored surfaces and highly textured surfaces. Second, it introduces inverse-intensity chromaticity space that clearly describes the correlation of image chromaticity and illumination chromaticity in a linear correlation.

Note that, while having ability to work on rough estimate of highlight regions is one of the advantages of our method, the problem of determining highlight regions is still an open challenging problem. Moreover, although the method does not require any other intrinsic camera characteristics, such as sensor sensitivity as well as an assumption of a narrowband sensor, it assumes that the output of the camera is linear to the flux of incoming light.

The remaining discussion of the chapter is organized as follows. In Section 2, the reflection model of inhomogeneous materials and image color formation is discussed. In Section 3, we explain the theoretical derivation of the correlation between image chromaticity and illumination chromaticity. In Section 4, we bring the theoretical derivation into a practical computational method to estimate illumination chromaticity. In Section 5, the distribution in inverse-intensity chromaticity space is discussed in detail in order to understand the main factors that determine the robustness of the estimation. We provide a brief description of the implementation, experimental results and the evaluations for real images in Section 6. Finally in Section 7, we conclude this chapter.

2.   Reflection Model

Optically, most objects can be divided into two categories: homogeneous and inhomogeneous objects. Homogeneous objects, which have a uniform refractive index throughout their surface and body, produce specular-only reflection [13]. On the contrary, inhomogeneous objects, which have varying refractive indices in their surfaces and bodies, exhibit diffuse reflection. In addition, because of the refractive index difference between the object's surfaces and the air, inhomogeneous objects also reflect specular reflection [23]. The amount of reflected light is governed by Fresnel's law, while the direction of the specular reflection is relative to the local surface normal. Thus, reflection of opaque inhomogeneous objects can be modeled as a linear combination of diffuse and specular reflections, which is known as the dichromatic reflection model [23] . The model states that the light reflected from an object is a linear combination of diffuse and specular reflections:

$$I(\lambda, \bar{\mathbf{x}}) = w_d(\bar{\mathbf{x}}) S_d(\lambda, \bar{\mathbf{x}}) E(\lambda, \bar{\mathbf{x}}) + w_s(\bar{\mathbf{x}}) S_s(\lambda, \bar{\mathbf{x}}) E(\lambda, \bar{\mathbf{x}}) \qquad (16.1)$$

where $\bar{\mathbf{x}} = \{r, s, t\}$ is the position of a surface point in a three-dimensional world coordinate system; $w_d(\bar{\mathbf{x}})$ and $w_s(\bar{\mathbf{x}})$ are the geometrical parameters for diffuse and specular reflection, respectively; their values depend on the geometric structure at location $\bar{\mathbf{x}}$. $S_d(\lambda, \bar{\mathbf{x}})$ is the diffuse spectral reflectance function; $S_s(\lambda, \bar{\mathbf{x}})$ is the specular spectral reflectance function; $E(\lambda, \bar{\mathbf{x}})$ is the spectral energy distribution function of the illumination.

For most dielectric inhomogeneous objects, the spectral reflectance distribution of the specular reflection component is similar to the spectral energy distribution of the incident light [19]. Researchers usually assume that both of them are the same [6, 26, 17, 3]. Lee *et al.* [19] named this well-known assumption the neutral interface reflection (NIR) assumption. All dichromatic-based methods, including our method, use this assumption as one of the basic assumptions. As a result, we can set $S_s(\lambda, \bar{\mathbf{x}})$ as a constant, and Equation (16.1) becomes:

$$I(\lambda, \bar{\mathbf{x}}) = w_d(\bar{\mathbf{x}})S_d(\lambda, \bar{\mathbf{x}})E(\lambda, \bar{\mathbf{x}}) + \tilde{w}_s(\bar{\mathbf{x}})E(\lambda, \bar{\mathbf{x}}) \qquad (16.2)$$

where $\tilde{w}_s(\bar{\mathbf{x}}) = w_s(\bar{\mathbf{x}})k_s(\bar{\mathbf{x}})$, with $k_s(\bar{\mathbf{x}})$ is a constant scalar w.r.t. the wavelength.

Image Formation. An image taken by a digital color camera can be described as:

$$I_c(\mathbf{x}) = w_d(\mathbf{x}) \int_\Omega S_d(\lambda, \mathbf{x})E(\lambda)q_c(\lambda)d\lambda +$$
$$\tilde{w}_s(\mathbf{x}) \int_\Omega E(\lambda)q_c(\lambda)d\lambda \qquad (16.3)$$

where I_c is the sensor response (RGB pixel values), which in this chapter we call *image intensity*, $\mathbf{x} = \{x, y\}$ is the two dimensional image coordinates and q_c is the three-element-vector of sensor sensitivity with index c represents the type of sensors (r, g, and b). The integration is done over the visible spectrum (Ω). Note that we ignore camera noise and gain. In addition, we assume a uniform color of illumination over the input image, so that the illumination spectral distribution $E(\lambda)$ becomes independent of the image coordinate ($\mathbf{x}$). For the sake of simplicity, equation (16.3) is written as:

$$I_c(\mathbf{x}) = w_d(\mathbf{x})B_c(\mathbf{x}) + \tilde{w}_s(\mathbf{x})G_c \qquad (16.4)$$

where $B_c(\mathbf{x}) = \int_\Omega S_d(\lambda, \mathbf{x})E(\lambda)q_c(\lambda)d\lambda$; and $G_c = \int_\Omega E(\lambda)q_c(\lambda)d\lambda$. The first part of the right side of the equation represents the diffuse reflection component, while the second part represents the specular reflection component.

3.   Inverse-Intensity Chromaticity Space

In this chapter, chromaticity or also commonly called *normalized rgb* is defined as:

$$\sigma_c(\mathbf{x}) = \frac{I_c(\mathbf{x})}{\Sigma I_i(\mathbf{x})} \qquad (16.5)$$

where $\Sigma I_i(\mathbf{x}) = I_r(\mathbf{x}) + I_g(\mathbf{x}) + I_b(\mathbf{x})$.

By considering the chromaticity definition in the last equation and the image intensity definition in Equation (16.4), for diffuse-only reflection component ($\tilde{w}_s = 0$), the chromaticity becomes independent from the diffuse geometrical parameter w_d, since it is factored out by using Equation (16.5). We call this *diffuse chromaticity* (Λ_c), with definition:

$$\Lambda_c(\mathbf{x}) = \frac{B_c(\mathbf{x})}{\Sigma B_i(\mathbf{x})} \qquad (16.6)$$

On the other hand, for the specular-only reflection component ($w_d = 0$), the chromaticity is independent of the specular geometrical parameter ($\tilde{w}_s$), which we call *specular chromaticity* (Γ_c):

$$\Gamma_c(\mathbf{x}) = \frac{G_c(\mathbf{x})}{\Sigma G_i(\mathbf{x})} \qquad (16.7)$$

By considering Equation (16.6) and (16.7), consequently Equation (16.4) can be written as:

$$I_c(\mathbf{x}) = m_d(\mathbf{x})\Lambda_c(\mathbf{x}) + m_s(\mathbf{x})\Gamma_c \qquad (16.8)$$

where

$$m_d(\mathbf{x}) = w_d(\mathbf{x})\Sigma B_i(\mathbf{x}) \qquad (16.9)$$
$$m_s(\mathbf{x}) = \tilde{w}_d(\mathbf{x})\Sigma G_i \qquad (16.10)$$

We can also set $\Sigma\sigma_i(\mathbf{x}) = \Sigma\Lambda_i(\mathbf{x}) = \Sigma\Gamma_i(\mathbf{x}) = 1$, without loss of generality. Note that we assume that the camera output is linear to the flux of incoming light intensity; in our method, using only that assumption allows the above chromaticity definitions to be applied to estimate illumination chromaticity.

3.1   Image Chromaticity and Image Intensity

By substituting each channel's image intensity in Equation (16.5) with its definition in Equation (16.8) and by considering pixel-based operation, the image chromaticity can be written in terms of the dichromatic reflection model:

$$\sigma_c = \frac{m_d\Lambda_c + m_s\Gamma_c}{m_d\Sigma\Lambda_i + m_s\Sigma\Gamma_i} \qquad (16.11)$$

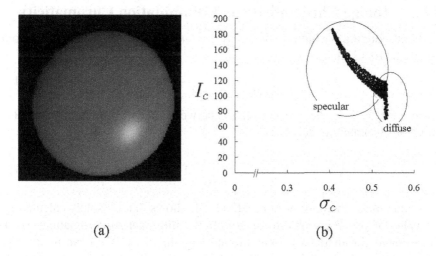

Figure 16.1. (a) Synthetic image with a single surface color, (b) projection of the diffuse and specular pixels into the chromaticity-intensity space, with c representing the green channel.

By deriving the last equation we can obtain the correlation between m_s and m_d:

$$m_s = \frac{m_d(\Lambda_c - \sigma_c)}{\sigma_c - \Gamma_c} \qquad (16.12)$$

From the above correlation, we know that m_s is encapsulated in the image chromaticity (σ_c). Then, by plugging Equation (16.12) into Equation (16.8), the correlation between image intensity (I_c) and image chromaticity (σ_c) can be described as:

$$I_c = m_d(\Lambda_c - \Gamma_c)\left(\frac{\sigma_c}{\sigma_c - \Gamma_c}\right) \qquad (16.13)$$

The last equation shows that the correlation between image intensity (I_c) and image chromaticity (σ_c) is not linear.

By projecting a uniformly colored surface into chromaticity-intensity space, according to Equation (16.13), the specular pixels will form a curved cluster (non-linear correlation), as illustrated in Figure 16.1.b. On the other hand, the diffuse pixels will form a straight vertical line, since the image chromaticity (σ_c) which is equal to diffuse chromaticity (Λ_c) is independent from image intensity (I_c).

3.2   Image Chromaticity and Illumination Chromaticity

By introducing p which we define as $p = m_d(\Lambda_c - \Gamma_c)$, we can derive from Equation (16.13) that:

$$\frac{I_c}{\sigma_c} = \frac{p}{\sigma_c - \Gamma_c} \tag{16.14}$$

Since $I_c/\sigma_c = \Sigma I_i$, then the correlation between image chromaticity and illumination chromaticity becomes:

$$\sigma_c = p\frac{1}{\Sigma I_i} + \Gamma_c \tag{16.15}$$

This equation is the core of our method. It shows that by solely calculating the value of p, we are able to determine the illumination chromaticity (Γ_c), since image chromaticity (σ_c) and total image intensity (ΣI_i) can be directly observed from the input image. The details are as follows.

If the values of p are constant and the values of ΣI_i vary throughout the image, the last equation becomes a linear equation, and the illumination chromaticity (Γ_c) can be estimated in a straightforward manner by using general line fitting algorithms. However, in most images, the values of p are not constant, since p depends on m_d, Λ_c and Γ_c. For the sake of simplicity, until the end of this subsection, we temporarily assume that the values of Λ_c are constant, making the values of p depend solely on m_d, as Γ_c has already been assumed to be constant.

Equation (16.9) states that $m_d = w_d\Sigma B_i$. According to the Lambert's Law [16], w_d is determined by the angle between lighting direction and surface normal, while ΣB_i is determined by diffuse albedo (k_d) and intensity of incident light (L). The angles between surface normals and light directions depend on the shape of the object and the light distribution. The angle will be constant if an object has planar surface and illumination directions are all the same for all points in the surface. While, if the surface is not planar or the illumination directions are not uniform, then the angle will vary. For a surface with a uniform color, the value of the diffuse albedo (k_d) is constant. The values of L (intensity of incident light) are mostly determined by the location of illuminants, which will be constant if the locations of the illuminants are distant from the surface. For relatively nearby illuminants, the values of L may vary w.r.t. the surface point. Considering all these aspects, as a result, in general conditions the value of m_d can be either constant or varied. Yet, in most cases the value of m_d will be varied because, most shapes of objects in the real world are not planar and the assumption on uniform illumination direction, in some conditions, cannot be held.

Consequently, Equation (16.15) poses two problems: first, whether there are a number of specular pixels that have the same m_d, and second, whether these pixels that have the same m_d also have different ΣI_i. If we consider a single surface color, then the solution of the first problem depends on w_d and L. In microscopic scale of the real world, the combination of w_d and L could be unique for certain circumstances. Fortunately, in the scale of image intensity, for some set of surface points, the differences of the combination of w_d and L are small and can be approximated as constant. We can take this approximation for granted, as current ordinary digital cameras automatically do it for us as a part of their accuracy limitation. Moreover, in Section 5, we will explain that the distribution of specular pixels for the same surface color is localized in a certain area in inverse-intensity chromaticity space, in which certain points have small difference of p and thus can be grouped together.

The second problem can be resolved by considering Equation (16.8). In this equation, two specular pixels will have the same m_d but different I_c, if their values of m_s are different. Equation (16.10) states that $m_s = \tilde{w}_s \Sigma G_i$. In Torrance and Sparrow reflection model [28], which is reasonably accurate to model specularity, $\tilde{w}_s$ is expressed as:

$$\tilde{w}_s = FG\frac{1}{cos\theta_r}exp(-\frac{\alpha^2}{2\phi^2}) \tag{16.16}$$

where F is the Fresnel reflection, G is the geometrical attenuation factor, θ_r is the angle of surface normal and viewing direction, α is the angle between the surface normal and the bisector of viewing direction and illumination direction, and ϕ is the surface roughness. Thus, if the two specular pixels have the same surface color lit by distant light source and have the same m_d which implies the same p, then m_s of both pixels will be different if their values of θ_r and α are different.

Hence, in general conditions, specular pixels can be grouped into a number of clusters that have the same values of p and different ΣI_i. For every group of pixels that share the same value of m_d, we can consider p as a constant, which makes Equation (16.15) become a linear equation, with p as its constant gradient. These groups of pixels can be clearly observed in inverse-intensity chromaticity space, with x-axis representing $1/\Sigma I_i$ and y-axis representing σ_c, as illustrated in Figure 16.2.a. Several straight lines in the figure correspond to several groups of different m_d values (several number of different p: $p_1, \ldots, p_j, \ldots, p_n$). These lines intersect at a single point on the y-axis, which is identical to the illumination chromaticity (Γ_c). Figure 16.3.a shows the projection of all pixels of a synthetic image in Figure 16.1.a into inverse-intensity chromaticity space. The horizontal line in the figure represents the diffuse points, since the image chromaticity of diffuse pixels will be constant regardless the change of ΣI_i. While, the slant cluster represents the specular points. If we focus on this cluster by removing the diffuse points, according to Equation (16.15) we will find that a number of straight lines, which compose the cluster,

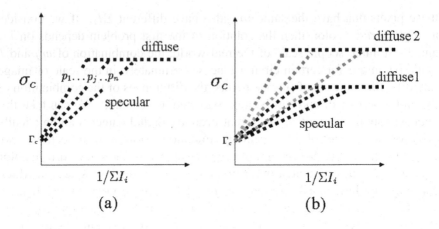

Figure 16.2. (a) Sketch of specular points of uniformly colored surface in inverse-intensity chromaticity space, (b) sketch of specular points of two surface different colors.

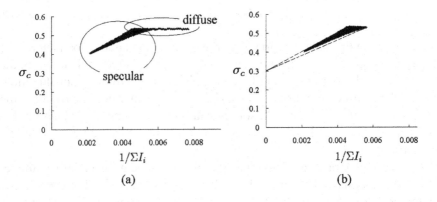

Figure 16.3. (a) Diffuse and specular points of a synthetic image (Figure 16.1.a) in inverse-intensity chromaticity space, with c representing the green channel, (b) the cluster of specular points which head for illumination chromaticity value in y-axis

head for the value of illumination chromaticity at y-axis, as shown in Figure 16.3.b.

Now we relax the assumption of a uniformly colored surface to handle multicolored surfaces. Figure 16.2.b. illustrates the projection of two different surface colors into inverse-intensity chromaticity space. We can observe that two specular clusters with different values of diffuse chromaticity head for the same value on the chromaticity axis (Γ_c). Since we consider only points that have the same values of p and Γ_c, then, even if there are many different clus-

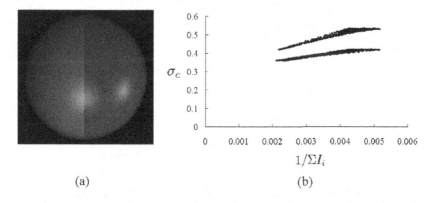

(a)   (b)

Figure 16.4. (a) Synthetic image with multiple surface colors, (b) specular points in inverse-intensity chromaticity space, with c representing the green channel.

ters with different values of Λ_c, as is the case for multicolored surfaces, we can still safely estimate the illumination chromaticity (Γ_c). This means that, for multicolored surfaces, the estimation process is exactly the same as the case of a uniformly colored surface. Figure 16.4.b shows the projection of high-tlighted regions of a synthetic image with two surface colors (Figure 16.4.a) into inverse-intensity chromaticity space.

4. Computational Method to Estimate Illumination Chromaticity

To estimate the illumination chromaticity (Γ_c) from inverse-intensity chro-maticity space, we use the Hough transform. Figure 16.5.a shows the transfor-mation from inverse-intensity chromaticity space into the Hough space, where its x-axis represents Γ_c and its y-axis represents p. Since Γ_c is a normalized value, the range of its value is from 0 to 1 ($0 < \Gamma_c < 1$).

Using the Hough transform alone does not yet give any solution, because the values of p are not constant throughout the image, which makes the intersection point of lines not located at a single location. Fortunately, even if the values of p vary, the values of Γ_c are constant. Thus, in principle, all intersections will be concentrated at a single value of Γ_c, with a small range of p's values. These intersections are indicated by a thick solid line in Figure 16.5.a.

If we focus on the intersections in the Hough space as illustrated in Figure 16.5.b, we should find a larger number of intersections at a certain value of Γ_c compared with other values of Γ_c. The reason is that, in inverse-intensity chromaticity space, within the range of Γ_c ($0 < \Gamma_c < 1$), the number of groups of points that form a straight line heading for certain value of Γ_c is

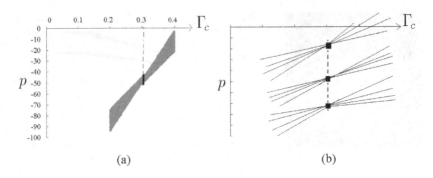

Figure 16.5. (a) Projection of points in Figure 16.3.b into Hough space, (b) sketch of intersected lines in Hough space.

more dominant than the number of groups of points that form a straight line heading for other values of Γ_c.

In practice, we count the intersections in the Hough space based on the number of points that occupy the same location. The details are as follows. A line in the Hough space is formed by a number of points. If this line is not intersected by other lines, then each point will occupy a certain location uniquely (one point for each location). However, if two lines intersect, a location where the intersection takes place will be shared by two points. The number of points will increase if other lines also intersect with those two lines at the same location. Thus, to count the intersections, we first discard all points that occupy a location uniquely, as it means there are no intersections, and then count the number of points for each value of Γ_c.

As a consequence, by projecting the total number of intersections of each Γ_c into a two-dimensional space, illumination-chromaticity count space, with y-axis representing the count of intersections and x-axis representing Γ_c, we can robustly estimate the actual value of Γ_c. Figure 16.6.a shows the distribution of the count numbers of intersections in the space, where the distribution forms a Gaussian-like distribution. The peak of the distribution lies at the actual value of Γ_c.

5.   Discussion

In this section we analyze the distributions of points of highlight regions in inverse-intensity chromaticity space. This analysis is important, since by understanding the distribution, we can find out the main factors that determine the accuracy and robustness of the illumination chromaticity estimation using the space. Note that, while in this discussion, for the sake of simplicity we as-

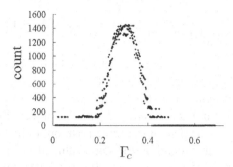

Figure 16.6. Intersection-counting distribution of green channel. The estimated illumination chromaticity is as follows: $\Gamma_r = 0.535$, $\Gamma_b = 0.303$, $\Gamma_b = 0.162$, the ground-truth values are: $\Gamma_r = 0.536$, $\Gamma_b = 0.304$, $\Gamma_b = 0.160$.

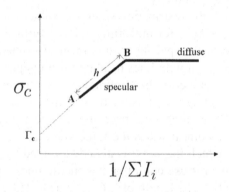

Figure 16.7. Distribution of specular and diffuse pixels in inverse-intensity chromaticity space, when m_d constant.

sume a single surface color, the analysis results can be applied for multicolored surfaces as well.

First, we analyze the distribution when the values of m_d are constant throughout the image. For a uniformly colored surface, this constant m_d makes p become identical for all specular points. As a result, the distribution of the specular pixels forms a single straight line in inverse-intensity chromaticity space, as shown in Figure 16.7. $\overline{AB}$, in the figure, represents the specular line whose gradient is determined by the value of p and whose length is represented by h, i.e., the distance between the brightest specular point and the corresponding diffuse point that has the same p value. Mathematically the value of h is determined by:

$$h = \left| \frac{m_s^A}{m_d^A(m_d^A + m_s^A)} \sqrt{1 + (m_d^A)^2(\Lambda_c - \Gamma_c)^2} \right| \qquad (16.17)$$

where m_s^A and m_d^A are the m_s and m_d value of the brightest specular pixel at A. The value of m_d^A is identical to the value of m_d^B.

Equation (16.17) implies that surface roughness, one of the components of m_s, significantly determines the value of h. Two objects that have the same shape and surface color, located at the same position, lit by the same illumination, viewed from the same location (the same value of m_d^B) will have different values of h if the surface roughness of the objects is different. The smaller surface roughness (larger value of m_s^A) will produce longer h. On the other hand, the larger surface roughness (smaller value of m_s^A) will produce shorter h. For our estimation method, the longer h is better, yet fortunately, even if h is short, as long as the highlight regions can be obtained, the illumination chromaticity estimation can be done accurately.

Second, we analyze the distribution when the values of m_d vary throughout the image. If m_d varies, for uniformly colored surfaces, p will also vary, which consequently makes specular points in inverse-intensity chromaticity space form a number of straight lines heading for a unique value in y-axis. If the change of m_d is assumed to be continuous (smooth surface), the straight lines will grow into a cluster as illustrated in Figure 16.8. $\overline{AB}$, in the figure, represents the specular straight line from the brightest specular point to the corresponding diffuse point that has the same value of p. The length of $\overline{AB}$ is represented by h, which the value is also determined by Equation (16.17). Point C represents the diffuse point that has the dimmest specular pixel (but its m_s is larger than 0). The length of $\overline{BC}$ is represented by v, which equals to $(V_{max} - V_{min})$. Where V_{max} and V_{min} are the values of inverse-intensity of diffuse pixels that have identical p to the dimmest specular pixel and to the brightest specular pixel, respectively. Note that the value of V_{min} is not necessary to be the lowest inverse-intensity value of diffuse pixels, since some diffuse pixels, in certain conditions, could have inverse-intensity value smaller than V_{min}.

The value of v, which is determined by V_{max} and V_{min}, does not depends only on m_d, but also on several factors that determine the value of m_s such as surface roughness. By considering Torrance-Sparrow reflection model in Equation (16.16), if the surface has small surface roughness, then the number of specular pixels (pixels whose m_s does not equal to zero) is relatively small, which could make the diversity of m_d in highlight regions also small. On the contrary, if the same surface has large surface roughness, then the number of specular pixels is relatively large, making the diversity of m_d in highlight regions also possibly large. As a result, since surface roughness affects the diversity of m_d in highlight regions, it also affects the value of v. In general

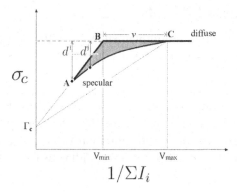

Figure 16.8. Distribution of specular and diffuse pixels in inverse-intensity chromaticity space, when m_d vary.

cases, smaller surface roughness will cause the value of v to be smaller, while larger surface roughness will cause the value of v to be larger.

Beside knowing the value of h and v, we also need to know the shape of the boundaries of the distribution. As explained previously, the shape of $\overline{AB}$ is a straight line in which the gradient is equal to p of the brightest specular pixel. The shape of $\overline{BC}$ is a straight horizontal line, since for all diffuse pixels, their image chromaticity values are identical regardless of the change of image intensity. Unlike both lines, the shape of $\overline{AC}$ in general cases is not a straight line. To determine the shape of the line, we need to define the vertical distances between points at $\overline{AC}$ and the diffuse horizontal line, which is represented by d, as shown in the figure. The values of d is determined by:

$$d^j = \left| \frac{m_s^j}{m_d^j + m_s^j}(\Lambda_c - \Gamma_c) \right| \tag{16.18}$$

where superscript j is the index of specular points located at $\overline{AC}$. m_d^j is the diffuse pixel that has identical p to the corresponding specular point located at $\overline{AC}$ with index j. From Equation (16.18), we can conclude that the shape of $\overline{AC}$ is a curve line, since according to Torrance and Sparrow reflection model m_s is a Gaussian function (Equation (16.16)).

Having understood the factors that determine the distribution of specular points when m_d varies, if the surface roughness is small, v will be small, h will be long, and $\overline{AC}$ will be more parallel to $\overline{AB}$. In this condition, the estimation using our computational method can be done accurately and robustly. On the contrary, if the surface roughness is large, then v will be large, h will be short, and $\overline{AC}$ will be more parallel to $\overline{BC}$, making the estimation in practice less robust compared with relatively smaller surface roughness.

6.   Experimental Results

We will briefly describe the implementation of the proposed method, and then present several experimental results on real images, as well as an evaluation of our method.

Implementation.   Implementation of the proposed method is quite simple. Given an image that has highlights, we first find the highlight regions by using thresholding on image intensity and saturation values. Following the method of Lehmann *et al.* [20], we define the thresholding as follows:

$$\tilde{I} = \frac{I_r + I_g + I_b}{3} > T_a \tilde{I}^{max}$$

$$\tilde{S} = 1 - \frac{min(I_r, I_g, I_b)}{\tilde{I}} < T_b \tilde{S}^{max} \qquad (16.19)$$

where $\tilde{I}^{max}$ and $\tilde{S}^{max}$ are the largest $\tilde{I}$ and $\tilde{S}$ in the whole input image, respectively. T_a and T_b are the thresholds of image intensity and saturation, respectively. In our implementation, we set T_a and T_b from $0.4 - 0.6$.

This thresholding technique cannot always produce precise highlight regions. Fortunately, in practice our estimation method does not need precise highlight regions, even if relatively small regions of diffuse pixels are included, the algorithm could work robustly. Of course, more preciseness is better. Then, for each color channel, we project the highlight pixels into inverse-intensity chromaticity space. From this space, we use the conventional Hough transform to project the clusters into Hough space. During the projection, we count all possible intersections at each value of chromaticity. We plot these intersection-counting numbers into the illumination-chromaticity count space. Ideally, from this space, we can choose the tip as the estimated illumination chromaticity. However, because noise always exists in real images, the result can be improved by computing the median of a certain percentage from the highest counts. In our implementation, we use 30% from the highest counted number.

Note that, first, in our current implementation we estimate three color channels of illumination chromaticity independently. In fact, since $\Sigma \Gamma_i = 1$, we can solely estimate two color channels instead of three. Second, the problem of determining highlight regions is still an open challenging problem, and our method could fail for specific domains that do not follow our thresholding described in Equation (16.19).

Experimental Conditions.   We have conducted several experiments on real images, which were taken using a SONY DXC-9000, a progressive 3 CCD digital camera, by setting its gamma correction at off. To ensure that the outputs of the camera are linear to the flux of incident light, we used a spectrometer: Photo Research PR-650. We examined the algorithm using four types of input, i.e., uniform colored surfaces, multicolored surfaces, highly textured surfaces, and a scene multiple objects. We used convex objects to avoid interreflection, and excluded saturated pixels from the computation. For the evaluation, we compared the results with the average values of image chromaticity of a white reference image (Photo Research Reflectance Standard model SRS-3), captured by the same camera. The standard deviations of these average values under various illuminant positions and colors were approximately $0.01 \sim 0.03$.

Result on a uniformly colored surface. Figure 16.9.a shows a real image of a head model that has a uniformly colored surface and relatively low specularity, illuminated by Solux Halogen with temperature $4700K$. Under the illumination, the image chromaticity of the white reference taken by our camera has chromaticity value: $\Gamma_r = 0.371, \Gamma_g = 0.318, \Gamma_b = 0.310$.

Figure 16.9.b shows the specular points of the red channel of chromaticity in inverse-intensity chromaticity space. Even though there is some noise, generally, all points form several straight lines heading for a certain point in the chromaticity axis. The same phenomenon can also be observed in Figure 16.9.c and Figure 16.9.d. Figure 16.10 shows the intersection-counting distribution in the illumination-chromaticity count space. The peaks of the distribution denote the illumination chromaticity. The result of the estimation was: $\Gamma_r = 0.378, \Gamma_g = 0.324, \Gamma_b = 0.287$.

Result on a multi-colored surface. Figure 16.11.a shows a plastic toy with a multicolored surface. The illumination is Solux Halogen covered with a green filter. The image chromaticity of the white reference under this illuminant taken by our camera was $\Gamma_r = 0.298, \Gamma_g = 0.458, \Gamma_b = 0.244$.

Figure 16.11.b, c, d show the specular points of multiple surface colors in inverse-intensity chromaticity space. From Figure 16.12, we can observe that, even for several surface colors, the peak of intersection counts was still at a single value of Γ_c. The result of the estimation was $\Gamma_r = 0.319, \Gamma_g = 0.439, \Gamma_b = 0.212$.

Result on highly textured surface. Figure 16.13.a shows a magazine cover with a complex multicolored surface, which was lit by a fluorescent light covered with a green filter. The image chromaticity of the white reference under this illuminant taken by our camera has a chromaticity value of $\Gamma_r = 0.283, \Gamma_g = 0.481, \Gamma_b = 0.236$. The result of the estimation was $\Gamma_r = 0.315, \Gamma_g = 0.515, \Gamma_b = 0.207$.

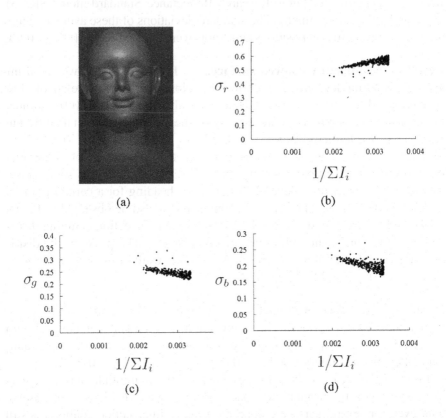

(a)

(b)

(c)

(d)

Figure 16.9.   (a) Real input image with a single surface color, (b) projection of the red channel of the specular pixels into inverse-intensity chromaticity space, (c) projection of the green channel of the specular pixels into inverse-intensity chromaticity space, (d) projection of the blue channel of the specular pixels into inverse-intensity chromaticity space.

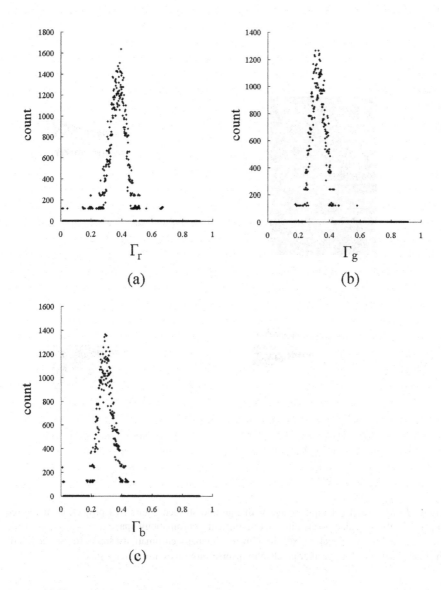

Figure 16.10. (a) Intersection-counting distribution for red channel of illumination chromaticity for image in Figure 16.9, (b) intersection-counting distribution for green-channel, (c) Intersection-counting distribution for blue channel.

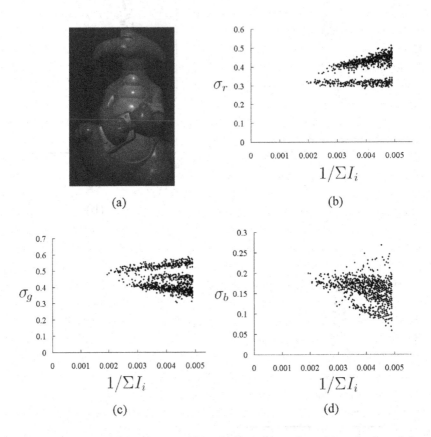

Figure 16.11.   (a) Real input image with multiple surface colors, (b) projection of the red channel of the specular pixels into inverse-intensity chromaticity space, (c) projection of the green channel of the specular pixels into inverse-intensity chromaticity space, (d) projection of the blue channel of the specular pixels into inverse-intensity chromaticity space.

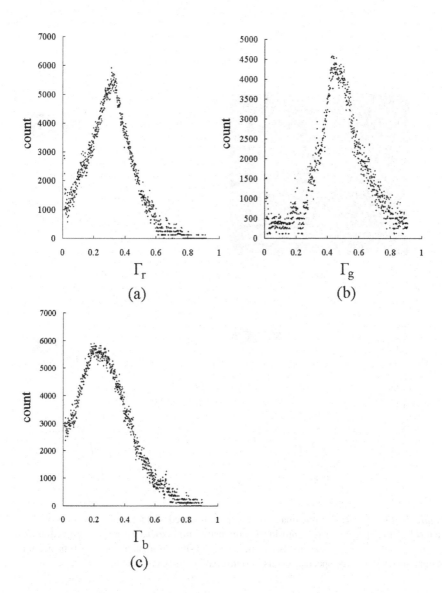

Figure 16.12. (a) Intersection-counting distribution for the red channel of illumination chromaticity for image in Figure 16.11, (b) intersection-counting distribution for the green channel, (c) intersection-counting distribution for the blue channel.

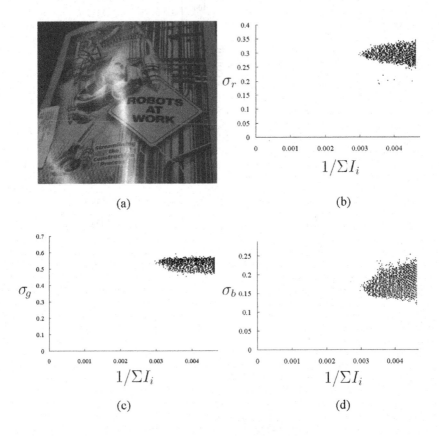

Figure 16.13. (a) Real input image of complex textured surface, (b) projection of the red channel of the specular pixels into inverse-intensity chromaticity space, (c) projection of the green channel of the specular pixels into inverse-intensity chromaticity space (d) projection of the green channel of the specular pixels into inverse-intensity chromaticity space.

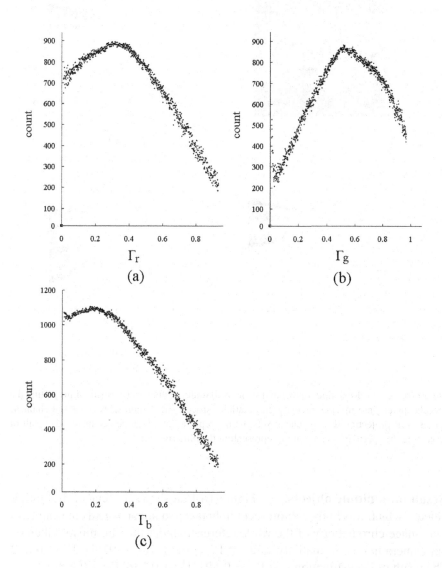

Figure 16.14.   (a) Intersection-counting distribution for the red channel of illumination chromaticity for image in Figure 16.13, (b) intersection-counting distribution for the green channel,
(c) intersection-counting distribution for the blue channel.

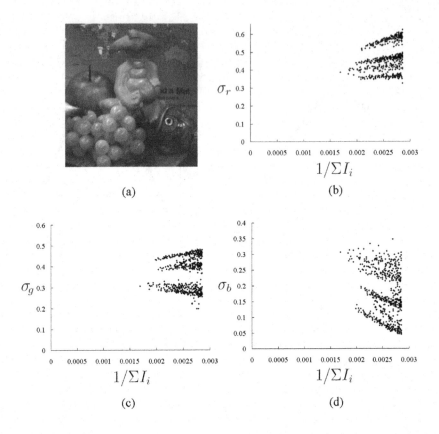

Figure 16.15.   (a) Real input image of a scene with multiple objects, (b) result of projecting the specular pixels into inverse-intensity chromaticity space, with c representing the red channel, (c) result of projecting the specular pixels, with c representing the green channel, (d) result of projecting the specular pixels, with c representing the blue channel.

Result on multiple objects.   Figure 16.15.a shows a scene with multiple objects, which was lit by a fluorescent light taken in uncontrolled environment. The image chromaticity of the white reference under this illuminant taken by our camera has a chromaticity value of $\Gamma_r = 0.337, \Gamma_g = 0.341, \Gamma_b = 0.312$. The result of the estimation was $\Gamma_r = 0.321, \Gamma_g = 0.346, \Gamma_b = 0.309$.

Evaluation.   To evaluate the robustness of our method, we have also conducted experiments on 6 different objects: 2 objects with a single surface color, 1 object with multiple surface colors, and 3 objects with highly textured surfaces. The colors of illuminants were grouped into 5 different colors: Solux Halogen lamp with temperature $4700K$, incandescent lamp with temperature around $2800K$, Solux Halogen lamp covered with green, blue and purple fil-

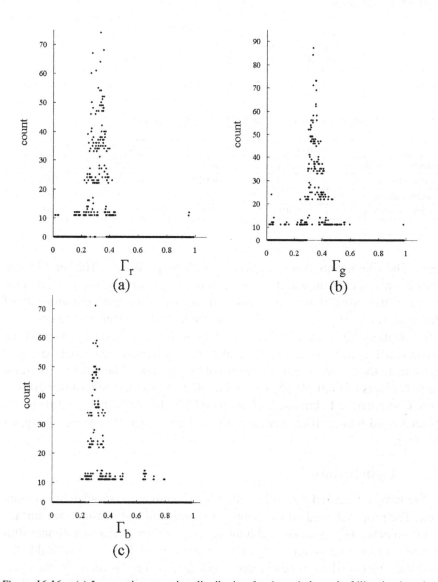

Figure 16.16. (a) Intersection-counting distribution for the red channel of illumination chromaticity for image in Figure 16.13, (b) intersection-counting distribution for the green channel, (c) intersection-counting distribution for the blue channel.

Table 16.1. The performance of the estimation method with regard to the image chromaticity of the white reference

	red	green	blue
average of error	0.0172	0.0141	0.0201
std. dev. of error	0.01	0.01	0.01

Table 16.2. The estimation results using Lehmann *et al.*'s Database

	average of Γ_r	std. dev of Γ_r	average of Γ_g	std. dev of Γ_g
unclipped, white ill.	0.320	0.02	0.329	0.02
clipped, white ill.	0.318	0.02	0.332	0.02
unclipped, yellow ill.	0.479	0.02	0.411	0.02
clipped, yellow ill.	0.469	0.02	0.399	0.02

ters. The illuminants were arranged at various positions. The total of images in our experiment was 43 images. From these images, we calculated the errors of the estimation by comparing them with the image chromaticity of the white reference, which are shown in Table 16.1. The errors are considerably small, as the standard deviations of the reference image chromaticity are around $0.01 \sim 0.03$. In addition, we also used Lehmann *et al.*'s database [20] to evaluate the accuracy and robustness of our method. The database contains various colors of multiple objects. Table 16.2 shows the result of our estimation. Compared to Lehmann *et al.* method [20], the method is more stable for general conditions of illumination colors and input images (unclipped/clipped images).

7. Conclusion

We have introduced a novel method for illumination chromaticity estimation. The proposed method can handle both uniform and non-uniform surface color objects. Given crude highlight regions, the method can estimate illumination color without requiring color segmentation. It is also applicable for multiple objects with various colored surfaces, as long as there are no inter-reflections. In this chapter, we have also introduced *inverse-intensity chromaticity space* to analyze the relationship between illumination chromaticity and image chromaticity. Advantages of the method include: first, the capability to cope with either single surface color or multiple surface colors; second, color segmentation inside highlighted regions and intrinsic camera characteristics are not required; third, the method does not use the strong constraints on illumination, which several existing color constancy methods use, such as blackbody radiator. The experimental results have shown that the method is accurate and robust even for highly textured surfaces.

Acknowledgments

This research was supported, in part, by Ministry of Education, Culture, Sports, Science and Technology under the Leading Project, "Development of High Fidelity Digitization Software for Large-Scale and Intangible Cultural Assets," and, in part, by Japan Science and Technology Agency, under the CREST program, "Automatic generation of virtual models of cultural heritage."

References

[1] H.J. Andersen, E. Granum, "Classifying illumination conditions from two light sources by colour histogram assessment", Journal of the Optical Society of America A, **17**(4), pp. 667-676, 2000.

[2] D.H. Brainard, W.T. Freeman, "Bayesian color constancy", Journal of the Optical Society of America A, **14**(7), pp. 1393-1411, 1997.

[3] D'Zmura, M., Lennie,P., "Mechanism of color constancy", Journal of the Optical Society of America A, **3**(10), pp. 1162-1672, 1986.

[4] G.D. Finlayson, "Color in perspective", IEEE Trans. on Pattern Analysis and Machine Intelligence **18**(10), pp. 1034-1036, 1996.

[5] G.D. Finlayson, B.V. Funt , "Color constancy using shadows", Perception **23**, pp. 89-90, 1994.

[6] G.F. Finlayson, G. Schaefer, "Solving for colour constancy using a constrained dichromatic reflection model", International Journal of Computer Vision, **42**(3), pp. 127-144, 2001.

[7] G.F. Finlayson, S.D. Hordley, "Color constancy at a pixel", Journal of the Optical Society of America A, **18**(2), pp. 253-264, 2001.

[8] G.D. Finlayson and G. Schaefer, "Convex and non-convex illumination constraints for dichromatic color constancy", in proceeding of IEEE Conference on Computer Vision and Pattern Recognition, pp. 598-605, 2001.

[9] G.D. Finlayson and S.D. Hordley and P.M. Hubel, "Color by correlation: a simple, unifying, framework for color constancy", IEEE Trans. on Pattern Analysis and Machine Intelligence **23**(11), pp. 1209-1221, 2001.

[10] B.V. Funt, M. Drew, J. Ho, "Color constancy from mutual reflection", International Journal of Computer Vision, **6**(1), pp. 5-24, 1991.

[11] J.M. Geusebroek, R. Boomgaard, S. Smeulders and H. Geert, "Color invariance", IEEE Trans. on Pattern Analysis and Machine Intelligence **23**(12), pp. 1338-1350, 2001.

[12] J.M. Geusebroek, R. Boomgaard , S. Smeulders, T. Gevers, "A physical basis for color constancy", in proceeding of The First European Conference on Colour in Graphics, Image and Vision, pp. 3-6, 2002.

[13] G. Healey, "Using color for geometry-insensitive segmentation", Journal of the Optical Society of America A, 6(6), pp. 920-937, 1989.

[14] G.J. Klinker , Shafer, S.A., Kanade, T., "The measurement of highlights in color images", International Journal of Computer Vision, 2, pp 7-32, 1990.

[15] G.J. Klinker , "A physical approach to color image understanding", PhD. Thesis, Carnegie Mellon University, May, 1988.

[16] J.H. Lambert , "Photometria sive de mensura de gratibus luminis, colorum et umbrae", Eberhard Klett: Augsberg, Germany, 1760.

[17] H.C. Lee , "Method for computing the scene-illuminant from specular highlights", Journal of the Optical Society of America A, 3(10), pp. 1694–1699, 1986

[18] H.C. Lee , "Illuminant color from shading", in Physics-based Vision Principle and Practice: Color, pp. 340-347, 1992, Jones and Bartlett.

[19] H.C. Lee , E.J. Breneman, C.P. Schulte, "Modeling light reflection for computer color vision", IEEE Trans. on Pattern Analysis and Machine Intelligence, 12(4), pp. 402-409, 1990.

[20] T.M. Lehmann , C. Palm, "Color line search for illuminant estimation in real-world scene", Journal of the Optical Society of America A, 18(11), pp. 2679-2691, 2001.

[21] C. Rosenberg, M. Hebert , S. Thrun, "Color constancy using KL-Divergence", in proceeding of IEEE International Conference on Computer Vision, pp.239-247, 2001.

[22] G. Sapiro , "Color and Illumination Voting", IEEE trans on Pattern Analysis and Machine Intelligence, 21(11), pp. 1210-1215, 1999.

[23] S.Shafer , "Using color to separate reflection components", Color Research and Applications, 10, pp. 210-218, 1985.

[24] S.Tominaga, "A multi-channel vision system for estimating surface and illumination functions", Journal of the Optical Society of America A, 13(11), pp. 2163-2173, 1996.

[25] S.Tominaga, S. Ebisui, B.A. Wandell , "Scene illuminant classification: brighter is better", Journal of the Optical Society of America A, 18(1), pp. 55-64, 2001.

[26] S.Tominaga, B.A. Wandell, "Standard surface-reflectance model and illumination estimation", Journal of the Optical Society of America A, 6(4), pp. 576-584, 1989.

[27] S.Tominaga, B.A. Wandell, "Natural scene-illuminant estimation using the sensor correlation", Proceedings of the IEEE **90**(1), pp. 42-56, 2002.

[28] Torrance, K.E., Sparrow, E.M., "Theory for off-specular reflection from roughened surfaces", Journal of the Optical Society of America, **57**, pp. 1105-1114, 1967.

[29] G. Wyszecki, W.S. Stiles, "Color science: concept and methods, quantitative data and formulae",Wiley Inter-Science,1982.

Chapter 17

SEPARATING REFLECTION COMPONENTS OF TEXTURED SURFACES USING A SINGLE IMAGE

Robby T. Tan and Katsushi Ikeuchi

Abstract   In inhomogeneous objects, highlights are linear combinations of diffuse and specular reflection components. A number of methods have been proposed to separate or decompose these two components. To our knowledge, all methods that use a single input image require explicit color segmentation to deal with multicolored surfaces. Unfortunately, for complex textured images, current color segmentation algorithms are still problematic to segment correctly. Consequently, a method without explicit color segmentation becomes indispensable, and this chapter presents such a method. The method is based solely on colors, particularly chromaticity, without requiring any geometrical information. One of the basic ideas is to iteratively compare the intensity logarithmic differentiation of an input image and its specular-free image. A specular-free image is an image that has exactly the same geometrical profile as the diffuse component of the input image, and that can be generated by shifting each pixel's intensity and maximum chromaticity non-linearly. Unlike existing methods using a single image, all processes in the proposed method are done locally, involving a maximum of only two neighboring pixels. This local operation is useful for handling textured objects with complex multicolored scenes. Evaluations by comparison with the results of polarizing filters demonstrate the effectiveness of the proposed method.

1.   Introduction

Separating diffuse and specular reflection components is an essential subject in the field of computer vision. Many algorithms in this field assume perfect diffuse surfaces and deem specular reflections to be outliers. However, in the real world, the presence of specular reflection is inevitable, since there are many dielectric inhomogeneous objects which have both diffuse and specular reflections. To properly acquire the diffuse only reflections, a method to separate the two components robustly and accurately is required. Moreover, once this separation has been accomplished, the specular reflection component can become advantageous since it conveys useful information of the surface properties such as microscopic roughness.

Theoretically, when a bundle of light rays enters an inhomogeneous opaque surface, some of the rays will immediately reflect back into the air, while the remainder will penetrate the body of the object. Some of these penetrating light rays will go through the body; the others will reflect back onto the surface and then into the air. The immediately reflected light rays are called specular or interface reflections, while those that have penetrated and then reflected back into the air are called diffuse or body reflections . Besides the two reflections, there is another reflection called *specular spike* [2, 21]. However, since its presence in inhomogeneous objects is very minor, we can ignore it. Thus, highlights which we usually observe in inhomogeneous objects are combinations of diffuse and specular reflection components.

In order to separate the two reflection components, it is necessary to know the optical differences between diffuse and specular reflections. Principally there are three differences. First, the reflections have different degrees of polarization (DOP) , where the DOP represents the ratio of the light being polarized. For unpolarized incident light, the DOP of specular reflection is larger than that of diffuse reflection for most angles of incidence light, meaning that specular reflection is generally more polarized than diffuse reflection [19, 3, 30, 32, 20]. Second, although recently a number of researchers [29, 22, 31] have introduced more complex models, the intensity distribution of diffuse reflections approximately follows Lambert's Law [12]. In contrast, the intensity distribution of specular reflections from the basis of geometrical optics follows the Torrance-Sparrow reflection model [28] and, from the basis of physical optics, follows the Beckmann-Spizzichino reflection model [2]. Third, for most inhomogeneous objects, the spectral power distribution (SPD) of specular reflection is determined by the object's interface spectral reflectance, which is mostly constant throughout the wavelength of visible spectrum, causing the SPD of specular reflections to be similar to the illumination's SPD [13], while the SPD of diffuse reflection is determined by the object's body spectral reflectance. This spectral power distribution (color) independence of diffuse and specular reflections was clearly described in the dichromatic reflection model proposed by Shafer [25].

1.1   Previous Work

Based on the three differences mentioned above, many methods have been developed for separating reflection components. Wolff *et al.* [32] used a polarizing filter to separate reflection components from gray images. The main idea of their method is that, for most incident angles, diffuse reflections tend to be less polarized than the specular reflections. Nayar *et al.* [20] extended this work by considering colors instead of using the polarizing filter alone. They identified specular pixels and the illumination color vector in RGB space by utilizing intensity variation produced by a polarizing filter. A specular pixel, which is partially composed of a specular reflection component, will have a different intensity if the polarization angle of the filter is changed. The combination of polarizing filter and colors is even for textured surfaces; however, utilizing such an additional filter is impractical in some circumstances. Sato *et al.* [24] introduced a four-dimensional space, temporal-color space, to analyze the diffuse and specular reflections based on colors and image intensity. While this method has the ability to separate the reflection components locally, since each location contains information of diffuse and specular reflections, it requires dense input images with variation of illuminant directions. Lee *et al.* [14, 15] introduced color histogram differencing to identify specularities. The key idea is that colors of diffuse pixels are independent of the changing of viewing positions, while colors of specular pixels are dependent on it. Later, Lin *et al.* [17] extended this method by adding multibaseline stereo. Criminisi et al. [4] developed an epipolar plane image (EPI) - based method to detect specularities. They found that, in two-dimensional spatio-temporal space, highlights' straight lines have larger gradients than diffusers' straight lines. Lin *et al.* [18], unlike previous methods, introduced a method using sparse images (at least two images) under different illumination positions. They suggested an analytical method that combines the finite dimensional basis functions [23] and a dichromatic model to form a closed form equation, by assuming that the sensor sensitivity is narrowband. This method can separate the reflection component locally.

The aforementioned methods are considerably effective in separating reflection components; unfortunately, for many applications, using multiple images is impractical. Shafer [25], who introduced the dichromatic reflection model, was one of the early researchers who used a single colored image. He proposed a separation method based on parallelogram distribution of colors in RGB space. Klinker *et al.* [11] then extended this method by introducing a T-shaped color distribution. This color distribution represents body and illumination color vectors. By separating these vectors, the reflection equation becomes a closed form equation and directly solvable. Unfortunately, for many real images, this T shape is hardly extractable due to noise, etc. Bajscy *et al.* [1] proposed an approach that introduced a three dimensional space composed of lightness, saturation and hue. In their method, the input image has to be neutralized to pure-white illumination using a linear basis functions operation. For every neutralized pixel, the weighting factors of the surface reflectance basis functions are projected into the three-dimensional space, where specular and diffuse reflections are identifiable due to the difference of their saturation values.

1.2   Contributions

All the above methods that use a single input image require color segmentation to deal with multicolored images. For non-complex multicolored images, current segmentation algorithms can produce reasonably correct results. However, in the real world that usually has complex scenes and textured surfaces, these algorithms are still problematic. To overcome this problem, we present a method that uses local operation, which consequently does not require explicit color segmentation. Briefly, our method is as follows.

Given a single colored image, we normalize the illumination color using known illumination chromaticity, which produces an image that has a pure white specular component. Using this image, we generate a *specular-free image* by simply shifting the intensity and maximum chromaticity of the pixels non-linearly while retaining their hue. This image has diffuse geometry exactly identical to the diffuse geometry of the input image; the difference is only in their surface colors. Thus, by using intensity logarithmic differentiation on both the normalized image and its specular-free image, we can determine whether the normalized image contains only diffuse pixels. This ability plays an important role as a termination condition in our iterative framework, which removes specular components step by step until no specular reflection exists in the image. All processes are done locally, involving a maximum of only two neighboring pixels.

In comparison with the existing methods that use a single input image, the proposed method offers some advantages: First, separation is done without requiring explicit segmentation. Klinker *et al.* [11] used color segmentation to obtain the T-shaped distribution for each surface color, thereby implying that failure in the segmentation would cause failure in identifying the T-shape. Bajcsy *et al.* [1] used region-growing algorithms for two steps of segmentation: hue-based segmentation and saturation-based segmentation. The main drawback of the hue-based segmentation is that, when two neighboring regions have different saturation but the same hue, the two different regions will be deemed as a single region, causing incorrect identification of the saturation value of diffuse pixels. Although they have proposed a solution for the problem, they did not have any suggestion on how the solution could be united into one whole framework. The solution is not simple; and, if it is applied to general cases where the problem might not occur, it will consume significant computational time and affect the robustness of the method. Moreover, the success of the method depends on the success of clustering the hues of specular pixels. If the specular pixels are mistakenly grouped into different hues, then the separation will produce incorrect results. Unlike the existing methods, our approach is based on chromaticity difference of two-neighboring pixels to detect color discontinuities, where the same hue but different saturation surfaces is no longer a problem. Although detecting color discontinuities is, in general, similar to the problem of color segmentation, in our framework we consider only local color discontinuity, in which the success of reflection separation does not necessarily imply the success of detecting global (all) color discontinuities. In other words, even if we mistakenly deem a number of two-neighboring pixels to be color discontinuities, it does not always affect the end result of separation. Second, the method uses simple and hands-on illumination color normalization. Unlike Bacjsy *et al.*'s neutralization that uses linear basis functions, we apply the normalization by simply dividing the input image with illumination chromaticity (without assuming narrow-band sensor). Third, we introduce specular-free image that has a geometrical profile identical to diffuse components of the input image and is free from the presence of highlights. This image could be useful for many algorithms in computer vision that do not need the object's actual color but suffer from highlights.

To separate reflection components correctly, our method requires several assumptions. First, diffuse pixels always occur in each color region regardless of their quantity. Second, the color constancy method can estimate illumination chromaticity correctly. Third, the surface color is chromatic ($R \neq G \neq B$), meaning the surface color is not a white, gray, or black color. These assumptions, particularly the last assumption, are commonly used by all methods that have only a single input image, since most of them are basically based on color; and, achromatic pixels simply mean that they have no color information.

1.3   Overview

The remainder of the chapter is organized as follows. In Section 2, we discuss the dichromatic reflection model, image color formation, chromaticity and normalization. In Section 3, we elaborate on a mechanism to obtain diffuse reflection component by deriving the correlation between image maximum chromaticity and image intensity, which we call specular-to-diffuse mechanism. Based on the mechanism, we describe a technique to generate a specular-free image and prove that the image has an identical geometrical profile to that of the input image. In Section 4, we explain the separation method derived from the specular-to-diffuse mechanism and specular-free image in detail. In Section 5, we provide a description of the implementation of the method and its algorithm. In Section 6, we discuss the effects of inaccurate estimation of illumination chromaticity in generating a specular-free image. We present several experimental results and evaluations for real images in Section 7. Finally, we offer our conclusions in Section 8.

2.   Reflection Model

Image Formation.   Most inhomogeneous objects, such as those made of plastics, acrylics, etc., exhibit both diffuse and specular reflections. The diffuse reflection is due to the varying refractive indices in the objects' surfaces and bodies, while the specular reflection is mainly due to the refractive index difference between objects' surfaces and the air. Considering these two reflection components, Shafer [25] introduced the dichromatic reflection model , which states that reflected lights of inhomogeneous objects are linear combinations of diffuse and specular reflection components. As a result, an image's pixel of inhomogeneous objects taken by a digital color camera can be described as:

$$
\begin{bmatrix} I_r(\mathbf{x}) \\ I_g(\mathbf{x}) \\ I_b(\mathbf{x}) \end{bmatrix} =
$$

$$
\begin{bmatrix} w_d(\mathbf{x}) \int_\Omega S(\lambda, \mathbf{x})E(\lambda)q_r(\lambda)d\lambda + w_s(\mathbf{x}) \int_\Omega E(\lambda)q_r(\lambda)d\lambda \\ w_d(\mathbf{x}) \int_\Omega S(\lambda, \mathbf{x})E(\lambda)q_g(\lambda)d\lambda + w_s(\mathbf{x}) \int_\Omega E(\lambda)q_g(\lambda)d\lambda \\ w_d(\mathbf{x}) \int_\Omega S(\lambda, \mathbf{x})E(\lambda)q_b(\lambda)d\lambda + w_s(\mathbf{x}) \int_\Omega E(\lambda)q_b(\lambda)d\lambda \end{bmatrix} \quad (17.1)
$$

in color vector we express as:

$$
\mathbf{I}(\mathbf{x}) = w_d(\mathbf{x}) \int_\Omega S(\lambda, \mathbf{x})E(\lambda)\mathbf{q}(\lambda)d\lambda + w_s(\mathbf{x}) \int_\Omega E(\lambda)\mathbf{q}(\lambda)d\lambda \quad (17.2)
$$

where $\mathbf{I} = \{I_r, I_g, I_b\}$ is the color vector of image intensity or camera sensor. The spatial parameter, $\mathbf{x} = \{x, y\}$, is the two dimensional image coordinates. $\mathbf{q} = \{q_r, q_g, q_b\}$ is the three-element-vector of sensor sensitivity. $w_d(\mathbf{x})$ and $w_s(\mathbf{x})$ are the weighting factors for diffuse and specular reflections, respectively; their values depend on the geometric structure at location $\mathbf{x}$. $S(\mathbf{x}, \lambda)$ is the diffuse spectral reflectance function, while $E(\lambda)$ is the spectral power distribution function of illumination. $E(\lambda)$ is independent of the spatial location ($\mathbf{x}$) because we assume a uniform illumination color. The integration is done over the visible spectrum (Ω). Note that we ignore the camera gain and camera noise in the above model, and assume that the model follows the neutral interface reflection (NIR) assumption [13], i.e., the color of specular reflection component equals the color of the illumination. For the sake of simplicity, Equation (17.2) can be written as:

$$
\mathbf{I}(\mathbf{x}) = w_d(\mathbf{x})\mathbf{B}(\mathbf{x}) + w_s(\mathbf{x})\mathbf{G} \quad (17.3)
$$

where $\mathbf{B}(\mathbf{x}) = \int_\Omega S(\lambda, \mathbf{x})E(\lambda)\mathbf{q}(\lambda)d\lambda$, and $\mathbf{G} = \int_\Omega E(\lambda)\mathbf{q}(\lambda)d\lambda$. The first part of the right side of the equation represents the diffuse reflection component, while the second part represents the specular reflection component.

Chromaticity.   Besides the dichromatic reflection model, we also use chromaticity or *normalized rgb* , which is defined as:

$$\sigma(\mathbf{x}) = \frac{\mathbf{I}(\mathbf{x})}{I_r(\mathbf{x}) + I_g(\mathbf{x}) + I_b(\mathbf{x})} \tag{17.4}$$

where $\sigma = \{\sigma_r, \sigma_g, \sigma_b\}$. Based on the equation, for the diffuse-only reflection component ($w_s = 0$), the chromaticity will be independent from the diffuse weighting factor w_d. We call this *diffuse chromaticity* (Λ) with definition:

$$\Lambda(\mathbf{x}) = \frac{\mathbf{B}(\mathbf{x})}{B_r(\mathbf{x}) + B_g(\mathbf{x}) + B_b(\mathbf{x})} \tag{17.5}$$

where $\Lambda = \{\Lambda_r, \Lambda_g, \Lambda_b\}$. On the other hand, for the specular-only reflection component ($w_d = 0$), the chromaticity will be independent from the specular weighting factor (w_s), and we call it *specular* or *illumination chromaticity* (Γ):

$$\Gamma = \frac{\mathbf{G}}{G_r + G_g + G_b} \tag{17.6}$$

where $\Gamma = \{\Gamma_r, \Gamma_g, \Gamma_b\}$. Consequently, with regard to Equation (17.5) and (17.6), Equation (17.3) becomes able to be written in term of chromaticity:

$$\mathbf{I}(\mathbf{x}) = m_d(\mathbf{x})\Lambda(\mathbf{x}) + m_s(\mathbf{x})\Gamma \tag{17.7}$$

where

$$m_d(\mathbf{x}) = w_d(\mathbf{x})[B_r(\mathbf{x}) + B_g(\mathbf{x}) + B_b(\mathbf{x})] \tag{17.8}$$

$$m_s(\mathbf{x}) = w_s(\mathbf{x})(G_r + G_g + G_b) \tag{17.9}$$

As a result, we have three types of chromaticity: image chromaticity (σ), diffuse chromaticity (Λ) and illumination chromaticity (Γ). The image chromaticity can be directly computed from the input image using Equation (17.4). In addition, from their definitions we can obtain $(\sigma_r + \sigma_g + \sigma_b) = (\Lambda_r + \Lambda_g + \Lambda_b) = (\Gamma_r + \Gamma_g + \Gamma_b) = 1$.

Based on the dichromatic reflection model and chromaticities definitions derived above, we describe our goal: given image intensities ($\mathbf{I}(\mathbf{x})$) whose illumination chromaticity (Γ) is known (estimated by using a color constancy method); we intend to decompose them into their reflection components: $m_d(\mathbf{x})\Lambda(\mathbf{x})$ and $m_s(\mathbf{x})\Gamma$.

Normalization.   In our method, to separate reflection components correctly, the color of the specular component must be pure white ($\Gamma_r = \Gamma_g = \Gamma_b$). However, in the real world, finding a pure white specular component is almost impossible. Most light sources are not wavelength-independent. Moreover, even if the light source is wavelength- independent, because of different sensitivities in color filters, the intensity value of the specular component for every color channel becomes varied, depending on camera sensitivity. Consequently, to obtain a pure white specular component, we need to normalize the input image. Here we use a simple method of normalization that does not require approximated linear basis functions such as in [1] and also does not assume narrowband sensor sensitivity.

Our normalization requires the value of Γ (the illumination chromaticity), which can be obtained by using a color constancy algorithm that can handle textured surfaces such as [26, 16]. We describe the estimated illumination chromaticity as Γ^{est}, with $\Gamma^{est} = \{\Gamma_r^{est}, \Gamma_g^{est}, \Gamma_b^{est}\}$, which enables the normalized image intensity to be expressed as:

$$\mathbf{I}'(\mathbf{x}) = m_d'(\mathbf{x})\mathbf{\Lambda}'(\mathbf{x}) + m_s'(\mathbf{x})\frac{1}{3} \qquad (17.10)$$

where $\mathbf{I}'(\mathbf{x}) = \frac{\mathbf{I}(\mathbf{x})}{\Gamma^{est}}$, the normalized image intensity. $m_d' = m_d\left[\frac{\Lambda_r(\mathbf{x})}{\Gamma_r^{est}} + \frac{\Lambda_g(\mathbf{x})}{\Gamma_g^{est}} + \frac{\Lambda_b(\mathbf{x})}{\Gamma_b^{est}}\right]$, $\mathbf{\Lambda}'$ is the chromaticity of $\left(m_d\frac{\mathbf{\Lambda}(\mathbf{x})}{\Gamma^{est}}\right)$, which we call the normalized diffuse chromaticity. We assume $\frac{\Gamma}{\Gamma^{est}} = \{1, 1, 1\}$, as a result the normalized specular chromaticity (Γ') equals $\{1/3, 1/3, 1/3\}$, and $m_s' = 3m_s$. The above normalization makes the specular reflection component become a scalar value.

Later, when the separation is done, to obtain the actual reflection components, we need to renormalize the separated components, simply by multiplying them $\left(m_d'(\mathbf{x})\mathbf{\Lambda}'(\mathbf{x}) \text{ and } m_s'(\mathbf{x})\frac{1}{3}\right)$ with Γ^{est}:

$$m_d(\mathbf{x})\mathbf{\Lambda}(\mathbf{x}) = \left[m_d'(\mathbf{x})\mathbf{\Lambda}'(\mathbf{x})\right]\Gamma^{est} \qquad (17.11)$$

$$m_s(\mathbf{x})\Gamma = \left[m_s'(\mathbf{x})\frac{1}{3}\right]\Gamma^{est} \qquad (17.12)$$

3.   Specular-to-diffuse mechanism

To separate the reflection components, we basically rely on the *specular-to-diffuse mechanism*. This mechanism is derived from *maximum chromaticity* and intensity values of diffuse and specular pixels. Following the chromaticity definition in Equation (17.4) we define maximum chromaticity as:

$$\tilde{\sigma}'(\mathbf{x}) = \frac{max(I_r'(\mathbf{x}), I_g'(\mathbf{x}), I_b'(\mathbf{x}))}{I_r'(\mathbf{x}) + I_g'(\mathbf{x}) + I_b'(\mathbf{x})} \qquad (17.13)$$

where $\{I_r'(\mathbf{x}), I_g'(\mathbf{x}), I_b'\}$ are obtained from a normalized image ($\mathbf{I}'$ in Equation (17.10)). Identically, we can express $\tilde{\sigma}'(\mathbf{x}) = max(\sigma_r'(\mathbf{x}), \sigma_g'(\mathbf{x}), \sigma_b'(\mathbf{x}))$,

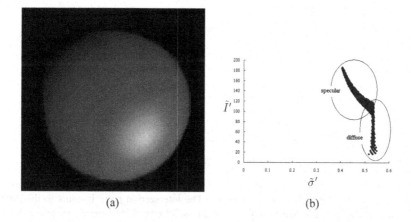

(a)   (b)

Figure 17.1.   (a) Synthetic image. (b) Projection of the synthetic image pixels into the maximum chromaticity intensity space.

where σ' is the image chromaticity of the normalized image. Unlike chromaticity (σ'), maximum chromaticity ($\tilde{\sigma}'$) is a scalar value.

For a uniformly colored surface that has been normalized, in a two-dimensional space: maximum chromaticity intensity space, where its x-axes representing $\tilde{\sigma}'$ and its y-axes representing $\tilde{I}'$, with $\tilde{I}' = max(I'_r, I'_g, I'_b)$, the diffuse points' maximum chromaticities of the image are always larger those of the specular points, due to the maximum chromaticity definition (17.13). Mathematically, it can be proved by comparing the values of maximum chromaticity ($\tilde{\sigma}'$) of diffuse and specular pixels defined in Equation (17.10):

$$\tilde{\sigma}'_{diff} > \tilde{\sigma}'_{spec} \tag{17.14}$$

$$\frac{\tilde{\Lambda}'}{\Lambda'_r + \Lambda'_g + \Lambda'_b} > \frac{m'_d\tilde{\Lambda}' + \frac{1}{3}m'_s}{m'_d(\Lambda'_r + \Lambda'_g + \Lambda'_b) + m'_s} \tag{17.15}$$

$$\tilde{\Lambda}' > \frac{1}{3} \tag{17.16}$$

where $\tilde{\Lambda}' = max(\Lambda'_r, \Lambda'_g, \Lambda'_b)$, the Λ'_c of $\tilde{I}'$ (with index c is identical to the color channel of $\tilde{I}'$), and $(\Lambda'_r + \Lambda'_g + \Lambda'_b) = 1$. Thus, since the values of $\tilde{\Lambda}'$ for chromatic pixels are always larger than $1/3$, the last equation holds true.

In addition, using either the chromaticity or the maximum chromaticity definition, the chromaticity values of the diffuse points will be constant, regardless of the variance of $m'_d(\mathbf{x})$. In contrast, the chromaticity values of specular points will vary with regard to the variance of $m'_s(\mathbf{x})$, as shown in Figure 17.1.b. From these different characteristics of specular and diffuse points in the maximum chromaticity intensity space, we devised specular-to-diffuse mechanism. The details are as follows.

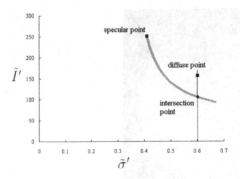

Figure 17.2. Specular-to-diffuse mechanism. The intersection point is equal to the diffuse component of the specular pixel. By knowing diffuse chromaticity from the diffuse pixel, the intersection point can be obtained.

When two normalized pixels, a specular pixel $\mathbf{I}'(\mathbf{x_1})$ and a diffuse pixel $\mathbf{I}'(\mathbf{x_2})$, with the same $\mathbf{\Lambda}'$ are projected into the maximum chromaticity intensity space, the location of the diffuse point will be at the right side of the specular point since, diffuse's maximum chromaticity is larger than specular's maximum chromaticity. Then, by subtracting every color channel of the specular pixel's intensity using a small scalar number iteratively, and projecting the subtracted values into the maximum chromaticity intensity space, we will find that the projected points form a curved line in the space, as shown in Figure 17.2. This curved line follows the following equation (see Appendix A for complete derivation):

$$\tilde{I}'(\mathbf{x}) = m'_d(\mathbf{x})(\tilde{\Lambda}'(\mathbf{x}) - 1/3)(\frac{\tilde{\sigma}'(\mathbf{x})}{\tilde{\sigma}'(\mathbf{x}) - 1/3}) \qquad (17.17)$$

The last equation proves that the distribution of specular points in maximum chromaticity intensity space forms a curved cluster if the values of m'_d vary (Figure 17.1.b).

In Figure 17.2, we can observe that a certain point in the curved line intersects with a vertical line representing the maximum chromaticity of the diffuse point. At this intersection, m'_s of the specular pixel equals zero, since the maximum chromaticity of the subtracted specular pixel becomes identical to that of the diffuse pixel. As a consequence, the intersection point becomes crucial, since it indicates the diffuse component of the specular pixel ($m'_d(\mathbf{x_1})\mathbf{\Lambda}'$). To obtain this value, we first compute $m'_d(\mathbf{x_1})$, which can be derived from Equation (17.17):

$$m'_d(\mathbf{x_1}) = \frac{\tilde{I}'(\mathbf{x_1})[3\tilde{\sigma}'(\mathbf{x_1}) - 1]}{\tilde{\sigma}'(\mathbf{x_1})[3\tilde{\Lambda}'(\mathbf{x_1}) - 1]} \qquad (17.18)$$

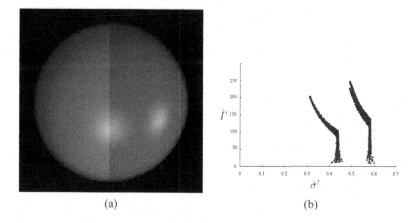

(a)   (b)

Figure 17.3. (a) Synthetic image with multicolored surface. (b) Projection of the synthetic image pixels into the maximum chromaticity intensity space.

To compute m'_d we need to know the value of $\tilde{\Lambda}'(\mathbf{x_1})$. This value can be obtained from the diffuse pixel since, if the two pixels have the same diffuse chromaticity, then $\tilde{\Lambda}'(\mathbf{x_1}) = \tilde{\Lambda}'(\mathbf{x_2}) = \tilde{\sigma}'(\mathbf{x_2})$. Upon knowing the value of $m'_d(\mathbf{x_1})$, we can directly obtain the value of $m'_s(\mathbf{x_1})$, since $m'_s(\mathbf{x_1}) = (I'_r(\mathbf{x_1}) + I'_b(\mathbf{x_1}) + I'_g(\mathbf{x_1})) - m'_d(\mathbf{x_1})$. As a result, the normalized diffuse reflection component of the specular pixel is able to obtain: $m'_d(\mathbf{x_1})\Lambda'(\mathbf{x_1}) = \mathbf{I}'(\mathbf{x_1}) - \frac{m'_s(\mathbf{x_1})}{3}$.

To correctly compute the diffuse component $(m'_d(\mathbf{x_1})\Lambda')$, the mechanism needs a linearity between the camera output and the flux of incoming light intensity. Moreover, in the case of the above two pixels, the mechanism can successfully obtain the reflection components because the diffuse chromaticity is known. Unfortunately, given a multicolored image as shown in Figure 17.3, the diffuse chromaticity for each color is unknown; this, in fact, is the main problem of separating reflection components by using a single multicolored image.

Although we cannot directly use specular-to-diffuse mechanism to separate the reflection components, the mechanism is still usefull, since it tells us that the diffuse component of a specular pixel lies somewhere in the curved line (Equation (17.17)). Furthermore, by using the mechanism, we are also able to generate a specular-free image, which is one of the crucial components in our proposed method.

3.1   Specular-Free Image

To generate a *specular-free image* , we simply set the diffuse maximum chromaticity ($\tilde{\Lambda}'$ in Equation (17.18)) equal to an arbitrary scalar value ($1/3 <$

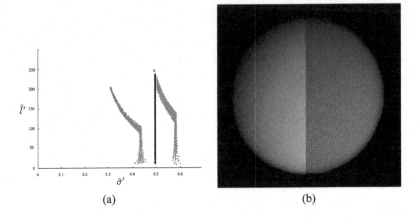

Figure 17.4. (a) Shifting all pixels into arbitrary $\tilde{\Lambda}'$. (b) Specular-free image.

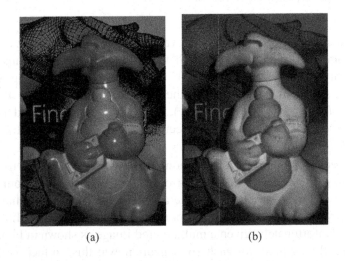

Figure 17.5. (a) Normalized input image. (b) Specular-free image by setting $\tilde{\Lambda}' = 0.5$. The specular components are perfectly removed, but the surface color is different.

$\tilde{\Lambda}' \leq 1$), for all pixels regardless of their color. For instance, we set $\tilde{\Lambda}'$ equal to 0.5 for image in Figure 17.1.a, which implies that the distribution of the points in maximum chromaticity-intensity space becomes a vertical line as shown in Figure 17.4.a. As a result, we can obtain an image that does not have specular reflections (Figure 17.4.b). Figure 17.5.a shows a real image of a multicolored scene. By setting $\tilde{\Lambda}' = 0.5$ for all pixels, we can obtain an image that is geometrically identical to the diffuse component of the input image (Figure 17.5.b). The difference of both is solely in their surface colors.

This technique can successfully remove highlights mainly because the saturation values of all pixels are made constant regarding to the maximum chromaticity, while retaining their hue [5, 1]. It is well known that, if the specular component's color is pure white, then diffuse and specular pixels that have the same surface color will have identical values of hue, with the hue defined as [8] :

$$H = cos^{-1} \left[\frac{\frac{1}{2}\left[(I'_r - I'_g) + (I'_r - I'_b)\right]}{\left[(I'_r - I'_g)^2 + (I'_r - I'_b)(I'_g - I'_b)\right]^{\frac{1}{2}}} \right] \qquad (17.19)$$

and difference saturation values, with saturation is defined as [8] :

$$S = 1 - \left[\frac{3}{I'_r + I'_g + I'_b} min(I'_r, I'_g, I'_b) \right] \qquad (17.20)$$

In our dichromatic reflection model (Equation 17.10), different saturation means different value of m'_s (the weighting factor of specular component), and the same hue means the same value of Λ' (the normalized diffuse chromaticity). As a consequence, in maximum chromaticity intensity space, for diffuse points with the same Λ', both saturation and hue values will be constant (since their m'_s values equal zero) while, for specular points with the same Λ', their saturation values will vary (since their m'_s values vary), and the hue values will be constant. Thus, shifting all points in maximum chromaticity intensity space into a certain arbitrary value using a specular-to-diffuse mechanism is identical to making all points' saturation values constant, but retaining their hue values intact. These constant-saturation values can make the highlights disappear from the image.

Formally, we describe the specular-free image as:

$$\mathring{\mathbf{I}}(\mathbf{x}) = \mathring{m}_d(\mathbf{x})\mathring{\mathbf{\Lambda}}(\mathbf{x}) \qquad (17.21)$$

where $\mathring{\mathbf{I}} = \{\mathring{I}_r, \mathring{I}_g, \mathring{I}_b\}$ is the image intensity of the specular-free image, $\mathring{\mathbf{\Lambda}} = \{\mathring{\Lambda}_r, \mathring{\Lambda}_g, \mathring{\Lambda}_b\}$ is the diffuse chromaticity, and $\mathring{m}_d$ is the diffuse weighting factor. In the following, we will prove that $\mathring{m}_d$ has the same geometrical profile to m'_d (the diffuse weighting factor of normalized image).

According to Equation (17.10) a normalized diffuse pixel is described as $\mathbf{I}'(\mathbf{x}) = m'_d(\mathbf{x})\mathbf{\Lambda}'(\mathbf{x})$. If we apply the specular-to-diffuse mechanism to the pixel by substituting the value of $\tilde{\Lambda}'$ in Equation (17.18) where $\tilde{\Lambda}' = max(\Lambda'_r, \Lambda'_g, \Lambda'_b)$ with an arbitrary maximum chromaticity whose value equals $max(\mathring{\Lambda}_r, \mathring{\Lambda}_g, \mathring{\Lambda}_b)$, then the equation becomes:

$$\mathring{m}_d(\mathbf{x}) = \frac{\tilde{I}'(\mathbf{x})[3\tilde{\sigma}'(\mathbf{x}) - 1]}{\tilde{\sigma}'(\mathbf{x})[3max(\mathring{\Lambda}_r, \mathring{\Lambda}_g, \mathring{\Lambda}_b) - 1]} \qquad (17.22)$$

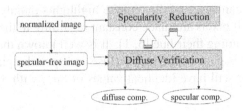

Figure 17.6.   Basic Flow of the proposed method.

Since $\tilde{I}'(\mathbf{x}) = m'_d(\mathbf{x})\tilde{\Lambda}'(\mathbf{x})$, and for diffuse pixels $\tilde{\Lambda}'(\mathbf{x}) = \tilde{\sigma}'(\mathbf{x})$, by defining $\tilde{\Lambda}^{new} = max(\mathring{\Lambda}_r, \mathring{\Lambda}_g, \mathring{\Lambda}_b)$, we can obtain:

$$\mathring{m}_d(\mathbf{x}) = m'_d(\mathbf{x}) \frac{3\tilde{\Lambda}'(\mathbf{x}) - 1}{3\tilde{\Lambda}^{new} - 1} \qquad (17.23)$$

$\tilde{\Lambda}^{new}$ is independent of the spatial parameter $(\mathbf{x})$, since we use the same value $\tilde{\Lambda}^{new}$ for all pixels regardless of their colors. Note that the same value of $\tilde{\Lambda}^{new}$ does not necessarily imply the same value $\mathring{\Lambda}$. As a result, for diffuse pixels with the same diffuse chromaticity (the same surface color), $\frac{3\tilde{\Lambda}'(\mathbf{x})-1}{3\tilde{\Lambda}^{new}-1}$ will be constant, thereby enabling us to describe the image intensity of specular-free image as:

$$\mathring{\mathbf{I}}(\mathbf{x}) = m'_d(\mathbf{x})k(\mathbf{x})\mathring{\mathbf{\Lambda}}(\mathbf{x}) \qquad (17.24)$$

where $k(\mathbf{x}) = \frac{3\tilde{\Lambda}'(\mathbf{x})-1}{3\tilde{\Lambda}^{new}-1}$. For pixels with the same diffuse chromaticity $(\mathbf{\Lambda}')$, k is a constant scalar value. For the proof for specular pixels, see Appendix B. Therefore, since $\mathring{m}_d(\mathbf{x}) = m'_d(\mathbf{x})k$, the diffuse geometrical profile of the specular-free image is identical to the geometrical profile of both the normalized image (17.10) and the input image (17.7).

Generating a specular-free image using specular-to-diffuse mechanism is a one-pixel-based operation that requires only a single colored image without any segmentation process. As a result, it is simple and could be useful for many applications in computer vision that do not need actual surface color but suffer from highlights. Note that caution should be taken in using a specular-free image, particularly for applications that require evaluating color discontinuities since, in the case of two adjacent colors that have the same hue but different saturation, color discontinuities of the two colors will disappear.

4.   Separation Method

Flowchart in Figure 17.6 illustrates the basic idea of our proposed method. First, given a normalized image, a specular-free image is generated. Based on these two images (the normalized image and the specular free image), the 'diffuse verification' verifies whether the normalized image has diffuse-only pixels. If it does, then the processes terminate. Otherwise, the 'specularity reduction' will decrease the intensity of the specular pixels of the normalized image. After that, the diffuse verification verifies once again whether the normalized image has diffuse-only pixels. These two processes are done iteratively until there is no specularity in the normalized image. All processes require only two adjacent pixels to accomplish their task; and, this local operation is indispensable in dealing with highly textured surfaces. The following subsections will show the detail of the two processes.

4.1   Diffuse Pixels Verification

Intensity Logarithmic Differentiation.   Given one colored pixel, to determine whether it is diffuse or specular pixel is completely an ill posed problem. Since in a linear equation such as equation (17.10), whether m'_s is equal to zero is undeterminable from a single $\mathbf{I}'$. In this section, instead of a single pixel, we will show that two-neighboring pixels can be the minimum requirement to determine whether both of them are diffuse pixels.

We base our technique on intensity logarithmic differentiation of the normalized image and the specular free image. Considering a diffuse pixel which is not located at color discontinuities in Figure 17.5.a, we can describe it as: $\mathbf{I}'(\mathbf{x_1}) = m'_d(\mathbf{x_1})\mathbf{\Lambda}'$. The spatial parameter $(\mathbf{x_1})$ is removed from $\mathbf{\Lambda}'$, since the pixel is not located at color discontinuities. If we apply logarithmic and then differentiation operation on this pixel, the equation becomes:

$$log(\mathbf{I}'(\mathbf{x_1})) = log(m'_d(\mathbf{x_1})) + log(\mathbf{\Lambda}') \qquad (17.25)$$

$$\frac{d}{d\mathbf{x}}log(\mathbf{I}'(\mathbf{x_1})) = \frac{d}{d\mathbf{x}}log(m'_d(\mathbf{x_1})) \qquad (17.26)$$

For the same pixel's location $(\mathbf{x_1})$, we can obtain a corresponding pixel in the specular-free image. We describe it as: $\mathring{\mathbf{I}}(\mathbf{x_1}) = m'_d(\mathbf{x_1})k\mathring{\mathbf{\Lambda}}$, where k and $\mathring{\mathbf{\Lambda}}$ are independent from spatial parameter. Thus, using the same operations, logarithmic and differentiation, we can obtain:

$$log(\mathring{\mathbf{I}}(\mathbf{x_1})) = log(m'_d(\mathbf{x_1})) + log(k) + log(\mathring{\mathbf{\Lambda}}) \qquad (17.27)$$

$$\frac{d}{d\mathbf{x}}log(\mathring{\mathbf{I}}(\mathbf{x_1})) = \frac{d}{d\mathbf{x}}log(m'_d(\mathbf{x_1})) \qquad (17.28)$$

The last equation has the same result to Equation (17.26). It means that the differential logarithmic of the diffuse pixels of the normalized image (Equation (17.26)) and the differential logarithmic of the corresponding pixels in the specular free image (Equation (17.28)) are exactly identical.

As a result, based on the intensity logarithmic differentiation operation, we become able to determine whether two-neighboring pixels are diffuse pixels:

$$\Delta(\mathbf{x}) \;=\; dlog(\mathbf{I}'(\mathbf{x})) - dlog(\mathring{\mathbf{I}}(\mathbf{x})) \tag{17.29}$$

$$\Delta(\mathbf{x}) \quad \begin{cases} = 0 & : \quad \text{diffuse} \\ \neq 0 & : \quad \text{specular or color discontinuity} \end{cases} \tag{17.30}$$

As shown in Equation (17.30), for pixels located at color discontinuities, there is still an ambiguity between specular and color discontinuity pixels. Since using two neighboring pixels that have different surface color, the difference of the logarithmic differentiation does not equal zero, although the pixels are diffuse pixels. Theoretically, by extending the number of pixels into at least four neighboring pixels, it is possible to distinguish them. However, in real images, camera noise and surface noise (surface variance) [9, 27] make such identification become error-prone; consequently, to deal with the color discontinuity problem, we need another more robust analysis which will be described in the next subsection.

Color Discontinuity.   A number of methods have been proposed to solve the color discontinuity problem, which is also known as the problem of material changes [10, 7]. Unlike those methods, we use a simple chromaticity-based method to handle the problem. We use the below decision rule:

$$(\Delta r > thR \quad \text{and} \quad \Delta g > thG) \begin{cases} true & : \quad \text{color discontinuity} \\ false & : \quad \text{otherwise} \end{cases} \tag{17.31}$$

where thR and thG are the small scalar numbers. $\Delta r(\mathbf{x}) = \sigma'_r(\mathbf{x}) - \sigma'_r(\mathbf{x} - 1)$ and $\Delta g(\mathbf{x}) = \sigma'_g(\mathbf{x}) - \sigma'_g(\mathbf{x} - 1)$, with $\sigma'_r = \frac{I'_r}{I'_r + I'_g + I'_b}$ and $\sigma'_g = \frac{I'_g}{I'_r + I'_g + I'_b}$. This simple technique is similar to the method proposed by Funt *et al.* [6].

For two neighboring pixels, this simple chromaticity thresholding is sufficient since when two neighboring pixels have the same surface color, their chromaticity difference is small, even for specular pixels. This is one of the advantages of our local, two-neighboring-pixels operation. Moreover, the above thresholding can also solve the problem of two adjacent objects that have the same hue but different saturation, as long as the saturation difference is not less than that of the thresholds. Fortunately, in practice, even if the saturation difference is less than the thresholds, it does not affect the result much; since it implies that the objects have almost the same color, so that it is unnecessary to distinguish them. In addition, we have no problem when the above thresholding wrongly deems the shadow boundary to be a color discontinuity, since we have nothing to do with shadow.

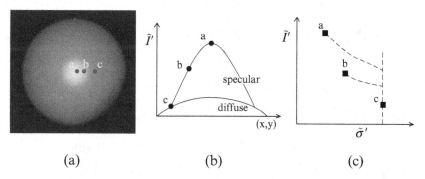

Figure 17.7. (a) Three points in an image. (b) The three points in spatial-intensity space. (c) The three points in maximum chromaticity intensity space.

4.2   Specularity Reduction

Specularity reduction is the second process of the two main processes we have proposed. The purpose of this process is to decrease the intensity of the specular pixels until we obtain diffuse-only reflections. All operations in this process are still based only on two-neighboring pixels. Figure 17.7.a shows three pixels: a, b, and c. For the sake of simplicity, for the moment we assume a uniformly colored surface and those the three pixels are adjacent spatially to each other. Pixel a is the highlight's brightest pixels, and pixel c is a diffuse pixel, and pixel b is a specular pixels located between pixels a and c. In spatial-image intensity space, the image intensity of pixel a will be the largest value followed by pixels b and c, as shown in Figure 17.7.b. If we transform the pixels into maximum chromaticity-intensity space, we will obtain a point distribution illustrated in Figure 17.7.c.

Figure 17.8 illustrates the basic idea of our specularity reduction. In considering a two-pixel operation, the iteration begins with comparing the maximum chromaticity of point a and point b in Figure 17.8.d . From the maximum chromaticity definition in Equation (17.13), we know that the smaller the m'_s is, the bigger the maximum chromaticity value. In other words, point b is more diffuse than point a. Thus, by shifting point a using the specular-to-diffuse mechanism w.r.t the maximum chromaticity of point b, the more diffuse pixel a can be obtained, i.e., the intensity of pixel a becomes decreased and its chromaticity becomes identical to point b's, as illustrated in Figure 17.8.b and 17.8.e, respectively. Using the same process in the second iteration, the maximum chromaticities of point b and point c are compared and then shifted. When the maximum chromaticity of point b equals the maximum chromaticity of point c, the intensity of pixel b becomes equal to its diffuse component. The same operation is done for all pixels iteratively until their maximum chromaticity

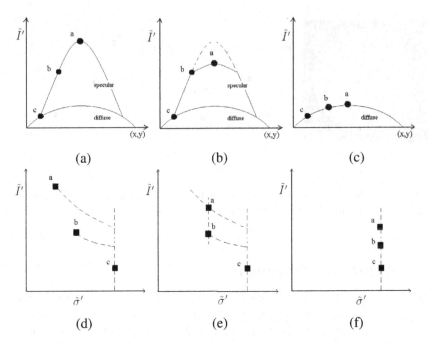

Figure 17.8. Basic idea of the iterative framework using local two-pixels operation. Top row, spatial-intensity space: (a) Initial condition. (b) First looping. (c) Final condition; Bottom row, chromaticity intensity space: (d) Initial condition. (e) First looping. (f) Final condition.

becomes the same (Figure 17.8.f), which as a result, produces the diffuse components of the three pixels (Figure 17.8.c).

However, the above termination condition, looping until the maximum chromaticities of all pixels are the same, is feasible only for a uniformly colored surface. In multicolored surfaces, such a termination condition will produce incorrect separation results. Therefore, to determine the termination we use the diffuse verification process explained in Subsection 4.1. We have learned that the process can identify whether an image has diffuse-only pixels, even for a multicolored image. Algorithm 5.1 shows the pseudo-code of the iteration method for both uniform and multicolored surfaces.

5.   Implementation

Algorithm 5.1 shows the pseudo-code of the iterative algorithm. It begins with executing function $delta(N, S, \epsilon)$, which computes the difference of the intensity logarithmic differentiation of the normalized image (N) and the specular-free image (S). In discrete operations, the logarithmic differentiation is done using: $dlog(I'_{tot}(\mathbf{x})) = log(\Sigma I'_i(\mathbf{x}+1)) - log(\Sigma I'_i(\mathbf{x}))$, where $\Sigma I'_i = (I'_r + I'_g + I'_b)$. Then, the function computes $\Delta = dlog(I'_{tot}(\mathbf{x})) - dlog(\mathring{I}_{tot}(\mathbf{x}))$, and labels the pixels of the normalized image: for pixels that have Δ more than ϵ (≈ 0), they are labeled 'specular', otherwise, they are labeled 'diffuse'.

Algorithm 5.1: ITERATION(N, S, ϵ)

comment: N=normalized-image; S= specular-free-image

(1) $\Delta = delta(N, S, \epsilon)$;
(2) **while** $any(\Delta(\mathbf{x}) > \epsilon)$
$\left\{\begin{array}{l} \textbf{for } \mathbf{x} \leftarrow 0 \textbf{ to } \text{sizeof(N)-1} \\ \left\{\begin{array}{l} (3) \textbf{ if } \mathbf{x}.flag == diffuse \\ \quad \textbf{then } \text{next}(\mathbf{x}); \\ (4) \textbf{ if } IsDiscontinuity(\mathbf{x}, \mathbf{x}+1) == true \\ \quad \textbf{then } \left\{\begin{array}{l} \mathbf{x}.flag = discontinuity; \\ (\mathbf{x}+1).flag = discontinuity; \\ next(\mathbf{x}); \end{array}\right. \\ (5) \textbf{ if } \tilde{\sigma}'(\mathbf{x}) == \tilde{\sigma}'(\mathbf{x}+1) \\ \quad \textbf{then } \left\{\begin{array}{l} \mathbf{x}.flag = noise; \\ (\mathbf{x}+1).flag = noise; \\ next(\mathbf{x}); \end{array}\right. \\ (6) \ M(\mathbf{x}) = Specular2Diffuse(\mathbf{I}'(\mathbf{x}), \mathbf{I}'(\mathbf{x}+1)); \\ next(\mathbf{x}); \end{array}\right. \\ N = M; \\ (7) \Delta = delta(N, S, \epsilon); \end{array}\right.$
return (N)
comment: N = normalized diffuse component

In Step 2 until Step 4, if there are any pixels labeled 'specular', for each of them, the algorithm examines whether the pixel and its neighbor are color discontinuity pixels. If so, then they are labeled 'discontinuity'; otherwise, then at least one of them must be a specular pixel. In Step 5, before we apply the specular-to-diffuse mechanism to both pixels, additional checking is necessary, i.e., whether both pixels' maximum chromaticity is the same. If they are the same, then the pixels are labeled 'noise'. The reason that they are noise and not specular pixels is because two-neighboring specular pixels never have the same maximum chromaticity.

In Step 6, using the specular-to-diffuse mechanism the intensity and maximum chromaticity value of the pixel that have smaller $\tilde{\sigma}'$ is shifted w.r.t. the pixel with bigger $\tilde{\sigma}'$. This is applied to all pixels, and produces a more diffuse normalized image. By setting N equal to this image (M), function $delta(N, S, \epsilon)$ is executed once again in Step 7. This time, pixels labeled 'discontinuity' and 'noise' are ignored (not included in the process). Finally, if there is still any Δ larger than ϵ, then the iteration continues; if not, the separation terminates, which consequently yields a diffuse component of the normalized image.

In our implementation, we define $\epsilon = 0$. For color discontinuity thresholds (thR and thG), we set them with the same number ranging from 0.05 to 0.1. The numbers are chosen by considering camera noise, illumination color variance, ambient light (some considerably small interreflections) and surface color variance (although human perception deems that the color surface is uniform, there is, in fact, still color variance due to dust, imperfect painting, etc. [27]).

Algorithm 5.2: CONTROLLEDTHRESHOLD(N, S)

comment: N=normalized-image; S= specular-free-image

$RemoveAchromaticPixels(N)$;
$stepTH = InitialThreshold$;
while $stepTH\epsilon$
$\begin{cases} \Delta = delta(N, S, \epsilon); \\ \textbf{if } any(\Delta(\mathbf{x}) > stepTH) \\ \quad \textbf{then } Iteration(N, S, stepTH); \\ stepTH = stepTH - \delta; \\ ResetAllLabels(); \end{cases}$
$Renormalization(N)$;
return (N);
comment: N=actual diffuse component

For a more stable and robust algorithm we add an algorithm that controls the decrease of the threshold of Δ step-by-step, as described in Algorithm 5.2. In function $Iteration(N, S, \epsilon)$, $stepTh$ will replace ϵ, which in our implementation its initial value is equal to 0.5. Ideally, the initial value should be set as large as possible; yet, by considering the time computation the number is chosen. To obtain more accurate results, the smaller subtracting number (δ) is preferable and, our implementation, we set it equal to 0.01. To anticipate regions having achromatic pixels ($I'_r = I'_g = I'_b$), which are inevitable in the real images, we remove them by using simple thresholding in maximum chromaticity; achromatic pixels of normalized image have maximum chromaticity near $1/3$.

6.   Discussion

In previous sections, we assumed that the estimated illumination chromaticity is exactly identical to the input image's illumination chromaticity, $\Gamma = \Gamma^{est}$ (Equation 17.10). However, to estimate illumination chromaticity accurately is not trivial; real images always have noises that make the estimation deviate from the actual value. In this section, we intend to describe the effect of illumination error in estimating the value of m_d by using the specular-to-diffuse mechanism.

Without normalizing an image intensity, the correlation between m_d and image intensity in Equation (17.18) becomes:

$$m_d = \tilde{I} \frac{\tilde{\sigma} - \tilde{\Gamma}}{\tilde{\sigma}(\tilde{\Lambda} - \tilde{\Gamma})} \tag{17.32}$$

where $\tilde{I} = max(I_r, I_g, I_b)$, with $\mathbf{I}$ is defined in Equation (17.7). While, $\tilde{\sigma}$, $\tilde{\Lambda}$ and $\tilde{\Gamma}$ are the σ_c, Λ_c and Γ_c of $\tilde{I}$ (with index c is identical to the color channel of $\tilde{I}$), respectively. We define the estimated illumination chromaticity equal $\tilde{\Gamma} + e^{ill}$, where e^{ill} is the error of illumination estimation, whose value can be either positive or negative. Thus, m_d of error illumination becomes:

$$m_d^{err} = \tilde{I} \frac{\tilde{\sigma} - \tilde{\Gamma} - e^{ill}}{\tilde{\sigma}(\tilde{\Lambda} - \tilde{\Gamma} - e^{ill})} \tag{17.33}$$

We express the error of computing m_d as: $err = \left| m_d - m_d^{err} \right|$. By plugging Equation (17.32) and Equation (17.33) into the error definition, we obtain:

$$err = \left| \frac{(\tilde{\Lambda} - \tilde{\sigma})}{(\tilde{\Lambda} - \tilde{\Gamma})(\tilde{\Lambda} - \tilde{\Gamma} - e^{ill})} \frac{\tilde{I}}{\tilde{\sigma}} e^{ill} \right| \tag{17.34}$$

The last equation means that the error of estimating m_d depends on:

- $(\tilde{\Lambda} - \tilde{\sigma})$, whose value is determined by m_s (the specular weighting factor). The bigger the value of m_s, the larger the difference between $\tilde{\sigma}$ and $\tilde{\Lambda}$.

- $(\tilde{\Lambda} - \tilde{\Gamma})$. The smaller difference causes the larger error. Consequently, the error will be larger for pixels whose $\tilde{\Lambda}$ is near $1/3$ (achromatic pixels).

- $\tilde{I}$. The brighter image intensity causes the larger error of estimated m_d. For raw images taken directly from a digital camera, the range of image intensity is $0 \sim 255$.

- $\tilde{\sigma}$, the image chromaticity of $\tilde{I}$. The smaller $\tilde{\sigma}$ produces the larger error. The smallest value of $\tilde{\sigma}$ is $1/3$ (for chromatic pixels, $\tilde{\sigma} > 1/3$).

Besides error in estimating illumination chromaticity, we also consider error in estimating actual diffuse chromaticity, $\tilde{\Lambda}$. We define the error as: $\tilde{\Lambda} + e^{ch}$, which makes Equation (17.33) become:

$$m_d^{err} = \tilde{I}\frac{\tilde{\sigma} - \tilde{\Gamma} - e^{ill}}{\tilde{\sigma}\left[(\tilde{\Lambda} + e^{ch}) - (\tilde{\Gamma} + e^{ill})\right]} \qquad (17.35)$$

Consequently, err of estimating m_d:

$$err =$$
$$\left|\frac{(\tilde{\sigma} - \tilde{\Gamma})}{(\tilde{\Lambda} - \tilde{\Gamma})(\tilde{\Lambda} + e^{ch} - \tilde{\Gamma} - e^{ill})}\frac{\tilde{I}}{\tilde{\sigma}}e^{ch} + \frac{(\tilde{\Lambda} - \tilde{\sigma})}{(\tilde{\Lambda} - \tilde{\Gamma})(\tilde{\Lambda} + e^{ch} - \tilde{\Gamma} - e^{ill})}\frac{\tilde{I}}{\tilde{\sigma}}e^{ill}\right|$$
$$(17.36)$$

For normalized images and chromatic surface color, $\tilde{\sigma} > \tilde{\Gamma}$ and $\tilde{\Lambda} > \tilde{\Gamma}$, where $\tilde{\Gamma} = 1/3$. The last equation shows that the error of estimating m_d is an accumulation of the errors caused by the illumination chromaticity and the diffuse chromaticity imprecise estimation.

7. Experimental Results

All images in our experiments were taken using a CCD camera: SONY DXC-9000 (a progressive 3 CCD digital camera) by setting the gamma correction off. The separations were processed using Intel Pentium III CPU 850 MHz Double Processors, with memory 700 MB RAM. We used convex-shaped objects to avoid inter-reflections, and did not take account of saturated or blooming pixels in our experiments. The illumination chromaticities were estimated using a color constancy algorithm [26]. This color constancy method requires crude highlight regions, which can be obtained using thresholding in both intensity and saturation.

Evaluation. We evaluated the estimation results by comparing the results of two polarizing filters. We placed one of the two filters in front of camera and the other in front of the light source. Theoretically, if we change the polarization angle of one of the two filters into a certain angle, we can obtain diffuse-only reflections. In our experiment, we changed the polarization angle of the filter placed in front of the camera. Figure 17.9.a, b and c show, respectively, the input image, the diffuse reflection component obtained using the two polarizing filters (ground truth) and reflection components estimated using our method. Figure 17.9.d, e and f show the difference of image intensity values of the input image (Figure 17.9.a) and the ground truth (Figure 17.9.b), in red, green and blue channels, respectively. The ranges of blue pixels in the figures are $0 \sim 5$. Green pixels are $6 \sim 15$, red pixels are $16 \sim 35$, while yellow pixels represent larger than 35. In regions exhibit highlights, we can observe large differences of the intensity values in all color channels. Also, in certain places near occluding boundaries, yellow and red pixels appear. The latter is caused by the difference of intensity distribution when the polarization angle is changed. Figure 17.9.g, h and i show the difference of image intensity values of the estimated reflection component (Figure 17.9.c) and the ground truth (Figure 17.9.b) in red, green and blue, respectively. In regions that originally exhibit highlights, the colors became blue, indicating that the estimation result was considerably accurate. Red and green pixels occurring in many places in the comparison were due to two main factors: inaccurate illumination chromaticity estimation, and dark noise. Despite these factors, the estimation results are considerably accurate, since the maximum value of dark noise of the camera (Sony DXC-9000) is around 10. Figure 17.9 shows another separation result using a different object. Note that, in this evaluation, we did not evaluate pixels whose image intensity was below camera dark (black pixels in the evaluation represent unevaluated pixels).

Figure 17.11 shows the separation result of Figure 17.5.a., where the objects were lit with a solux halogen lamp. For a more complex textured surface, Figure 17.12.a shows an image of a textured surface under fluorescent lights in an uncontrolled environment. The specular-free image, which was generated by setting $\tilde{\Lambda}^{new}$ equal to 0.5 is shown in Figure 17.12.b. Figure 17.12.c and 17.12.d show the separated components of the object. To separate the diffuse and specular components from the image (with size 640x480), the computational time using our machine was 2 minutes and 36 seconds. Figure 17.13.a shows a complex scene lit with fluorescent lights in an uncontrolled environment. The specular-free image result is shown in Figure 17.13.b. Figure 17.14.a and Figure 17.14.b show the diffuse and specular reflections, respectively. In the estimated diffuse component (Figure 17.14.a) and the specular-free image (Figure 17.13.b), regions which are originally white become dark. The reason is that the specular-to-diffuse mechanism failed to handle achromatic pixels (Section 1.2). The computational time for processing the image (with size 640x480) was 6 minute and 6 seconds. For more separation results, please visit our website:
www.cvl.iis.u-tokyo.ac.jp/~robby/textureSeparation/results.html

8.   Conclusion

We have proposed a novel method to separate diffuse and specular reflection components. The main insight of the method is in the chromaticity-based iteration with regard to the logarithmic differentiation of the specular-free image. Using the method, the separation problem in textured surfaces with complex multicolored scene can be resolved without requiring explicit color segmentation. It is possible because we base our method on local operation by utilizing the specular-free image. The three crucial factors and thus, the main contribu-

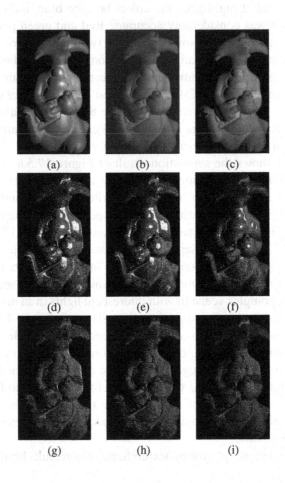

Figure 17.9.   Top row: (a) multicolored input image. (b) Ground truth. (c) Estimation. Middle row: comparison of image (a) and (b): (d) R channel. (e) G channel. (f) B channel. Bottom row: comparison of image (c) and (b): (g) R channel. (h) G channel. (i) B channel.

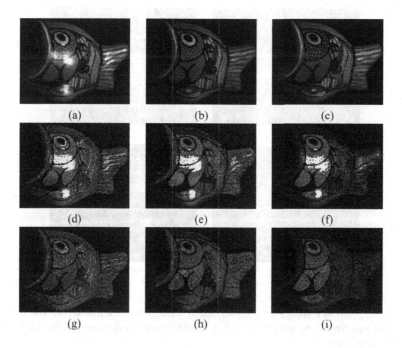

Figure 17.10. Top row: (a) textured input image. (b) Ground truth. (c) Estimation. Middle row: comparison of image (a) and (b): (d) R channel. (e) G channel. (f) B channel. Bottom row: comparison of image (c) and (b): (g) R channel. (h) G channel. (i) B channel.

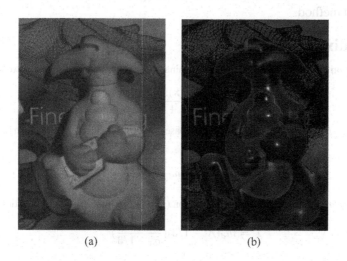

Figure 17.11. (a) Diffuse component of Figure 17.5.a. (b) Specular component of Figure 17.5.a

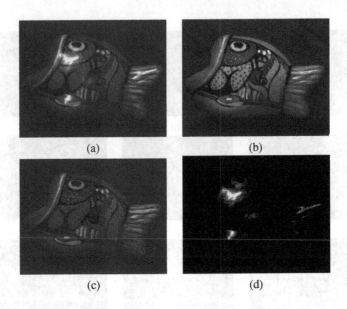

Figure 17.12. (a) A complex textured surface lit with fluorescent lights. (b) The specular-free image was created by setting $\tilde{\Lambda}' = 0.5$. (c) Diffuse reflection component. (d) Specular reflection component.

tions of our method, are the specular-to-diffuse mechanism, the specular-free image, and the logarithmic differentiation-based iteration framework. The experimental results on complex textured images show the effectiveness of our proposed method.

Appendix: A

Derivation of the correlation between illumination chromaticity and image chromaticity.

$$\tilde{\sigma}'(\mathbf{x}) = \frac{m'_d(\mathbf{x})\tilde{\Lambda}'(\mathbf{x}) + \frac{1}{3}m'_s(\mathbf{x})}{m'_d(\mathbf{x})[\Lambda'_r(\mathbf{x}) + \Lambda'_g(\mathbf{x}) + \Lambda'_b(\mathbf{x})] + m'_s(\mathbf{x})} \qquad (17.A.1)$$

where $[\Lambda'_r + \Lambda'_g + \Lambda'_b] = 1$. For local (pixel based) operation the location $(\mathbf{x})$ can be removed. Then:

$$m'_s = m'_d \frac{(\tilde{\Lambda}' - \tilde{\sigma}')}{(\tilde{\sigma}' - 1/3)} \qquad (17.A.2)$$

Substituting m'_s in the definition of $\tilde{I}$ (Equation (17.10)) with m'_s in the last equation:

$$\tilde{I}' = m'_d(\tilde{\Lambda}' - 1/3)(\frac{\tilde{\sigma}'}{\tilde{\sigma}' - 1/3}) \qquad (17.A.3)$$

Appendix: B

A diffuse pixel from a normalized image can be described as: $\mathbf{I}'(\mathbf{x}) = m'_d(\mathbf{x})\mathbf{\Lambda}'(\mathbf{x})$. In Section 3.1, we have shown that using specular-to-diffuse mechanism by substituting $\tilde{\Lambda}'$ with

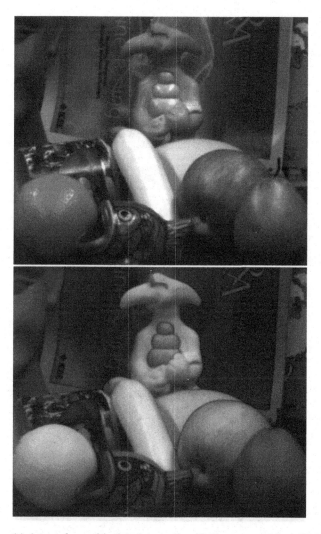

Figure 17.13.   (a) A complex multicolored scene lit with fluorescent lights. (b) The specular-free image by setting $\tilde{\Lambda}' = 0.5$

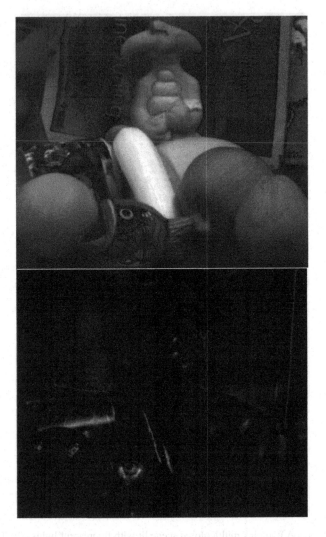

Figure 17.14.   (a) Diffuse reflection component. (b) Specular reflection component

an arbitrary value ($\tilde{\Lambda}^{new}$) whose value is between $1/3 \sim 1$, we can obtain:

$$\mathring{\mathbf{I}}(\mathbf{x}) = \mathring{m}_d(\mathbf{x})\mathring{\mathbf{\Lambda}}(\mathbf{x}) = m'_d(\mathbf{x})k(\mathbf{x})\mathring{\mathbf{\Lambda}}(\mathbf{x}) \qquad (17.B.1)$$

where, for pixels with the same diffuse chromaticity, k is a constant scalar value. Thus, we can obtain that the geometrical profile of specular-free image is identical to that of diffuse reflection component. The proof for specular pixels is as follows:

A specular pixel with identical diffuse geometrical profile to the above diffuse pixel is described as: $\mathbf{I}'(\mathbf{x}) = m'_d(\mathbf{x})\mathbf{\Lambda}'(\mathbf{x}) + \frac{m'_s(\mathbf{x})}{3}$. By applying specular-to-diffuse mechanism (Equation (17.23)) to the specular pixel with the same value of $\tilde{\Lambda}^{new}$, we can obtain:

$$\mathring{m}_d(\mathbf{x}) = \frac{\tilde{I}'(\mathbf{x})[3\tilde{\sigma}'(\mathbf{x}) - 1]}{\tilde{\sigma}'(\mathbf{x})[3\tilde{\Lambda}^{new} - 1]} \qquad (17.B.2)$$

where $\tilde{I}'(\mathbf{x}) = m'_d(\mathbf{x})\tilde{\Lambda}'(\mathbf{x}) + \frac{m'_s(\mathbf{x})}{3}$, and $\tilde{\Lambda}^{new}$ is the arbitrary maximum chromaticity. Unlike diffuse pixels, for specular pixels, $\tilde{\sigma}' \neq \tilde{\Lambda}'$. Then, the last equation becomes:

$$\mathring{m}_d(\mathbf{x}) = \left[m'_d(\mathbf{x})\tilde{\Lambda}'(\mathbf{x}) + \frac{m'_s(\mathbf{x})}{3} \right] \frac{[3\tilde{\sigma}'(\mathbf{x}) - 1]}{\tilde{\sigma}'(\mathbf{x})[3\tilde{\Lambda}^{new} - 1]} \qquad (17.B.3)$$

Since we argued that in specular-free image specular reflection disappear ($\mathring{m}_s = 0$), then $\mathring{m}_d$ of the specular pixel should equal to $\mathring{m}_d$ of the diffuse pixel:

$$\mathring{m}_d^{diff} = \mathring{m}_d^{spec} \qquad (17.B.4)$$

$$m'_d \left[\frac{3\tilde{\Lambda}'(\mathbf{x}) - 1}{3\tilde{\Lambda}^{new} - 1} \right] = \left[m'_d(\mathbf{x})\tilde{\Lambda}'(\mathbf{x}) + \frac{m'_s(\mathbf{x})}{3} \right] \frac{[3\tilde{\sigma}'(\mathbf{x}) - 1]}{\tilde{\sigma}'(\mathbf{x})[3\tilde{\Lambda}^{new} - 1]} \qquad (17.B.5)$$

$$m'_d(\mathbf{x}) \left[3\tilde{\Lambda}'(\mathbf{x}) - 1 \right]\tilde{\sigma}'(\mathbf{x}) = m'_d(\mathbf{x})\tilde{\Lambda}'(\mathbf{x}) \left[3\tilde{\sigma}'(\mathbf{x}) - 1 \right] + \frac{m'_s(\mathbf{x})}{3} \left[3\tilde{\sigma}'(\mathbf{x}) - 1 \right] \qquad (17.B.6)$$

$$m'_d(\mathbf{x}) \left[\tilde{\Lambda}'(\mathbf{x}) - \tilde{\sigma}'(\mathbf{x}) \right] = m'_s(\mathbf{x}) \left[\tilde{\sigma}'(\mathbf{x}) - 1/3 \right] \qquad (17.B.7)$$

$$m'_s(\mathbf{x}) = m'_d(\mathbf{x}) \frac{(\tilde{\Lambda}'(\mathbf{x}) - \tilde{\sigma}'(\mathbf{x}))}{(\tilde{\sigma}'(\mathbf{x}) - 1/3)} \qquad (17.B.8)$$

the last equation is identical to Equation (17.A.2) in Appendix A, which proves that $\mathring{m}_d^{diff} = \mathring{m}_d^{spec}$ holds true. Therefore, all pixels in a specular-free image have no specular reflection component and its geometrical profile is identical to the diffuse component of the input image.

Acknowledgments

This research was supported, in part, by Ministry of Education, Culture, Sports, Science and Technology under the Leading Project, "Development of High Fidelity Digitization Software for Large-Scale and Intangible Cultural Assets," and, in part, by Japan Science and Technology Agency, under the CREST program, "Automatic generation of virtual models of cultural heritage."

References

[1] R. Bajscy, S.W. Lee, and A. Leonardis. Detection of diffuse and specular interface reflections by color image segmentation. *International Journal of Computer Vision*, 17(3):249–272, 1996.

[2] P. Beckmann and A. Spizzochino. *The scattering of electromagnetic waves from rough surfaces*. Pergamon, New York, 1963.

[3] M. Born and E. Wolf. *Principles of Optics*. Cambridge, seventh edition, 1999.

[4] A. Criminisi, S.B. Kang, R. Swaminathan, S. Szeliski, and P. Anandan. Extracting layers and analysis their specular properties using epipolar plane image analysis. *Microsoft Research Technical Report MSR-TR-2002-19*, 2002.

[5] M. D'Zmura and P. Lennie. Mechanism of color constancy. *Journal of Optics Society of America A.*, 3(10):1162–1672, 1986.

[6] B.V. Funt, M. Drew, and M. Brockington. Recovering shading from color images. *in proceeding of European Conference on Computer Vision (ECCV)*, pages 124–132, 1992.

[7] R. Gershon, A.D. Jepson, and J.K. Tsotsos. Ambient illumination and the determination of material changes. *Journal of Optics Society of America A.*, 3(10):1700–1707, 1986.

[8] R.C. Gonzales and R.E. Woods. *Digital Image Processing*. Addison-Wesley, 1993.

[9] G. Healey and R. Kondepudy. Radiometric ccd camera calibration and noise estimation. *IEEE Trans. on Pattern Analysis and Machine Intelligence*, 16(3):267–276, 1994.

[10] J.M.Rubin and W.A.Richard. Color vision: representing material changes. *AI Memo 764, MIT Artificial Intelligence Lab. Cambridge, Mass.*, 1984.

[11] G.J. Klinker, S.A. Shafer, and T. Kanade. The measurement of highlights in color images. *International Journal of Computer Vision*, 2:7–32, 1990.

[12] J.H. Lambert. Photometria sive de mensura de gratibus luminis, colorum et umbrae. *Eberhard Klett: Augsberg, Germany*, 1760.

[13] H.C. Lee, E.J. Breneman, and C.P.Schulte. Modeling light reflection for computer color vision. *IEEE Trans. on Pattern Analysis and Machine Intelligence*, 12:402–409, 1990.

[14] S.W. Lee. *Understanding of surface reflections in Computer vision by color and multiple views*. PhD thesis, University of Pennsylvania, 1991.

[15] S.W. Lee and R. Bajcsy. Detection of specularity using color and multiple views. *Image and Vision Computing*, 10:643–653, 1992.

[16] T.M. Lehmann and C. Palm. Color line search for illuminant estimation in real-world scene. *Journal of Optics Society of America A.*, 18(11):2679–2691, 2001.

[17] S. Lin, Y. Li, S.B. Kang, X. Tong, and H.Y. Shum. Diffuse-specular separation and depth recovery from image sequences. In *in proceeding of European Conference on Computer Vision (ECCV)*, pages 210–224, 2002.

[18] S. Lin and H.Y. Shum. Separation of diffuse and specular reflection in color images. In *in proceeding of IEEE Computer Society Conference on Computer Vision and Pattern Recognition (CVPR)*, 2001.

[19] D. Miyazaki, R.T. Tan, K. Hara, and K. Ikeuchi. Polarization-based inverse rendering from a single view. *in proceeding of IEEE International Conference on Computer Vision (ICCV)*, 2003.

[20] S.K. Nayar, X.S. Fang, and T. Boult. Separation of reflection components using color and polarization. *International Journal of Computer Vision*, 21(3), 1996.

[21] S.K. Nayar, K.Ikeuchi, and T. Kanade. Surface reflection: Physical and geometrical perspectives. *IEEE Trans. on Pattern Analysis and Machine Intelligence*, 13(7):611–634, 1991.

[22] M. Oren and S.K. Nayar. Generalization of the lambertian model and implications for machine vision. *International Journal of Computer Vision*, 14(3):227–251, 1995.

[23] J.P.S. Parkkinen, J. Hallikainen, and T. Jasskelainen. Characteristic spectra of munsell colors. *Journal of Optics Society of America A.*, 6, 1989.

[24] Y. Sato and K. Ikeuchi. Temporal-color space analysis of reflection. *Journal of Optics Society of America A.*, 11, 1994.

[25] S. Shafer. Using color to separate reflection components. *Color Research and Applications*, 10:210–218, 1985.

[26] R. T. Tan, K. Nishino, and K. Ikeuchi. Color constancy through inverse intensity chromaticity space. *Journal of Optics Society of America A.*, 21(3):321–334, 2004.

[27] R. T. Tan, K. Nishino, and K. Ikeuchi. Separating reflection components based on chromaticity and noise analysis. *IEEE Trans. on Pattern Analysis and Machine Intelligence*, to appear, October 2004.

[28] K.E. Torrance and E.M. Sparrow. Theory for off-specular reflection from roughened surfaces. *Journal of Optics Society of America*, 57:1105–1114, 1966.

[29] L. Wolff, S.K. Nayar, and M. Oren. Improved diffuse reflection models for computer vision. *International Journal of Computer Vision*, 30(1):55–71, 1998.

[30] L.B. Wolff. Polarization-based material classification from specular reflection. *IEEE Trans. on Pattern Analysis and Machine Intelligence*, 12(11):1059–1071, 1990.

[31] L.B. Wolff. A diffuse reflectance model for smooth dielectrics. *Journal of Optics Society of America A.*, 11(11):2956–2968, 1994.

[32] L.B. Wolff and T. Boult. Constraining object features using polarization reflectance model. *IEEE Trans. on Pattern Analysis and Machine Intelligence*, 13(7):635–657, 1991.

Chapter 18

CREATING PHOTOREALISTIC VIRTUAL MODEL WITH POLARIZATION-BASED VISION SYSTEM

Takushi Shibata, Toru Takahashi, Daisuke Miyazaki, Yoichi Sato, Katsushi Ikeuchi

Abstract   Recently, 3D models are used in many fields such as education, medical services, entertainment, art, digital archive, etc., because of the progress of computational time and demand for creating photorealistic virtual model is increasing for higher reality. In the field of computer vision, a number of techniques have been developed for creating the virtual model by observing the real object in computer vision field. In this chapter, we propose the method for creating photorealistic virtual model by using laser range sensor and polarization based image capture system. We capture the range and color images of the object which is rotated on the rotary table. In geometrical aspects, an object surface shape is reconstructed by merging multiple range images of the object. In optical aspects, color images are captured under fixed point light source. By using reconstructed object shape and sequence of color images of the object, parameter of a reflection model are estimated in a robust manner. As a result, we can make photorealistic 3D model in consideration of surface reflection. The key point of the proposed method is that, first, the diffuse and specular reflection components are separated from the color image sequence, and then, reflectance parameters of each reflection component are estimated separately. In separation of reflection components, we use polarization filter. This approach enables estimation of reflectance properties of real objects whose surfaces show specularity as well as diffusely reflected lights. The recovered object shape and reflectance properties are then used for synthesizing object images with realistic shading effects under arbitrary illumination conditions.

1.   Introduction

It has become more and more important to develop easy methods for getting the accurate reflectance information as the interest in virtual reality is growing. Currently, virtual reality system is used in a wide variety of applications including electronic commerce, simulation-and-training, and virtual museum walk-through. In spite of these many needs for virtual reality models, most of the virtual reality systems utilize models that are manually created by programmers. If we can build a system that automatically create the models for virtual reality system, we can drastically decrease modeling costs for virtual reality systems.

One major approach to building the virtual object model is the one which reconstructs the input images taken by camera. In recent years, many techniques have been proposed for interpolating between views by warping input images, using depth information or correspondences between multiple images. The general notion of generating new views from pre-acquired imagery is called image-based rendering. Apple's QuickTime VR is one example. Gorter et al. [5] proposed the method for capturing the complete appearance of the real objects and scenes, and rendering the images of the objects from new view positions. Unlike the traditional shape capturing method which is used in computer vision, they don't use the fine geometric representation. Instead, they use the 4D function called Lumigraph. The Lumigraph is a subset of the complete plenoptic function which represents the complete flow of light at all positions in all directions. Levoy et al.[7] also proposed the subset of the plenoptic function called Light Field. They interpretes the input images as two slices of 4-D function. This function can completely characterizes the flow of light through unobstructed space in a static scene with fixed illumination.

Nishino et al.[10] proposed another approach for image-based rendering. They used a fine geometric model and the eigen-texture which was texture-patches made of pictures taken from various points of view and reduced its data set by principal-component analysis. Wood et al.[19] also proposed the method which used a fine geometric model and point-based color information called Lumisphere. Lumisphere also reduced information quantity with the use of principal-component analysis. Georghiades[4] proposed the method recovering BRDF to render under novel illumination and 3D shape of the object at the same time from a small number of photographs without information about the position and intensity of the light-source and the position of the camera. The method is under assumption that image is monochrome and the parameters are constant across the surface. Debevec et al.[2] proposed the method to acquire the reflectance filed of a human face and use these measurements to render the face under arbitrary changes in lighting and viewpoint. They acquire images of the face from a small set of viewpoints under a dense sampling of incident illumination directions using the setup named Light Stage. Then they construct a reflectance function image for each observed image pixel to generate images of the face from the viewpoints in any form of sampled or computed illumination. This method has been extended[3] to composite a live performance of an actor into a virtual set wherein the actor is consistently illuminated by the virtual environment using sphere of inward-pointing RGB light. Furthermore, Wenger et al.[17] have extended it to time-multiplexed illumination and high-speed photography to capture time-varying reflectance properties of a live performance in a way that the lighting and reflectance of the actor can be designed and modified in postproduction.

The other approach to the problem is called model-based rendering. Usually, model-based rendering uses information of a fine geometry and a physical surface property. Sato et al.[13] built a virtual model which is made of a fine geometric model and reflectance parameters used in a particular reflectance model. They fixed the position of the camera and point light source and, then, put the real object on the rotary table.

When we make a model of reflectance properties by observing real objects, we need to consider two reflection components: the specular reflection component and the diffuse reflection component. If we only map the observed image onto the object shape model as observed surface texture, we cannot reproduce the appearance of the object under different viewing and illumination conditions correctly. When highlights are observed in the original images, those highlights are fixed on a certain position of the object surface permanently regardless of illumination and viewing conditions. Therefore, in order to model the reflection properties correctly, we have to separate the specular reflection and diffuse reflection.

Several techniques to separate the reflection components have been developed. One major approach to the problem uses color as a clue. Most of color based methods are based on the dichromatic reflection model proposed by Shafer[15]. The dichromatic reflection model suggests that reflected lights from dielectric material have different spectral distributions between the specular and the diffuse reflection components. The specular component has a similar spectral distribution to that of the illumination. On the other hand, the diffuse component has an altered distribution by the colorants in the surface medium. Consequently, the color of an image point can be viewed as the sum of of two vectors with different directions in color space. Klinker et al. [6] observed that color histogram of a uniformly colored object surface makes the shape of *skewed T* with two limbs in the color space. One limb represents the purely diffuse points while the other represents highlight regions. Based on this observation, Klinker et al.[6] proposed an algorithm for automatically identifying the two limbs and using them to separate the diffuse and specular reflection components at each surface point. Sato and Ikeuchi[12] used a sequence of color images taken under actively varying light direction, and successfully separated the reflection components for each object surface point even if object surface is not uniformly colored.

Nayer et al.[9] used not only color but also polarization to separate the reflection components. Their proposed algorithm used the partial polarization included in the reflection in order to determine the color of specular component independently for each image point. The specular color imposes constraints on the color of the diffuse component and the neighboring diffuse colors that satisfy these constraints are used to estimate the diffuse color vector for each image point.

All of these separation methods based on the dichromatic reflection model suffer from the common weakness in that they cannot work if the specular and diffuse reflection vectors have same direction in a color space. In this chapter, we propose a new method for separating the reflection components using polarization. Unlike the previously proposed methods, our method does not require the diffuse color and the specular color to be different. In order to separate the reflection components in a robust manner, we use a controlled illumination which is linearly polarized, and we take the images of an object through a polarization filter. Our method is able to separate the diffuse and specular reflection components for each image pixel independently, and therefore, it can be applied to objects with complicated surface textures.

This chapter is organized as follows: Section 2 describes the representative reflection models and especially, Torrance-Sparrow reflectance model which is used in this chapter is described in detail. Section 3 explains polarization mechanism which is used to separate the reflection components is explained. In Section 4, data acquisition system which contains the CCD camera, the light stripe range sensor, polarization filter, point light source, and rotary table, is described. In Section 5, the details of the algorithm is described and the separation result is examined. In Section 6, the parameters of the Torrance-Sparrow are estimated, and the result is presented. In Section 7, by the estimated parameters, We synthesize the virtual images. Finally, Section 8 concludes the chapter.

2.   Reflection Mechanism

A number of reflectance models have been proposed in the past by the researchers in the fields of applied physics and computer vision. In general, these models are classified into two categories: a specular reflectance model and a diffuse reflectance model.

2.1   Diffuse Reflection

A diffuse reflectance model represents reflected rays resulted from internal scattering inside surface medium. When light strikes an interface between two different medias, some percentage of the light passes through the boundary and the remaining portion of light is reflected. The penetrating light hits the internal pigments of objects, and is re-emitted randomly(Figure18.1). This re-emitted light is called diffuse reflection, and Lambert is the first who modeled

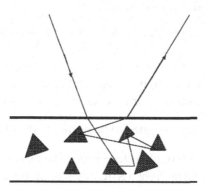

Figure 18.1.   Diffuse reflection resulting from the internal scattering mechanism

this phenomenon. The formula Lambert deduced is:

$$I_{diff} = C_{diff}\vec{N} \cdot \vec{S}$$
$$= C_{diff}\cos\theta_i \qquad (18.1)$$

where I_{diff}, C_{diff}, $\vec{N}$, $\vec{S}$, θ_i are the brightness, a proportional constant, the surface orientation, the light source direction, the angle between the light source direction and the surface orientation, respectively. The diffuse component does not depend on the angle of reflection but does depend on the incident light.

2.2   Specular Reflection

A specular reflectance model, on the other hand, represents light rays reflected on the surface of the object. The surface may be assumed to be composed of microscopic planar elements, each of which has its own surface orientation different from the macroscopic local orientation of the surface. The result is the specular reflection component that spreads around the specular direction and that depends on the surface roughness for the width of the distribution.

Specular reflectance model can be derived from the two completely different approaches: physical optics based and geometrical optics based. The physical optics based approach uses electromagnetic theory and Maxwell's equations to study the propagation of light. On the other hand, geometrical optics based approach uses assumption of the short wave length of light and treats the propagation of light geometrically. The representative physical optics based model is the Beckmann-Spizzichino model, and the representative geometrical optics based model is the Torrance-Sparrow model[16].

2.2.1   Physical Optics Based Model

The physical models are directly derived from electromagnetic wave theory by using Maxwell's equations. Beckmann and Spizzichino deduced their reflectance model by solving the Maxwell's equations by using Helmholts integral with Kirchoff's assumption on a perfect conductor surface. They made some assumptions to make up their reflectance model, as follows:

- The surface height is assumed to be normally distributed.

- The radius of curvature of surface irregularities is large compared to the wavelength of incident light (Kirchoff's assumption).

- The surface is assumed to be a perfect conductor.

- The shadowing and masking of surface points by adjacent surface points is ignored.

- The light is assumed to be reflected only once and not to bounce between surface facets before scattered in the direction of the observer.

- The incident wave is assumed to be perpendicularly polarized.

- The incident wave is assumed to be a plane wave. This assumption is reasonable when the light source is at a great distance from the surface relative to the physical dimensions of the surface.

The Beckmann-Spizzichino model consists of the specular lobe and specular spike component. The specular spike component is represented as a delta function and causes very sharp reflection when reflection angle equals to the incidence angle(specular angle). The specular lobe component is represented as a Gaussian function and causes widely spreading reflection.

2.2.2   Geometrical Optics Based Model

The geometrical models are derived from simplifying many of the light propagation problems. Torrance and Sparrow obtained their reflectance model by assuming as follows:

- The surface is modeled as a collection of planar microfacets, and the facet slopes are assumed to be normally distributed.

- The size of planar facets is much greater than the wave length of incident light. Therefore, it can be assumed that incident light rays are reflected by each facet in its specular direction only.

- Each facet is one side of a symmetric V-groove cavity.

- The light source is assumed to be at a great distance from the surface so that all incident rays are regarded to be parallel to one another.

The Torrance-Sparrow model is represented by a Gaussian function of the surface roughness parameters.

2.3   General Reflectance Model

The Torrance-Sparrow model is aimed for modeling rough surface of any materials. The Beckmann-Spizzichino model describes the reflection from rough to smooth surface. The Torrance-Sparrow model is good approximation of the Beckmann-Spizzichino model when it is applied to a rough surface. So, physical optics based model is more general than the geometrical optics based. But, physical optics based model has very complex mathematical forms and is difficult to manipulate. Geometrical optics based model, however, has very simple function form, but it can not be applied to the smooth surface materials.

In order to combine the reflection models for the smooth surface and the rough surface, Nayer, Ikeuchi, and Kanade[8] proposed the general reflectance model. This model consists of three components: specular spike, specular lobe, and diffuse. Each of these components is represented by, respectively, these three functions: the delta function, the Gaussian function, and the Lambertian's cosine function.

We assume that the surface is located at the origin of the coordinate frame, and that surface normal vector is in the direction of the Z axis. The beam illuminating the surface lies in the X-Z plane, and it's incident on the surface is at an angle, θ_i. The observer is located at (θ_r, ϕ_r).

Under this geometry, general reflectance model is represented as follows

$$I = C_{ss}\delta(\theta_i - \theta_r)(\phi_r) + C_{sl}\frac{\exp\left(-k\alpha^2\right)}{\cos\theta_r} + C_{diff}\cos\theta_i \qquad (18.2)$$

C_{ss}, C_{sl}, C_{diff} are constants which respectively represent the strength of the specular spike, specular lobe, and diffuse components. The α is the angle between the surface normal and the bisector of the viewing and surface directions. The k is the parameter related to the Torrance-Sparrow surface roughness parameter.

The ratio C_{sl}/C_{ss} is dependent on the optical roughness of the surface. Mathematically, optical roughness is defined as

$$g = (2\pi\frac{\sigma_h}{\lambda}(\cos\theta_i + \cos\theta_r))^2 \qquad (18.3)$$

where σ_h, λ are the root-mean-square of the height distribution, and the wavelength, respectively. For smooth surface $(g \ll 1)$, the spike component is dominant. As the roughness increase, however, the spike component shrinks

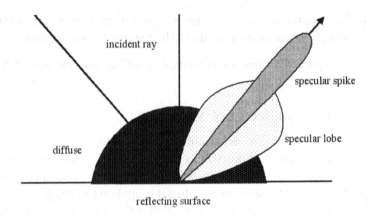

Figure 18.2.   Diagram of the Unified Reflectance Model

rapidly, and for rough surface $g \gg 1$, the lobe component begins to dominate. It is only for a small range of roughness values that C_{sl} and C_{ss} are both significant. In this chapter, the Torrance-Sparrow model is used for representing the diffuse and specular components.

$$I_m = I_{D,m} \cos \theta_i + I_{S,m} \frac{1}{\cos \theta_r} e^{-\alpha^2/2\sigma^2} \quad m = R, G, B \qquad (18.4)$$

where θ_i is the angle between the surface normal and the light source direction, θ_r is the angle between the surface normal and the viewing direction, α is the angle between the surface normal and the bisector of the light source direction and the viewing direction, $I_{D,m}$ and $I_{S,m}$ are the scaling factor for the diffuse and specular components, and σ is the standard deviation of a facet slope of the Torrance-Sparrow model.

In this model, the reflections bounced only once from the light source are considered. Therefore, this model is valid only for the convex objects. So, in this research, we use the objects so that inter-reflection does not affect our analysis significantly.

We refer to $I_{D,m}$ as the diffuse reflection parameters, and $I_{S,m}$ and σ as the specular reflection parameters.

3.   Polarization

Polarization has been used for several decades in the remote sensing research. Wolff and Boult[18] have proposed an algorithm which analyzes linear polarization states of highlights removal and material classification. Boult and Wolff[1] have also studied the classification of scene edges based on their polarization characteristics. Recently, Saito et al.[11] have proposed a method for measuring surface orientation of a transparent object using the degree of linear polarization in highlights observed on the object. Schechner et al.[14] have presented the method for classifying the transmitted image and the reflected image to the transparent sheet.

The method presented in this chapter uses two linear polarization filters. One is placed in front of a point light source in order to polarize the light source linearly, and the other is placed in front of a camera to capture images through the linear polarization filter.

For an ideal filter, a light wave should be passed unattenuated when its electric field is aligned with the polarization axis of the filter, and the energy is attenuated as a trigonometric function when the filter is rotated.

As described in the previous section, the image brightness value taken by sensor is described as:

$$I = I_d + I_s \tag{18.5}$$

where I_d represents the diffuse component and I_s represents the specular component.

When incident light is linearly polarized, the diffuse component tends to be unpolarized due to its internal scattering. In contrast, the specular reflection component tends to remain linearly polarized. Therefore, the observed brightness of the specular component can be expressed as a trigonometric function for polarization filter angle, and that of the diffuse component can be expressed as a constant. Thus the image brightness observed through a linear polarization filter is described as:

$$I = I_c + I_v(1 + \cos 2(\theta - \beta)) \tag{18.6}$$

where θ is the angle of the polarization filter and β is the phase angle determined by the projection of the surface normal onto the plane of the filter.

It should be noted that in the above equation I_c is not equal to the real diffuse intensity, and $2 \times I_v$ is not equal to the real specular intensity. The diffuse reflection component which is unpolarized is always attenuated by the polarization filter and the specular reflection component is also attenuated by the difference of the reflectivity between the light waves which are parallel or perpendicular to the incidence plane. [1]

The polarization state of reflected light dependents on several factors including the material of the reflecting surface element, and the type of reflection component, i.e. diffuse or specular. In order to describe the state of polarization of the reflected light, the Fresnel reflection coefficients $F_\perp(\eta, \psi)$ and $F_\parallel(\eta, \psi)$ are used [18]. The Fresnel reflection coefficients determine the polarization of reflected light waves in the directions perpendicular and parallel to the plane of incidence respectively, and determine the maximum and the minimum intensities which are observed when the angle θ of the polarization filter varies. The parameter η is the complex index of reflection of the surface medium and the parameter ψ is the incidence angle. Since we use a linearly polarized light source, we can assume that the intensity of the specular component observed through a linear polarization filter is guaranteed to become equal to zero at a certain angle. Hence, we obtain the following relation between I_v and specular reflection intensity:

$$q = \frac{F_\perp(\eta, \psi)}{F_\parallel(\eta, \psi)} \tag{18.7}$$

$$2I_v = \frac{q}{1+q} I_s \tag{18.8}$$

where I_s equals the specular reflection intensity.

It is known that the diffuse component is also polarized when the viewing angle is close to 90 degrees, e.g., near the occluding contour of an object. However, the diffuse component becomes linearly polarized only in narrow region and the degree of polarization in the diffuse reflection component is generally negligible. Hence, we assume that the diffuse component is unpolarized in our analysis. The intensity of unpolarized light is attenuated by half when it passes a linear polarization filter. As a result, I_c and the diffuse component have a relation as below:

$$I_c = \frac{1}{2} I_d \tag{18.9}$$

where $\frac{1}{2} I_d$ is the intensity of the diffuse reflection.

Figure 18.3 shows the relation between the image brightness and the angle of the polarization filter.

4.   Data Acquisition System

The experimental setup for the image acquisition system used in our experiment is illustrated in Figure 18.4. An object to be modeled in this experiment is placed on the rotary table. A sequence of range images and color images are captured as the object is rotated at a certain angle step. For each rotation step, one range image and thirty five color images, which are taken every five degrees of polarization filter rotation in front of the CCD camera, are obtained.

A range image is obtained using a light-stripe range finder with a liquid crystal shutter and a color CCD video camera. Each range image pixel represents an (X, Y, Z) location of a corresponding point on an object surface. The same color camera is used for acquiring range images and color images. Therefore, pixels of the range images and the color images directly correspond. Color images are taken through a polarization filter.

The range finder is calibrated to produce a 3×4 projection matrix which represents the translation between the world coordinate system and the image coordinate system. The location of the rotary table with respect to the world coordinate system is calibrated before image acquisition. Therefore, object location is uniquely determined by the translation matrix.

A xeon lamp is used as a light source. The lamp is small and is placed far enough from the object so that we can assume that it is a point light source. In order to illuminate the object with linearly polarized light, a linear polarization filter is placed in front of the lamp.

5. Separation of Reflection Components

In our experiments, images of a target object are taken every five degrees of filter rotation, i.e., 35 images in total. Then, the maximum intensity I_{max} and the minimum intensity I_{min} are determined for every image pixel. Theoretically, only three images are sufficient for determining I_{max} and I_{min}. However, for increasing robustness of estimation of I_{min} and I_{max}, we uses more images by rotating the polarization filter. If $I_{min} - I_{max}$ for a certain pixel is less than a threshold, we consider the pixel to contain only the diffuse component. If $I_{max} - I_{min}$ is larger than a threshold value, we consider that the pixel contains the specular component and that $I_{max} - I_{min}$ is equal to $2I_v$ and I_{min} is equal to I_c.

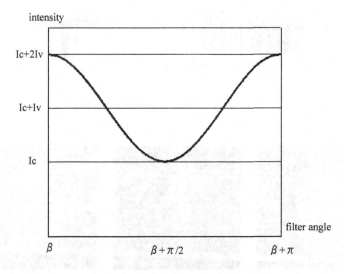

Figure 18.3. Imge brightness plotted as a function of the orientation of a polarization filter

In summary, our separation technique is proceeded as follows. First, a linear polarization filter is placed in front of the light source and camera. Second, input images of an object are captured for every 5 degrees of rotation of the polarization filter in front of the camera. Third, I_{max} and I_{min} are determined for each pixel. If $I_{max} - I_{min}$ is larger than a threshold value, we determine that the pixel contains the specular component and the intensity of the specular component is obtained from $I_{max} - I_{min}$. I_{min} is used for determining the intensity of the diffuse component.

Figure 18.5 shows an example of reflection component separation by using our proposed method. For comparison, we show another image which was captured without a polarization filter. It shows that the specular and diffuse reflection components were successfully separated even if they have the similar color.

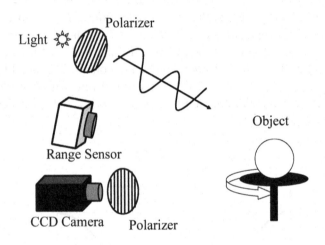

Figure 18.4. Image acquisition system

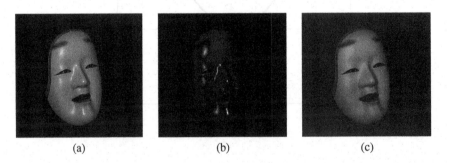

(a)   (b)   (c)

Figure 18.5. (a)Original image, (b)Specular component, (c)Diffuse component

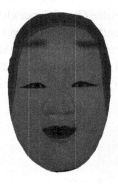

Figure 18.6.   Estimated diffuse parameter image

6.   Parameter Estimation

After separating the reflection components, we determine the reflection parameters using the separated reflection component images.

6.1   Diffuse Parameters Estimation

Using the separated diffuse reflection image, we can estimate the diffuse reflection parameters $(I_{D,R}, I_{D,G}, I_{D,B})$ without undesirable effects from the specular reflection component.   The incidence angle θ_i can be obtained by range sensors and camera calibration.

Figure 18.6 shows the estimated diffuse parameter image. We can see the object surface color which is not attenuated due to the incidence angle.

6.2   Specular Parameters Estimation

After estimating the diffuse parameters, we also estimate the specular parameters $(I_{S,R}, I_{S_G}, I_{S_B}, \sigma)$ using the angle α and the angle θ_r as a known information.

As described in the Section 3, separated specular images are attenuated by a certain ratio determined by Fresnel reflection coefficients.   But attenuation ratio is constant overall highlight region, we can correctly estimate the specular parameters. More precisely, the Fresnel reflection coefficients are dependent on the incidence angle. However, the Fresnel coefficients are constant around the incidence angle of less than 30 degrees, and the specular reflection is observed only near the surface normal   direction in our experimental setup. Therefore, by setting the light and camera in the same direction, we can assume that the Fresnel reflection coefficients are constant.

There is a significant difference between estimation of the diffuse and specular reflection. Diffuse reflection can be observed all across the object surface illuminated by a light. On the other hand, specular reflection is observed from a limited viewing direction, and is observed over a narrow area of the object surface. So, we have to select the sampling pixel carefully for specular parameters estimation. We used the same strategy described in [13]. Figure 18.7 shows the estimated σ and I_S which are projected on the mesh model.

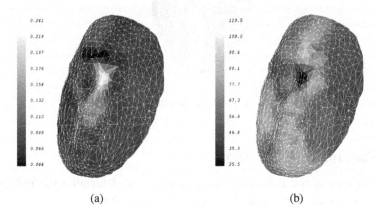

(a)   (b)

Figure 18.7.   (a)Specular parameter(σ) image, (b)Specular parameter(I_S) image

7.   Synthesized Images

Using the diffuse and specular reflection parameters estimated in the previous section, and the surface mesh model of the object, we synthesized virtual images of the object under different illumination and viewing conditions. Figure 18.8 shows the comparison between original images and synthesized images viewed from different directions.

Comparing the synthesized images with the original images, we notice that synthesized images are darker than the original images. This is probably caused by the variation of the polarizer's optical density with respect to the wavelength. In order to avoid this problem, we should calibrate white balance before capturing images without the polarizer and before capturing images through the polarizer.

8.   Conclusion

In this chapter, we proposed a new method for separating the reflection components using polarization. Unlike the previously proposed methods, our method does not require the difference of color between the specular reflection and diffuse reflection. So, our method can robustly separate the reflection components even if objects have a white texture and illumination color is white. After reflection component separation, we estimate the parameters of a

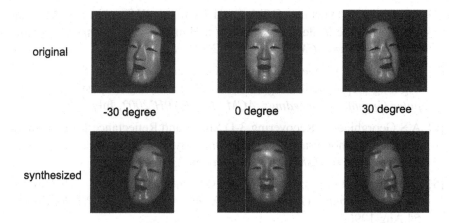

Figure 18.8. Comparison between input images and synthesized images

reflection model by using the separated reflection components. By synthesizing virtual images under the arbitrary illumination and viewing environment, we have shown that the reflection parameters are successfully estimated from the separated reflection components. Future work includes calibrating white balance because synthesized images are darker than the original images. We would attempt to use circular polarizer for separating specular and diffuse components easier. For large scale data, we will consider data compression for efficiency.

Acknowledgments

This research was supported, in part, by Ministry of Education, Culture, Sports, Science and Technology under the Leading Project, "Development of High Fidelity Digitization Software for Large-Scale and Intangible Cultural Assets," and, in part, by Japan Science and Technology Agency, under the CREST program, "Automatic generation of virtual models of cultural heritage." Special thanks to Yuko Matsumoto, who helped this research. The authors thank Joan Knapp for proofreading and editing this chapter.

Notes

1. The incidence plane includes the surface normal and the illumination direction.

References

[1] T.E.Boult and L.B.Wolff, "Phisically based edge labeling," *Proceedings of Computer Vision and Pattern Recognition* ,pp.656-663,Maui,Hawaii,June 1991.

[2] P.Debevec, T.Hawkins, C.Tchou, H-P.Duiker, W.Sarokin and M.Sagar "Acquiring the Reflectance Field of a Human Face," *Computer Graphics Proceedings, ACM SIGGRAPH'2000*, Aug.2000

[3] P.Debevec, A.Wenger, C.Tchou, A.Gardner, J.Waese and T.Hawkins "A Lighting Reproduction Approach to Live-Action Compositing," *Computer Graphics Proceedings, ACM SIGGRAPH'2002*, July.2002

[4] A.S.Georghiades "Recovering 3-D Shape and Reflectance From a Small Number of Photographs," *Eurographics Symposium on Rendering:14th Eurographics Workshop on Rendering*, pp230-240, 2002

[5] S.J.Gorter, R.Grzeszczuk, R.Szeliski and M.F.Cohen, "The Lumigraph," *Computer Graphics Proceedings,ACM SIGGRAPH'96*, pp.43-54,Aug.1996.

[6] G.J.Klinker, S.A.Shafer and T.Kanade, "The measurement of highlights in color images," *International Journal of Computer Vision*, Vol.2,No.1,pp-7-32,1990.

[7] M.Levoy and P.Hanrahan, "Light Field Rendering," *Computer Graphics Proceedings,ACM SIGGRAPH'96*, pp.31-42,Aug.1996.

[8] S.K.Nayer, K.Ikeuchi, T.Kanade, "Surafece Reflection: Physical and Geometrical Perspectives," *IEEE Trans. on Patte5rn AAnalysis and Machine Intelligence*, Vol.13, No.7, pp.611-634, July 1991.

[9] S.K.Nayer,X.Fang, T.E.Boult, "Removal of specularities using color and polarization,"*Proceedings of Computer Vision and Pattern Recognition '93*, pp.583-590, New York City, NY,June 1993.

[10] K.Nishino, Y.Sato and K.Ikeuchi, "Eigen-Texture Method: Appearance Compression and Synthesis based on a 3D Model," *IEEE Transactions on Pattern Analysis and Machine Intelligence*, Vol.23,No.11,pp.1257-1265, Nov.2001.

[11] M.Saito,Y.Sato,K.Ikeuchi,H.Kashiwagi, "Measurement of Surface Orientations of Transparent Objects Using Polarization in Highlight," *IEEE Trans.on Computer Vision and Pattern Recognition '99*, Vol.1,pp.381-386, Fort Collins,Colorado, June 1999.

[12] Y.Sato and K.Ikeuchi, "Temporal-color space analysis of reflection," *Journal of Optical Society of America A*, vol.11, no.11,pp.2990-3002,November 1994.

[13] Y.Sato,M.D.Wheeler,K.Ikeuchi, "Object Shape and Reflectance Modeling from Observation," *Computer Graphics Proceedings,ACM SIGGRAPH'97*,pp. 379-387,Aug 1997.

[14] Y.Y.Schechner, J.Shamir and N.Kiryati, "Polarization-based Decorrelation of Transparent Layers: The Inclination Angle of an Invisible Sur-

face," *Proceedings of International Conference on Computer Vision '99*,pp.814-819, 1999.

[15] S.Shafer, "Using color to separate reflection components," *Color Research and Applications*, Vol.10,pp.210-218,1985.

[16] K.E.Torrance and E.M.Sparrow, "Theory of off-specular reflection from roughened surfaces," *Journal of the Optical Society of America* Vol.57, pp.1105-1114, 1967.

[17] A.Wenger, A.Gardner, C.Tchou, J.Unger, T.Hawkins and P.Debevec "A Lighting Reproduction Approach to Live-Action Compositing," *Computer Graphics Proceedings, ACM SIGGRAPH'2005*, to be appear.

[18] L.B.Wolff and T.E.Boult, "Constraining Object Features using a Polaization Reflectance Model," *IEEE Trans. on Pattern Analysis and Machine Intelligence*, Volo.13,No.7,pp.635-657, July 1991.

[19] D.N.Wood, D.I.Azuma, K.Aldinger, B.Curless, T.Duchamp, D.H.Salesin and W.Stuetzle, "Surface Light Fields for 3D Photography," *Computer Graphics Proceedings,ACM SIGGRAPH'00*, Aug.2000.

IV

DIGITIZING CULTURAL HERITAGE

Chapter 19

CLASSIFICATION OF BAYON FACES

Mawo Kamakura, Takeshi Oishi, Jun Takamatsu, and Katsushi Ikeuchi

Abstract   Digital 3D models of historic buildings or cultural heritage objects are useful
for preservation. Not only can we store them permanently, but the models can
supply a clear guideline for the restoration process. 3D models also provide
sufficient information about geometrical characteristics that may help archaeologists to inspect and classify the objects. Currently, we are working on a 3D
digital-archiving project of the Bayon Temple. It is a building of stonework that
was built in the 12th century in Cambodia. It is famous for its towers with four
faces at the four cardinal points. According to research by JSA (Japanese government team for Safeguarding Angkor), the faces can be classified into three
groups based on subjective criteria. In this chapter, we explore a more objective
way to classify the faces by using measured 3D geometrical models. After alignment of 3D faces in the same coordinate system, orientation, and normalization,
we captured in-depth images of each face and then classified them by several
statistics methods.

1.   Introduction

Over the past years, much research has been done on automatically obtaining 3D shapes of art objects and cultural heritage objects using laser range
sensors. The performance of computers has improved rapidly, so research in
the fields of image processing and computer vision have also advanced. Measuring real world objects and converting them to 3D digital models are well-
known applications of computer vision. We are currently working on digital
preservation of large-scale cultural heritage objects by using computer vision
techniques and laser range sensors. We have worked on the Great Buddha
Project [1] and have preserved cultural heritage objects such as the Kamakura,
Nara, and Atchana Great Buddha and at the same time have researched and
developed advanced modeling techniques.

Our work is on measuring and preserving the 3D shape of the Bayon faces
using laser range sensors (Fig. 19.2). The Bayon is a temple constructed in
the 12th century and is located in the center of the Angkor Thom. An enor-

Figure 19.1. left: pictures of the Bayon temple, right: picture of Bayon face

mous site with a size of 100m x 100m and towers reaching about 40m at the highest, it is famous for its towers, each with four faces carved on each side. Figure 19.1 shows pictures of Bayon temple and Bayon Face. The Bayon Digital Archiving Project started in 2003 and until now six missions have been executed [2]. Figure 19.3 shows the measurement result of the entire Bayon Temple. In addition to modeling of the whole site, we have been modeling and constructing libraries of the faces. There are 52 towers in Bayon with faces on them, and 173 faces have endured damage or collapse. We have completed measurement of all 173 faces in the previous six missions. Figure 19.4 shows the picture of a face and the measurement result of the 3D face model.

From the 3D models acquired from the measurement, we made an objective classification of the faces. According to research by the JSA (Japanese government team for safeguarding Angkor) [3], the 173 faces can be classified into three types: Deva, Asura, and Devata. It is known that the Deva type face is dominant. However, this classification is based on subjective evaluation. We expect to scientifically confirm the classification results of JSA, and if not, to present a new classification which would be impossible to achieve by human eyes.

The outline of the rest of this chapter is as follows. Section 2 gives a description of the Bayon faces. Section 3 explains the pre-classification normalization process and the classification methods. In Section 4 we present experimental results. Finally, in Section 5 we summarize and conclude this chapter.

2. Bayon face

The Art History team of JSA investigated the Bayon faces on the towers of the Bayon Temple to see if they might provide insight into the purpose of the construction of the temple. According to the JSA, as a result, the faces can be

Figure 19.2. picture of laser range sensor

Figure 19.3. measurement result of entire Bayon temple

Figure 19.4. left: picture of face, right: measurement result of 3D face model

classified into roughly three types: Deva, Asura, and Devata [3]. These faces are classified based on the outlines of the faces. Some degree of regularity could be identified in the locations where each of the types was found. JSA found that the faces looking out from temple are all the Asura type; those on the inner facing center tower are the Deva type; and those looking toward the central sanctuary are the Devata type. The four-faced tower is thus a composite of guardian deities, giving protection of the deities Deva and Asura, with the goddess Devata attendant on the main deities. Figure 19.5 shows pictures, 3D models and shape lines of three types Bayon faces. Typical face of each type is 35N (Asura), 51S (Deva), 50E (Devata).

The Deva face is calm and noble, representing God. It is plump and rounded in shape. The Devata face is a comparatively narrow face with a harsh expression. The Asura face is angular in shape with a square jaw and a rather grim, heavy expression (Devil). It is known that the Deva type face is the dominant one of these three types.

However, on some of the four-faced towers of the Bayon temple are many other faces that are difficult to classify with accuracy. This is thought to be related to the division of labor between different craftsmen, and the differences in their techniques. Also, differences may have been created by other influences like weathering and destruction. JSA examined the degree of completion of the faces on the towers, and found that although some examples are very nearly finished, overall there is high number of unfinished examples. Furthermore, the Bayon temple was built in a short period of time, so the work must undoubtedly have been divided between many different craftsmen. As mentioned above, it can be gathered that the same group completed the four faces in a single tower. It is highly likely that the same group completed two or more towers at the same time. Furthermore, consistent variations can be identified in the shapes and expressions of the faces that enable us to classify them roughly into the three types listed above: Deva, Devata, and Asura. However, other places were found where the craftsmen could not have worked with any awareness of creating one of these three types. There are many instances of clear differences between the left and right sides of the face, suggesting the possibility that separate groups of craftsmen worked on left and right sides. Given this situation, 173 faces of four-faced towers of Bayon temple are classified, but the classification is not exact.

3.   Classification technique

3D models with Bayon faces acquired by measurement are used and classified. First of all, we convert all the faces into homogeneous in-depth images, that is, normalization. Afterward, we classify them by several statistic techniques using the converted images.

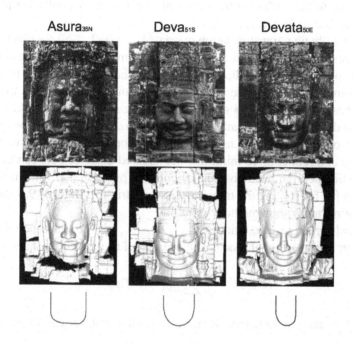

Figure 19.5. pictures, 3D models and shapes line of 3 types of Bayon faces.

3.1   Normalization

First of all, we normalize an arbitrary 3D Bayon face as a standard face. This normalization removes difference between the sizes and also between the directions of the faces in the same size images. It also suppresses the influence of data excluding the face to a minimum. The 3D Bayon face model as a standard face is in a consistent position and orientation, and its in-depth image from an appropriate viewpoint is displayed in the entire specified area. According to the research by JSA, faces are classified based on the outline of the face. So we fit the outline of the face with image size manually. At this time, the moving matrix is M_{ref}.

Next, we obtain a transformation matrix M_{tar},i (i=1,...,N) for displaying all face images similar to the standard face. N is number of faces being classified. First, we obtain three coordinate points of a characteristic face; two points from the inner corners of the eyes and one from a point between the mouth and the nose. Let the points of a characteristic standard face model be (x_1, x_2, x_3) and the points of characteristic normalized face models be (y_{1i}, y_{2i}, y_{3i}). We obtain R: rotation matrix, t: translation matrix, and c: variable of expansion and reduction to minimize the squared distance between these two points. This theorem is an absolute orientation problem [4]. Shown below is the technique for solving the transformation matrix [5]. Figure 19.6 shows the outline of normalization method.

Let $X=\{x_1, x_2, \ldots, x_n\}$ and $Y=\{y_1, y_2, \ldots, y_n\}$ be corresponding point patterns in m-dimensional space. The average of the squared distances is,

$$e^2(R, t, c) = \frac{1}{n} \sum_{i=1}^{n} \|y_i - (cRx_i + t)\|^2. \tag{19.1}$$

Transformation parameters (R, t, c) to minimize the equation are given as follows:

$$R = USV^T \tag{19.2}$$

$$t = \mu_y - cR\mu_x \tag{19.3}$$

$$c = \frac{1}{\sigma_x^2} tr(DS) \tag{19.4}$$

$$\sigma_x^2 = \frac{1}{n} \sum \|x_i - \mu_x\|^2 \tag{19.5}$$

$$\sigma_y^2 = \frac{1}{n} \sum \|y_i - \mu_y\|^2 \tag{19.6}$$

where μ_x and μ_y are mean vectors of x_i and y_i, UDV^T is the singular value decomposition of a covariance matrix between x_i and y_i, S in (19.4) must be chosen as

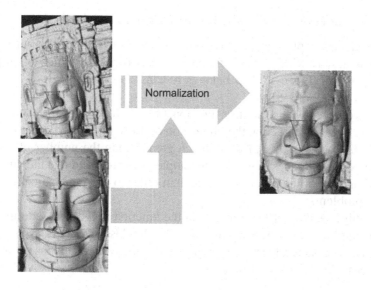

Figure 19.6. outline of normalization method

$$S = \begin{cases} I & \text{if } \det(U)\det(V) = 1 \\ \operatorname{diag}(1, 1, \cdots, 1, -1) & \text{if } \det(U)\det(V) = -1. \end{cases} \qquad (19.7)$$

3.2　3D Shape Analysis

In this chapter, we examine two types of analysis: supervised and unsupervised analysis. The purpose of the supervised analysis is to clarify the differences among the given classes. JSA has already classified all faces into three types based on its subjective evaluations. Through such an analysis, we can verify correctness of the process of JSA's classification, and then objectively evaluate the differences using statistical analysis methods.

In contrast, the purpose of the unsupervised analysis is to discover new knowledge through classification of the faces without any a priori standards. This analysis may be able to produce a novel and detailed classification. As a result, it may reveal undiscovered historical secrets. In this section, we first describe these analysis methods.

At the end of this section, we describe a method to visualize classification criteria. Although conventional methods for object recognition only pay attention to improvement in recognition ability, it is more important in this chapter to clarify the criteria.

3.2.1   Supervised Analysis: Linear Discriminant Analysis

Consider a sample space R^m. Given two classes G_1, G_2, discriminant analysis provides us with a scalar function $f(\mathbf{x})$ to decide which class points pbelong to ; if $f(\mathbf{x}) > 0$, **p** belongs to Class G_1 and if $f(\mathbf{x}) < 0$, **p** belongs to Class G_2 [6–8].

In this chapter, we use a linear function $f(\mathbf{x}) = \mathbf{n} \cdot \mathbf{x} + d$ as the classification function. The reason is that the dimension of the sample space, that is, image size (= 64×64, in this case), is much greater than the number of samples; there are only 173 faces in the Bayon temple. It is preferred that the dimension and parameters of the function are small in order to prevent a so-called "overfitting" problem.

Roughly speaking, the parameters of the function $\mathbf{n}, d$ can be determined by maximizing S_B/S_T, where S_B and S_T are intraclass and interclass variances, respectively. Concretely, it is necessary only to solve simultaneous linear equation in $S\mathbf{n} = \bar{\mathbf{x}}^{(1)} - \bar{\mathbf{x}}^{(2)}$, where

$$
S = \frac{1}{n_1 + n_2 - 2} \left(\sum_{i=1}^{n_1} \left(\mathbf{x}_i^{(1)} - \bar{\mathbf{x}}^{(1)} \right) \left(\mathbf{x}_i^{(1)} - \bar{\mathbf{x}}^{(1)} \right)^T \right.
$$
$$
\left. + \sum_{i=1}^{n_2} \left(\mathbf{x}_i^{(2)} - \bar{\mathbf{x}}^{(2)} \right) \left(\mathbf{x}_i^{(2)} - \bar{\mathbf{x}}^{(2)} \right)^T \right),
$$

n_i is the number of samples including Group i, $\mathbf{x}_j^{(i)}$ is the jth sample of Group i, and $\bar{\mathbf{x}}^{(i)}$ is the average of Group i.

Also $d = -\frac{1}{2} \left(\mathbf{n} \cdot \left(\bar{\mathbf{x}}^{(1)} + \bar{\mathbf{x}}^{(2)} \right) \right)$. Because the matrix S is not full-rank matrix, we solve the equation using the singular value decomposition (SVD) method while minimizing $|\mathbf{n}|$.

3.2.2   Unsupervised Analysis: Hierarchical Cluster Analysis

Cluster analysis provides us with some classification of samples according to distances among them. In this study, we employ agglomerative hierarchical cluster analysis. This analysis begins with each sample being considered as each cluster and then proceeds to combine the nearest two clusters until all samples belong to one cluster. As the result of this analysis, we obtain a dendrogram as shown in Fig. 19.9. Unfortunately, we cannot determine the correct number of clusters from this analysis only. However, distances between the combined two clusters are useful to determine the number.

Before using the analysis, it is necessary to define the distance between any two samples. We naturally define it as the Euclidean distance in the distance image space [9, 10]. It is also necessary to define the distance between the combined cluster and the other cluster. In this study, we calculate the distance based on the Ward method, which is superior in practical use.

3.2.3   Visualization of Differences between two Classes

As mentioned above, it is quite important to clarify the classification criterion, especially for this study. Suppose we have two classes and a linear discriminant function to classify them. The value of a linear discriminant function expresses the distance between a sample point and the hyper-plane expressed by the function. The greater the distance becomes, the more similar the sample looks to faces in the class G_1, vice versa. That is, variance of the distance helps visualize the differences between the two classes. Because the variance is equal to displacement of the point along the direction of the normal of the plane, the direction just expresses the classification criterion. The visualization is quite easy.

4.   Experiments

Original 3D models of faces used in this experiment are obtained by the following steps: We first measured 3D models of Bayon faces by the laser range sensors, Cyrax2500 [11] and Vivid910 [12]. Next, we applied the alignment [13] and refinement [14] methods to these models. After obtaining the models, we made their in-depth images using the normalization method as mentioned above. The sizes of these images were 64 x 64. In this experiment we assume that the image data is only a 4096 dimensional vector and that usual vector operations are applicable for the data. In this experiment we used 88 images. We preformed the following two analyses: the supervised and unsupervised analysis.

4.1   Supervised analysis

In this experiment, we preformed the supervised analysis based on the JSA's classification. Figure 19.7 illustrates the result of the analysis. The graph is obtained by projecting all vector points of faces on the 2D flat surface that are determined by two linear discriminant functions in order to most clearly express the classification result.

The former discriminant function classifies Devata (goddess) and Deva (god) and the separate plane corresponds to the y-axis. That means the right side area of the Y axis is a female area and the left side area a male area. Although Asura images are not used for determining the function at all, almost all of Asura (male) data are in the male area.

The latter function classifies Deva (god) and Asura (devil) and the separate plane corresponds to the diagonal line. That means the upper side area of the diagonal line is a god area and the lower side area is a Devil area. Because Devata is a goddess, and not a devil, almost all of Devata data are in the god area.

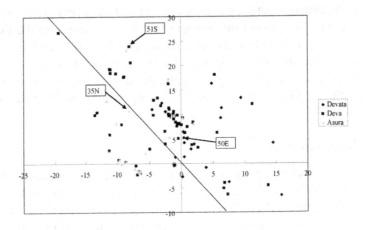

Figure 19.7.   result of the supervised analysis

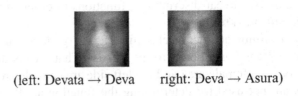

(left: Devata → Deva   right: Deva → Asura)

Figure 19.8.   visualization of differences between two classes

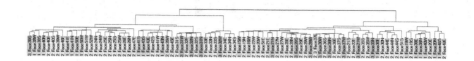

Figure 19.9.   dendrogram obtained by unsupervised analysis

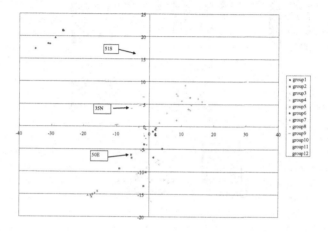

Figure 19.10.   scatter diagram of unsupervised analysis result

Additionally, Fig. 19.8 shows visualization of differences among three classes. Two images reveal that when some face of the former group is morphed to become similar to a face of the latter group, the blue area is dented and the red area bulges. On the left side image, we find that the bite of Deva is dented and the chin bulges more than Devata's. In the same manner, we also find out about the right side image, that the bite of Asura is dented and the chin bulges more than Deva's. We find that this result corresponds to characteristics of the three types.

4.2   Unsupervised analysis

The dendrogram as shown in Fig. 19.9 is the result of unsupervised analysis. This dendrogram shows that, as expected, the face data of the same tower is in the same cluster.

In order to examine the result of this analysis, we used the scatter diagram shown in Fig. 19.10. Because each vector is 4096 (not two) dimensional, a map is needed to draw the diagram. We determine the map using the PCA

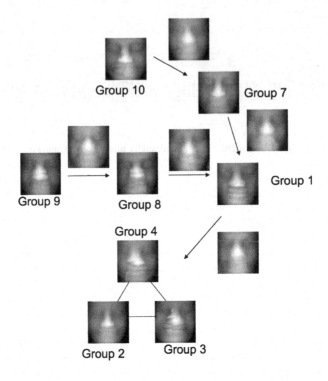

Figure 19.11.   visualization of the clusters and their differences

(principal component analysis). PCA can determine the map to minimize the reduction of Euclidean distances caused by the map. Each color expresses one cluster.

In this analysis, we don't have any a priori knowledge. This diagram shows distributions of the clusters. Although this diagram includes some outliers (group: 5, 6, 11 and 12), almost all clusters concentrate in one area. Especially three clusters including the typical faces are near the boundary and respectively far away from each other. That is, we find that JSA correctly selected the more distinguished faces as the typical faces.

Figure 19.11 shows visualization of the clusters and their differences. Each gray image in the figure expresses an average face of the corresponding cluster. The images on transitions express differences between the two clusters linked by arrows. Faces included in group 1 look unlike the three typical faces. That proves it may be impossible to classify all the faces into the three types in the first place.

5.   Conclusion

In this chapter, we classified the Bayon faces using their precise 3D models. As mentioned above, the Art History team of JSA classified all faces into three types, but this classification was based on subjective criteria. Therefore, we tried classification based on objective criteria using 3D models.

To achieve our purpose, we first measured the 173 faces by laser range sensors. As the result of measurement of the faces, we made libraries of the Bayon faces. In this experiment, we used these face model libraries.

We tried to classify using two analysis methods: One was supervised analysis based on linear discriminant analysis and the other was unsupervised analysis based on hierarchical cluster analysis.

We actually classified the three types using supervised analysis. Furthermore, we visualized differences among the three types of faces by our objective criteria. The result justified JSA's classification criteria. The classification of our result and that of JSA's were almost same. However, these two classifications did not coincide perfectly. In our future work, we should determine whether this is caused by failure of our analysis or by JSA's misclassification.

Also we showed classification of all the faces using unsupervised analysis. This analysis assumes no a priori knowledge. In this analysis, we illustrated the justification of the selection of the typical faces and found that these pieces of data are not on an overlapping area of clusters, but on an area where the boundary is relatively clear. This analysis also showed difficulties in classification. We determined that it may be impossible to classify all the faces into three categories; there are some faces unlike Deva, Devata, or Asura. In the future, we should further investigate results obtained by our analysis methods.

Acknowledgments

This research was supported, in part, by Ministry of Education, Culture, Sports, Science and Technology under the Leading Project, "Development of High Fidelity Digitization Software for Large-Scale and Intangible Cultural Assets," and, in part, by Japan Science and Technology Agency, under the CREST program, "Automatic generation of virtual models of cultural heritage."

References

[1] K. Ikeuchi, A. Nakazawa, K. Hasegawa, T. Oishi, "The Great Buddha Project: Modeling Cultural Heritage for VR Systems through Observation," *Proc. The second IEEE and ACM International Symposium on Mixed and Augmented Reality (ISMAR2003)*, Oct. 2003.

[2] K. Ikeuchi, K. Hasegawa, A. Nakazawa, J. Takamatsu, T. Oishi and T. Masuda, "Bayon Digital Archival Project," *Proc. the Tenth International Conference on Virtual System and Multimedia*, pp. 334-343, Nov. 2004.

[3] http://www.angkor-jsa.org/

[4] B. K. P. Horn, "Closed-form solution of absolute orientation using unit quaternions", *Journal of the Optical Society of America A*, vol.5, no.7, pp. 1127-1135, 1987.

[5] S. Umeyama, "Least-Squares Estimation of Transformation Parameters Between Two Point Patterns," *IEEE Transactions on Pattern Analysis and Machine Intelligence*, vol.13, no.4, Apr. 1991.

[6] P. N. Belhumeur, J. P. Hespanha, and D. J. Kriegman, "Eigenfaces vs. Fisherfaces: Recognition Using Class Specific Linear Projection," *IEEE Trans. Trans. Pattern Analysis and Machine Intelligence*, Vol. 19, No. 7, Jul. 1997.

[7] K. Etemad, R. Chellappa, "Discriminant Analysis for Recognition of Human Face Images," *J. Optical Society of America A*, Vol. 14, No. 8, pp. 1724-1733, Aug. 1997.

[8] T. Heseltine, N. Pears and J. Austin, "Three-Dimensional Face Recognition: A Fishersurface Approach," *Proc. Int'l Conf. Image Analysis and Recognition*, vol. 2, 2004, pp. 684-691.

[9] G. Gordon, "Face Recognition Based on Depth and Curvature Features," *IEEE Int'l Conf. Computer Vision and Pattern Recognition*, pp. 808-810, 1992.

[10] W. Zhao, R. Chellappa, A. Rosenfeld, and P.J. Phillips, "Face Recognition: A Literature Survey," *ACM Computing Surveys*, pp. 399-458, 2003.

[11] http://www.cyra.com.

[12] http://konicaminolta.com/products/
     instruments/vivid/vivid910.html.

[13] T. Oishi, A. Nakazawa, R. Kurazume and K. Ikeuchi, "Fast Simultaneous Alignment of Multiple Range Images using Index Images," *Proc. The 5th International Conference on 3D Digital Imaging and Modeling*, pp. 476-483, 2005.

[14] R. Sagawa, T. Oishi, A. Nakazawa, R. Kurazume, K. Ikeuchi, "Iterative Refinement of Range Images with Anisotropic Error Distribution," *Proc. IEEE/RSJ International Conference on Intelligent Robots and Systems*, pp. 79-85, 2002.

Chapter 20

ILLUMINATION SIMULATION FOR ARCHAEOLOGICAL INVESTIGATION

Tomohito Masuda, Yosuke Yamada, Nobuaki Kuchitsu, and Katsushi Ikeuchi

Abstract   In the research of such cultural assets as wall sculptures or paintings, archæologists have paid much attention to the appearance of the painting at that time it was created and have argued about illumination conditions by observing or simulating the appearance of these assets in various ways.

Since observation or simulation is often not allowed to use actual cultural assets because they must be protected from destruction and deterioration, the use of 3D data is necessary for the verification of archaeological hypotheses. This process enables us to reproduce the 3D appearance realistically according to the properties of the light sources.

1.   Introduction

In the research of caves and tumuli, archaeologists often argue over when the sculptors and painters created the carvings, since they usually imagine that it was dark inside the cave. The idea that ancient sculptors and painters used artificial light sources has been considered; however, this is generally questionable since there is no firm evidence of it. For example, the use of torches would have caused soot on the wall and the ceiling, but almost no soot can be found there [1].

In Fugoppe Cave in northern Japan, we consider that the natural light emitted by the sun could have reached the interior of the cave. The reason is that the cave probably had the same entrance as the current entrance, which is large enough for the sunlight to pass through.

We also studied the Ozuka Tumulus in Kyushu Island, which has murals using six pigments. If the tumulus was built with wall stones that were already decorated, we imagine that these stones were painted under the natural light of sunshine. But if the wall was decorated after it was built, it is possible that the paintings were done under artificial light, such as light from taper. In the latter case, it is doubtful whether ancient artists could see well enough to paint these decorations by the taper light.

In this chapter, we verify the possibility that they were decorated in the sunlight focusing on the shading or shadowing over the carvings in Section 5 and the recognition of colors used for murals under sunlight or taper light in Section 6. We consider only the change of shade and shadow as time passes in a day, namely, the change of areas illuminated by natural light resulting from the sun in Section5. In Section 5, we do not consider the color spectrum because the Fugoppe cave has no color in the area where carvings were done. In Section 6, we consider the color appearance difference under different light sources (spectrum) in Section 6. In Section 6, we do not consider the spectrum change as time passes; we use the daylight spectrum as observed at noon in the spring equinox (fine weather).

Our targets for this study are the Fugoppe Cave in the former case, and the Ozuka Tumulus in the latter case. As topics in this chapter, we describe researches similar to ours, and then we explain how to obtain geometric and photometric information to reproduce their 3D appearance of these objects in computer graphics. After that, we show the results of our simulation of the Fugoppe Cave and the Ozuka Tumulus. Finally, we describe the knowledge obtained from the simulation.

2.   Related Work

Archaeologists analyzed the spectrum of each color or the 2D information of pictures taken by a camera [2, 3]. But we argue that the 3D shape information is essential in order to restore the whole appearance of decorated walls with complicated 3D shapes that are sculptured or painted on a wall.

Caves and tumuli are usually located under the ground, and it is hard to accurately recognize their relative positions with regard to the earth's surface. A number of researchers have argued that the use of the 3D data is suitable for the investigation of the caves, and have proposed their 3D models [4, 5]. Sellers et al.[6] measured the Kitley cave in England by using an ultrasonic sensor. Beraldin restored the 3D textured model of Byzantine Crypt at Santa Cristina in Carpignano, Italy [7], which has many frescos that are preserved in good condition. Brown et al. [8] measured the frieze of the Cap Blanc in France, and Deblin et al. [9] used their data for their archaeological study. They restored the appearance under the torches inside the cave in order to investigate shadow and shade motion and the visual effect resulting from the flames of the torches. Cruz-Neira et al. [10] developed a projection system, called "CAVE" in order to express the atmosphere unique to the inside space of the cave as virtual reality contents. Similarly, Toppan printing Co., ltd. used

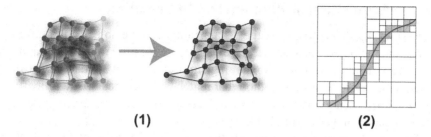

Figure 20.1. (1) Merging. Merging can integrate multiple aligned data sets (left side) into the single data set (right side). (2) Voxel division by octree. Octree provides the effective merging because voxel division is adaptively performed only where the object surfaces exist.

its theater for an interactive virtual reality display of cultural assets and world heritage objects [11].

3. Acquisition of Geometric Information

The entire 3D shape of the Fugoppe Cave is measured by using two types of laser range sensors. The first one can cover a wide area, but cannot guarantee a highly accurate measurement: it cannot capture the decoration on the wall. The other covers a much narrower area, but can measure the 3D shape with much higher accuracy than the first one. We therefore measured the whole shapes and the decorated areas by using the CYRAX 2500 and the VIVID 900, respectively, and then aligned two types of the measured data sets. The registration we used here [12] adopts the simultaneous strategy of alignment ordering, so it can reconstruct their 3D models accurately.

As a wide range sensor, we used the CYRAX 2500 (Leica) in the Fugoppe Cave, and the Imager (Z+F) in the Ozuka Tumulus. As an accurate and narrow range sensor, we used the VIVID 900 in both sites. We obtained 18 data sets in the Fugoppe Cave, and 171 (54 by CYRAX and 117 by VIVID) data sets in the Ozuka Tumulus.

As the last step of the 3D shape restoration, the registered multiple data sets are integrated into a single mesh (merging) (Figure 20.1-(1)). This is performed by calculating the signed distance between the center of the lattice and the object surface on each lattice. Calculated signed distance fields are converted into a single mesh model by using the marching cubes method [13].

Since each measured data set has random measurement errors that can affect the final results, the consensus is taken among the multiple measured data sets representing the same surface [14]. Also, octree representation is employed to adaptively and effectively divide the lattice unit that covers only the object surface (Figure 20.1-(2)).

4.   Acquisition of Photometric Information

Besides 3D shape, to restore the 3D appearance of the object, color information about the object's surface (texture) is needed. Texture images are captured separately from the 3D data, so the registration between 3D data and texture is required. Here we use a method that matches the characteristic property of a 2D texture image and the edge of reflectance image subsequently obtained from the laser range sensor [15].

The reflectance image represents the reflection intensity of laser light on each measurement point, and these are measured simultaneously by the same laser range sensor; thus, the reflectance image coincides with the 3D measured data.

The reflectance image and color image have similar characteristics in the respect that they affect the material, shape and color of the object's surface. For example, the Cyrax 2500 uses a green laser diode; in this wavelength, the reflectance changes according to the difference of surface color and material, so their boundary is shown as the edge in the reflectance image. On the other hand, the color image has similar boundary edges, since the different material generally has the different color. The jumping edge and contour are similarly shown in both images.

Registration between the 3D shape data and 2D color image is performed by iteratively minimizing the squared sum of the corresponding edge of the reflectance and the color image in a 3D coordinate. In order to reduce the influence of the outliers, this iterative minimization is implemented by using conjugate gradient method and the maximum likelihood method whose distribution function is a Lorentz function.

For the texture of the Fugoppe Cave, we used the pictures acquired by the Yoichi Town Board of Education (Figure 20.2-(1)). They are captured by a camera made by HASSELBLAD, inc., with a strobe light and illumination. In the Ozuka Tumulus, we used the pictures captured by D1x (Nikon).

5.   Fugoppe Cave

The Fugoppe Cave is a natural cave in tertiary tufaceous rocks located in the Yoichi town, Hokkaido, in northern Japan. The cave has a lot of petroglyphs (rock carving) of Zoku-Jomon period (A.D. 1C - 5C), and has been designated as a national historical site. Inside the Fugoppe Cave, there was an observation room that consists of windowpanes until 2001. The windowpanes were temporally removed for reconstruction, and on that occasion we measured the 3D data inside the cave for preservation of the present condition. Later, the new windowpanes were built (Figure 20.3), and it became impossible to observe the natural light incidence in direct observation. This presented a difficulty, since we began our project to solve the problem of the lighting inside the cave after

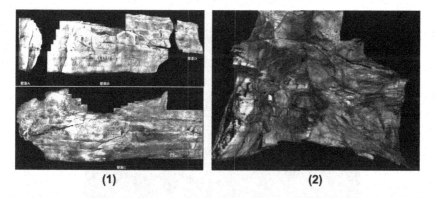

Figure 20.2. (1) Color images of the Fugoppe Cave, used as the texture. (2) Acquired whole shape of the Fugoppe Cave with texture. (Data Informant: Yoichi Town Board of Education)

Figure 20.3. Inside and outside the observation room of the Fugoppe Cave. (Data Informant: Mr. Nobuaki Kuchitsu (National Research Institute for Cultural Properties, Tokyo.))

the rebuilding. As a consequence, we required computer simulation by using the 3D data we had already obtained (Figure 20.2-(2)). As the environmental information in this simulation, we took the correspondence between the 3D model of the cave and its position on the earth's surface, calculate the ecliptic at the latitude of the cave, and then reproduced the change of appearance to the inside according to the position of the sun in our coordinate system.

5.1 Correspondence between 3D Model and its Position on Earth's Surface

In order to restore the interior appearance of Fugoppe Cave under sunlight, the correspondence between 3D model and its position on the earth's surface has to be taken. The surface registration of the cave model was performed by using principal component analysis for the estimation of the cave surface data,

Figure 20.4. Carvings inside the Fugoppe Cave. (Data Informant: Mr. Nobuaki Kuchitsu (National Research Institute for Cultural Properties, Tokyo.))

which was extracted from the whole 3D model (Figure 20.5-(1)). Direction registration was performed by using multiple reference points, including the 3D model, where the latitude, longitude, and altitude were known (Figure 20.5-(2)).

5.2   Orbit and Light Sources Setting for the Sunlight

The ecliptic was assumed here to be a simple circular orbit which is defined from the gradient of the earth's axis, the latitude, and the earth's position in the revolution surface. The circular orbit is translated according to the earth's position in the revolution, that is, the season (Figure 20.5-(3)). In order to simplify the time setting of a day, mean solar time was adopted. The sun always crosses the meridian at noon under mean solar time.

In existing computer graphics techniques, the sunlight is usually assumed to be parallel light rays. However, to be more physically correct, the entire light from the sky, resulting in sunlight, should be represented as the skylight. Skylight is the hemispheric light of infinite radius as the collection of surface light patches changing the brightness distribution according to the position of the sun. The rays emitted from the sun are diffused because of the floating matter in the atmosphere and such diffused light is regarded as the indirect light from the entire celestial sphere. Perez proposed the ALL-WEATHER MODEL in which all the sky models were classified into eight categories [16].

Skylight changes according to the season, time of the day and the state of the atmosphere. The International Commission on Illumination (CIE) defines the

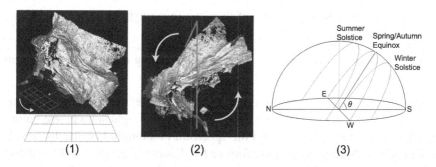

Figure 20.5. (1) Registration of the ground surface. (2) Registration of the direction. (3) Ecliptic according to the season and the time.

typical brightness distribution of the skylight as "CIE Standard Sky Luminance Distribution". This distribution is determined by direct horizontal irradiance (the irradiance of the direct light) and the diffuse horizontal irradiance (the irradiance of the indirect light, namely, the light diffused by the floating matter in the atmosphere).

5.3 Light Interreflection

The cave is illuminated by the direct sunlight and the indirect light that is reflected by the surfaces inside the cave. In computer graphics, indirect light is usually created by the radiosity method which considers the interreflection of light among objects. In the radiosity method, the illumination brightness of the object's surface, which is assumed to be the Lambertian surface, is calculated as the sum of the brightness of the direct sunlight and the indirect light from other surfaces.

In this chapter, we first assume parallel and direct light; and later, we relax the assumption by using the skylight and the entire light, including the indirect light. In our simulation that considers indirect light as well, we use radiance [17] which enables the radiosity method. Although, in the real world, indirect light is reflected repeatedly; radiance is approximated by the gradual radiosity method that sets the number of interreflections of the light. In this method, one or two interreflections are enough for the creation of the shadow and shade, and more than four interreflections are needed for calculation of the illumination. In our simulation, we use four interreflections.

5.4 Simulation of the Appearance of the Cave in Sunlight

We reproduce the appearance inside the Fugoppe Cave under the above conditions, as shown in previous sections, with the computer graphics. Here we consider the following issues.

- The changes in appearance of the cave in sunlight at each equinox and solstice.

- The shadow movement of the sculptor standing against the south wall and the west wall.

In this chapter, we describe how we first observe the shadow cast by using direct light and assuming that the sunlight is a parallel light source. We ignore the changes of the luminance and the spectrum of sunlight because the inside of the cave is illuminated for only four or five hours. The region that the direct light reaches is shown by its color obtained as the photometric information, and other regions are shown as black. We use a proper 3D human model created by CAD for the shadow movement simulation of the sculptor.

The simulation results are shown in Figures 20.6 and 20.7. We first observe the deepest part of the south wall inside the cave. At the winter solstice, direct sunlight does not reach the wall during the daytime (Figure 20.6-(1)). At the spring/autumn equinox, it reaches the wall at 6:00 a.m., but it soon becomes dark (Figure 20.6-(2)). On the other hand, the sunlight reaches the wall from 4:00 a.m. to 9:00 a.m. during the summer solstice (Figure 20.6-(3)). In summary, the direct sunlight reaches even the deepest part of the cave during fine weather for over half of a year, and lasts for about five hours a day at the summer solstice. Moreover, even if a sculptor stands there under the direct sunlight, the shadow is not cast on the wall, and has no effect on his or her work (Figure 20.7).

The simulation result under the interreflected light as well as direct light, is shown in Figure 20.8. This result shows that it is sufficiently bright to sculpt inside the cave.

5.5   Consideration of Ancient Outside Effect

From this simulation, it is known that direct sunlight reaches the deepest part of the Fugoppe Cave at a certain time. But this simulation is based on the current conditions of the cave, and it is possible that the ancient conditions were different.

It is too difficult to accurately estimate the ancient conditions. The Fugoppe Cave probably had the similar entrance in the same direction as the present, since the ancient cave dwellers are imagined to pass through the entrance, judging from the distribution of the excavated relics. First, the floor of the cave is presumed to be lower than it is at present because there are a lot of carvings nearby the floor, so this added depth would have made the cave brighter in ancient times. Second, the width of each wall would be different from the present width since the carvings remain near the current entrance. Third, the current ceiling may be higher than the ancient ceiling because there is evidence that the ceiling of the cave crumbled and raised the height level, but the shadow cast in the deepest part before and after the direct sunlight reaches it results from the wall, so the ancient illumination condition would be almost the same as the present. In other words, the height of the ceiling would not have brought a significant change in the lighting.

Then we consider the outside obstacles for the sunlight. To the east of the Fugoppe Cave, there is no high mountain that can obstruct the sunlight; instead, there is a hill of $\pm 50m$ in height, which does not yield a shadow inside the Fugoppe Cave, judging from the numerical analysis of the data on the map. It is difficult to know the ancient vegetation, but the entrance would not have been covered by some plants other than those currently present since ancient vegetation is consider to have been similar to the present one [1]. Therefore we think that the ancient illumination condition of the cave would be almost the same as the simulation result.

In other words, we consider that the direct sunlight would reach inside the Fugoppe Cave in ancient times at certain times and seasons, although the simulation may not be exact, because of the subtle differences in the ancient conditions. Moreover, the simulation that considers the interreflected light shows that it would be sufficiently bright inside the cave for a sculptor to work.

Finally, we consider the distribution of the carvings according to the effect shadows might have on the sculptor. As shown in Figure 20.7-(1), the shadow of the sculptor standing against the south wall would have been cast on the right side. If he or she were right-handed, the illumination condition would be better there. In the case of the west wall, it would have been worse because the shadow would have been cast just at the front as shown in Figure 20.7-(2). Actually, more carvings remain on the south wall than on the west, and this fact coincides with our theory.

6. Ozuka Tumulus

The Ozuka tumulus is a burial mound with a square front and a round back (Figure 20.10), located in the town of Keisen in Fukuoka prefecture in Kyushu Island (Figure 20.9). It is said to have been built in the middle of the six century A.D., and has been designated as a Special Historic Site because of its brilliantly painted inside wall (Figure 20.11). Six colors are used for the painting, namely, red, yellow, white, black, green and gray [18]. The inside paintings (murals) are supposed to have been done in commemoration of those who are buried in the tumulus, and thus they are valuable as ancient burial accessories (Figure 20.11). In order to verify the color recognition, we would need to take the tumulus to pieces, and to burn a taper for light inside the cave, but they are impossible. Instead, we used 3D techniques to restore the appearance of the painting in sunshine and taper light and to represent the appearance in computer graphics.

6.1   Texture Images and Color Spectrum

Our aim is to investigate the difference in appearance of paintings in sunlight and in taper light, so the color appearance has to be theoretically restored. We explain the details of their color tone correction in this section.

In 3D textured modeling, we usually use pictures taken by a digital camera as texture images. Though such pictures can be captured in high resolution, they do not represent accurate colors because the color tone changes according to environmental conditions, such as a lighting condition. This effect is formulated as follows.

$$I(\lambda) = E(\lambda)S(\lambda), \qquad (20.1)$$

where

I : reflected spectral color signal (measured object color),

E : illumination spectral power distribution (illuminated light color),

S : surface spectral reflectance,

λ : visible wavelength.

The appearance of an object is very different if illuminated under a different light, for example, incandescent light vs. fluorescent light.

Moreover, to capture color for each pixel, most cameras record the values of three colors (usually red, green, and blue, RGB) for visible wavelength, but the values depend on the type of camera. This fact is described in a mathematical form extended from equation (20.1) as follows:

$$P_k = \int E(\lambda)S(\lambda)R_k(\lambda)d\lambda, \qquad (20.2)$$

where

k : color channel; RGB,

P_k : camera response,

R_k : spectral response curve for each channel.

Note that R_k changes if a camera changes.

An accurate acquisition method for color information is spectrometry [19], which can obtain color signals of continuous spectrum $I(\lambda)$ independent of the type of camera. Since we can measure illumination spectral color $S(\lambda)$ as a spectral color signal of a reference object (usually a white object) illuminated by objective light, we can calculate $I(\lambda)$ from equation (20.1). By using spectral color signals, we restore the color appearance of an object under an arbitrary light in computer graphics more accurately than using RGB data because we have more accurate color information [20] [21].

Additionally, these spectral data can be converted to RGB data. However, the resolution of spectrum images cannot compare with that of camera images. So using spectrometry takes a huge amount of time to obtain the whole color of objects.

In order to take advantage of both methods, we apply spectrum information to high-resolution camera images [22]. Our method needs the spectrum of an environmental light and an object within the environment, as well as camera images, as input data. The environmental light is an illumination color distribution component, and the reflection component of an object is calculated from the spectrum of the environmental light and the object's surface. The surface spectral reflectance component information is registered into the camera images.

Finally, the color appearance is restored by using the reflection component and illumination component of the environmental light under which the scene is observed.

In our photometric measurement, we obtained about 600 pictures and 21 spectrum data sets by using D1x (Nikon) and SpectraScan (Photo Research Inc.), respectively.

6.2   Sunlight and Artificial Taper Spectrum

As the environmental information in this simulation, we used spectrum information of two kinds of environmental light: sunlight and taper light. To obtain the spectrum of sunlight, we measured the white reference illuminated by the sunlight as observed at noon in the spring equinox (fine weather). The spectrum of taper light was measured by a spectrometer. We also measured the spectrum of the white reference illuminated by the fire in the fireplace constructed from bricks in the exhaust system (Figure 20.12). Figure 20.13 shows the obtained spectrum.

6.3   Experimental Results and Consideration

On the basis of the above method, we restored the textured 3D model of the Ozuka tumulus. Here we assumed that the amount of light of an artificial taper is the same as that of sunlight because we do not know what the ancient artists actually used as an artificial light, so we cannot gauge the brightness of an artificial light.

We focused on continuous triangle patterns (Figure 20.15) as typical ones of the Ozuka tumulus. Figure 20.14 shows the result when the wall was exposed to daylight (no ceiling cover) and also when the wall was illuminated by tapers from the two stands inside the tumulus while the ceiling was covered. In the former case, we can recognize the triangle patterns. But in the latter case, we cannot recognize them.

7.   Summary

In this chapter, we showed the illumination simulation for archaeological simulation using 3D shape model. From the above simulations, we can assert, against the established theory of ancient sculptors having to do their carving with an artificial light in the dark environment, and we can support the possibility that they worked inside the cave in sunlight if they chose the optimum season and time for working.

In such a model as caves and tumuli, it is difficult to reconstruct the whole 3D shape by aligning their partial data. The registration we developed employs the simultaneous strategies, so the complete reconstruction is enabled.

Our simulation results of Fugoppe Cave and Ozuka Tumulus were exhibited at Fugoppe Cave Museum in the Yoichi town, Hokkaido, and Kyushu National Museum in the Dazaifu city, Fukuoka. Our approaches to the archaeological hypotheses are considered to be useful in this field.

Acknowledgments

This research was supported, in part, by Ministry of Education, Culture, Sports, Science and Technology under the Leading Project, "Development of High Fidelity Digitization Software for Large-Scale and Intangible Cultural Assets," and, in part, by Japan Science and Technology Agency, under the CREST program, "Automatic generation of virtual models of cultural heritage."

References

[1] Otaru City Board of Education. *Symposium on Temiya Cave(in Japanese)*. Otaru City Board of Education, 1997.

[2] M. Kamii. *Ho-oh-do at Byodoin Temple - Restoration of Original Color at Heian Period -*. Tohoshuppan, 2002. This book is available in Japanese only, and the title is translated in English by the authors of this paper.

[3] Y. Katagiri and A. Arenas. *Restoration of The Last Supper*. Japan Broadcast Publishing Co.,Ltd., 2000. This book is available in Japanese only, and the title is translated in English by the authors of this paper.

[4] W. I. Sellers, R. Orton, and A. T. Chamberlain. Computer-aided visualisation of archaeological caves.
http://www.shef.ac.uk/~capra/3/sellers.html, 2001.

[5] M. Roe. The brighter the light the darker the shadows: how we perceive and represent underground spaces.
http://www.shef.ac.uk/~capra/2/roe.html, 2000.

[6] W. I. Sellers and A. T. Chamberlain. Ultrasonic cave mapping. In *Journal of Archaeological Science*, pp. 283–289, March 2001.

[7] J-A. Beraldin, M. Picard, S. F. El-Hakim, G. Godin, V. Valzano, A. Bandiera, and C. Latouche. Virtualizing a byzantine crypt by combining high-resolution textures with laser scanner 3d data. In *Proceedings of the 8th International Conference on Virtual Systems and MultiMedia (VSMM2002)*, pp. 3–14, September 2002.

[8] K. A. R. Brown, A. Chalmers, T. Saigol, C. Green, and F. d'Errico. An automated laser scan survey of the upper palaeolithic rock shelter of cap blanc. In *Journal of Archaeological Science*, pp. 867–873, September 1998.

[9] K. Devlin, A. Chalmers, and D. Brown. Predictive lighting and perception in archaeological representations. In *UNESCO World Heritage in the Digital Age 30th Anniversary Digital Congress*, October 2002.

[10] C. Cruz-Neira, D. J. Sandin, and T. A. DeFanti. Surround-screen projection-based virtual reality: The design and implementation of the cave. In *Proceedings of SIGGRAPH 1993*, pp. 135–142, August 1993.

[11] Interactive Media Lab at Toppan Printing Co.,ltd. VR Theater at Toppan Koishikawa Building.
http://www.toppan.co.jp/products+service/vr/intro_e.htm.

[12] T. Masuda, Y. Hirota, K. Ikeuchi, and K. Nishino. Simultaneous determination of registration and deformation parameters among 3d range images. In *Proceedings of the 5th International Conference on 3-D Digital Imaging and Modeling (3DIM 2005)*, pp. 369–376, June 2005.

[13] B. Curless and M. Levoy. A volumetric method for building complex models from range images. In *Proceedings of ACM SIGGRAPH 96*, pp. 303–312, August 1996.

[14] R. Sagawa K. Nishino, M.D. Wheeler, and K. Ikeuchi. Parallel processing of range data merging. In *IEEE/RSJ International Conference on Intelligent Robots and Systems*, Vol. 1, pp. 577–583, October 2001.

[15] R. Kurazume, Z. Zhang K. Nishino, and K. Ikeuchi. Simultaneous 2d images and 3d geometric model registration for texture mapping utilizing reflectance attribute. In *Proceedings of Fifth Asian Conference on Computer Vision*, pp. 99–106, January 2002.

[16] Perez R., Seals R., and Michalsky J. All-weather model for sky luminance distribution - preliminary cofiguration and validation. *Solar Energy*, Vol. 50, No. 3, pp. 235–245, 1993.

[17] Ward Gregory J. The radiance lighting simulation and rendering system. In *Proceedings of SIGGRAPH 1994*, pp. 459–472, July 1994.

[18] N. Kuchitsu and W. Kawanobe. Green and "Blue" Pigments used for Mural Paintings of Old Tombs in Kyushu -Especially in Fukuoka Prefecture-. In *Science for Conservation*, Vol. 39, pp. 24–32, March 2000.

[19] G. E. Healey, S. A. Shafer, and L. B. Wolff. *Physics-Based Vision Principles and Practice*. Jones and Bartlett Publishers, 1992.

[20] R. T. Tan, K. Nishino, and K. Ikeuchi. Color constancy through inverse-intensity chromaticity space. *Journal of the Optical Society of America A*, Vol. 21, No. 302, March 2004.

[21] A. Ikari, R. T. Tan, and K. Ikeuchi. Separating illumination and surface spectral from multiple color signals. In *Proceedings of the 6th Asian Conference on Computer Vision (ACCV2004)*, pp. 264–269, January 2004.

[22] A. Ikari, T. Masuda, T. Mihashi, K. Matsudo, N. Kuchitsu, and K. Ikeuchi. High quality color restoration using spectral power distribution for 3d textured model. In *Proceedings of the Eleventh International Conference on Virtual Systems and MultiMedia (VSMM 2005)*, pp. 453–462, October 2005.

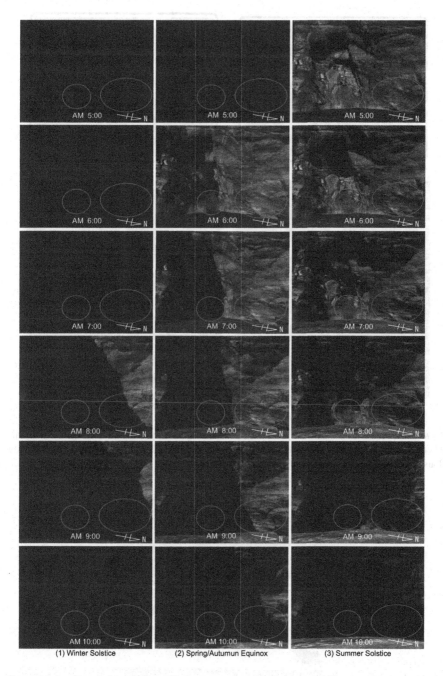

Figure 20.6. Simulation results. There are carvings inside the area illustrated by red circles. As the season changes from winter to summer, the direct sunlight reaches the walls for more hours.

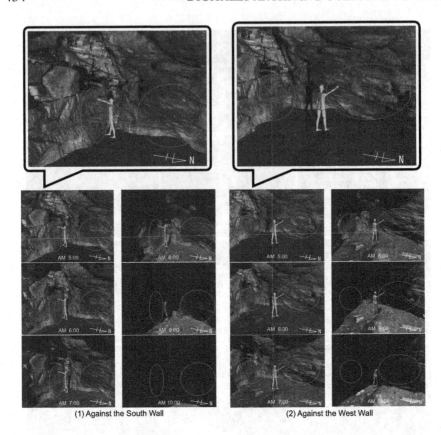

(1) Against the South Wall   (2) Against the West Wall

Figure 20.7.   Simulation results on the summer solstice with a man standing against the wall. There are carvings inside the area illustrated by red circles. This shows the sculptor's shadow does not darken his or her working space.

Figure 20.8.   Simulation result considering the sunlight interreflection. This result shows the inside is brighter than expected.

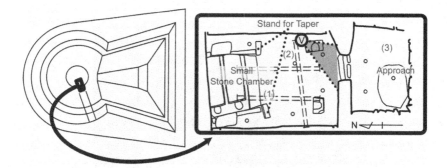

Figure 20.9.   The projection map of the Ozuka tumulus. The right figure is the enlarged view of the thick line area in the left figure. (Data Informant: Kyushu National Museum)

Figure 20.10.   The aerial map of the Ozuka tumulus. The tumulus is located at the circular area. (Data Informant: Keisen Town Board of Education.)

Figure 20.11. The mural inside the Ozuka tumulus. Various patterns were painted in the tumulus to decorate the tombs of those buried there.

Figure 20.12. The spectrum measurement of a taper light. In this experiment, we measured the light from burned wood as an artificial light.

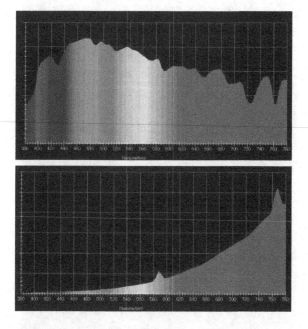

Figure 20.13. The obtained spectrum data. The upper and lower histograms respectively show the spectrum data of sunlight and a taper light.

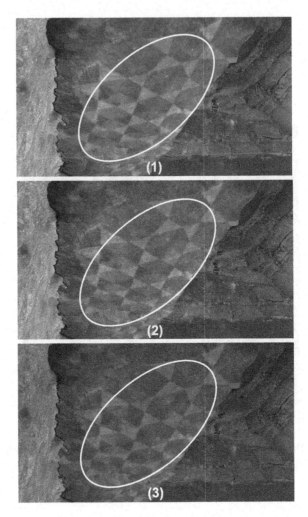

Figure 20.14. Simulation Results. The color appearance, in the area enclosed by curves in Figure (1), is restored. Figure (2) and (3) show the color appearance restoration under the sunlight and taper light, respectively. We can recognize the pattern in the former figure much more clearly than that in the latter.

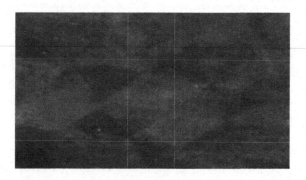

Figure 20.15. Continuous triangle pattern.

Chapter 21

EDITING, RETRIEVAL, AND DISPLAY SYSTEM OF ARCHEOLOGICAL INFORMATION ON LARGE 3D GEOMETRIC MODELS

Yasuhide Okamoto, Takeshi Oishi, and Katsushi Ikeuchi

Abstract   One of the promising directions for utilizing scanned 3D models is to provide computer graphics models with various types of archeological information. However, very huge models and variety of information cannot be handled easily on common PCs because of limits to performance of the hardware and to compatibility between a variety types of data format. In this chapter, we propose a system which enables users to browse 3D models, retrieve information, and edit associations. Firstly, on our system, users can browse models and information easily and quickly. For real-time 3D browsing, it achieved highly interactive rendering by adopting multi-resolution meshes. Secondly, users can associate and edit information with 3D models with easy mouse actions. In these procedures, users can effectively select specified regions by interactive tools using Lazy Snapping algorithm and by mapping interface of drawing images.

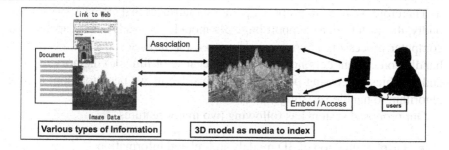

Figure 21.1.   The usability by relating 3D models and other information

1.   Introduction

In the field of computer vision, there is an application that converts real objects into digital 3-Dimensional models for the preservation of cultural properties ([6, 8], and described in previous chapters). The obtained models can be used for many purposes, for example, scientific analysis and simulation for archeological research, digital storage, repairing, and public viewing.

At the same time, many cultural properties have been researched by archeologists for a long time, and the information about them have been stored in various forms such as text documents, images, drawings, and numerical tables, which have cultural and academic value. In some objects, the quantity of stored information is so huge that the information cannot be managed efficiently for non-experts. So, the information is not effectively utilized except in few specialistic research.

To effectively utilize such information, the management system for many kinds of information is desired. 3D models are very appropriate as tools to visualize managing operation of related information (Fig. 21.1). In this chapter, we propose such a management and visualizing system.

There are some applications that associate 3D models and related information. However, most of those focus on simple 3D models with a small number of triangles such as CAD models, and are unavailable for massive meshes. The system proposed in [3], locates the related information on the 3D model obtained by scanning. Information displayed includes analysis of research such as graphs and charts, and many kinds of images and pictures. Some web applications have been proposed that map information and notes on landmarks to a 3D map of the earth; i.e. Nasa World Wind[2] and Google Earth[1]. These applications propose 3D geometry information, texture images, and embedded information as landmarks through networks.

When implementing management system using 3D models, we have some problems. Firstly, this system must enable general users to view and edit information and 3D models intuitively. In the case of conventional 3D software, the operating methods are very complex and users must learn how to operate it. Therefore we need to propose operation interfaces that are easy to use. Secondly, the system must support huge 3D models. Nowadays the capability of computer processing is growing. However, the huge scanned data cannot be handled on current common computers because of limits to memory capacity and graphics processing performance. To solve it, we need to adopt a novel algorithm to handle very huge data.

Our proposed system has following two major features.

- Display function of 3D models and related information

- Editing association function between 3D models and information

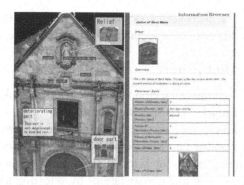

Figure 21.2.　Access to related information from 3D models

For efficient rendering of huge 3D models, we adopt multiresolution scheme, and minimize the processing cost. Users can also access associated information with the model when they browse it in real-time. Because related information is recorded as link to the real data, users can access the information regardless of the data format. Additionally, users can associate information with a specific region on the 3D model. These operations in the associating procedures are realized by easy mouse action such as clicking, dragging and dropping.

In this chapter, we describe the overview of our proposed system in the section 2, explain about the view and browsing function in section 3, and the function editing associations in section 4. After that, we explain the result of experiments in section 5, and conclude in section 6.

2.　　Overview of Proposed System

Our proposed system has two major functions. One is the browsing function; which users can view a 3D model in real-time and can access related information to the model. The other is the function for editing associations between 3D models and related information.

2.1　　3D Model and Information Browser

By using the system users can interactively view the 3D model in real-time from desired viewpoints. To avoid processing stall when rendering huge models, we adopt the multiresolution rendering. The method converts the input model into tree structure which has hierarchical resolution, and traverse and load only the nodes which are needed when rendering.

At the same time users view a 3D model, users can access and browse related information which is associated with the specific region on the 3D model (see Fig. 21.2). When users select a specific region in viewing, the system outputs the overview and detail of associated information on the system's browser.

2.2   Association Editor

The function for editing associations enables users to make and edit associations between information and specified regions.

To make associations, users firstly define specific regions on the target 3D model. To define regions can be operated by easy mouse actions. We implements some types of tools for selecting specific regions intuitively. After defining regions, users can make associations by selecting files storing related information or database records, and moving them to the defined region by mouse actions. The data formats of associated information which our system supports are text documents, images, database records (tables), and links to web pages or files.

3.   Browsing

On our proposed system, users can freely view the target 3D model from desired viewpoints in real-time, and can browse the information associated with the model.

In the case of rendering 3D models with a very huge number of triangles, the conventional method cannot maintain interactivity because of limits to memory capacity and graphics processing performance. Therefore, we need the novel method for real-time rendering.

In this section, we explain about the detail of efficient rendering algorithm and browsing function of information of proposed system.

3.1   Real-Time Rendering for Huge Meshes

On our system, we use LOD method for huge mesh rendering; which represents huge meshes in hierarchical design. There are two major rendering method using points ([9, 11]) and polygon ([4, 12]) as rendering primitives. We chose polygon based method because of rendering quality on our system. We use a binary tree as the hierarchical structure described in [4].

3.1.1   Building Hierarchy

We build the hierarchical representation in the following procedures.

1 Recursively splitting the input mesh into two meshes, and building a binary tree.

2 Traversing in the bottom-up order, and recursively merging and simplifying intermediate nodes.

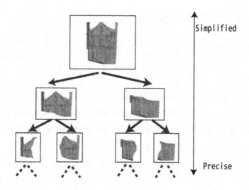

Figure 21.3. The hierarchy of patches for multiresolution rendering

The input meshes are split by using graph-cut algorithm which use the distances between neighboring normals as weights of the graph. We implemented the splitting procedure by using the Metis library [7]. Splitting operation is continued recursively until the number of polygons of each node is under predefined number 21.3.

After that, we traverse the binary tree in the bottom-up order. In traversing time, we merge two child nodes, simplify it until the size is under the predefined number, and assign it to the parent node. For the simplifying algorithm, we use the method in the way described in [5]. When simplifying step, the consistency between neighbouring sub-split meshes in different simplified levels cannot be maintained. This inconsistency can generate holes or artificial patches along the boundaries. To avoid it we constrain the simplifying operation not to be applied to the polygons along the boundaries.

3.1.2 Multiresolution Rendering

When rendering time, we traverse the built hierarchy in the top-down order and select appropriate nodes which can be rendered with enough resolution on the screen. The system loads only selected nodes from secondary memory and renders. In the traversing procedure, for efficiency, invisible nodes obviously on screen and those sub-tree can be skipped because the meshes are outside of view frustum or the normal vectors are out of the view direction. Judgement whether the node is rendered depends on the quadric error value of the child nodes. If the scale of error value on screen is under the desired accuracy, we load and render the node. Otherwise, traverse is continued recursively. For memory efficiency, the data of each node is managed by FIFO algorithm, unused data for a period of time is released from main memory.

3.2 Browsing Information

At the same time that users are viewing a 3D model, they can find the related information to the object. On the viewer, the regions with which information is associated are highlighted. In particular users point the associated region by mouse, the associated information with the region is displayed on the temporary dialog; which shows the label, thumbnail, and the summary. If users click the highlighted region, they can browse the list of associated information on the system's browser (see Fig. 21.2).

The associated information is managed with some parameters; which are ID of associated region, summary, detailed description, thumbnail images, and tag words; in the database system. When users access, the recorded information is retrieved by using existing database function. Retrieved information is casted as HTML format, and output on the browser. On the browser, users can view related documents, images, other linked web pages and files to the model. In addition to this, users can add, edit, delete information on the browser.

4. Associating Information

On our system users can edit associations between the target 3D models and related information. The associations procedure is operated by the following way.

 1 Defining the specified regions to which information will be assigned

 2 Associating the information by drag-and-drop

 3 Editing the ID, summary, and description of associated information

Firstly, users define the specified regions on the target 3D model which they want to associate related information with. We propose very interactive tools for region definition to support the regions with very complex boundaries.

4.1 Region Definition

There are some conventional tools for selecting specified regions on 2D images. However, common users cannot handle those tools skillfully without enough training. In the case of 3D images, particularly, it is harder to select precisely because of the depth on images. In addition to it, the 3D models obtained by laser scanning are very huge and complex, so it is costly for users. Therefore we propose users very effective tools to select complex 3D regions intuitively and without extra cost.

4.1.1 Interactive Tools

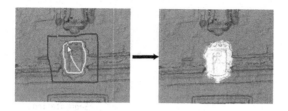

Figure 21.4. Segmentation of 3D regions by Lazy Snapping (The yellow marker means foreground, and the blue marker means background)

Lasso tool. Lasso tool is the most common method to select specified regions on 2D images. By tracing the boundaries by lasso, users can select a region intuitively. However, it is difficult and time consuming for common users to precisely select a region by this tool using mouse actions.

We implemented the lasso tool available on 3D images. The system projects the resulting region which users select on the 2D image onto the original 3D model. To avoid selection backface which users do not want to select, we split the input model into small segments, and select only the segments which are rendered on screen by checking the segment ID.

Selection tool using Lazy Snapping. Lazy Snapping[10] is a very interactive method to split a 2D image into foreground and background areas. We apply this method to the definition of specified regions on the 3D images.

In the methodology of Lazy Snapping, firstly, users draw two types of markers: the ones are yellow markers for foreground, and the others are blue for background (see Fig. 21.4). We describe the 2D image as a graph G, and solve the labelling problem of G starting from F and B which are nodes drawn by users' markers. To solve it, we convert the labelling problem into the minimization problem of the following equation. Moreover, we apply the Lazy Snapping method to 3D images like the method described in [13].

$$E(X) = \sum_{i \in V} E_1(x_i) + \lambda \sum_{(i,j) \in E} E_2(x_i, x_j) \qquad (21.1)$$

In equation 21.1, E_1 is the distance energy between each node and belonging set (foreground or background). And E_2 is the similarity between neighboring nodes along the boundaries of foreground set and background set. As parameters of each node the color is used in the 2D image version. We also use the normal vector and depth value in the 3D image version. After labelling, users can obtain the desired region on the 3D model.

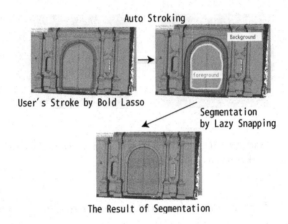

Figure 21.5.   Segmentation by Lazy Snapping Like Lasso Tool

Lazy Snapping selection like lasso.   Lazy Snapping selection requires less work than lasso selection because of the robustness and the automation. However, in the some case users need more operations. Lazy Snapping method is not intuitive because users cannot smoothly connect drawn markers by themselves to selected regions obtained by Lazy Snapping algorithm. That is why users may need to draw extra markers when selecting fuzzy regions.

To support those case, we propose another selection tool which combined lasso and Lazy Snapping. The procedures of this method are described in Fig. 21.5. Firstly users draw a lasso marker along the boundaries. We set the size of lasso marker to be bold for robustness. Secondly, the yellow markers and blue markers are drawn automatically and invisibly for users as in Fig. 21.5. After that, the resulting region is calculated by Lazy Snapping algorithm.

This tool has both intuitive affordance and robustness of a lasso tool and Lazy Snapping . So, it is very effective tool. We describe the effectiveness in section 5.

4.1.2   Automated Selection Using Drawings

The selection tools described above, are very effective when users want to record note or comment on the target model sporadically. However, in the case that researchers hope to associate information with every part on target object and manage systematically, these tools are inadequate. For example, in the case of the restoration activity of a cultural building constructed by stones, experts engaging in restoration hope to record the state of each stone. In this case, it is hard to define regions of all stones by mouse actions.

In those restoration activities for cultural properties, researchers often record the drawings of target objects. Therefore, we implemented another selecting

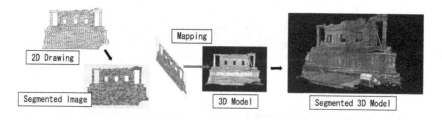

Figure 21.6. The region definition by using drawing.

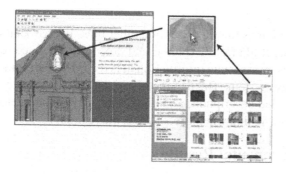

Figure 21.7. The relating operation by simple actions

tool which can define the specified regions on entity of the building by using the recorded drawings.

The procedure of selection by drawings is as follows, and is described in Fig. 21.6.

1. Inserting a drawing from one side of the target object

2. Editing the resulting segments on a 2D image split by automatic segmentation

3. Mapping the segments onto the 3D model

In step 2 of the above procedure, we use a simple region growing method to split the drawing image into small segments. After that, users select required segments and delete needless ones. Finally, the resulting segments are mapped onto the target 3D model. For mapping of the resulting segmentation, we implemented the interface on which users can map it manually.

4.2 Edition of Association

After definition of regions, users can associate many types of data with those regions; our system supports text documents, images, records, tables

model	Mercede Church	Nara Buddha	Bayon Face	Bayon Towers
Input[tris]	1,148,939	3,109,824	5,922,790	9,343,426
Preprocessing[sec]	340	818	1641	3055
Rendering time[fps]	32.8	24.7	13.8	16.4

Table 21.1. The result of preprocessing time, rendering speed, and amount of occupied memory

in database, and links to web pages and other files. For association, users drag an icon of a target file from Explorer, and drop it on a defined region (see Fig. 21.7). When users associate information, it is recorded with some other parameters in database system. The parameters are an ID of associated region, label, summary, detailed description, and thumbnail. Those parameters are used to retrieve the information when users access the region.

5. Experimental Result

In this section, we evaluate the performance of our proposed system. We evaluate rendering performance and region definition tools by experiments and user study. In addition, we introduce the project using our system.

We have experimented on commodity PC, for rendering on an ATI Radeon 9800XT, processing on a 3.2 GHz Intel Pentium4 processor with 2GBytes of RAM. Our system runs on Windows XP, and it has been implemented using C++ with OpenGL.

5.1 Rendering Performance

We evaluated the performance of building multiresolution model and rendering speed. We describe the result in Fig. 21.1. We test four models whose number of polygons is from one million to ten million.

The time consumed in constructing multiresolution model is shown in the row of Preprocessing. In the case of Mercede Church (1M polys), it took 6 minutes in preprocessing. In other case, we can find the commensurate results with the input size. The order of consuming time is practical enough.

For evaluation of rendering performance, we measured the frame rate described in the row of Rendering time. In the case of Bayon Face (6M polys), the average frame rate is 13.8 fps, it is quick enough to render in real-time. In the other case, we can observe that the frame rates are faster. The reason is because we use multiresolution scheme for rendering.

From those results, our system can build the multiresolution model, and render it.

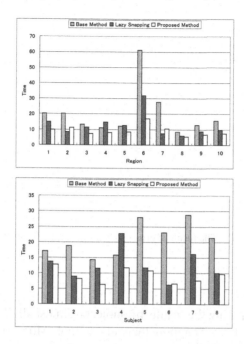

Figure 21.8. The result of consumed time for segmentation (upper:by regions, lower:by users)

5.2 User Study for Selection Tools

To test the usability of our interactive selection tools, we have conducted a usability study. We select eight subjects; two subjects are novices, other two are experts for 3D softwares, and others are intermediate users. The study of selecting operations have two times. We gave subjects ten region selecting tasks by using three selecting tools; which are a lasso tool, a Lazy Snapping tool, and a selection tool combined lasso and Lazy Snapping. We measured the consumed time and error rate which is the area selected in error. We describe the result in the followed charts (see Fig. 21.8, 21.9).

In figure 21.8, we describe the average consumed time by using three different tools. The upper one shows the results by regions and the lower one shows ones by subjects.

Firstly, by comparing a lasso tool with Lazy Snapping by regions, we can find advantages in the case of region 1, 2, 6, and 7, which are larger than other regions. But in the other case, we cannot find a decisive advantage. Comparing a lasso tool with a combined tool in a similar way, we can find major advantages in any region.

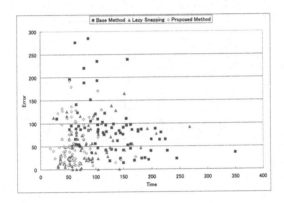

Figure 21.9.   The result of errors to consumed time for segmentation

Secondly, comparing the results by subjects, almost all of subjects required less time by using Lazy Snapping than a lasso tool. Moreover, the results of a combined tool are much less than those of Lazy Snapping.

Finally, we evaluate the time and error by three selecting methods. On this diagram the lower the value of both parameters, the better the results are. Observing the distributional condition, we figure that the most effective method is the combined selecting tool. The distribution of samples of the method and Lazy Snapping is very analogical with regard to error. However, the combined method has an advantage from the aspect of time.

From these experimental results, we are sure that the combined selection method is the most efficient operation of the three methods.

5.3   Case Study

Our target is to build a system for South Library of Bayon Temple in Cambodia. To save Bayon Temple from destruction, The members of Japanese government team for safeguarding Angkor (JSA) engage in restoration activity. We are developing this system as a part of the activity.

The drawings of South Library are drawn from four cardinal directions for recording of the state of every stone. In the same way, with our system, users can record information in region of every stone. We can define the regions assigned to every stone by using the interface described in 4.1.2.

In this mission, we are developing the 3D database system for restoration of South Library. Figure 21.10 is a snapshot of the database system. In this system researchers can record and manage each stone's information such as stone ID, the condition, and photographs.

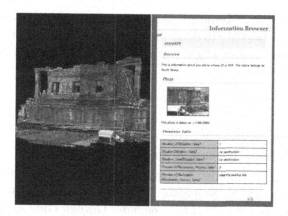

Figure 21.10.　The 3D Database System for South Library of Bayon Temple.

6.　Conclusion

In this chapter, we proposed the system in which users can deal with both 3D models and other information. In this system, users can view the target 3D model and access the associated information at the same time. In addition to it, users can associate information to specified regions on the 3D model. We proposed some interactive tools which enabled users to define the specified regions by easy mouse actions. We combine the Lazy Snapping and the conventional lasso tool, and developed a more efficient selecting tool. We also proposed the function for automatic definition of many specific regions by using drawings.

From experimental results, we observed the rendering capacity of our system has enough efficiency to render huge 3D models with over ten million polygons in real-time. Moreover, we observed that users can define specified regions in less time and with less error by using our proposed selecting tool than by other tools.

For future work, we hope to sophisticate the rendering and region selecting algorithm which are more efficient and more robust. Finally, we hope to extend this system to the network version. It is inefficient and unuseful for many users to store huge amount of data on local disks. To solve the problem we hope to develop a database system which enables users to share the huge 3D models and related information with other people through internet.

Acknowledgments

This research was supported, in part, by Ministry of Education, Culture, Sports, Science and Technology under the Leading Project, "Development of High Fidelity Digitization Software for Large-Scale and Intangible Cultural Assets," and, in part, by Japan Science and Technology Agency, under

454 DIGITALLY ARCHIVING CULTURAL OBJECTS

the CREST program, "Automatic generation of virtual models of cultural heritage." And we would like to thank the members of Japanese government team for safeguarding Angkor (JSA) for assistance when the scanning of Bayon Temple in Cambodia.

References

[1] http://earth.google.com.

[2] http://worldwind.arc.nasa.gov/index.html.

[3] M. Callieri, P. Cignoni, F. Ganovelli, G. Impoco, C. Montani, P. Pingi, F. Ponchio, and R. Scopigno. Visualization and 3d data processing in david's restoration. In *IEEE Computer Graphics and Applications*, volume 24(5), pages 16–21, 2004.

[4] Paolo Cignoni, Fabio Ganovelli, Enrico Gobetti, Fabio Marton, Federico Ponchio, and Roberto Scopigno. Adaptive tetrapuzzles: Efficient out-of-core construction and visualization of gigantic multiresolution polygonal models. In *ACM Trans. on Graphics (SIGGRAPH 2004)*, volume 23(3), pages 796–803, 2004.

[5] Michael Garland and Paul S. Heckbert. Surface simplification using quadric error metrics. In *Proceedings of SIGGRAPH 97*, pages 209–216, 1997.

[6] Katsushi Ikeuchi, Kazuhide Hasegawa, Atsushi Nakazawa, Jun Takamatsu, Takeshi Oishi, and Tomohito Masuda. Bayon digital archival project. In *Proceedings of Virtual Systems and Multimedia*, pages 334–343, 2004.

[7] George Karypis and Vipin Kumar. Multilevel k-way partitioning scheme for irregular graphs. *Journal of Parallel and Distributed Computing*, 1998.

[8] Marc Levoy, Kari Pulli, Brian Curless, Szymon Rusinkiewicz, Dave Koller, Lucas Pereira, Matt Ginzton, Sean Anderson, James Davis, Jeremy Ginsberg, Jonathan Shade, and Duane Fulk. The digital michelangelo project: 3d scanning of large statues. In *Proceedings of SIGGRAPH 2000*, pages 131–144, 2000.

[9] Szymon Rusinkiewicz. Marc Levoy. Qsplat:a multiresolution point rendering system for large meshes. In *Proceedings of ACM SIGGRAPH 2000, Computer Graphics Proceedings*, pages 343–352, 2000.

[10] Yin Li, Jian Sun, Chi-Keung Tang, and Heung-Yeung Shum. Lazy snapping. In *ACM Trans. Graph*, volume 23(3), pages 303–308, 2004.

[11] Carsten Dachsbacher. Christian Vogelgsang. Marc Stamminger. Sequential point trees. In *Proceedings of ACM SIGGRAPH 2003, Computer Graphics Proceedings*, pages 657–662, 2003.

[12] Sung-Eui Yoon, Brian Salomon, Russell Gayle, and Dinesh Manocha. Quick-vdr: Interactive view-dependent rendering of massive models. In *Proceeding of IEEE Visualization*, 2004.

[13] Xiaoru Yuan, Hui Xu, Minh X. Nguyen, Amit Shesh, and Baoquan Chen. Sketch-based segmentation of scanned outdoor environment models. In *Proceeding of the 2nd Eurographics Workshop on Sketch-Based Interfaces and Modeling*, pages 19–26, 2005.

Chapter 22

VIRTUAL ASUKAKYO:
REAL-TIME SOFT SHADOWS IN MIXED
REALITY USING SHADOWING PLANES

Tetsuya Kakuta, Takeshi Oishi, and Katsushi Ikeuchi

Abstract   This chapter introduces fast shading and shadowing method in Mixed Reality. We create realistic soft shadows of virtual objects in a fast and efficient way using shadowing planes and a set of pre-rendered basis images. In the preparatory stages, we generate shadowing planes from convex hulls of objects and render basis images with basis lights which approximate the illumination of the real world. We then synthesize basis images with luminance parameters and generate shadow images which correspond to the current illumination. Finally we map shadow images onto shadowing planes and express soft shadows of objects in real-time. The proposed method can support both dynamic changes of illumination and movements of user's viewpoint. We successfully achieve the consistency of illumination and improve the quality of synthesized image in MR-systems.

1.   Introduction

Mixed Reality (MR) systems allow us to see real scenes that contain computer-generated virtual objects [1, 2]. Recently, outdoor MR applications which are intended to represent lost cultural heritages with MR-systems have become feasible. Considering the problem of cost and archaeological concerns, it is preferable to reconstruct the cultural heritages with Computer Graphics (CG) rather than rebuild them. Using the MR technology, we can show visitors reconstructed CG models directly on historical sites. Furthermore, we can easily correspond to the update of restoration plan by modifying CG models. Against such a background, we started Virtual Asukakyo project to reconstruct Asukakyo city, the earliest historical capital of Japan in 7th century.

For the seamless integration of virtual and real objects in MR, it is important to achieve the consistency of illumination. First of all, the shading of the virtual objects needs to match that of other objects in the environment. Also, the virtual objects must cast a correct shadow onto the real scene. However, it is not easy to obtain correct illumination because real scenes usually include both direct and indirect illumination distributed in a complex way. In addition, computing global illumination and soft shadow in real-time is a difficult task. Therefore the consistency of illumination in MR is a challenging problem.

There are some previous works related to the illumination in MR. Jacobs and Loscos provide a detailed survey of illumination methods for MR[3]. They classify the various techniques based on their input requirements of geometry and radiance of real environment[4–8]. Most of these techniques are demonstrated in indoor scenes and few of them are carried out at interactive update rates. To simulate the naturally illuminated architectural environment, Nimeroff et al. presented an efficient re-rendering method using pre-rendered basis images[10]. Sato et al. applied this technique for MR and achieved a fast image synthesis with natural shading[9]. Nevertheless, their method is applicable only to still images and fixed viewpoints.

We propose a fast shadowing method for interactive MR applications. We generate basis images to express the shadows of virtual objects and set them onto other planate objects (hereafter called the shadowing planes) so that they correspond to both the arbitrary viewpoints and changing illumination of the real environment. The major contributions of this chapter are as follows:

- Realistic soft shadows in real-time using pre-rendered basis images.

- Model-based shadowing that allows user to move the viewpoint.

- Hardware acceleration is available in the synthesis of basis images.

The proposed method is workable in real-time using the GPU(Graphics Processing Unit) and supports the movement of user's viewpoint. Therefore it is applicable to interactive MR applications.

The rest of the chapter is organized as follows. In section 2, we explain how to generate shadowing planes and basis images. In section 3, we describe the real-time shadowing process using pre-rendered basis images and shadowing planes. In section 4, we show the experimental result and confirm the effectiveness of our shadowing method. Then in section 5, we introduce the "Virtual Asukakyo Project" which aims to reconstruct the ancient Asukakyo. Finally, in section 6, we present concluding remarks.

2.   Generation of Shadowing Planes and Basis Images

We propose the idea of shadowing planes to make the soft shadow possible in MR application. Shadowing planes are planate objects set on the surface of real and virtual objects in the scene. In order to express soft shadow in real-time, we synthesize basis images and generate shadow images according to the illumination of the real scene. Then we map shadow images onto shadowing planes and express simulated cast shadow on other objects. In this section, we describe the process of generating shadowing planes and basis images in the preprocessing stage.

2.1 Setting up of Shadowing Planes

We set up the shadowing planes on the surface of objects in the scene. As shown in Figure22.1, each shadowing plane covers the surface of object roughly, and is offset a little in the direction of a user's viewpoint so as to avoid the stitching or z-fighting of polygons. Therefore shadowing planes are put between the objects and camera.

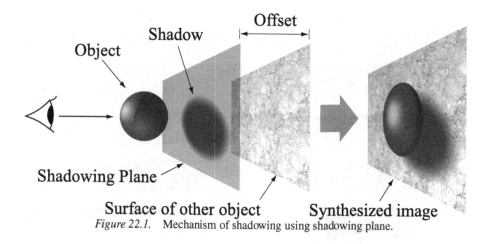

Figure 22.1. Mechanism of shadowing using shadowing plane.

Shadowing planes are generated from convex hulls of objects. In the simple scene, shadowing planes approximately correspond to the original objects. Though in case of complicated scene, we need to divide the objects into some clusters previously. Figure 22.2 shows the generating process of shadowing planes from complex architectural model. We divide the object manually and pick up shadowing planes from convex hulls of each clusters.

2.2 Approximation of the Illumination

In order to generate the basis images from shadowing planes, we approximate the illumination of the real scene by the number of basis lights.

First, we assume that the illumination in the scene is a hemispheric surface light source as illustrated in Figure 22.3(a)[11]. In this model, we can compute the irradiance E of the point A with whole surface light source as

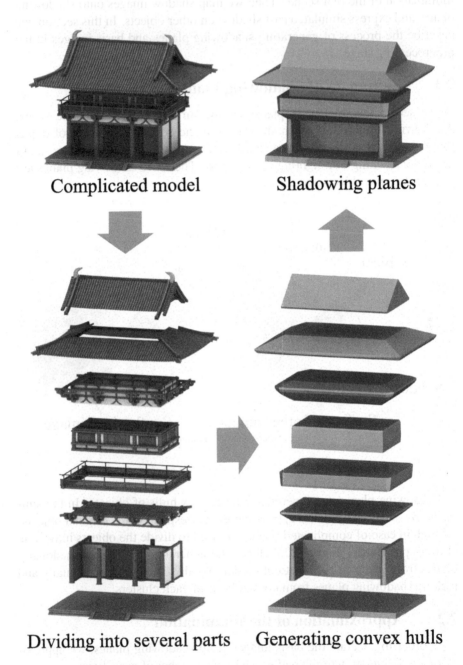

Complicated model   Shadowing planes

Dividing into several parts   Generating convex hulls

Figure 22.2.   Generation of shadowing planes from a complicated model using convex hulls.

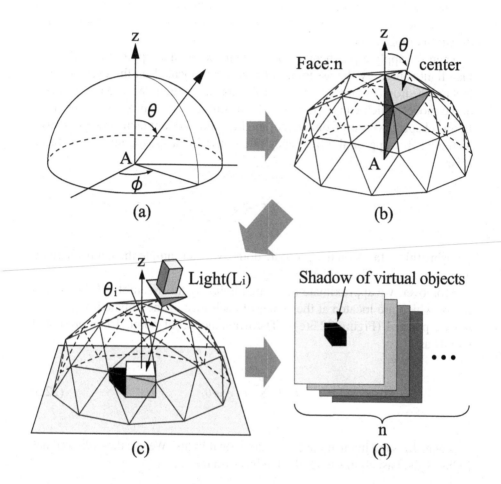

Figure 22.3. Approximation of the illumination; (a) hemispheric surface light source; (b) area lights on the face of a polyhedron; (c) rendering with directional lights; (d) generation of basis images.

$$E = \int_{-\pi}^{\pi} \int_{0}^{\frac{\pi}{2}} L_0(\theta_i, \phi_i) \cos \theta_i \sin \phi_i d\theta_i d\phi_i \qquad (22.1)$$

where $L_0(\theta_i, \phi_i)$ is the luminance per unit solid angle from the direction of (θ_i, ϕ_i), and $\cos \theta_i$ is the parameter which means the attenuation relating to the direction of incidence.

Then we apply a polyhedron to this hemisphere, and approximate the surface light source by the assembly of area lights located on the every face of this polyhedron (Figure 22.3(b)). For the approximation, We use the geodesic dome model which can divide the spheric surface into almost the same area. In this chapter, we start from an icosahedron and divide it using the alternative method[12]. Suppose the frequency of the division as f, the number of faces n is,

$$n = 20f^2 \qquad (22.2)$$

Using this n faces on the geodesic dome, we can sample the hemisphere by almost the same solid angle($\delta\omega = \frac{2\pi}{n}$).

Moreover, we approximate these area lights by the assembly of directional lights, which are located at the center of each face of the polyhedron looking toward point A (Figure 22.3(c)). The irradiance E of point A is represented simply as:

$$E = \sum_{i=1}^{n} L_i \cos \theta_i \qquad (22.3)$$

where L_i is the intensity of every directional lights. We use these directional lights as the basis lights to render the basis images.

2.3   Generation of Basis Images

After setting up m shadowing planes $P_j (j = 1, 2, ..., m)$ and n directional lights $L_i (i = 1, 2, .., n)$, the virtual objects are rendered with each light. Virtual cameras, which look towards each shadowing plane perpendicularly, capture the shadows of virtual objects cast on the shadowing planes. This rendering process is done off-line, so we can compute global illumination using radiosity method and the like. Finally, we obtain basis images $Ib_{j,i}(j = 1, 2, ..., m, i = 1, 2, ..., n)$ with every shadowing planes and lights (Figure 22.3(d)).

3. Real-Time Shadowing Process

3.1 Acquiring the Luminance of the Scene

We obtain the information in the luminance of the scene with an omnidirectional image taken by a video camera with a fisheye lens. Then we project the polyhedron noted above onto the omni-directional image, and compute the sum total value of internal pixels per each triangular region (Figure 22.4(a)). At this point, we bring in the luminance parameter $S_i (i = 1, 2, .., n)$ to represent the radiance scale of each light source.

For the shading of virtual objects, we set six virtual directional lights in the scene. The intensity of every light is determined by the parameter Si (Figure.22.4(b)). With that we can express correct shadings of virtual objects responding to the real scene.

Luminance paramters Si   Directional lights in the scene

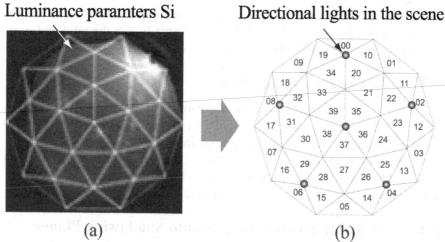

(a)   (b)

Figure 22.4. Acquisition of the luminance; (a) omni-directional image of the real scene; (b) distribution of lights in the scene.

3.2 Synthesis of Basis Images

Meanwhile, we compute the linear combination of basis images $Ib_{j,i}$ with S_i as shown in Figure 22.5.

$$Isum_j = \sum_{i=1}^{n} S_i \times Ib_{j,i} \tag{22.4}$$

$$Asum_j = \sum_{i=1}^{n} S_i \times a_{j,i} \tag{22.5}$$

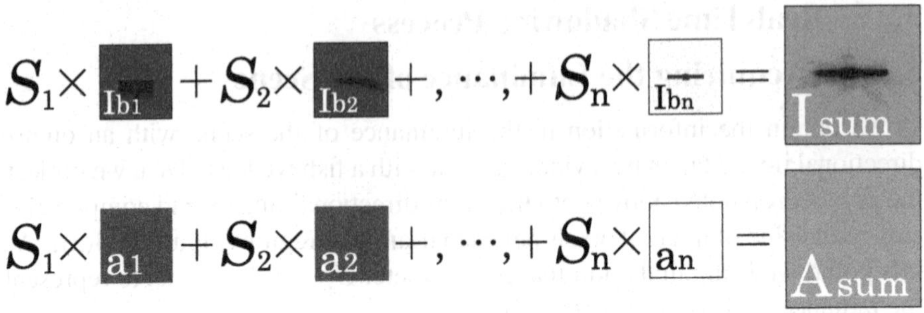

$$S_1 \times \boxed{\text{Ib1}} + S_2 \times \boxed{\text{Ib2}} +, \cdots, + S_n \times \boxed{\text{Ibn}} = \boxed{I_{\text{sum}}}$$

$$S_1 \times \boxed{\text{a1}} + S_2 \times \boxed{\text{a2}} +, \cdots, + S_n \times \boxed{\text{an}} = \boxed{A_{\text{sum}}}$$

Figure 22.5. The linear combination of luminance parameters and basis images

where $Isum_j$ is the synthesized soft shadow image, $a_{j,i}$ make up the area of remaining unaffected by any shadow of virtual objects in basis images, and $Asum_j$ shows the sum total of no shadowing area so that the ratio of $Isum_j$ and $Asum_j$ represent the effect of shadows of virtual objects.

3.3   Hardware Acceleration

Note that the computation of linear combination of basis images and luminance parameters is executable rapidly by recent GPU. Figure 22.6 shows the computation process of the linear combination explained in previous section in the fragment shader. Using multiple texture unit in GPU and assigning grayscale basis images to each RGBA channel, we can compute the linear sum of basis images and luminance parameter efficiently and execute it in real-time.

3.4   Mapping Shadow Images onto Shadowing Planes

Finally, we superimpose virtual objects onto a real image. We set soft shadow images synthesized from basis images onto shadowing planes as an alpha texture. Then we render the virtual scene and synthesize it with the real scene. Virtual objects are properly shaded with light sources responding to the illumination of the real scene.

The shadowing planes can represent simulated shadows of virtual objects over both the real image and objects themselves. And also, they can express the shadows on virtual objects cast by real objects using basis images which store shadows generated from objects corresponding to the real scene.

4.   Experimental Result

In this section, we explain the experimental result in both an indoor and outdoor scene. In order to confirm the effect of our shadowing method, we superimpose the virtual objects onto a real image using a video see-through

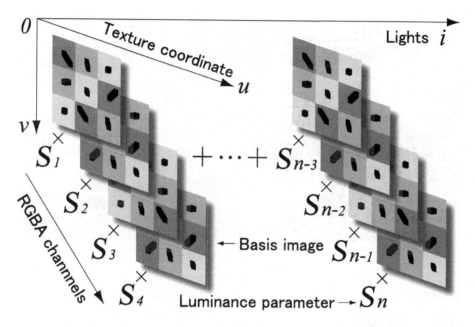

Figure 22.6. Synthesize of basis images using fragment shader.

head mounted display. We compare two synthesized images, one is a simple synthesized image which exclude the consistency of illumination, and another is a improved synthesized image in which we apply the proposed shadowing method. At first, we describe the component of our MR-system. Then we show the experimental result in an indoor and outdoor scene.

4.1   MR-System

Our system is mainly based on Canon's MR Platform system [13], which includes a video see-through head mounted display. We also used the Polhemus's Fastrak, six degree-of-freedom (DOF) electromagnetic tracking sensor, for the alignment of camera position and rotation to the real image. In the experiment to be described later, we use Windows PC (2.40GHz Core^{TM} 2 Duo E6600 CPU, 1024MB RAM, nVIDIA GeForce7950GT GPU). The appearance of our equipment is shown in Figure.22.7, and the detail of our MR-system is shown in Figure.22.8. As can be seen from the right side of Figure.22.7 and left bottom corner of Figure.22.8, we add a CCD camera with a fisheye lens to the MR Platform system in order to capture the illumination of the real scene.

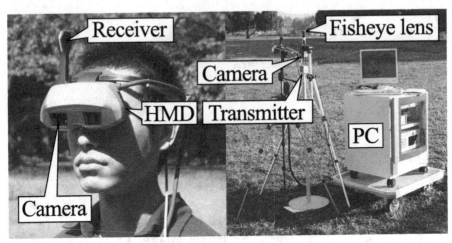

Figure 22.7. Appearance of our system

4.2 Result

Figure.22.9 shows the synthesized images of the indoor experiment. Note that the ground surface beneath the virtual box on the right side of images, the reality of synthesized image becomes better by adding the shadow of virtual object. We can confirm the effect shadowing of virtual object.

Figure.22.10 shows the result of the outdoor experiment using an old Japanese temple model. In Figure.22.10(b), we can see that the self-shadow of virtual buildings is apparent on their walls and both the shading and the shadow of virtual building are reasonably well matched to the real scene.

In the experiment of an outdoor scene, we used 1520 basis images generated from 40 directional lights and 38 shadowing planes. The size of each basis image is 128×128 pixels and the resolution of the synthesized image is 640×480 pixels. We implemented the calculation of the linear combination of basis images on the fragment shader to making use of GPU acceleration. The virtual objects consist of 58500 polygons and we achieved about 18fps frame rate.

5. Virtual Asukakyo Project

We apply the shadowing method to an outdoor MR-application called "Virtual Asukakyo Project". This project aims to restore the ancient Asukakyo virtually and exhibit it in the Asuka village on-site. In this section, we introduce the outline of the Virtual Asukakyo Project.

The Asukakyo was the oldest city of Japan. It was located in the Asuka village, about 25 kilometers south of Nara city. Through excavations continued in Asuka capital district over the past thirty years, it has become clear that the

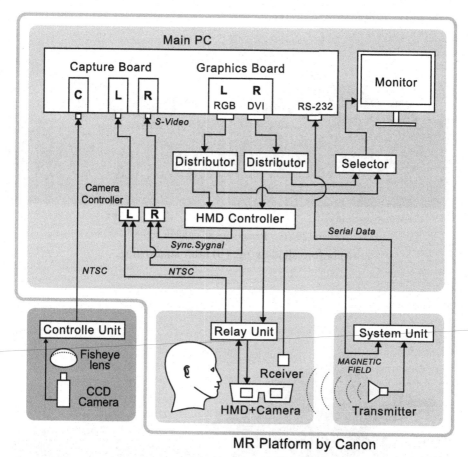

Figure 22.8. Detail of the MR-system

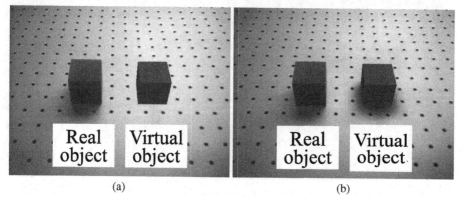

(a)   (b)

Figure 22.9. Results for an indoor scene;
(a) before shadowing; (b) after shadowing.

(a)   (b)

Figure 22.10.   Results for an outdoor scene;
(a) before shadowing; (b) after shadowing.

Figure 22.11.   Concept of Virtual Asukakyo.

political and cultural center of Japan existed in this area in the 7th century. The Kawaradera temple, located in the southwest side of Asuakyo, was one of the oldest temple like famous Horyuji. It is considered to have had its beginning during the reign of Emperor Tenji and came to flourish as the national religion. In the 8th century, Kawaradera declined because of the capital relocation to Heijokyo in Nara, and was eventually burned down in the late Muromachi period. Nowadays, the main buildings are lost and only the foundation and cornerstones are left just like many of the ruins of wooden temples of those days.

The Asukakyo receives much attention and many tourists visit the site, but they are disappointed to find that so little remains of the original structure. So we decided to begin the Virtual Asukakyo project, by which we intend to virtually restore Asukakyo and Kawaradera temple to its original state. The purpose of this project is not only to present a CG model of those days, but also to exhibit the restoration model with MR-systems for tourists. In the process of constructing the CG model of Asukakyo and Kawaradera, we referred to the detailed restoration proposal based on the result of the excavation.

6. Conclusion

This chapter proposed a fast shading and shadowing method for MR. We approximate the illumination in the scene and generate the basis images using the shadowing planes. Soft shadow images, corresponding to the illumination of the real scene, are synthesized from basis images. Then we map these shadow images onto shadowing planes as alpha texture and express soft shadows of virtual objects in real-time. Though the proposed method is applicable only to static scene, it is effective for a specific application (e.g. MR-based restoration of cultural heritages in outdoor scene). Our method can achieve the consistency of illumination and improve the quality of synthesized image in MR-systems. And we applied the method to an outdoor MR-application "Virtual Asukakyo", in which we aim to reconstruct the ancient Asukakyo. Using the MR technology, we can show visitors reconstructed CG models directly on historical sites, and also we successfully improved the reality of synthesized image with proposed shadowing method.

Acknowledgment

This research was, in part, supported by the Ministry of Education, Culture, Sports, Science and Technology, under the program, "Development of High Fidelity Digitization Software for Large-Scale and Intangible Cultural Assets." The experiment in Asuka Village was supported by the Ministry of Land, Infrastructure and Transport. We are also grateful to the village office of Asuka, the Archaeological Institute of Kashihara and the National Research Institute for Cultural Properties.

References

[1] R. Azuma, "A Survey of Augmented Reality," In *Presence: Teleoperators and Virtual Environments,* pp. 355-385, 1997.

[2] R. Azuma, Y. Baillot, R. Behringer, S. Feiner, S. Julier, and B. MacIntyre, "Recent Advances in Augmented Reality," *IEEE Computer Graphics and Applications,* pp. 34-47, 2001.

[3] K. Jacobs and C. Loscos, "Classification of Illumination Methods for Mixed Reality," *Proc. Eurographics State of the Art Report(STAR),* pp. 95-118, 2004.

[4] I. Sato, Y. Sato, and K. Ikeuchi, "Acquiring a radiance distribution to superimpose virtual objects onto a real scene," *IEEE Trans. on Visualization and Computer Graphics,* pp. 1-12, 1999.

[5] M. Haller, S. Drab, and W. Hartmann, "A real-time shadow approach for an augmented reality application using shadow volumes," *Proc. Symp. on ACM Virtual Reality Software and Technology(VRST'03),* pp. 56-65, 2003.

[6] S. Gibson, J. Cook, T. Howard, and R. Hubbold, "Rapid shadow generation in real-world lighting environments," *Proc. Eurographics Symp. on Rendering (EGSR03),* pp. 219-229, 2003.

[7] P. Debevec, "Rendering synthetic objects into real scenes: bridging traditional and image-based graphics with global Illumination and high dynamic range photography, *Proc. SIGGRAPH '98,* pp. 189-198, 1998.

[8] O. Bimber, A. Grundhofer, G. Wetzstein, and S. Knodel, "Consistent Illumination within Optical See-Through Augmented Environments," *Proc. IEEE and ACM Int. Symp. on Mixed and Augmented Reality (ISMAR03),* pp. 198-207, 2003.

[9] I. Sato, M. Hayashida, F. Kai, Y. Sato, and K. Ikeuchi, "Fast Image Synthesis of Virtual Objects in a Real Scene with Natural Shading," *The Institute of Electronics, Information and Communication Engineers, D-II (in Japanese),* pp. 1234-1242, 2001.

[10] J. S. Nimeroff, E. Simoncelli, and J. Dorsey, "Efficient re-rendering of naturally illuminated environments,", *Proc. Eurographics Workshop on Rendering (EGWR94),* pp. 359-373, 1994.

[11] B. K. Horn, "Robot vision," *The MIT Press,* 1986.

[12] A. Pugh, "Polyhedra: a visual approach," *University of California Press,* 1986.

[13] S. Uchiyama, K. Takemoto, K. Satoh, H. Yamamoto, and H. Tamura, "MR Platform: A Basic Body on Which Mixed Reality Applications Are Built," *Proc. Int. Symp. on Mixed and Augmented Reality (ISMAR02)*, pp. 246-253. 2002.

Chapter 23

DIGITAL RESTORATION OF THE NARA GREAT BUDDHA

Takeshi Oishi and Katsushi Ikeuchi

Abstract   This chapter describes the attempt to digitally restore the original appearance of cultural heritage objects. The chapter focuses on the Nara Great Buddha statue in the Todaiji Temple, Japan. The Todaiji Temple has been destroyed by natural and artificial disasters a number of times. The current building and statue were rebuilt hundreds of years ago, but their shapes are different from the original shapes. In order to recreate their original appearance, we have utilized 3D geometric models that are obtained from the current Buddha statue. We have also recreated the appearance of buildings by using laser range sensors. The original Great Buddha statue was reconstructed by morphing the model of the current Great Buddha statue based on a literature survey. The Buddha's Palace was reconstructed by assembling partial 3D models of the other temple that was constructed during the same period as the Todaiji temple. By combining the original Buddha's Palace and the original Buddha statue, we created the virtual appearance of the Nara Great Buddha at the time it was created.

1.   Introduction

Currently, a large number of cultural heritage objects around the world are deteriorating or being destroyed because of natural weathering, disasters, and civil wars. Among them, Japanese cultural heritage objects, in particular, are vulnerable to fires and other natural disasters because most of them were constructed of wood and paper.

One of the best ways to prevent these objects from loss and deterioration is to digitally preserve them. Digital data of heritage objects can be obtained by using modern computer vision techniques. Once these data have been acquired, they can be preserved permanently, and then safely passed down to future generations.

Another advantage of obtaining digital data of cultural heritage objects is to modify those data and display the original appearance of the object. After we obtain the precise geometric information about cultural heritage objects in

Figure 23.1.   Nara Great Buddha

their current state, we can modify the current data into a hypothesized original state for multimedia contents. In order to demonstrate this ability, this chapter describes an example of this type of modification: the restoration of the Buddha Statue and its Buddha Palace (Fig. 23.1).

2.   Toudaiji and the Great Buddha

The Nara Great Buddha is one of the most important heritage objects in Japan. The Buddha Statue is sitting in the Buddha Palace at the Toudaiji Temple in Nara, Japan. The history of Toudaiji Temple starts in the year 728. A temple called Kinshousenji was build by the Shomu emperor for his child who had died. In 743, the emperor ordered the construction of the Buddha Statue. Originally, the Buddha Statue was to be built inside a temple located in an area which nowadays is known as Shiga Prefecture. However, forest fires and earthquake had struck this area frequently, which forced the emperor to relocate the construction site to Kinshousenji Temple in 745. Around this time, this temple has started to be referred to as Toudaiji Temple. From 747, construction of the Buddha Palace began alongside the Buddha Statue itself. Both of these were completed in the year 751, and in 752, a ceremony was held to celebrate the completion of the Buddha Statue.The original Buddha Statue is made of bronze and coated with gold. In 1181, Toudaiji had been set a fire during a civil war. Parts of the temple including the Buddha Palace had been burned down during this war. Reconstruction was carried out, and was completed in 1203. The temple was burned down again in 1567 due to another civil war. The restoration of the Buddha Statue was completed in 1691, and the reconstruction of the Buddha Palace took until 1709.

Although most parts on the Buddha Statue were either repaired or reconstructed, there are some pieces which have not been destroyed. The height of the Buddha Palace has not changed, but the width has been shrunk to about two-thirds of the original size.

The remainder of this chapter is organized as follows. Section 2 and 3 reports our efforts to restore the original appearance of the Buddha statue and the Buddha palace using acquired digital data and a literature survey. Section 3 describes the analysis of the restored 3D model to demonstrate the effectiveness of digital restoration. Section 4 summarizes this chapter.

3.   Restoring the Buddha Statue

As the first step, we acquired the complete 3D mesh model of the Nara Great Buddha Statue in its current state by using the geometrical modeling techniques described in this book. We collected 114 partial mesh models using CYRAX sensors. Those partial mesh models were aligned using the parallel alignment algorithm[1] on a PC cluster and merged[2–4] into a unified mesh model with 70M polygon.

We synthesized the original state by morphing the 3D mesh of the model from this mesh model. From some literature inherited at various temples, we knew the sizes of various face parts such as the nose and mouth. "Enryaku-so-rokubun," "Daibutsuden-hibun," "Hichidaiji-nikki," and "Gokokuji-honnsyoji-engisho" are representative documents that contain those sizes. Unfortunately, however, those numbers often contradict each other. Some researchers investigated which number is the most reliable one. We followed their method to compare them and determined a common figure for each part.

Table 1 shows the obtained estimated and the current dimensions of various face parts. Here, all the documents employ the unit called "shaku." We interpreted shaku as the tempyo shaku, and one shaku is assumed to be 0.2964 meters among the various interpretations of shaku. Notice that relatively large differences exist in height measurements.

Using these data, we designed a two-step morphing algorithm. First, we globally changed the scale of the whole portions (for example, Height when sitting, Face Length, Nose Length); these are gradually modified. In the second stage, vertices were moved one by one iteratively, similarly to the constraint propagation algorithm, using smoothness and uniform constraints. The two-stage morphing enabled us to obtain the complete model of the original Great Buddha. Figure 23.2 shows the 3D models of the current (a) and the original

Table 23.1.   Current and estimated dimensions of various face parts

Parts Name	Current (m)	Original (m)
Height when sitting	14.98	15.85
Eye length	1.02	1.16
Face length	3.20	2.82
Ear length	2.54	2.52
Palm length	1.48	1.66
Foot length	3.74	3.56
Nose height	0.50	0.47
Mouth length	1.33	1.10

Great Buddha (Tempyou Buddha) (b). We can easily recognize that the original Buddha is larger and rather thin.

(a) (b)

Figure 23.2.   Comparison in 3D models. (a) Current Buddha, (b) Original Buddha

4.   Restoring the Buddha Palace

The Buddha Palace of the Toudaiji Temple was built during the same decades as those of the Great Buddha (8th century). It was also rebuilt twice: in the 12th and 17th centuries. In the 12th century, Tenjiku architecture was imported from China, and the Buddha Palace was rebuilt in a totally different architecture style. The rebuilding in the 18th century followed the same new style. As a result, the style of the current Buddha Palace is entirely different from that of the original building.

Fortunately, the Toudaiji Temple has been displaying a miniature model of the original hall, constructed for the Paris Expo in 1900, as shown in Figure 23.3. We digitized it using the Pulsteck TDS-1500 and scaled it up to the original size as shown in Figure 23.5(a). The TDS-1500 can scan a range from 3.5 meters through 10 meters with the accuracy of 0.5mm to 5mm and the spatial resolution of 420 X 280. We obtained 12 range images from various observation directions. As shown in Figure 23.5(b), due to the limits of the sensor's accuracy and constraints of observation directions, though the model provides rough dimensions of locations of columns and walls, it does not provide a precise and accurate picture of the detailed parts.

According to Prof. Keisuke Fujii, who is a professor of architecture at the University of Tokyo and one of the experts on building style in the era, the Toudaiji and Toushoudaiji temples share a similar format. The main hall of the Toushoudaiji Temple was also built during the same period (8 th century). We have decided to combine the detailed part model of the Toushoudaiji Temple with the rough whole model of the Todaiji temple.

We digitized various key parts of the main hall at Toushoudaiji. Using the suggestions of Prof. Fujii, we chose 20 important parts of the main hall. Figure 23.5 shows 4 parts among 20 important parts. We employed Cyrax 2004 and Pulsteck TDS-1500, which have a range from 0.5 meter through 1meter, with resolution of 0.23 mm through 0.83 mm, to obtain 780 range images. Figure 23.6 shows the obtained range images of the detailed parts.

We pasted these partial range data of Touhoudaiji parts (Fig. 23.6) to the scaled-up range data of the Toudaiji (Fig. 23.4(b)), using as a scale the average size difference between those temples, roughly 1 to 2.3[5]. Figure 23.7(a) shows the original Buddha's Palace digitally restored by our method. By combining the original Buddha's Palace and the original Buddha, we created the virtual appearance of the Nara Buddha in the 8 th century, as shown in Fig. 23.7(b-c). The virtual appearance of this and other historic objects can be used for education about and promotion of our cultural heritage.

5. Analysis

As one of the demonstrations of utilizing digital restoration, we conducted an experiment to determine the amount of gold used to plate the surface of the Buddha. It is well known that the original Buddha was golden due to gold plating of its surface. However, several contradictory numbers exist in documents. For example, "Daibutu-den-hibun" and "Enryaku-sorokubun" say it required 5412 ryou and 4187 ryou of gold, respectively, to cover the body of the Buddha statue. Moreover, there were two interpretations of "ryou"; A large ryou was 42 g, while a small ryou was 14 g. Thus, there are four interpretations determining the amount of gold required.

Figure 23.3.   Miniature model of Buddha palace

Table 23.2.   Four interpretations determining the amount of gold used

Document name	Written amount in the document	Interpretation	
		Large ryou (42g)	Small ryou (14g)
Daibutu-den-hibun	5412 ryou	227 kg	76 kg
Enryaku-sorokubun	4187 ryou	176 kg	59 kg

(a) a cloud of points representation

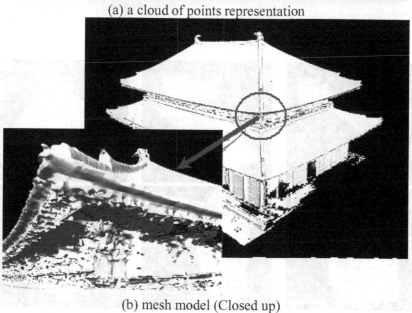

(b) mesh model (Closed up)

Figure 23.4. 3D model acquired from the Miniature model.

Figure 23.5.   Key parts of the main hall at Tousho-daiji digitized

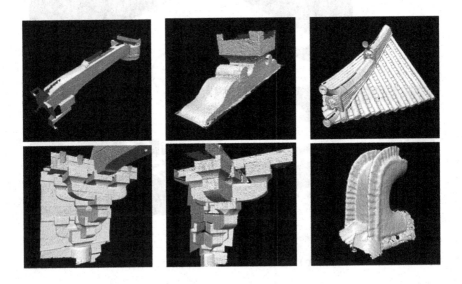

Figure 23.6.   3D models of those key parts

In order to disambiguate this discussion, we used our restored digital model of the Tempyou great Buddha Statue. The surface area, $597m^2$, is obtained from the restored digital model by taking a summation of all surface areas of triangular meshes. For comparison, the surface area of the current Buddha is $556m^2$. From the documents, it is known that the amalgam method was used to put gold over the Buddha's surface. Usually, this method uses 6 $\sim$ $10mg/cm^2$. This number was also confirmed by examining the thickness of gold plate on various treasures stored in Sho-so-in. By multiplying the surface area of Tempyo and the current Buddha with this number, we obtained the gold amount as 36kg $\sim$60kg and 33kg $\sim$ 56kg. Those numbers indicate that the interpretation of "enryaku-sorokubun" with a small ryou is most likely.

6.   Conclusion

Digital restoration of lost cultural heritage objects has a great advantage compared with other restoration methods such as physical construction of actual temples, because we can examine various hypotheses without any physical changes or long building periods. We demonstrated the effectiveness of this method through the restoration of the Nara Great Buddha Statue and the Buddha Palace. We have also utilized this method to obtain important data such as the probable amount of gold used to cover the body of the great Buddha. These findings would play a significant role in clarifying debates concerning ambiguous historical facts.

(a) Outside appearance

(b) Inside appearance

(c) Inside appearance

Figure 23.7.   Restored Nara Buddha

Acknowledgments

This research was supported, in part, by Ministry of Education, Culture, Sports, Science and Technology under the Leading Project, "Development of High Fidelity Digitization Software for Large-Scale and Intangible Cultural Assets," and, in part, by Japan Science and Technology Agency, under the CREST program, "Automatic generation of virtual models of cultural heritage." The authors also would like to thank to the staffs of Todaiji Temple and Toshodaiji Temple in Nara, Japan.

References

[1] T. Oishi, R. Sagawa, A. Nakazawa, R. Kurazume, and K. Ikeuchi, "Parallel Alignment of a Large Number of Range Images on PC Cluster," *Proc. Int'l Conf. 3-D Digital Imaging and Modeling*, pp. 195-202, Oct. 2003.

[2] R. Sagawa, K. Nishino, M.D. Wheeler and K. Ikeuchi, "Parallel Processing of Range Data Merging," *Proc. IEEE/RSJ Int'l Conf. Intelligent Robots and Systems,* Vol. 1, pp. 577-583, 2001.

[3] R. Sagawa, T. Masuda, and K. Ikeuchi, "Effective Nearest Neighbor Search for Aligning and Merging Range Images," *Proc. Int'l Conf. 3-D Digital Imaging and Modeling,* pp. 79-86, Oct. 2003

[4] R. Sagawa and K. Ikeuchi, "Taking Consensus of Signed Distance Field for Complementing Unobservable Surface," *Proc. Int'l Conf. 3-D Digital Imaging and Modeling,* pp. 410-417, Oct. 2003

[5] T. Masuda, Y. Hirota, K. Ikeuchi and K. Nishino, "Simultaneous Determination of Registration and Deformation Parameters among 3D Range Image," *Proc. Int'l Conf. 3-D Digital Imaging and Modeling,* pp369-376, Jun. 2005

V

GALLERY

1. Kamakura Great Buddha, Kamakura Japan. (October 2000)

2. Ishibutai Ancient Tomb, Asuka Japan. (March 2001)

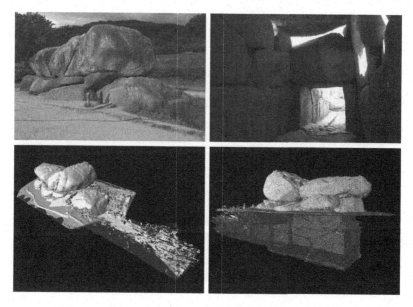

3. Sakafune-ishi site, Asuka Japan. (March 2001)

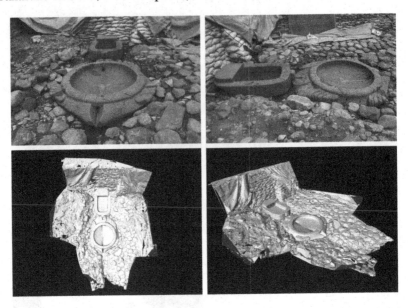

4. Original Campus of Institute of Industrial Science, the University of Tokyo, Tokyo Japan. (May 2001)

5. Nara Great Buddha, Nara Japan. (May 2001)

6. Toshodaiji Temple, Nara Japan. (July 2001)

7. Komaba Dormitory, the University of Tokyo, Tokyo Japan. (September 2001)

8. Ryumon Stone Buddha, Nara Japan. (November 2001)

9. Usuki Magai Buddha, Usuki Japan. (December 2001)

10. Asuka Great Buddha, Nara Japan. (January 2002)

11. Facade of La Merçhed Church, Panama. (February 2002)

12. Wat Sri Chum, Sukhothai Thailand. (March 2002)

13. Fugoppe Ruin, Yoichi Japan. (June 2002 & September 2002)

14. Koumoku-ten Clay Figure, Todaiji Temple, Nara Japan. (June-July 2002)

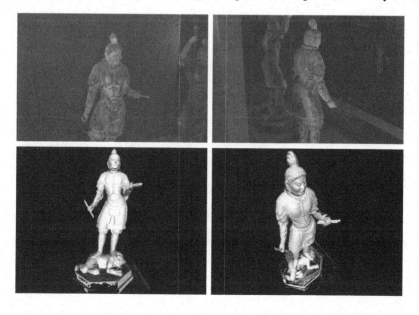

15. Ohzuka Tomb, Japan. (November 2003, April 2004)

16. Peplophoros., Somma Vesuviana Italy. (October 2003)

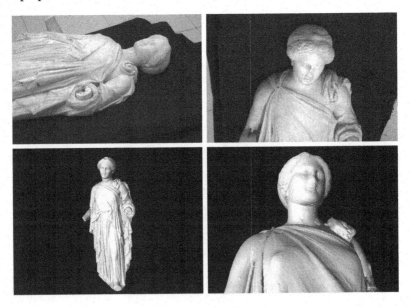

17. Somma Vesubiana Site Italy. (October 2003-2006)

18. Sambor Prei Kuk Monuments, Cambodia. (December 2003, December 2005)

19. Bayon Temple, Angkor Thom Cambodia. (February 2003 to December 2006)

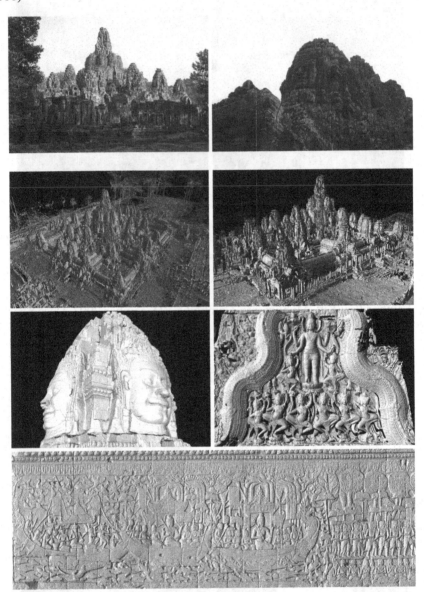

References

[1] A. Banno and K. Ikeuchi, "Shape Recovery of 3D Data Obtained from a Moving Range Sensor," *Proc. Int'l Conf. Computer Vision*, pp. 792-799, 2005.

[2] K. Matsui, S. Ono, and K. Ikeuchi, "The Climbing Sensor: 3-D Modeling of a Narrow and Vertically Stalky Space by Using Spatio-Temporal Range Image," *Proc. Int'l Conf. Intelligent Robots and Systems*, pp. 3997-4002, 2005.

[3] D. Miyazaki and K. Ikeuchi, "Inverse Polarization Raytracing: Estimating Surface Shape of Transparent Objects," *Proc. Int'l Conf. Computer Vision and Pattern Recognition*, pp. 910-917, 2005.

[4] K. Nishino and K. Ikeuchi, "Robust Simultaneous Registration of Multiple Range Images," *Proc. Asian Conf. Computer Vision*, pp. 454-461, 2002.

[5] T. Oishi, A. Nakazawa, R. Kurazume, and K. Ikeuchi, "Fast Simultaneous Alignment of Multiple Range Images using Index Images," *Proc. Int'l Conf. 3-D Digital Imaging and Modeling*, pp. 476-483, 2005.

[6] T. Oishi, R. Sagawa, A. Nakazawa, R. Kurazume, and K. Ikeuchi, "Parallel Alignment of Large Number of Range Images," *Proc. Int'l Conf. 3-D Digital Imaging and Modeling*, pp. 195-202, 2003.

[7] T. Masuda, Y. Hirota, K. Nishino, and K. Ikeuchi, "Simultaneous Determination of Registration and Deformation Parameters among 3D Range Images," *Proc. Int'l Conf. 3-D Digital Imaging and Modeling*, pp. 369-376, 2005.

[8] R. Sagawa, K. Nishino, M. D. Wheeler, and K. Ikeuchi, "Parallel Processing of Range Data Merging," *Proc. Int'l Conf. Intelligent Robots and Systems*, pp. 577-583, 2001.

[9] R. Sagawa, K. Nishino, and K. Ikeuchi, "Adaptively Merging Large-Scale Range Data with Reflectance Properties," *IEEE Trans. Pattern Analysis and Machine Intelligence*, vol. 27, no. 3, pp. 392-405, 2005.

[10] R. Sagawa, T. Oishi, A. Nakazawa, R. Kurazume, and K. Ikeuchi, "Iterative Refinement of Range Images with Anisortropic Error Distribution," *Proc. Int'l Conf. Intelligent Robots and Systems*, pp. 79-85, 2002.

[11] R. Sagawa and K. Ikeuchi, "Taking Consensus of Signed Distance Field for Complementing Unobservable Surface," *Proc. Int'l Conf. 3-D Digital Imaging and Modeling*, pp. 410-417, 2003.

[12] R. Kurazume, K. Nishino, Z. Zhang, and K. Ikeuchi, "Simultaneous 2D images and 3D geometric model registration for texture mapping utilizing reflectance attribute," *Proc. Asian Conf. Computer Vision*, pp. 99-106, 2002.

[13] R. Kawakami, R. T. Tan, and K. Ikeuchi, "Consistent Surface Color for Texturing Large Objects in Outdoor Scenes," *Proc. Int'l Conf. Computer Vision*, pp. 1200-1207, 2005.

[14] A. Ikari, R. T. Tan, and K. Ikeuchi, "Separating Illumination and Surface Spectral from Multiple color Signals," *Proc. Asian Conf. Compuyrt Vision*, pp. 264-269, 2004.

[15] R. T. Tan, K. Nishino, and Katsushi Ikeuchi, "Color constancy through inverse-intensity chromaticity space," *J. Optical Society of America A*, vol. 21, no. 3, pp. 321-334, 2004.

[16] R. T. Tan and Katsushi Ikeuchi, "Separating reflection components of textured surfaces using a single image," *Trans. Pattern Analysis and Machine Intelligence*, vol. 27, no. 2, pp. 179-193, 2005.

[17] T. Shibata, T. Takahashi, D. Miyazaki, Y. Sato, and K. Ikeuchi, "Creating Photorealistic Virtual Model with Polarization Based Vision System," *Proc. SPIE*, vol. 5888, pp. 25-35, 2005.

[18] M. Kamakura, T. Oishi, J. Takamatsu, and K. Ikeuchi, "Classification of Bayon Faces Using 3D Model," *Proc. Int'l Conf. Virtual Systems and Multimedia*, pp. 751-760, 2005.

[19] T. Masuda, Y. Yamada, N. Kuchitsu, and K. Ikeuchi, "Sunlight Illumination Simulation for Archaeological Investigation -Case Study of the Fugoppe Cave," *Proc. Int'l Conf. Virtual Systems and Multimedia*, pp. 850-859, 2004.

[20] Y. Okamoto, J. Takamatsu, M. Kagesawa, K. Okada, and K. Ikeuchi, "3D Database System of Mercede Church: The Use of 3D Models as an Interface to Information," *Proc. Int'l Conf. Virtual Systems and Multimedia*, pp. 163-172, 2005.

[21] T. Kakuta, T. Oishi, and K. Ikeuchi, "Shading and Shadowing of Architecture in Mixed Reality," *Int'l Symposium on Mixed and Augmented Reality*, pp. 200-201, 2005.

[22] K. Ikeuchi, A. Nakazawa, K. Hasegawa, T. Ohishi, "The Great Buddha Project: Modeling Cultural Heritage for VR Systems through Observation," *Int'l Symposium on Mixed and Augmented Reality*, pp. 7-16, 2003.

Index